Sufi Heirs of the Prophet

Sufi Heirs of the Prophet

The Indian Naqshbandiyya and the Rise of the Mediating Sufi Shaykh

ARTHUR F. BUEHLER
Foreword by Annemarie Schimmel

University of South Carolina Press

STUDIES IN COMPARATIVE RELIGION
Frederick M. Denny, Series Editor

Cloth edition published by the University of South Carolina Press, 1998
Paperback edition published in Columbia, South Carolina,
by the University of South Carolina Press, 2008

www.sc.edu/uscpress

Manufactured in the United States of America

17 16 15 14 13 12 11 10 09 08 10 9 8 7 6 5 4 3 2 1

The Library of Congress has cataloged the cloth edition as follows:

Buehler, Arthur F.
Sufi heirs of the Prophet : the Indian Naqshbandiyya and the rise of the mediating sufi shaykh / Arthur F. Buehler.
p. cm. — (Studies in comparative religion)
Includes bibliographical references and index.
ISBN 1-57003-201-7
1. Naqshabandīyah—India—History. 2. Sufism—India—History. I. Title. II. Series: Studies in comparative religion (Columbia, S.C.)
BP189.7.N35B84 1998
297.4'8—dc21 97–40145

Parts of chapter 3 of the present work appeared in a different version in "The Naqshbandiyya in Tīmūrid India: The Central Asian Legacy," *Journal of Islamic Studies* 7/2 (1996): 2008–28.

Quotation from the translation of Aḥmad Riḍā Khān's poem is from Usha Sanyal, "In the Path of the Prophet: Maulana Ahmad Riza Khan Barelwi and the Ahl-e Sunnat wa Jama ʿat Movement in British India, c. 1870–1921," Ph.D. dissertation, Columbia University, © 1990 Usha Sanyal. Reprinted by permission of Usha Sanyal.

ISBN: 978-1-57003-783-2 (pbk)

CONTENTS

List of Illustrations vii

Foreword by Annemarie Schimmel ix

Editor's Preface xiii

Preface and Acknowledgments xv

1. Patterns of Sufi Religious Authority 1
2. From Teaching-Shaykh to Directing-Shaykh 29
3. The Naqshbandiyya in India from Their Foundation to the Colonial Period 55
4. Genealogy as a Source of Authority 82
5. Spiritual Travel as a Source of Authority 98
6. Bonding the Heart with the Shaykh 131
7. From Initiation to Shaykhdom 147
8. Mediational Sufism and Revivalist Currents in British Colonial India 168
9. Redefining the Shaykh's Role in the Naqshbandī Sufi Tradition 190
10. The Role of the Naqshbandī Sufi in Pakistan 224

Appendixes

1. Written Sources for Spiritual Exercises 234
2. Mujaddidī Contemplations 241
3. The Intentions Guiding the Disciple through the Mujaddidī Contemplations 249
4. Examples of Teaching Certificates 254

Bibliography 260

Index 285

ILLUSTRATIONS

Ḥakīm Muḥammad Mūsā xxi

Calendar depicting the tomb of Aḥmad Sirhindī 67

Genealogical tree with the Naqshbandī lineage as the trunk and the other lineages as flowers 91

Jamāʿat ʿAlī Shāh, circa 1935 193

The tomb building in Alipur Sharif where Jamāʿat ʿAlī is buried 221

Jamāʿat ʿAlī's grave 222

Poster advertising the arrival at the Lahore airport of the Afghan sufi shaykh Sayfurraḥmān 231

Maps

Central and South Asia 57

The Panjab before 1901 173

Figures

1. Normative sufi hierarchies 7
2. Sources of Islamic personal authority 19
3. Mujaddidī genealogy 76
4. Naqshbandī genealogy 86
5. Model of Naqshbandī cosmology 107
6. Mujaddidī correspondences of *laṭīfas* 111
7. Diagram of the Mujaddidiyya path 124

FOREWORD

Just at the time when Arthur Buehler's manuscript was going to the press an international conference on Bahā'uddīn Naqshband took place in Bukhara, Uzbekistan. At the large shrine of the fourteenth-century saint, scholars from Uzbekistan, Kazakhstan, and Germany gathered to discuss the relevance of Khwāja Naqshband's teachings for present-day Uzbekistan. The Central Asian scholars rightly considered the emphasis that the Naqshbandiyya put on silent remembrance of God and on the practice of *khalwat dar anjuman* suitable for modern life. To turn one's heart in full concentration to the Divine Beloved while working in this world for the improvement of society seemed to them an attitude that could help them master the different and difficult tasks that modern people face. Therefore, almost every speaker dwelled upon the adage *dast be-kār, dil be-yār*—"The hand at work, the heart with a Friend"—a saying that is written in various calligraphic styles around the walls of the library where our meeting took place.

In an area where people lived for seven decades under a regime that allowed no religious activities whatsoever but where some of the sufi lineages secretly continued their work to preserve the Islamic heritage, this impressive attempt at integrating Naqshbandī teaching into the modern world shows the strength of the Naqshbandī order. Six hundred years after the death of its founder it has lost nothing of its vigor. Rather, it has not only been growing steadily in its place of origin and in Central Asia in general; but it also influenced Mughal India and increasingly the Near East as well. The late Turkish prime minister, Turgut Özal, a follower of Khwāja Bahā'uddīn Naqshband, contributed largely to the restoration of the shrine. Once dilapidated, it is now an attractive building surrounded by a rose garden, and it is equipped with a library and meeting hall. Pious men and women regularly visit the tomb of the founder, circumambulating counterclockwise the small cubic stone building thrice while reciting their prayers. They may take a drink from a fountain beneath a huge tree, the water of which is considered holy and wholesome.

While listening to the discussions of the pious Uzbeks about the necessity of a "Naqshbandī approach" to the contemporary world, we also observed that the number of publications about the order in Europe has grown amazingly during the last few decades. We can mention only a few outstanding examples here. A major sourcebook compiled by M. Gaborieau, A. Popovic, and T. Zarcone after a 1989 congress devoted to the Naqshbandiyya was published in Istanbul; the studies of Jürgen Paul discuss the political implications of the order and its role in Central Asia; and Fritz Meier of Basel, the author of many indispensable works on medieval Central Asian sufis such as Najmuddīn Kubrā, Abū Saʿīd-i Abū'l-Khayr, and Bahā-i Valad, has recently devoted several articles and an important book to the inner life, the theology, and the psychology of the Naqshbandiyya. It seems that the quiet but intense inner way of this order, which "begins where other orders end," is proudly claiming to be better suited to a modern mind than the ecstatic flights and sometimes strange behavior of some of the older orders. Averse to dance and music, the sober Naqshbandīs' way of life seems to appeal more to practically minded people than does the emphasis on poverty, otherworldliness, and rapture found among certain other lineages—as much as the lovely music of the Chishtīs and the whirling dance of the Mevlevīs attract beauty-loving souls. Was not the first Naqshbandī sufi, whom I encountered more than forty years ago in Ankara, a highly successful business manager who took his strength from his nightly vigils and regular meditation? The success of the Naqshbandiyya in the west, especially that of the Khālidiyya branch, is remarkable. One of the members of our delegation to Bukhara was a German lady doctor, a brigadier in the army who was an active follower of the widely known Naqshbandī Shaykh Nazim, from Cyprus.

Given these observations, it seems that Arthur Buehler's book comes just at the right moment. His original aim was to study the role of the Naqshbandī shaykhs in contemporary Pakistan, especially in the Panjab, but the book has outgrown the author's first goal. Thanks to his contacts with a number of masters and the perusal of numerous hitherto unknown manuals and treatises in Arabic, Persian, and Urdu, he has traced the rules of succession and the inner journey in a fascinating way, concentrating on the role of the shaykh vis-à-vis his disciples, upon whom the shaykh concentrates his inner powers. Buehler shows the changes that have taken place in the last century among the Indo-Pakistani branches of the order and discusses the most difficult feature of the Naqshbandī theories and practices, namely the inner growth of the seeker's soul during his wandering through the *laṭīfas*, the spiritual fine points, in a kind of helezonic upward-and-inward movement.

I am convinced that the author's analysis of both the theoretical and the practical aspects of the Naqshbandiyya, including their role in the present-day Panjab, will lead to a better understanding not only of this order but also of some important aspects of Pakistani religious life as well.

Annemarie Schimmel

EDITOR'S PREFACE

The fascination with sufi spirituality of both the general public and the professional scholars has been important to the development of Islamic studies in the West. This series has contributed several significant works to sufi studies that are founded on original yet accessible scholarship, based both in texts and on field work. Earle H. Waugh's pioneering *The Munshidīn of Eqypt: Their World and Their Song* (1989) explored the world of sufi singers. Then Th. Emil Homerin traced the fortunes of the saint cult of a great medieval Egyptian sufi in *From Arab Poet to Egyptian Saint: Ibn al-Fāriḍ, His Verse, and His Shrine* (1994). And Valerie J. Hoffman has given us a new way of thinking about Islamic mysticism in her major work *Sufism, Mystics, and Saints in Modern Egypt* (1995).

Now we have Arthur F. Buehler's study of the sufi master as mediating agent in Indian Naqshbandī sufism. *Sufi Heirs of the Prophet* probes the relatively little known area of sufi leadership traditions and styles. The Muslim community—known as the Umma—is a charismatic community that both represents and embodies Muḥammad's authority as founder and, through the cultivation of his Sunna (teachings and deportment), his continuing inspiration. This study reveals many important dimensions of how sufi shaykhs represent and embody the Prophet, whether as spiritual directors, as in traditional sufism, or, increasingly in the twentieth century, as mediating presences that enable Muslims to pursue a spiritual path within the conflicting and contending pressures and institutions of modern life. This study, based on historical records and field investigations, will be of interest not only to historians of sufi teachings and practices; it will also appeal to social scientists wanting to understand the structures, dynamics, and processes of sufi communal life today.

Frederick Mathewson Denny

PREFACE AND ACKNOWLEDGMENTS

In this study I explore the development of the Islamic institution of sufism in general and in particular the exercise of personal authority in one international sufi lineage, the Naqshbandiyya, named after Bahā'uddīn Naqshband (791/1389), who, among other things, pioneered spiritual practices. He is buried near Bukhara in present-day Uzbekistan.[1] This lineage later became known as the Naqshbandiyya-Mujaddidiyya (often abbreviated Mujaddidiyya) after an influential reformer, the Indian Aḥmad Sirhindī (d. 1034/1624), known as the "renewer" (*mujaddid*) of the second Islamic millennium. The Naqshbandiyya exercised leadership by modeling themselves after the most compelling of personal Islamic symbols, the Prophet Muḥammad. Linked to Muḥammad through a spiritual genealogy, traveling the same inner path as the Prophet, and exemplifying the Prophet in every thought and action, Naqshbandī shaykhs (Arabic literally, "elder"; Persian *pīr*) were thought literally to embody him. As obedient disciples modeled themselves after their mentors and confirmed the Prophetic reality through spiritual practice, the Naqshbandī heirs of the Prophet spread throughout the world. Their sufi communities became replicas of the paradigmatic seventh-century community of the Prophet and his Companions. Indian Naqshbandī-Mujaddidīs, by effectively implementing the system of underlying, mostly unconscious conceptual patterns (an "Islamic paradigm"), made an impact on social action far beyond their small numbers and limited popularity.

In this continuity of purpose, significant changes occurred, represented by three overlapping configurations of personal authority—teaching-shaykhs, directing-shaykhs, and mediating-shaykhs—among sufi masters. These three types of sufi shaykh utilized various sources of authority—lineage, spiritual traveling,

[1]When two dates or centuries are juxtaposed, the first is the Islamic lunar *hijrī* date followed by a slash and the Common Era date. When a century is written out, only the Common Era date will be used. All date conversions were calculated with Professor John Woods's "Taqwim" software, using Julian equivalents for the *hijrī* era up to 4 October 1582 and Gregorian equivalents thereafter. Except for technical discussions and post sixteenth-century developments I use Naqshbandiyya to designate the Naqshbandiyya-Mujaddidiyya.

acting as a Prophetic exemplar, and transmission of religious knowledge—to mediate the various divine-human, interpersonal, and sociopolitical dimensions of Muslim society. At the nexus between the divine and human, sufis, as veritable heirs of the Prophet, occupied a borderline, "liminal" position from which they endeavored to re-create the ideal community of the Prophet and his Companions and to act as intermediaries in mundane concerns, just as the Prophet himself had done.

Sources of authority, varieties of sufi guides, and the shifting processes of mediation integrally interconnect with inner spiritual practice that virtually defines who is and who is not a Naqshbandī (or Mujaddidī), who is or is not a directing-shaykh, and who is and who is not a mediating-shaykh. Spiritual practice, a topic often ignored by historians, sociologists, and anthropologists, vitally interacted with historical processes and sociocultural dynamics in Muslim societies. This is so because any paradigm is both an underlying conceptual framework and a set of agreed-upon techniques to verify and confirm it.[2] The "Naqshbandī paradigm" had its shared practices which "generated knowledge" for those who went on a spiritual journey under the guidance of a directing-shaykh. A transformed understanding of the earthly world when they returned from spiritual journeys allowed Mujaddidīs to unite spiritual experience and worldly action and propelled many of them into influential positions in the Muslim community. As Victor Turner's antistructure is the "hidden foundation" of structure, the commanding positions in Muslim societies occupied by Naqshbandīs (historically verifiable) point to extensive but unseen transformation processes (historically unverifiable) that have occurred.[3]

These spiritual experiences, as well as other aspects of the "Naqshbandī paradigm," do not lend themselves automatically to categorization as material or spiritual, legal or mystical, shariʿa or *ṭarīqa*, orthopraxy or orthodoxy, cosmology or credal dogma, or spiritual practice or daily life. The Naqshbandīs as consummate mediators in society, however, were able to integrate these diverse, apparently conflicting aspects of experience into a coherent religious practice for large numbers of people over the centuries. Their early success in India, Central Asia, and Turkey and

[2]Those who use the term *paradigm* generally acknowledge the first aspect (often reduced in popular usage to a theory, any theory) but neglect the second. "Men whose research is based on shared paradigms are committed to the same rules and standards for scientific practice" (Thomas S. Kuhn, *The Structure of Scientific Revolutions*, p. 11).

[3]See Turner's *Dramas, Fields, and Metaphors: Symbolic Action in Human Society*.

later in the entire Islamic world indicates that their practices harmonized well with both the sociocultural milieu and the conceptual framework underpinning the Islamic worldview. Their prominence over centuries demonstrates that Naqshbandī shaykhs continued to maintain the delicate balance between social mediation and acting as transformative presences, veritable "masters of the heart."

Many years ago I left California to see the world and reached Egypt, where I spent the next two years before going to Yemen for three years. By then I had become enamored of the Arabic language and its dialects, but I still knew little about the Islamic tradition. Then another unexpected turn led to Harvard University, where I specialized in the study of sufism under the guidance of one of its foremost experts, Professor Annemarie Schimmel. Since Professor Schimmel had done much work in Indo-Pakistan, learning Urdu in Pakistan was a logical next step for me, and I left Harvard for Lahore in October 1987.

The following spring, in the Northwest Frontier Province, I made the acquaintance of Mubārak Ṣāḥib, the first Naqshbandī shaykh and the first sufi I had encountered in Pakistan. The way to his sufi lodge was about as direct as my path to the study of sufism, and one might well wonder why anyone would go to visit a sufi almost six hundred kilometers from Lahore when one could find hundreds of sufis nearer to hand. I had been asking Pakistanis if they knew someone who taught a contemplative discipline like the sufi mystics I had read about in my studies. In their minds this question usually translated into the whereabouts of a "genuine pir" (*ḥaqīqī pīr*), and they were unable to help me. The assumption behind this, as I realize all too clearly now, was that I expected a sufi to be a mystic. Finally, through two leads, one from an Iranian in Islamabad and another from a Pakistani scholar in Multan, I learned of a sufi in the hinterlands of the Northwest Frontier Province.

At that time, the male dress code outside Peshawar still included a submachine gun, a bandolier, and a pistol. Undaunted, I proposed a three-week independent study program to the director of the language program in Lahore and was granted a three-week leave. Two months later I arrived in the Northwest Frontier Province with a letter of introduction and the name of someone who would conduct me to the shaykh. When I found him, he did not give me a warm reception. After a mild interrogation, my would-be liaison informed me of the dangers of traveling in tribal areas where the only government was the individual and unpredictable armed tribesmen. In addition he was not eager to take on the burdens of protecting me on the road or incurring the displeasure of his shaykh if I proved to be *non grata.* He told me to come back.

Later in the week he finally agreed to make the long journey to the shaykh's lodge, passing fortress-houses with rows of strategically placed slits in the walls along the way. We arrived late one afternoon. Shaykh Mubārak Ṣāḥib, after shaking my hand and giving me a big hug, read my letter and gave me permission to stay. While I was there, he and everyone else were too busy with more important business to answer my elementary questions, so I was left in the odd position of observing sufi activities, some of which I briefly read about but never witnessed, without any conceptual or experiential frame of reference to organize my observations. The lodge was designed for disciples to spend time with their shaykh to learn and refine their spiritual practice and to receive amulets and cures; it served also for the learned to discuss fine points of Islamic law. It was clearly not a place for outsiders to study sufism.

When I returned to Pakistan a year later, I spent the next two years (1989–1991) gathering books about the Naqshbandīs, whose puzzling practices I had witnessed. In Lahore there were qualified scholars and extensive book collections for investigating the Naqshbandiyya during the nineteenth century, because more Naqshbandī activity had taken place in colonial Panjab than in any other region in the world. I visited prominent and also not-so-prominent Naqshbandī lodges, mainly in the Panjab, but as it turned out, Mubārak Ṣāḥib's lodge was the only one where I witnessed Naqshbandīs practicing the spiritual exercises according to the long-established Naqshbandī-Mujaddidī tradition described in the books.

It soon became apparent that directing-shaykhs in Panjabi Naqshbandī lodges had been supplanted by what I decided to call "mediating-shaykhs," that is, shaykhs who had abandoned the spiritual practices and display of spiritual energy used by their directing-shaykh predecessors. To pinpoint when this shift occurred in any given lineage is impossible, since traditional Indian sufi materials do not tell us. All that can be reasonably ascertained is whether or not a certain shaykh acted as a directing-shaykh, that is, whether a shaykh advised his disciples on fine points of practice. If one can find questions or answers concerning established Naqshbandī spiritual practices and phenomenological evidence of spiritual energy transference in collected letters or the published discourses of the shaykh, one can be reasonably certain that the shaykh taught Naqshbandī practices, but the lack of such evidence does not prove the opposite. In other words with textual evidence one might be able to verify that a deceased directing-shaykh was a spiritual director, but there is no way to verify that Naqshbandī practices had been abandoned by a deceased mediating-shaykh on the basis of traditional written evidence or its lack.

Near the end of my two-year research trip I came across a twenty-year collection of monthly magazines from a group led by a prominent pre-independence Naqshbandī shaykh named Jamāʿat ʿAlī Shāh (1841–1951), who had been selected as the Leader of the Muslim Community in 1935. This kind of detailed printed material had no Indian sufi precedent before the twentieth century. It provided ample evidence that Jamāʿat ʿAlī was a paradigmatic mediating-shaykh, an entirely new kind of Naqshbandī leader. Although there had been hereditary shaykhs and shrine caretakers whose primary function was mediatory and who were not known to have taught involved spiritual practices with transmission of spiritual energy, they are not mentioned in Naqshbandī literature. The fortunate discovery of the magazines allowed me to use Jamāʿat ʿAlī as a case study of what was taking place at a time when colonial Panjab was vibrantly alive with Naqshbandī revival activity.

The transformation from directing-shaykh to mediating-shaykh is only rivaled in magnitude of change by the earlier shift from teaching-shaykh to directing-shaykh in the tenth century. But throughout this change one consistent thread continues in the Naqshbandī style of juristic sufism: the conscious striving to duplicate the Prophetic model, inner and outer, centered on a living heir of the Prophet within a "charismatic" community. Whether directing-shaykhs or mediating-shaykhs, Naqshbandī shaykhs engage the hearts of their disciples aspiring to achieve intimacy with God. In this enterprise these spiritual guides prove themselves to be eminently resourceful "masters of the heart."

The largest share of my fieldwork was taken up by a never-ending search for sufi materials scattered in countless private and public collections all over Pakistan and India. The key to what books had been written and where they were located rested in one person, Ḥakīm Muḥammad Mūsā Ṣāḥib, a veritable living bibliographical database and living authority on sufism. Ḥakīm Ṣāḥib is a sufi who practices Greek (*yūnānī*) medicine. I would visit him a couple times a week at his clinic/pharmacy, where he presided over a mixed audience of scholars and writers while a steady stream of patients filed in and out. In the midst of simultaneously following three conversations and writing prescriptions, he would assign me tasks, ostensibly meant to track down books around the city of Lahore. When I completed these errands I would report back, and he would give me another set of assignments. After about a year these errands involved going out to rural Panjab and the Northwest Frontier Province. Although I did not appreciate it at first, ignorantly thinking only in terms of books, I ended up in places where I would never have gone otherwise—Qur'ān schools, mosques, and even a cloth shop. Many times I did not find the books that were supposed to be there, but I learned a great deal about the culture and religion of Muslims living in the Panjab.

The source material by and for the Naqshbandīs is in Arabic, Persian, and Urdu. Most of it is in Lahore, the cultural and literary capital of western Panjab. It falls into three general categories: hagiographical literature, collections of letters written by sufis, and recorded sufi discussions. Hagiography predominates in Indian sufi literature; the latter two categories are usually edited and embedded as separate sections in hagiographical works. When that happens, the complete primary source frequently becomes unavailable, and the hagiographical version becomes the authoritative compilation for posterity.

The limitations of hagiographical sources are aptly described by Amadou Hampaté Bā, the African disciple and hagiographer of a Tijānī sufi named Cerno Bokar (d. 1359/1940) of Mali: "He [the disciple] cannot *not* love his spiritual master because he *is* his master. For him, he has accomplished everything; otherwise he would not have chosen him as his master. He is his model. For example, I can say that for me Cerno Bokar is [*al-*]*insān al-kāmil*, a perfected man. But that does not mean that he is, *in fact*, [*al-*]*insān al-kāmil*, because he himself would not accept it. But for me he is [*al-*]insān al-kāmil because I have never seen anyone whom I would place above him."[4] This passage is a poignant reminder that glorification of the master overrides all other concerns of the hagiographer. Any other context, historical or otherwise, is subordinated to or even obliterated in this primary sentiment.

A research enterprise such as mine cannot avoid all methodological pitfalls; it is difficult to establish the existence of directing-shaykhs on the basis of scattered and incomplete sufi sources and nearly impossible to verify anything about deceased mediating-shaykhs. The major textual "find" was the twenty-year set of monthly sufi magazines of Jamā'at 'Alī Shāh. Although extensive

[4]Brenner, *West African Sufi: The Religious Heritage and Spiritual Search of Cerno Bokar Saalif Taal.* Comments in brackets are my additions.

Ḥakīm Muḥammad Mūsā, well-known sufi, scholar, and Greek medical doctor of Lahore

research has yet to be done, it appears that Jamāʿat ʿAlī's leadership style as a mediating-shaykh has become the norm among his successors and among the recognized institutional successors of the other notable Naqshbandīs in British India and in many other parts of the Islamic world. If the two hagiographic works written on Jamāʿat ʿAlī had been the only sources available to me, there would have been no evidence for this decisive shift in charismatic leadership. Fortunately, these two sources could be augmented with extensive, almost day-to-day information gleaned from twenty years of continuous publication of Jamāʿat ʿAlī's magazine, *Risāla-yi Anwār al-Ṣūfiyya*. Such documentation contrasts sharply with the information available for Naqshbandīs prior to the twentieth century, when historical research depends on random shards of material. In this regard, modern researchers are fortunate that the Naqshbandiyya had so many prolific writers whose works have been preserved. But the sources remain uneven.

In the matter of translation, using the conventions of contemporary American English ignores a considerable part of a cultural tradition. For example, if one translates honorifics from Arabic/Persian/Urdu into English an unwieldy text results; but without these descriptors, pious Muslims would consider the style disrespectful. This, for instance, is how Naqshbandīs would introduce Dōst Muḥammad Qandahārī (d. 1284/1867): "Pilgrim of the two sacred places, the Sign of following the precedents of the chief of the two universes, Sultan of the lovers, Lover of lovers, Chief of those attracted [to God], Support of those traveling [on the Path to God], Leader of the gnostics, Origin of outward miracles, Source of dazzling auspiciousness, Pole of the age, Succor of the age, Appearance of Truth's beauty, Proof of God the Creator's glory, the Presence of our master, Pilgrim Dōst Muḥammad Ṣāḥib 'Associate of the prayer niche,' The poor one (*dāmānī*) from Qandahar, we glorify God almighty with His holiest secrets . . ."[5] In American English this becomes a mere "Dōst Muḥammad Qandahārī."

Although this is a particularly elaborate example, the principle of expressing superior hierarchical rank through titles or appended Arabic phrases of blessing is frequently encountered in Islamic texts as a literary representation of a hierarchical paradigm of religious authority that pervades Islamic culture. Here the use of honorifics has generally been avoided to facilitate con-

[5]Muḥammad Ismāʿīl, *Mawāhib raḥmāniyya fī fawāʾid wa-fuyūḍāt-i ḥaḍarāt thalātha dāmāniyya: al-tajallīyāt al-dōstiyya* [hereafter *Al-tajallīyāt al-dōstiyya*], p. 2.

sistency of names. Designations omitted include "presence" (*ḥaḍrat*), "our lord" (*maulānā*), "master" (*khwāja*), "elder" or "master" (*shaykh* and *pīr*), and "descendants of the Prophet" (*sayyid*), except when such titles have become a part of a person's name—for example, Maulānā Rūmī. Similarly when I refer to a single sufi shaykh "he" is used rather than the formal "they," and a third-person singular rather than the third-person Urdu plural is used to refer to a religiously honored person. Pious Muslims would be astonished by these Western linguistic practices, as many Europeans coming to the United States are shocked the first time a stranger casually addresses them by their first name.

Following convention, Prophet and Prophetic are capitalized when referring to Muḥammad, as are *Companion* and *Successor*, terms referring to individuals of the first and second generations of Muslims, respectively. Formulae for pious blessings are indicated by conventional abbreviations used by Muslims themselves:

"(J)," standing for *jalla jalāluhu*, often follows the word *Allāh*, meaning "May His Majesty be exalted."

"(S)," standing for *ṣallā Allāhu ʿalayhi wa-sallam*, is the preferred eulogy for the Prophet Muḥammad, meaning "God bless him and grant him salvation."

"(s)," standing for *ʿalayhi as-salām*, is used for prophets, meaning "on him (or them, *ʿalayhim*, if plural) be peace."

"(R)," standing for *raḍiya Allāhu ʿanhu*, follows the names of Companions of the Prophet and is sometimes found in Indian sufi texts attached to the names of other pious persons, meaning "May God be pleased with him" (or her, *ʿanhā;* two of them, *ʿanhumā;* three or more of them, *ʿanhum*).

"(r)," standing for *raḥmat Allāh ʿalayhi* or *raḥimahullāh*, follows the names of sufis and other deceased religious authorities or pious Muslims, meaning "May God have mercy upon him" (or her or them, with the appropriate pronoun suffixes, above).

Polite Muslims always add pious phrases in Arabic when mentioning God or pious deceased Muslims. Some pious Muslims do not put a book on their library shelves until they have appended hundreds of such eulogies to names in Urdu and Persian books lacking such niceties.

Neither Persian nor Urdu has gendered pronouns, although Urdu has feminine verb forms. Since it is unacceptable to use masculine forms for both sexes in popular American English, inclusive language is used when there is textual substantiation that both men and women have been regularly involved, e.g., in sufi initiation. There may have been sufi shaykhs who did not have female disciples, but I have no evidence of any such exclusion. On the contrary, the proper method of initiating women was considered important enough to discuss.

There is, however, no written evidence that Naqshbandī *shaykhas* (the feminine of *shaykh*) existed in British India, though sufi *shaykhas* have been prominent from the earliest times.[6] Among the Naqshbandiyya, Muḥammad Faḍlullāh refers to his mother as Shaykha Bībī Ṣāḥiba (d. 1218/1803).[7] Women have ascended to some of the higher reaches of the Islamic spiritual hierarchy. Ibn al-ʿArabī (d. 638/1240), when mentioning the forty substitutes (*abdāl*), makes the special point that there were women among them.[8] Undoubtedly many Indian Muslim women went on to become Naqshbandī *shaykhas*, but their names did not surface in male-dominated sufi writing. The intriguing investigation of Naqshbandī *shaykhas* in India awaits textual evidence; until that time the discussion must be confined to shaykhs.

The transliteration system used here for Arabic, Persian, and Urdu is based on the Library of Congress system (Bulletin 118, Summer 1976, and Bulletin 125, Spring 1978), with the following exceptions:

1. Persian and Urdu consonants are transliterated the same as Arabic. When the same word occurs in more than one language, the Arabic spelling is used if the word is originally an Arabic word and is frequently used in Arabic.
2. The Persian *iḍāfa* is expressed by either -i or -yi and is not usually included for personal names (except Abū Saʿīd-i Abū'l-Khayr). Aspirants in Urdu are indicated by an apostrophe; for example, T'hānawī—to be distinguished from consonants; for example, Thanāullāh.
3. Arabic words ending in *hā'* and *tā' marbūṭa* are written with

[6]Many hagiographic compendia include sections on women sufis (usually at the end). See ʿAbdurraḥmān as-Sulamī, *Kitāb ṭabaqāt aṣ-ṣūfiyya;* ʿFarīduddīn ʿAṭṭār, *Tadhkirat al-awliyā'*; ʿAbdurraḥmān Jāmī, *Nafaḥāt al-uns min ḥaḍarāt al-quds;* and ʿAbdulḥaqq Dihlawī, *Akhbār al-akhyār.*

[7]Muḥammad Faḍlullāh, *ʿUmdat al-maqāmāt*, pp. 445–78.

[8]Muḥyīddīn Ibn al-ʿArabī, *Al-futūḥāt al-makkiyya*, vol. 11, pp. 277–78. The head of the spiritual hierarchy is the pole, surrounded by three directors, four pillars, seven pious ones, and forty substitutes. See Annemarie Schimmel, *Mystical Dimensions of Islam*, p. 200.

a final -a. In the latter case when the *tā'* is followed by a vowel a *-t* is written instead, for example, *sunna* and *sunnat an-nabī.*

4. The diphthong *alif-waw* is transliterated *aw* unless the pronunciation is clearly *au;* for example, *maulwī.* The diphthong *alif-yā* is transliterated *ay.*
5. Personal names are written as they are pronounced, without a separate definite article *al-*, while book titles, the names of groups, and quotations are transliterated as they are written, using the definite article *al-*. In personal names *ibn* (son of) is conventionally abbreviated b.
6. Words used frequently and recognized by scholars of religion are not italicized or transliterated; for example, shaykh, pir, ulama, shariʿa, hadith, sunna. Place names (unless they are part of a name) are treated as English words, and therefore are not transliterated. Repeated discussions among Pakistani scholars on correct voweling of place names confirm Panjab instead of Punjab and Qusur rather than Qasur. There is no consensus on place-name spelling. *Sufi* begins with a lowercase, along with *imam, ulama,* and other terms for Muslim holy persons, as does sufism.
7. Whenever possible I have made plurals of transliterated words by adding -s to avoid burdening the nonspecialist with new vocabulary items.

Without the generosity of the many people and organizations who have assisted me in this project I could not have begun this research, much less complete it. This study has reached timely closure under the auspices of a Rockefeller grant for the year 1995–1996 administered through the Triangle South Asia Consortium in North Carolina. For the study of South Asian Islam it would be difficult to find a more dynamic multidisciplinary group of scholars. The stimulating feedback and advice of Carl Ernst, Kathryn Ewing, David Gilmartin, and Qasim Zaman provided fresh perspectives and necessary correctives to the project throughout the year. Bruce Lawrence returned from a leave in Damascus to convey a year's insights in three short months.

Colgate University has been extremely supportive in this endeavor. In addition to granting a year's leave for the Rockefeller grant, they graciously awarded me a major faculty grant for research at the London India Office and at the Bibliothèque Nationale in Paris. The previous year Colgate University facilitated a research trip to Pakistan through the combined funding of the

Humanities Faculty Development Fund, the Faculty Research Council, and the Faculty Development Council of Colgate University.

This entire enterprise began at Harvard University, where Annemarie Schimmel patiently introduced me to the study of sufism and guided me around the many pitfalls of dealing with the numerous overlapping languages and cultures of South Asia. She has seen the slow evolution of this research project over a period of five years and has kindly written the foreword. Ali Asani and William A. Graham also saw this project through its first incarnation and provided invaluable support. Sue Lonoff of the Derek Bok Center assisted me in developing a writing style more suited for a nonspecialist audience. A number of other individuals provided valuable feedback, including William Chittick, Carl Ernst, Aḥmad Jāvīd, Bruce Lawrence, Fritz Meier, and Iqbāl Mujaddidī. To them and to my other teachers, friends, and colleagues I am indebted for their wisdom and intellectual guidance. They are not responsible for the shortcomings of this book.

The first part of this research was supported by a grant from the American Institute of Pakistani Studies in 1989–1990, followed by a grant from the Institute of International Education in 1990–1991. Suhayl ʿUmar, assistant director of the Iqbal Academy in Lahore, Pakistan, warmly facilitated my research in Pakistan. An accomplished scholar himself, he guided me to the resources needed to begin my project. The Iqbal Academy, my institutional sponsor, and the people working there, especially Aḥmad Jāvīd, have made many aspects of this project possible. The erudite advice of Professor Iqbāl Mujaddidī, one of the foremost historians of the Indian Naqshbandiyya, alerted me to the many difficulties and misconceptions an outsider encounters in studying this lineage. Peter and Erica Dodd of the United States Educational Foundation gave me both personal and institutional support while in Pakistan. I could not have conceived of this project without the timely visit to Mubārak Ṣāḥib; its fulfillment would have been impossible without Ḥakīm Ṣāḥib. Throughout my studies at Harvard, the Center for the Study of World Religions provided financial and academic assistance, in addition to a congenial personal and social atmosphere, thanks to both John B. Carman, the former director, and Lawrence Sullivan, the present director.

The staff at numerous libraries that cooperated in providing the books and manuscripts used for this study have been a constant source of support. Thanks are due the staff at the Punjab University Library, Punjab Public Library, Iqbal Academy Library, Diyal Singh Library, Islamic Research Institute Library in

Islamabad, and Widener Library at Harvard University. Special thanks to the former director of the Iran-Pakistan Institute of Persian Studies in Islamabad, Dr. Tamīmdārī. The scholar-librarian Dr. Tasbīḥi and scholar-bibliographer Dr. Aḥmad Munzavī of this Institute have provided invaluable services to scholars for many years. I cannot mention all the Pakistanis who generously helped me in this work; they have my gratitude.

I thank my parents, Mr. and Mrs. F. F. Buehler, who prepared me well many years ago to do this kind of work. The manuscript has benefited greatly from the accomplished editing of Margaret Ševčenko, and my editors at the University of South Carolina Press, Joyce Harrison and Peggy Hill, have been a joy to work with. Most important, I would like to thank my wife, Emi Morita, who did not anticipate what it would be like to share her husband with a three-year writing project. All the diagrams are her artistic creations and are only a small part of her contribution to this work.

Sufi Heirs of the Prophet

CHAPTER 1

Patterns of Sufi Religious Authority

Even during Muḥammad's lifetime some of his followers expressed a desire to enter into a more intimate relationship with God than could be achieved by performing required ritual practices. Over the next three centuries a discipline of pious self-examination and refined religious psychology, now known as sufism, developed with its own specialized technical vocabulary that came directly from the Qur'ān.[1] The Muslims who engaged in these pious activities became known as sufis, presumably because they wore simple woolen (*ṣūfī*) robes as tokens of their piety. Since those early times, sufism (*taṣawwuf*) has come to represent both an Islamic religious science and the collective spiritual practices of people who desire to have a more encompassing experience of submitting to God (the literal meaning of *islām*).

Because such dramatic transformations in sufism occurred between the ninth and eleventh centuries, it is only from this time that one can even speak of sufism as an Islamic institution. By the eleventh century there was already a practice centered around a directing-shaykh who commanded absolute obedience from his disciples. Instead of being an ascetic who wandered about from teacher-shaykh to teacher-shaykh as they had in the past, each obedient disciple had to be properly initiated by one master who alone could authorize his travel. Formal allegiance (*bay'a*) to this directing-shaykh became common, as did the sufi robe (*khirqa*), the tangible manifestation of this bond. The disciple's attitude revolved around one underlying operating principle: an unquestioning compliance to an infallible shaykh. The Qur'ān had first

[1]See Paul Nywia, *Exégèse coranique et langage mystique: Nouvel essai sur le lexique technique des mystiques musulmanes*. The best introduction to sufism in English is Annemarie Schimmel's *Mystical Dimensions of Islam*.

been interpreted to equate obedience to God with obedience to Muḥammad; the equation now extended to include the shaykh. Going against the spiritual mentor meant opposing God. By the twelfth century a disciple, rather than submitting his or her ego (*nafs* including the lower, carnal soul) to God (*fanā' fi'llāh*),[2] was first expected to annihilate the ego in the directing-shaykh (*fanā' fi'l-shaykh*).[3] Instead of surrendering to God as if to the hands of a corpsewasher (a saying attributed to Sahl b. ʿAbdullāh at-Tustarī [d. 283/896]), the disciple was supposed to surrender to the spiritual mentor as if to the hands of the corpsewasher.[4] This authority of the sufi pir within his inner circle of disciples extended also to the rest of the Muslim community, which increasingly expected him to harness supernatural power on their behalf.

Sufis legitimized this broadened scope of authority—which did not go unchallenged by other religious specialists—in a typically Islamic fashion by creating spiritual lineages, continuous chains (*isnāds*) of pious sufis leading back to the Successors. Jaʿfar al-Khuldī (d. 358/959) first noted such a spiritual pedigree. In the following generation, sufis had extended these spiritual lineages back to the Prophet himself. Starting in the eleventh century, a number of international pan-Islamic sufi *ṭarīqas* named after founder figures flourished, including the Kāzarūniyya or Murshidiyya (named after Abū Iṣḥāq al-Kāzarūnī [d. 426/1035], known as Shaykh-i Murshid), followed by the Qādiriyya (named after ʿAbdulqādir al-Jīlānī [d. 561/1166]), the Kubrawiyya (named after Najmuddīn Kubrā [d. 618/1221]), and the Suhrawardiyya (named after Abū Ḥafṣ Suhrawardī [d. 632/1234]).

By the tenth century, influential sufis had their own sufi centers, lodges (known variously as *khānaqāh, ribāṭ, zāwiya*)[5] where

---

[2]By ego I mean "das Ich" in the Freudian sense of I-ness, in contrast to a more objective "Es" or "it" commonly translated as id.

[3]Farīduddīn ʿAṭṭār, *Dīwān-i qaṣā'id wa-ghazaliyāt,* p. 347, cited by Annemarie Schimmel, *Mystical Dimensions,* p. 237.

[4]The first text is cited by Abū'l-Qāsim al-Qushayrī (d. 465/1072) in his *Al-risāla al-qushayriyya fī ʿilm al-taṣawwuf,* and the second by ʿAynulquḍāt (martyred 525/1132). See Fritz Meier, "Ḫurāsān und das Ende der klassischen Ṣūfik" in *La Persia nel medioevo,* p. 555.

[5]The most extensive study of *khānaqāhs* in the eastern Islamic world is Muḥsin Kiyānī's *Tārīkh-i khānaqāh dar Īrān.* According to Kiyānī there were places called *khānaqāhs* in Damascus from the eighth century ca. 150/767, on ʿAbbadan Island in the Persian Gulf (177/793), and in Ramla, the capital of Palestine. Fritz Meier doubts whether these were actual sufi lodges; see his *Abū Saʿīd-i Abū l-Ḫayr (357–440/967–1049): Wirklichkeit und Legende,* pp. 296–312. Since Nishapur was the Tahirid center for administrative and religious affairs, the first *khānaqāhs* in Khurasan were built there around the beginning of the ninth century. See Kiyānī,

they were free to perform initiation rituals and spiritual practices. Sufi manuals detailing correct conduct toward the shaykh and suitable behavior in the lodge were written to orient newcomers. When the Turkish Saljūq dynasty established their rule in Khurasan during the eleventh century, they reorganized some private religious schools into official institutions, and sufis established joint sufi *khānaqāh-madrasa* complexes, a combination which had become widespread by the twelfth century.[6]

This institutionalization did not occur in isolation but overlapped with developments in other groups trying to consolidate their authority. The ulama defined religious knowledge as comprising the Qur'ān and hadith and derivative texts. They assumed the role of authoritative interpreters of both the holy scripture and its practical applications. Their power did not become an issue until ʿAbbasid times (132/750–656/1258), when they became administrators, judges, and officials of the government and utilized their religious authority for legitimizing purposes. Their influence over religious knowledge was enhanced by the compilation of what were to become the two most authoritative Sunnī hadith collections, the two *Ṣaḥīḥs*.[7] Under the ʿAbbasids the concentration of authority transformed schools of jurisprudence from regional authorities for Kufans, Medinans, or Syrians to "personal schools" identified with an imam, for example, Abū Ḥanīfa (d. 150/767) and Muḥammad ash-Shāfiʿī (d. 204/820).[8] Just as the disciple was supposed to have only one sufi master, by the tenth century a Muslim was expected to follow only one imam in jurisprudence.[9] Politically, much of this crucial period of institutional growth overlapped with what Marshall Hodgson

pp. 137–84. Kiyānī states that lodges to house sufi masters and their circle of permanent disciples date from the tenth century. See ibid., p. 149. Often the term *ribāṭ* refers to a military outpost on the Christian-Muslim frontier.

[6]One of many examples of this combination is the *madrasa* of al-Qushayrī's teacher, Abū ʿAlī Daqqāq, later named Madrasa al-Qushayrī, located in Nishapur and founded in 391/1001. See Richard W. Bulliet, *The Patricians of Nishapur: A Study in Medieval Islamic Social History*, p. 250; and appendix 1 of his volume.

[7]During the ninth century the eminent hadith specialists al-Bukhārī (d. 256/870) and Muslim (d. 261/875) compiled these two *Ṣaḥīḥs* which, in addition to four others, were soon considered canonical by the Sunnī community. Shīʿī collections, accepting only traditions of the imams, followed with the *Al-Kāfī* of Kulaynī (d. 328/939), *Al-uṣūl al-kāfī fī ʿilm al-dīn*.

[8]George Makdisi, *The Rise of Colleges: Institutions of Learning in Islam and the West*, p. 5.

[9]So intense was the personal identification with one's law school in Nishapur that bitter fighting broke out regularly between Ḥanafīs and Shāfiʿīs. Members of different law schools did not live in the same areas nor did they intermarry; see Bulliet, *The Patricians of Nishapur*.

calls "the Shīʿī Century" (333/945–447/1055).[10] Historically speaking, the institutional development of sufism overlapped with other intellectual and political developments of early Islam, including groups focused on infallible imams, known later as Twelver Shīʿīs and Ismāʿīlīs.[11]

Islam and Sufism

In terms of personal experience, *islām* and sufism (*taṣawwuf*) represent two of the aspects or modes of spiritual involvement of three domains of Muslim practice described in an early hadith of the Prophet, "Gabriel's hadith," which describes works (*islām*), faith (*īmān*), and perfection (*iḥsān*).[12] In this hadith it is related that one day a man came walking out of the desert and met the Prophet and his Companions. He proceeded to ask the Prophet a few questions. He asked first about submitting to God (*islām*) and Muḥammad replied that Islam consists of five pillars (attestation of one God and Muḥammad as the Messenger of God, prayer, fasting, alms, and pilgrimage). To everyone's shock, the guest remarked that the Prophet had spoken correctly. He then inquired about faith (*īmān*), and the Prophet responded by listing the articles of faith mentioned in the Qur'ān, namely, God, His messengers, angels, scriptures, and the Day of Judgement. His last question was about virtue or perfection (*iḥsān*), and the Prophet answered that *iḥsān* was worshiping God as if you see Him; if you do not see Him He sees you. At that point the visitor left, and Muḥammad informed his astounded Companions that the angel Gabriel had just visited them in human form.

This threefold conception of religion assumes that the faithful

---

[10]The Shīʿī Buwayhids (320/932–447/1062) ruled Iraq and Persia as the Hamdanids (336/947–392/1002) exercised political authority from Aleppo. It is not certain whether the Buwayhids were Zaydī or Twelver Shīʿīs but "without the smallest doubt, Twelver Shīʿism owes to the Buwayhid régime not only this organisation, but even a part of its doctrinal structure"; see C. Cahen, "Buwayhids or Būyids." Other Shīʿī groups still had their imams who continued to exercise political authority. The Fatimid Ismāʿīlī imams still ruled Egypt and parts of North Africa (297/909–567/1171); Zaydī imams ruled the area of Daylam near the Caspian Sea on and off from 250/864 to 520/1126; and other Zaydī imams first ruled in Yemen from 284/897 to 569/1174.

[11]In a future article I will discuss the confluences between the sufi shaykh and Imāmī imam in early Islamic history.

[12]This hadith is found in the hadith collections of both Bukhārī and Muslim and in English translation. See Tabrīzī, *Mishkāt al-masābīh,* 1:5 (it is the first hadith cited); and William Chittick's *Faith and Practice of Islam: Three Thirteenth-Century Sufi Texts,* which lays out this threefold framework in detail.

have varying potential, inclination, and ability for spiritual activities. The vast majority of Muslims seek salvation through their daily practice of *islām*, informed by faith (*īmān*). Anyone who desires to proceed further into either of these dimensions of the Islamic tradition can spend a lifetime studying each field of knowledge, guided by a teaching-shaykh. Sufism encompasses the activities by which one works toward the field of consciousness and experience represented by perfection (*iḥsān*). Such an enterprise, explicit in the Naqshbandī context, assumes a firm foundation in the practice of submitting to God (*islām*) and in faith (*īmān*) before achieving an extraordinary degree of proximity to God.

Abū'l-Ḥusayn an-Nūrī (d. ca. 295/908) and al-Ḥakīm at-Tirmidhī (d. ca. 298/910) expanded this threefold pattern to a fourfold framework of correspondences in the heart (represented by concentric circles; see figure 1).[13] Accordingly, the breast (*ṣadr*) is connected to the external aspect of religion, *islām*, the domain of jurists; the first interiorization is *īmān* located in the heart (*qalb*), the specialty of theologians and philosophers; the inner heart (*fu'ād*) is the locus of intuitive "gnosis" (*ma'rifa*), associated with perfection (*iḥsān*); and the innermost essence of the heart (*lubb*) represents the ultimate experience of Oneness (*tawḥīd*). The latter two domains are typically those of sufis.

Conceptually both Gabriel's and Nūrī's framework are interlocking hierarchies, that is, each of these inner levels of the heart (see the lower left quadrant of figure 1) encompasses and transcends the other. For example, one can perform the outward obligations of Islam, such as prayer or fasting, without any inner commitment whatsoever. Qur'ān 49:14 describes such a situation: "Say [to the Bedouin] 'You do not have faith.' Instead say 'We have submitted;' since faith has not yet entered your hearts." Faith transcends works while including them; just as perfection (*iḥsān*) includes both faith and works. According to this normative sufi construct, one cannot practice sufism without acting outwardly as a Muslim and having a sincere commitment to the faith.[14]

The principle of encompassing hierarchies also applies to hierarchies of knowledge associated with these levels. Al-Ḥakīm at-

[13] Annemarie Schimmel, *Deciphering the Signs of God: A Phenomenological Approach to Islam*, pp. xiv–xv.

[14] This is one of many reasons why sufism cannot be properly separated from the Islamic tradition. Sufism's unfortunate linguistic status as a capitalized "ism" encourages the tendency to think of it as outside the Islamic tradition.

Tirmidhī in his *Kitāb bayān al-ʿilm* refutes the jurist's equating of jurisprudence (*fiqh*) with the entirety of religious knowledge (*ʿilm*), citing a hadith in which the Prophet declares these three kinds of knowledge. For at-Tirmidhī these three types of knowledge are jurisprudence (*fiqh*), wisdom (*ḥikma*), and gnosis (*maʿrifa*). The sufis are the only ones who combine all three types and thus know both the lawful and unlawful and the realm of the supernatural (*ʿālam al-malakūt*) while feeling God's majesty in their hearts.[15] As the notable sufi Abū'l-ʿAbbās al-Mursī (d. 686/1287) bemoaned, "We have partaken of the knowledge of jurists but they have not partaken of ours."[16] Transformed by spiritual experiences, sufis found jurists, who specialize in external visually observed actions, to be particularly myopic when they claimed exclusive authority over the entire spectrum of religious knowledge.

Sufis, particularly those who studied hadith, respected the oral transmission of scripture, but it was difficult for them to accept a limited notion of religious knowledge (*ʿilm*) based solely on rote memorization of transmitted material.[17] "Gnosis" (*maʿrifa*), claimed by sufis to be a higher form of infallible and certain knowledge, was devoid of the errors found in the ordinary, acquired knowledge of the ulama. One who had certainty (*yaqīn*) through direct intuitive knowledge of God surpassed ordinary ulama who had to rely on long chains of transmitters, some of whom might not have been reliable. In the words of Abū Saʿīd-i Abū'l-Khayr (d. 440/1049), "Having seen, who needs reports?"[18] Speaking from the depths of spiritual experience, Abū Yazīd al-Bisṭāmī (d. 261/875) proclaims, "You have had your knowledge from a dead man who had it from a dead man while we had our knowledge from the living one who never dies."[19]

In figure 1 an-Nūrī's formulation has been expanded into three additional quadrants. These categories approximate the hierarchies and are not intended to harmonize around each circle (for

---

[15]Franz Rosenthal, *Knowledge Triumphant: The Concept of Knowledge in Medieval Islam*, pp. 179–81.

[16]Tarif Khalidi, *Arabic Historical Thought in the Classical Period*, p. 213.

[17]Rosenthal, in his *Knowledge Triumphant*, p. 166, notes (citing al-Qushayrī) that before the development in the ninth century of the separate categories of knowledge, theology, and mysticism, *ʿilm* and *maʿrifa* were identical and every scholar (*ʿālim*) was also a gnostic (*ʿārif*).

[18]Muḥammad b. Munawwar, *Asrār al-tawḥīd fī maqāmāt Shaykh Abī Saʿīd*, p. 102; translated by John O'Kane, *The Secrets of God's Mystical Oneness*, p. 188.

[19]ʿAbdurra'ūf al-Munāwī, *Al-kawākib al-durriyya fī tarājim al-sadāt al-ṣūfiyya*, British Museum ms. add. 23369; cited in Kamil Mustafa Al-Shaibi, *Sufism and Shiʿism*, p. 65.

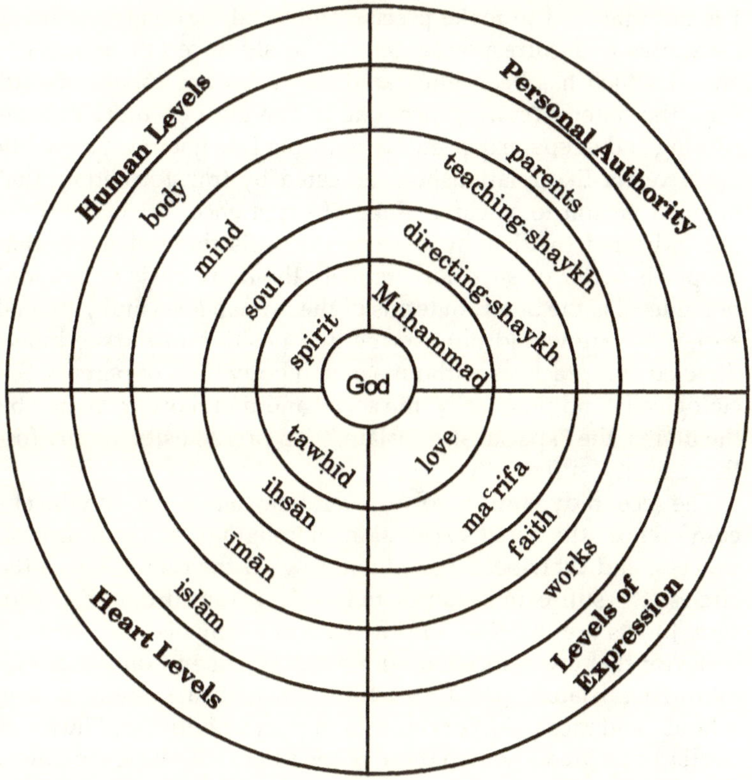

Figure 1. Normative sufi hierarchies

example, soul, directing-shaykh, *iḥsān* and *maʿrifa*) even though rough correspondences do exist. The upper left quadrant and lower right quadrant are mirror images of each other: works are accomplished by observable bodily actions; faith is developed through increased knowledge (*ʿilm*); gnosis (*maʿrifa*) unfolds through a purified, tranquil soul (*al-nafs al-muṭmaʾinna*); and love, the most subtle of human expressions, is communicated through the most rarified human aspect, the spirit. Sumnūn, a tenth-century sufi living in Baghdad, exclaimed: "A thing can be explained only by something that is subtler than itself. There is nothing subtler than love—by what, then, shall love be explained?"[20] The upper right quadrant traces the usual sequence of religious teachers for Muslims, each of whose teaching tends to have greater transformative potential as one moves toward the center, the presence of Muḥammad being the most transformative. Figure

[20]Cited in Schimmel, *Mystical Dimensions*, p. 140.

1 is not intended to make precise, universal, mutually exclusive categories and correspondences but to show certain processes, one of which has been illustrated above: as one moves inward from the outer circumference, one is moving into more encompassing and deeper experience. By deeper I do not mean a quality but a vector-like relationship, indicated by transformation, that opens a person to a wider range of experience. What clearly is not indicated (neither by me nor the sufis themselves) is that deeper is better or superior. Actually the more basic or foundational level is the outer. In terms of the human level and personal authority, one would not ever be in a position to pursue inner-directed sufi practices without a sound body born of parents. Sociologically and practically, the social and moral order created by the ulama, the "specialists of islām," is a prerequisite for any further activity, sufi or otherwise.

The second dynamic involves lateral movement around the circumference (the jurist expression of religion), a legitimization process, and centripetal movement toward the center across the circles (the sufi expression of religion), a transformational process. Jurists are interested in the external symbols and outward behavior that are associated with maintaining and outwardly legitimizing Islamic social structures through a system of law, schools, and mosques. For this reason their activities and interests overlap considerably with those of the rulers who have the power to enforce such concerns and who need such legitimacy to keep their power. It is the ulama who justify war in the name of *jihād* and who provide the basis for salvation to give meaning to such endeavors (martyrs go immediately to heaven). This outer level supplies soteriological formulae, important psychologically, to enforce the dictates of society (if one does these things one goes to heaven; otherwise one goes to hell). The jurist's expression of religion integrates and stabilizes societal structures, a necessary precondition for sufi expressions which are internally revolutionary in their transformative quality. The shariʿa is the kernel that protects, legitimizes, and tempers the precious seed of spiritual practice. The jurist's expression represents structure and the sufi's expression represents anti-structure.[21]

This anti-structure, required for the integration and stabilization of the outer social structure, presumes movement, change, and transformation within the individual. Instead of *jihād* as war, sufis stress *jihād* as the "inner struggle" on the path to God, to

[21]See the discussion of the sufi lodge in chapter 2. Juristic sufism overlaps both spheres.

control the desires and ignorance of one's lower carnal nature (*nafs*). This refers to the hadith where the Prophet is reported to have said, "I have returned from the lesser *jihād* to the greater *jihād*."[22] The transformation implies a transcending of prior states and perceptions which in the sufi environment results from the spiritual experiences associated with the performance of sufi exercises. By mystical or spiritual experience I mean a form of awareness beyond the conventional space-time consensus reality. Although it is transrational, i.e., beyond mental, emotional, and physical processes, part of the referent associated with mystical/spiritual experience is associated with the ordinary cultural matrix of the individual. Discipline under a preceptor enables mystical experience slowly to transform the individual. For most people it requires decades of disciplined work with a directing-shaykh.

Gifted and persevering travelers on the Naqshbandī-Mujaddidī path could reach a state of greater intimacy, returning to the everyday world transformed by their experiences. Like gifted monks and nuns in the Zen Buddhist tradition, they normally show no outward signs of their extraordinary achievements: they are extraordinarily ordinary. Their inner commitment is no longer merely the appearance of faith (*sūrat-i īmān*), but the reality of faith (*ḥaqīqat-i īmān*). After having traveled in the spiritual depths, they appear to bend over and prostrate themselves in prayer just as they had before embarking on the Path. Rather than merely having the appearance of worship (*ṣūrat-i 'ibādat*), however, their ritual practices manifest the reality of worship (*ḥaqīqat-i 'ibādat*). When the traveler comes back radically changed to the temporary abode of the phenomenal world, every action performed in this world takes on an extraordinary quality. In Muḥammad 'Umar Bīrbalī's words, it is a "revolution of Reality" whereby "the disciple experiences such a revolution in his own carnal soul that, having lost his first [way of] being, he experiences in his existence the certainty of another [way of] being. [It is] in regard to this great revolution [that] I have named my book *Revolution of Reality* (*Inqilāb al-ḥaqīqat*)."[23]

To summarize briefly, the difference between the center and the circumference in figure 1 represents the polarities of center vs. periphery, inspired action vs. uninspired action, charismatic

[22]Often *jihād* is translated as "holy war," but I suspect most Muslims have not agreed that such wars are primarily "in the path of God."

[23]Muḥammad 'Umar Bīrbalī, *Inqilāb al-ḥaqīqat*, pp. 6–7 (introduction).

vs. routinized authority, and extraordinary vs. ordinary.[24] This figure, conforming to sufi notions, will serve as the basis for a later discussion of transformation and the various configurations associated with sources of authority. In its simplest form figure 1 is one circle of sharīʿa with many radii or paths (the sufi *ṭarīqas*) leading to the center (*ḥaqīqa*).

In actual human life abstractions such as circles, vectors, and radii have little meaning. Practicing sufis work and live in the everyday world where they try to live a quasi-monastic life, which includes an emphasis on ritual purity, the segregation of sexes, and a plethora of utterly mundane details. The genius of these sufi practices is that they enable the ordinary householder to imbue his or her life with spirituality. Although this study emphasizes the importance of a meditative discipline this is only a small slice of what sufi activities mean to contemporary South Asian Muslims who visit sufis. A tour of sufi lodges in South Asia demonstrates that the primary activities of sufis are assisting believers in their worldly affairs, counseling them in mental/physical health problems, and making amulets to protect them. Although not well documented in sufi literature, sufism probably always has had this worldly component since the development of the sufi lodge in the tenth century. I suspect that only a minority of those going to sufi shaykhs ever have yearned for mystical experience, but those relative few had importance beyond their numbers.[25] Few twentieth-century Indian Naqshbandī shaykhs emphasize a contemplative discipline and guide others along the Path. Rather than directing their disciples to approach God themselves, disciples depend on the intercession of mediating-shaykhs who in turn intercede with Muḥammad.

Mediation and Sufi Shaykhs

According to Sunnī dogma, God's messengers (sing. *rasūl*) brought God's scripture to human beings; of them the Prophet Muḥammad was the latest, the last, and the most exalted, though

[24]For an analysis of these terms, see Edward Shils, *Center and Periphery: Essays in Macrosociology*.

[25]Katherine Ewing has done groundbreaking work researching the sufi's role as healer, dream interpreter, and exorciser. See her "Sufi as Saint, Curer, and Exorcist in Modern Pakistan," in E. Valentine Daniel and Judy F. Pugh, eds., *South Asian Systems of Healing;* and "The Dream of Spiritual Initiation and the Organization of Self Representations Among Pakistani Sufis," which appeared in *American Ethnologist*.

even he had God's message revealed to him through the mediation of the angel Gabriel. For humanity Muḥammad is the divine mediator par excellence, the intermediary through whose voice the Qur'ān becomes revealed to humanity. Once the door to divine mediation opens, people will ask for assistance with more immediate worldly concerns. It was under these circumstances that representatives from Yathrib (later Medina) came to ask Muḥammad to act as an arbiter in settling disputes between conflicting factions. There are numerous examples of Muslims asking Muḥammad for something as a prophetic mediator between God and humans and receiving a reply in a dream.[26] After Muḥammad's death people soon assumed that he would intercede with God concerning their affairs, especially if one visited his grave ("Whoever visits my grave will be given intercession").[27]

Since the ninth century Muslims have expected sufi pirs, as "heirs of the Prophet," to perform similar (if non-prophetic) mediatory functions, for example, between God and humans, between individuals, and between factions. The sufi shaykh, like the Prophet, also becomes an intermediary (*barzakh*) between the two worlds of the Creator and the created. Of the three dimensions of mediation, however, divine-human mediation forms the basis, at least until modern times, for sufi interpersonal and sociopolitical action. To clarify these mediating channels linking the divine and human, I identify four sources of authority—lineage, spiritual travel, being a Prophetic exemplar, and transmission of religious knowledge—that characterize and undergird sufi legitimacy.

The most circumscribed form of mediation, that utilized by religious scholars and teaching-shaykhs, involves the oral transmission of divine scripture. The directing-shaykh expanded that scope of mediation considerably. Having arrived close to God after spiritual travels, the Naqshbandī directing-shaykh returns to teach humanity. In this the directing-shaykh follows what the Naqshbandīs call the "inner" model of the Prophet (*sunna*), as

[26]Muḥammad Ḥasan Jān, *Al-uṣūl al-arbaʿ fī-tardīd al-wahhābiyya*, p. 34; and Abū Ḥāmid al-Ghazzālī, *The Remembrance of Death and the Afterlife*, pp. 156–59.

[27]Most likely this stems from a hadith passage from one of the oldest collections that confirms the Prophet's intercession on the Last Day: "Then He Says: 'Oh Muḥammad, lift your head, ask, and you will be given; intercede, and you will be granted [what you ask]!' I lift my head and say: 'O Lord, *ummatī, ummatī:* my community, my community!' " See Andrae, *Die Person Muhammads*, pp. 236–38. A slightly different wording is found in Asad b. Mūsā, *Kitāb al-zuhd*, pp. 73–76. Both of these sources are cited in Annemarie Schimmel, *And Muhammad Is His Messenger: The Veneration of the Prophet in Islamic Piety*, p. 85 (brackets are in original text).

opposed to its complement, outwardly imitating exemplary Prophetic behavior, or the "outer" sunna. Through a psycho-behavioral modeling process, those in the directing-shaykh's retinue become transformed by the borderline power that comes from being prophet/non-prophet. For Sunnīs there is an ontological divide between prophets and non-prophets and, no one after Muḥammad by definition can be a prophet, only prophetlike. As an heir of the Prophet the directing-shaykh approaches the threshold of prophethood, an asymptotic situation allowing some disciples to view "the actual Muḥammad" through their sufi shaykh. Combined with a spiritual lineage connecting the directing-shaykh back to Muḥammad, the resulting liminal power becomes channeled into wider networks as the directing-shaykh mediates both interpersonal and sociopolitical concerns in the larger interests of the community.

Just as the term "directing-shaykh" points to a new focus on directing not just spiritual practices but the daily lives of initiated disciples, in contrast to the teaching-shaykh, so the term "mediating-shaykh" identifies the pir as the sole intermediary between Prophet and disciple. While the activities of a directing-shaykh enable disciples to arrive near God themselves, the mediating-shaykh "transmits" the disciples' needs to Muḥammad, who then in turn intercedes with God. The disciple's activity is centered on cultivating an unconditional love to facilitate this mediational process. Both the directing-shaykh and mediating-shaykh have multidimensional mediatory functions, but for the latter the sphere of spiritual practice has been transformed completely into a mediatory process.

Over time the sufi shaykh continually adapted to the religious and sociopolitical interstices, until he functioned as a religious and sociopolitical facilitator or social lubricant. This was most noticeable after the transformation from teaching-shaykh to directing-shaykh. Instead of mediating transmitted knowledge, both scriptural and mystical, to a small group of roving students, the directing-shaykh typically had an inner circle of initiates whom he rigorously directed and a much larger outer circle of people who came for assistance in more mundane concerns. In the Naqshbandī case both activities involved divine mediation. God's spiritual grace/energy transmitted through the shaykh was experienced by disciples as supernatural power, and facilitated their spiritual travel. Others, recognizing the shaykh as a nexus of supernatural power, requested him to use this divine grace for their mundane concerns. Conflicting political or social factions often made use of a directing-shaykh's mediation. With the advent of the sufi lodge these roles became institutionalized.

Unlike Naqshbandī directing-shaykhs, who were found throughout the Islamic world for over five centuries, Naqshbandī mediating-shaykhs are a relatively recent development. Hereditary shaykhs and sufi shrine caretakers have existed at least from the eleventh century, apparently performing roles during the premodern period which correspond to those of Naqshbandī mediating-shaykhs in the modern period.[28] In the case study presented here, Jamāʿat ʿAlī's mediating-shaykh activity exhibits an inner-outer dichotomy in terms of initiates versus non-initiates, but the distinction becomes blurred, since love is the focus of spiritual practice. The world in which he mediated is very different from the milieu of the earlier directing-shaykh. As a religious figure, Jamāʿat ʿAlī's authority had no legitimacy with the British, and he mediated in a sufi circle composed of an unprecedented combination of rural, urban, and anglicized disciples. Compared to the directing-shaykh, his scope of mediation had considerably increased, while his power was diffused both geographically and within the master-disciple relationship.

Heirs of the Prophet

A Muslim holy person is considered to be a friend or protégé of God, a *walī Allāh,* whether a pious person, religious scholar (*ʿālim*), sufi, or Shīʿī imam. God's friends usually come in one of two kinds: those who intentionally exercise power (*taṣarruf*), both worldly and supernatural, over others and those through whom God works as He wills.[29] In other words, one *walī Allāh* is per-

---

[28]Further research on both kinds of shaykhs needs to be done. See P. M. Currie, *The Shrine and Cult of Muʿīn al-Din Chishtī of Ajmer.*

[29]The first type of protégé of God has *wilāya,* a tangible power which he can decide to wield over others. The second type has *walāya,* which means that any expression of divine power involuntarily manifests through him. See Muḥammad Hidāyat ʿAlī Jaipūrī, *Miʿyār al-sulūk wa-dāfiʿ al-awhām wa'l-shukūk,* p. 152; and Naṣrullāh Pūrjawādī, *Sulṭān-i ṭarīqat: sawānih zindagī wa-sharh-i athār-i Khwāja Aḥmad Ghazzālī,* pp. 223–25. In both sources *walāya* has superior rank to *wilāya.* The former type of closeness to God has an astonishing potential for abuse (in conventional terms). Grammatically both these two terms and *walī* are derived from the same Arabic root "w = l = y." For all practical purposes (except for occasional hairsplitting grammatical discussions) the two meanings have become conflated for two reasons: (1) People do not care whether the power surging from a holy person comes from his own volition or involuntarily: the source is perceived to be the same and the effect is equally beneficial or devastating; and (2) The short vowels are rarely written in Arabic and Persian script languages so one cannot

ceived as God working for His friend and the other is God working through His friend. Even though scholars occasionally discuss the differences between these two types of *walī Allāh* in grammatical terms, sociologically the result is the same: God's protégés are feared and respected. The theoretical framework underlying the concept of a friend of God assumes that all power and authority originate with God. When a person is close or intimate to God then that person is God's friend or protégé acting as an intermediary between humans and God in much the same way as a person having close connections to a king can help others. There are characteristic ways in which Muslims have connected to this power, but to be close to God is to have access to divine power in one form or another.

All three major types of religious figures in the Muslim community—jurists, sufis, and Shīʿī imams—have considered themselves "heirs of the Prophet." In Islamic terms, no person can legitimately claim to be a prophet or an heir of a prophet unless he has achieved intimacy with God (*wilāya*) in some fashion.[30] The authority of the ulama is derived from transmitted knowledge based on scriptural sources. Sufis typically establish their legitimacy through a spiritual lineage often combined with religious experience. In general, ulama derive their knowledge from books transmitted orally by teachers; sufis learn from the personal experience of sufi pirs. The Shīʿī imams emphasize physical as well as spiritual lineage, but some also derive their authority from spiritual experience.

Sufis flourished throughout the Islamic world more than any other type of personal authority because their mediatory skills were required for the smooth functioning of an agrarian-nomadic economy with a decentralized form of government.[31] This media-

distinguish between the two words. Following scholarly convention, I will use the term *wilāya* to denote proximity or intimacy with God. The most detailed grammatical explanation on these two terms and the notion of *walī* is Michel Chodkiewicz, *Le sceau des saints: Prophètie et sainteté dans la doctrine d'Ibn Arabî*, pp. 35–39; translated by Liadain Sherrard, *Seal of the Saints: Prophethood and Sainthood in the Doctrine of Ibn ʿArabī*, pp. 17–25.

[30]Hamid Dabashi, following the dogma of Weber's sociological theory, found *wilāya* to be too general and vague a term to use for Muḥammad's charismatic authority. Dabashi argues that since *wilāya* did not include the idea of domination and legitimate use of physical force, two concepts necessary for Weber's theory of charisma, it was not a meaningful term to describe Muḥammad's charismatic authority. His other objection was that it was a term not specific to Muḥammad. See Hamid Dabashi, *Authority in Islam*, pp. 39–40.

[31]After the Safavids sufi activity diminished considerably in Iran. Yet even in contemporary Iran sufi ideas are influential with Shīʿī clerics, e.g., the late Ayatullāh Rūḥullāh Khomeinī. See Alexander Knysh, "*Irfan* revisited: Khomeini and

tory authority was itself grounded in multiple connections to a deeper symbolic Prophetic authority, often enacted through the institution of the lodge where sufis could supervise the specialized practices of their disciples without interference. Legitimizing spiritual lineage, religious learning, and practices imitating ceremonies once used to declare allegiance to the Prophet rounded out the institutional trappings of sufi shaykhs. The fragile nature of prophetic charisma made institutional balance an extremely challenging proposition. Too much property and worldly success were as inimical to its rejuvenation as a scarcity of resources.

At the heart of this institution was the spiritual guide. Sufis, interpreting Muḥammad's prophetic experience on the basis of the Qur'ān and hadith texts, legitimized their pattern of authority by claiming to have experienced the depths of spiritual experience. They then returned, eminently qualified to help others proceed along the same path. In common parlance, the shaykh was someone who was a friend/intimate of God and therefore possessed the ability to act as an intermediary between humanity and God. Although the sufi shaykh could rarely be separated from the institutional practices that evolved from the tenth century, his or her authority was legitimized by having duplicated on a lesser scale the spiritual journey of the Prophet. In this fashion the personal authority of the sufi pir was necessarily dependent on that of Muḥammad and other prophets. He was their heir.

Instead of imitating the political or military exploits of the Prophet, sufi shaykhs attempted to duplicate his practical function as a "spiritual magnet.[32] To the extent that he attracted followers, he repelled enemies. The "atoms" of his entire being, whether physical, psychological, emotional, or spiritual, were aligned in one direction, pointing to and in harmony with God. A prophet or an intimate of God was like a praying lodestone whose internal structure had become magnetized after the atoms

---

the Legacy of Islamic Mystical Philosophy," in *Middle East Journal*. Whether Khomeini could be called a sufi is another matter, particularly in view of the Twelver Shīʿī (believing in twelve imams) environment. Khomeini wrote commentaries on Ibn al-ʿArabī's *Fuṣūṣ al-ḥikam* and on Muḥammad b. Hamza Fanarī's (d. 834/1431) *Miṣbāḥ al-uns*, a commentary on Ṣadruddīn al-Qūnawī's (d. 673/1273–74) *Miftāḥ al-ghayb*. Ismāʿīlī imams still lead their international groups.

[32]This metaphor is used by twentieth-century Naqshbandīs referring to the "magnetic pull of God" and how being in the company of the shaykh and other disciples "creates a magnetic charge which remains afterwards." (*Risāla-yi anwār al-ṣūfiyya* 1, no. 1: 9).

had lined up in one direction and whose external shape was precisely aligned in the direction of the Kaʿba.

The pir functioned as a combination touchstone/lodestone for the disciple's ego. Once one's ego is effaced in the shaykh, it is, for all practical purposes, subordinated directly to God because the shaykh has duplicated the Prophetic realities so closely. As an heir of the Prophet he functions like the Prophet (for Muslims this is not an ontological equivalence). Those with their egos in harmony with God merely needed fine tuning to become magnets in their own right. At the other extreme, some were not even lodestones. The majority, however, could not help but continually rub against the magnet of the spiritual mentor. All behavioral rules and psychological conditioning were purposely designed (or experimentally discovered) to be effective in this magnetizing process. Such an activity did not eliminate the ego but eventually aligned it in the same direction as the shaykh's will, which had already been aligned with that of God. The focused spiritual energy (*tawajjuh*) of the master was like an electromagnetic force. The Kaʿba, like the magnetic north pole, was the point toward which a praying Muslim or a freestanding magnet would turn. If, however, a strong presence was in the immediate vicinity, this would override all other spiritual and magnetic fields. For a sufi the goal of the human being is to reconcile the contradictory upper and lower aspects of reality within oneself. To develop fully each person has to become a bridge between the mundane and the supramundane without becoming caught in one or the other. The ways of connecting to God are the sources of authority by which Prophetic heirs have exercised leadership.

Sources of Personal Authority

I went to Ḥaḍrat Ḥājjī Muḥammad Afḍal's [house] to receive divine grace (*tawajjuh*) and, when I requested this, he said to me, "From your spiritual perception you have progressed far on the Path and have achieved the station of revealed knowledge. I do not have this kind of knowledge and therefore I cannot assist you on the advanced spiritual path (*bi-ṭarīq-i iḥsān*)." So I did not [expect to] benefit from Ḥaḍrat, but during hadith lessons from the divinely emanating grace and energy (*fuyūḍ*) of his blessed inner self I received divine energy (*fayḍ*) and my connection to God (*nisbat*) was strengthened. During Ḥaḍrat Ḥājjī Muḥammad Afḍal's hadith lesson I used to acquire the presence (*ḥuḍūr*) of the Prophet's connection. Many lights and blessings (*barakat*) used to manifest [themselves]. Essentially I used to be in companionship (*ṣuḥbat*) with God's messenger. During this time I experienced the Prophet's [focused] divine energy (*tawajjuh*) and spiritual countenance (*alṭafāt*). It was splendid from its perfect Prophetic connection (*nisbat*), expansive, and full of light. The meaning of "religious scholars are the heirs of the prophets" became clear.[33]

These radiant words of a famous sufi of Delhi, Mīrzā Maẓhar Jān-i jānān (assassinated in 1195/1781), succinctly describe the power of person-centered religious authority and implicitly show the contrast with scripture-centered authority. It beautifully demonstrates the ways Muslims can endeavor to be in the Prophet Muḥammad's presence, to re-enact for themselves the paradigmatic relationship that the Companions had with Muḥammad. For Indian Naqshbandīs this is what personal authority is all about: a heart-to-heart connection leading to a vividly intense experience of Muḥammad. For Muslims no human was ever nearer to God than the Prophet; therefore linking oneself with Muḥammad signifies intimacy with God.

The many ways of linking oneself to the Prophet are typically conceived as exclusive to a given specialist: transmitted religious knowledge is the domain of religious scholars, spiritual experience the domain of sufis. The foregoing passage adroitly sets the reader up to think in that way: why would an advanced sufi like Mīrzā Maẓhar, with direct access to God's revealed knowledge (*kashf*), sit at the feet of a teacher to memorize hadith? Muḥammad Afḍal's humility is a ritualized response for both Mīrzā Maẓhar and the reader. Instead of being just an ordinary religious scholar, Muḥammad Afḍal proves to be a catalytic Prophetic exemplar, allowing Mīrzā Maẓhar to have an astounding and unexpected psychospiritual experience. The transformative potential of such an intense personal experience matches anything one could have with a sufi master.[34] How shariʿa-minded juristic sufis, particularly the Naqshbandīs, have gone about linking themselves to their beloved Prophet is the subject of this study.

Establishing a connection with the Prophet also serves to authenticate Muslim claims to religious authority. The four ways of linking oneself to the Prophet (see figure 2, reading horizontally) are the sources of authority associated with different kinds of Muslim religious figures. Spiritual travel is typically a specialty of sufis which involves a transformative spiritual experience. By the eighth century sufis had become noted as protégés of God

[33]Ghulām ʿAlī Shāh, *Maqāmāt-i maẓharī*, pp. 287–88.

[34]Muḥammad Afḍal spent many years in the company of Naqshbandīs and learned the science of hadith from them, but he never received formal instruction in the spiritual methods of the Naqshbandiyya. See ibid., pp. 244–46.

(*awliyāʾ*) who often exhibited supernatural power. Being an exemplar involved modeling one's behavior on the Prophetic example (*sunna*). Originally associated with pious behavior, by the fifteenth-century the sunna had become a necessary requirement to the exercise of religious authority in some shariʿa-minded sufi lineages. Biological and spiritual lineage leading back to the Prophet often legitimized leadership. Among Shīʿīs, the Imāmī community and the Nizārī Ismāʿīlī community both have used an ancestral pedigree traced back to Muḥammad to designate imams who are said to have received the divine knowledge of the prophets.[35] Religious knowledge is the source associated with religious scholars who transmit the holy words received via an unbroken sequence of reputable Muslims. All four of these sources of authority—spiritual travel, the sunna, lineage, and religious knowledge—converge upon one central figure: the Prophet.

Early sufis acquired authority as a result of their piety and mystical experiences, understood in the Islamic context as non-prophetically replicating the Prophet's own physical ascension, a spiritual journey ending close to God. This is the explanation for the belief that sufis had supernatural powers and why many in the Muslim community came to expect them to function as healers, exorcists, and counselors.[36] For Naqshbandīs, who developed a shariʿa-minded juristic expression of sufism, spiritual travel was integrated, even subordinated, to ritual practice. Spiritual wayfaring was justified by and organized around the principle of duplicating the Prophet's own experience to the fullest extent possible. The prophetic path, argued the Naqshbandīs, required a return to the physical world to assist others to become better Muslims after a spiritual journey towards God. This inner connection enabled Naqshbandīs, as heirs of the Prophet, to exhibit tangible supernatural power that anyone visiting a directing-shaykh's sufi circle could witness.

---

[35]The Imāmīs, sometimes called "proto-Shīʿīs," become a formally distinct Shīʿī group (believing in twelve imams) in the tenth century. There are also Shīʿī groups who believe in only the first five or seven of the Twelver imams, called Zaydīs and Ismāʿīlīs respectively. The latter two groups have an ideal of the imam (in principle) whose functions include acting both as head of state and as the supreme religious authority.

[36]In Islam and in Judaism there is a hidden spiritual hierarchy whose members usually appear to be normal individuals. See Annemarie Schimmel, *Mystical Dimensions of Islam*, p. 200; and Gershom G. Scholem, *On the Kabbalah and Its Symbolism*, p. 6. Ibn al-ʿArabī states that "for the Muhammadan heir, the signs *(âyât)* are interior, making it difficult for an ordinary person to recognize." See Michel Chodkiewicz, *An Ocean Without a Shore: Ibn ʿArabî, The Book, and the Law*, p. 96.

	Sources of Personal Authority			
	Spiritual Travel/ Supernatural Power	Exemplar	Lineage	Transmitted Religious Knowledge
Divinely Inspired Ones (*majdhūbs*)	●			
Tablīghī Jamāʿat		●		
Shrine Caretakers Hereditary Shaykhs			●	
Ulama		○	○	●
Imāmī imāms/ Āghā Khān	○	●	●	●
Sufi Teaching-Shaykh	●	●	○	○
Sufi Directing-Shaykh	●	●	●	○
Sufi Revivalist Mediating-Shaykh	○	●	●	○

● indicate sources of authority that define the category

○ indicate optional sources of authority that do not define the category

Figure 2. Sources of Islamic personal authority

Early in Islamic history a set of intricately detailed, culturally appropriate rules for behavior and good manners (*adab*) became a characteristic ideal. Pious conduct and dress followed the Prophetic sunna, which, selectively interpreted, formed the framework for ritualized manners. Students and disciples constantly tried to imitate these exemplary patterns.[37] The conscious modeling of one's inward and outward behavior on that of Muḥammad also became an explicit source of authority for sufis, particularly among the Moroccan Jazūliyya from the fifteenth century and the Indian Mujaddidiyya from the seventeenth century.

In the Naqshbandī case a spiritual guide, as heir of the Prophet, was expected to be the living embodiment of the exemplary model of Muḥammad. In British India, behavior and dress conforming to the Prophetic model combined with a spiritual lineage

[37]A proper religious education involved students faithfully modeling their teachers. See Michael Chamberlain, *Knowledge and Social Practice in Medieval Damascus, 1190–1350*, pp. 122–25; and Barbara Metcalf, *Islamic Revival in British India: Deoband, 1860–1900*, pp. 138–97.

enabled sufis of many lineages to be recognized as revivalist pirs. The living pir brought Muḥammad's own vitality and charisma into direct contact with Muslims who venerated the Prophet. In nineteenth-century India, the disciples of Chishtī scholar Rashīd Aḥmad Gangōhī (d. 1322/1905) compared their shaykh's speech to that of Muḥammad: "[W]hen Rashid Ahmad spoke, it was like the Prophet speaking. My heart opened like a flower."[38] The contemporaries of Muḥammad Qāsim Nānautawī (d. 1294/1877), a Chishtī shaykh-scholar at Deoband, continually compared him to the Prophet.[39] A century earlier Mīrzā Maẓhar had similar experiences with Muḥammad Afḍal.

Tracing back one's genealogy to Muḥammad follows the same principle that hadith scholars had used to validate transmitted reports of Muḥammad's sayings and actions. Muslims certified "valid" sufis in the same fashion as they verified "correct" hadiths, i.e., by identifying chains of reliable transmitters that confirmed their spiritual training and teaching lineage. The sufism of pan-Islamic lineages did much to eliminate antinomian tendencies by the fourteenth century, and Naqshbandī-Mujaddidīs discouraged potentially disruptive Uwaysī initiations in the seventeenth century. Later, a spiritual lineage became increasingly necessary to legitimize sufi authority, even if this pedigree was unhistorically extended to include "charismatic transmissions," commonly known as Uwaysī initiations. By the eleventh century in the eastern Islamic world, spiritual pedigree alone, without any mystical experience, bestowed a spiritual authority upon sufis who had inherited their office as *sajjādanishīn* (principal successor, literally, "one who sits on the prayer carpet").[40]

Lineage, which Naqshbandīs have understood as a conduit for spiritual energy from God, became a prerequisite for mystical practice. What originally served as a means of verifying authority itself became a second, independent source of prestige. The authority of both Imāmīs and sufis who inherit their position as *sajjādanishīn*, without having done any spiritual journeying, stems from biological lineage.[41]

---

[38]Metcalf, *Islamic Revival*, p. 174.

[39]Ibid., p. 166. Both these pirs taught at Deoband, a prominent Indian Islamic seminary near Delhi.

[40]The Chishtiyya at Chisht, east of Herat in present-day Afghanistan, began designating hereditary successors from the eleventh century. See Lawrence Potter, "The Kart Dynasty of Herat: Religion and Politics in Medieval Iran," p. 110.

[41]Shīʿīs believed religious authority was communicated by certain lineal descendants of ʿAlī, the Prophet's cousin, and Fāṭima, the Prophet's daughter, the *ahl al-bayt*. From this legacy, *sayyids* or *ashrāf*, that is, descendants of the Prophet, have continued to be particularly respected in the Shīʿī community. Sunnīs, too, have

Scholars of Qur'ān and hadith often devoted their lives to the study and preservation of the holy scripture in order to transmit this sacred knowledge faithfully. Their involvement in the transmission of sacred knowledge connected them directly back to the Prophet. In the culture of the learned ulama, the pursuit of religious knowledge (*ʿilm*) and truth through studying scripture enabled the jurist to deliver a legal opinion (*fatwā*) which would be amply rewarded in the hereafter.[42] Critics denounced many of these scholars, especially hadith scholars, whose rote book learning they derisively compared to "donkeys carrying books without any understanding of their contents" (referring to Q. 62:5). This did not deter both rulers and common people from appreciating and utilizing the authority of the jurists who were the living exemplary receptacles of *ʿilm*. Shīʿī imams are believed to possess a special secret knowledge which was divinely inspired and transmitted through the designation (*naṣṣ*) of the preceding imam. By definition, this knowledge and an ancestral lineage from Muḥammad are sources of the imam's authority.

Muslim religious specialists have "jerry-rigged bits and pieces" of all of these sources of authority in a "charismatic bricolage" to assemble resources of superhuman power and to legitimize their authority. Figure 2 organizes approximate permutations of these sources.[43] At the top are types with one predominant source of authority whose influence has usually been to legitimize outer structures of society, only partially accessing Prophetic charismatic authority. These three types contrast with the imams and sufis at the bottom who utilize multiple sources of authority and who have through extraordinary action mobilized charismatic resources associated with the central symbol of the Prophet. Predictably, greater personal authority results from more types of actual or symbolic influence. Less obvious is the synergistic effect of someone with multiple sources of authority: these persons have transformative potential for social action.

Starting at the top of figure 2, the category of divinely inspired individuals (*majdhūbs*) represents uncontrolled, spiritually intoxi-

---

given high social status to the descendants of the Prophet. These are examples of physical pedigree being a source of authority.

[42]George Makdisi, *The Rise of Colleges: Institutions of Learning in Islam and the West*, p. 281.

[43]These sources and categories of religious figures are meant to be used as an analytical tool whose value reflects how satisfactorily it serves the goals of the inquiry instead of its disputable precision (there are always exceptions). Ideally this type of analysis will advance a better cross-traditional understanding of holy persons.

cated individuals who are generally respected and feared but who rarely have disciples.[44] Individuals from the Tablīghī Jamāʿat group, founded by the Indian Muḥammad Ilyās (d. 1944), stress the importance of strict adherence to the ritual requirements of Islam and outwardly following the Prophetic sunna, which they believe gives them the authority to propagate Islam.[45] Their Islamic dress code duplicates that of modern revivalist Indian sufis, but without any master-disciple relationship, traditional religious education, sufi initiation ritual, or inclination toward spiritual practice.[46]

Shrine caretakers and hereditary shaykhs illustrate the classic Weberian transformation of a shaykh's extraordinary charisma into lineage charisma.[47] These descendants of shaykhs or successors of shaykhs, often quite influential locally, routinely perform mediatory functions. Individuals with hereditary or "exemplar" connections with the Prophet perform necessary roles in the harmonious integration of others into the day-to-day functioning of society; their legitimizing actions maintain social structures and

---

[44]In Western society most of these individuals, judged by their outward behavior, would be classified as mentally ill. In the Islamic context crazy wise men (*ʿuqalāʾ al-majānīn*) are examples of permanently liminal persons. See Ḥasan b. Muḥammad al-Nīsābūrī, *Kitāb ʿuqalāʾ al-majānīn*. For a fascinating account of a modern Egyptian sufi, Aḥmad Raḍwān (d. 1967), who was supposed to be "the president of the *majdhūbs*," see Valerie J. Hoffman, *Sufism, Mystics, and Saints in Modern Egypt*, pp. 257–70.

[45]In two articles, one by Christian Troll, "Two Conceptions of Daʿwá in India: Jamāʿat-i Islamī and Tablīghī Jamāʿat," and the other by Barbara D. Metcalf, "Living Hadīth in the Tablīghī Jamaʿāt [*sic*]," it is clear that the Tablīghīs emphasize outward ritual performance in their strident missionary activity. Sufi terminology has been incorporated in their practices, e.g., *dhikr* and *chilla*, but with entirely new outwardly directed meanings. "Living hadith" has to do with acting out formulaic injunctions from an abridged missionary manual based on hadith rather than striving to transform oneself by connecting to the Prophet. Like other categories in this chart this one is based on a generalized view of Tablīghīs of which there are certain exceptions, one of whom might have been the founder. For example, in Christian Troll's opinion, Muḥammad Ilyās was a person who "comes accross [*sic*] as an ascetic and as a man of genuine mystical experience." See "Two Conceptions," p. 124.

[46]Directing-shaykhs consider such an outward expression of the sunna significant to the extent that it is accompanied by spiritual travel, the "inner" sunna. When this combination occurs, the shaykh personifies a living exemplar of the Prophet which enables him to transform the inner being of his disciples, who endeavor to replicate their every action on the Prophetic model.

[47]Max Weber posited a notion of "pure charisma" which became routinized, either through lineage or office. One example would be a prophet whose successor is his eldest son or who occupies a hierarchical position, e.g., as a Catholic priest. See Max Weber, *Economy and Society: An Outline of Interpretive Sociology*, 2 vols., 2:1135–41.

usually involve "uninspired action."[48] In other words, when sufis derive their authority solely from outward behavior or lineage, whether spiritual or biological, they have a technical connection to the Prophet but not necessarily an intimate relationship with him. Persons having many sources of personal authority, in contrast, are generally more deeply connected with the personal symbolic center of a culture,[49] in this case, the Muḥammadan reality. Sufis and imams not only perform the everyday activities and functions of religious types, but as living heirs of the Prophet they are capable of invoking profound transformations. Such extraordinary individuals have significantly affected the social order.

For sufi teaching-shaykhs and directing-shaykhs, the several sources of authority—spiritual travel, following the Prophetic model, and spiritual lineage from one's initiation—are all related; spiritual wayfaring is the inner sunna, and behavioral conformity to the Prophetic model is the outer sunna. In the case of the Naqshbandī directing-shaykh, connecting to the Prophet allows the resulting spiritual energy to flow through the chain of transmitters (a spiritual energy circuit represented by a genealogical chart). Eventually these three sources fuse into one as the connection develops. Through a modeling process and by channeling emotions (enhanced by the genealogical connection), the mediating-shaykh becomes intensely and lovingly connected to the Prophet. In the Shīʿī case, the Twelver imams and some of the Āghā Khāns functioned in many ways like sufi shaykhs, expressing their piety through sufi forms which Marshall Hodgson calls "ṭarīqa Shīʾīsm."[50] All of these types of individuals embodying several sources of authority have exhibited their potential to influence others. Their "inspired action" over the centuries slowly changed their respective cultures which have become notably Islamic.

Illustrating the effect of combining many sources of authority,

---

[48]Here I am indebted to the insights in Edward Shils's discussion of charisma in *Center and Periphery: Essays in Macrosociology*, p. 129.

[49]There are multiple and overlapping symbolic centers in Islamic societies, e.g., political and scriptural; local and universal. The geographical ritual center would be the physical Kaʿba; the scriptural ritual center would be God's word, the Qurʾān. To a large extent these are distant in comparison to the communal ritual center, the primordial Muslim community (duplicated in the sufi lodge) with the Prophet (and by extension his heir) as its center.

[50]Marshall G. S. Hodgson, *The Venture of Islam: Conscience and History in a World Civilization*, 3 vols., 2:494. It appears that imams have many parallels with directing-shaykhs and the Āghā Khāns with mediating-shaykhs.

the ulama are positioned as a "borderline" example between the two broadly defined groups described above in the chart. A religious scholar whose only qualification is transmitted religious knowledge has tended usually to belong to the three "peripheral types" (*majdhūbs*, Tablīghīs, and hereditary shaykhs located above the ulama category in figure 2). Like the hereditary shrine pir, he often holds an office, not necessarily hereditary but strictly defined by an educational role or a governmental position. Ulama sometimes appear more respected and influential than most religious figures on the chart, but this is almost always because they have access to political power, a qualitatively different notion of power than noncoercive personal authority. A scholar with only transmitted religious knowledge usually wants only to legitimize Islamic societal structures outwardly, not to change people or society.

Ar-Rāmhurmuzī, for example, a hadith scholar from the Buyid period (334/945–447/1055), writes, "It is sufficient nobility for the transmitter that his name be joined with the name of the Prophet and be mentioned along with mention of Him and of His family and His companions. . . . [a nobleman said,] 'I want, in the first place, to see my name united with that of the Prophet in a single line.' What better relatives (*'aṣabah*) could be desired than a group that includes ʿAlī b. al-Ḥusain b. ʿAlī and his descendants that followed him, and the family of the Prophet, and the sons of the Muhājirūn and the Anṣār, as well as the generation that succeeded them in piety, and the ascetics and the *fuqahā*ʾ and most of the caliphs, and countless numbers of *ʿulamā*ʾ and men of nobility, excellence, distinction, and importance?"[51] No doubt the transmission of hadith created a sense of community with previous generations of Muslims leading back to the Prophet. In this regard transmitted hadith connected to the Prophet, but in terms of transformative potential it is only a shadow of Mīrzā Maẓhar's experience with his hadith teacher who had internalized the Prophetic sayings to the point of embodying them.[52] Like previous generations of Prophetic heirs, sufi and non-sufi, such a "charismatic combination" enabled Muḥammad Afḍal to transform those receptive to his penetrating teaching.[53]

[51]Roy Mottahedeh, *Loyalty and Leadership in an Early Islamic Society*, pp. 140–41.

[52]Sufis, for example, have shown unusual proficiency in harmonizing transmitted religious knowledge, particularly hadith study, into their spiritual practices. See George Makdisi, *The Rise of Colleges*, p. 10.

[53]Many jurists and scholars have possessed qualities which attracted large numbers of followers. One of the best known is Aḥmad Ibn Ḥanbal (d. 241/855), the famous religious scholar and eponymous founder of the Ḥanbalī school of jurisprudence, who suffered punishment by the Caliph instead of denying the uncreated nature of the Qur'ān. Ibn Taymiyya (d. 728/1328) is another.

The consistent thread in these apparent changes is that the authority of Muslim religious specialists has depended on the degree to which they have linked themselves to the Islamic exemplar of human extraordinariness, the Prophet.[54] The ability to connect to Muḥammad spiritually, genealogically, behaviorally, and intellectually often has made the sufi a personal embodiment of the Prophet. Discussing charisma, Clifford Geertz asks, "Just what it is that causes some men to see transcendency in others, and what it is they see."[55] For many Muslims it has been the multifaceted symbolic vision/experience of Muḥammad, many generations removed but at times vibrantly present.

The idea that Muḥammad was superhuman developed soon after his death with the doctrine that God protected the Prophet from sin (*ʿiṣma*). The Qur'ān that was revealed to Muḥammad needed an immaculate vessel, an absolutely sinless prophet, to convey God's Word.[56] Having established an impeccable Prophet, it was only one more small step to declare that the faithful owned Muḥammad unquestioning and absolute obedience, especially in view of the numerous Qur'ānic verses that required it, for example, "Whoever obeys the messenger obeys God" [4:80].[57] By the eighth century the primacy of the Prophetic model included all Muḥammad's words and deeds. It was this exemplary model that later was said to have been cultivated by the earliest Muslims and transmitted by the living presence of religious scholars and sufis. Abū Bakr aṣ-Ṣiddīq (d. 13/634), Muḥammad's successor, is said to have exclaimed, "I do not omit anything of the things the Mes-

---

[54]By the ninth century, Muslim consensus had made Muḥammad the most perfect human with superhuman status, confirming that Muḥammad had become the celebrated symbolic focus of legitimate personal authority. For example, Sahl at-Tustarī (283/896) developed the themes of Muḥammad's pre-eternal light *(nūr Muḥammadī)*. See Annemarie Schimmel, *And Muhammad Is His Messenger: The Veneration of the Prophet in Islamic Piety*, pp. 125–26; Gerhard Böwering, *The Mystical Vision of Existence in Classical Islam: The Qur'ānic Hermeneutics of the Sufi Sahl at-Tustarī (d. 283/896)*; and U. Rubin, "Preexistence and Light: Aspects of the concept of Nūr Muḥammad."

[55]Clifford Geertz, *Local Knowledge: Further Essays in Interpretive Anthropology*, p. 122.

[56]For sources dealing with the veneration of Muḥammad in Islam, see Andrae, *Die Person Muhammads in Lehre und Glaube seiner Gemeinde* and Schimmel, *And Muhammad Is His Messenger*.

[57]Another twelve Qur'ānic citations [3:32,132;4:59;5:92;8:1,20,46; 24:52,54;47:33;58:13;64:12] usually state "Obey God and the messenger." Qur'ānic passages (e.g., 24:54; 72:21–22) that declare the Prophet as "merely human" or his own prayers expressing his feeling of weakness and sinfulness have been regarded as instructions to the believers to follow instead of being taken as Muḥammad's very human feelings. See Schimmel, *And Muhammad Is His Messenger*, p. 59.

senger of God has done, for I am afraid that if I should omit it, I could go astray."[58] Over the centuries these living models of the Prophet have striven to transmit his living virtues, defining the interpersonal and ethical ideals of Islam in the process. The sunna has had such compelling significance for Muslims that many followers of the Shāfi'ī school and most of those of the Mālikī school assumed that it was absolutely obligatory to imitate the Prophet even in ethically neutral actions.[59] Although the Qur'ān as duly respected and revered as the word of God, the Prophetic model became the means for applying Qur'ānic ideals to daily personal and community life.[60]

This pattern of prophetically legitimized authority first becomes inculcated in the family. Often Muḥammad is portrayed as a respected elderly paternal figure whom one can trust absolutely. A Muslim child first learns the "familial mode" of Prophetic authority at home where an unquestioning obedience and reverence to elders, particularly the father and grandfather, become ingrained at an early age. Later, with his family experience as the frame of reference for intimate relationships, the student is admonished to respect the teaching-shaykh even more than his father "since his father brought him into the world of perdition, [while] his teacher leads him to the world of eternal life."[61]

Personal Authority of the Teaching-Shaykh

The teaching-shaykh derives his social prestige from exemplary custodianship of sacred knowledge. Located in mosques and pri-

---

[58]Al-Qāḍī 'Iyāḍ (d. 544/1149), *Kitāb al-shifā fī ri'āyat ḥuqūq al-Muṣṭafā* cited in ibid., p. 31.

[59]Citing al-Qāḍī 'Iyāḍ in ibid., p. 194.

[60]By the ninth century there is an alleged hadith stating that the sunna interprets the Qur'ān rather than the Qur'ān judging the sunna. See William A. Graham Jr., "Traditionalism in Islam: An Essay in Interpretation," p. 504. This hadith is found in 'Abdurraḥmān ad-Dārimī's (d. 255/869) introduction to his *Kitāb al-sunan, bāb* 49.

[61]Al-Anṣārī, *Al-lu'lu'*, pp. 6–7, cited in Jonathon Berkey, *The Transmission of Knowledge in Medieval Cairo: A Social History of Islamic Education,* p. 36. See also Michael Chamberlain, *Knowledge and Social Practice,* pp. 108–9. Sufis also say that disciples experience a "spiritual" birth *(al-wilādat al-ma'nawiyya).* The lifelong commitment to a king is often expressed in terms of a familial loyalty pattern. If a king or noble mentions his *ṣanī'a* or *ghulām* it means that he had reared, educated, and trained that person. See Mottahedeh, *Loyalty and Leadership,* pp. 82–83. This quotation refers specifically to the Buyid dynasty (334/945–447/1055) but is representative of many similar patron-client relationships in government throughout Islamic history.

vate homes, the atmosphere of religious study circles (later including those in madrasas) cultivates a set of refined and stringent behavioral patterns to safeguard the transmission of religious knowledge. Based upon the sunna, an elaborate set of rituals developed, which Michael Chamberlain terms the "ritualization of religious knowledge."[62] Students were informed of appropriate ritual behavior: "Do not look at anything but the teacher, and do not turn around to investigate any sound, especially during discussion. Do not shake your sleeve. The student should not uncover his arms, nor should he fiddle with his hands or feet or any part of his body parts, nor should he place his hand on his beard or his mouth, or pick his nose or play with it, or open his mouth or gnash his teeth. . . . nor should he turn his back or his flank to his shaykh . . . . It is a sign of respect to the shaykh not to sit between him and the direction of prayer, nor to his side, nor on a cushion."[63] Mālik b. Anas (d. 179/796), the hadith scholar and eponymous founder of the Mālikīs, kept his student in such fear of moving in class that they acted as if there were birds on their heads.[64]

The culture and ritual of religious learning, both of sufis and ulama, required personal contact with an exemplary teaching-shaykh. Most traditional religious learning was practical in nature and extended to every aspect of the student's life. In this context the medieval Egyptian jurist al-ʿUthmānī asserts, "One should not study with another who himself studied only from books, without having read [them] to a learned shaykh . . . Whoever does not take his learning [*ʿilm*] from the mouths of men is like he who learns courage without ever facing battle."[65]

Personal instruction is a key component to authority. Biographical collections of medieval scholars, both in Egypt and in India, always stress the person's teachers (at least in colonial India until the 1870s when they came to be identified with a school such as Deoband or Aligarh).[66] The chain of teachers (*isnād*) validates the person's learning; institutional affiliation, al-

---

[62]Chamberlain, *Knowledge and Social Practice*, pp. 125–30.

[63]Muḥammad b. Ibrāhīm Ibn Jamāʿa (d. 733-34/1333), *Tadhkirat al-sāmiʿ wa'l-mutakallim*, pp. 98–100, cited in Chamberlain, p. 130.

[64]Al-Qādī ʿIyāḍ, *Tartīb al-madārik wa-taqrīb al-masālik li-maʿrifat aʿlām madhhab Mālik*, pp. 153–66, cited in Fritz Meier, "Ḫurāsān und das Ende der klassischen Ṣūfik," in *La Persia nel medioevo*, p. 562.

[65]Muḥammad b. ʿAbdurraḥmān al-ʿUthmānī, *Īḍāḥ al-taʿrīf bi-baʿḍ faḍāʾil al-ʿilm al-sharīf*, cited in Berkey, *The Transmission of Knowledge*, p. 26 (brackets are in original text).

[66]For the Egyptian case, see Berkey, *The Transmission of Knowledge*, pp. 21–27.

though it could enhance prestige (for example, being a shaykh at Al-Azhar in Cairo), is secondary. Legitimacy is always based on the unbroken chain going back to the author of the book or to the Prophet (in the case of hadith and Qur'ān study in particular). The shorter the chain the more authoritative the person becomes. When someone could relate hadith with an unusually short sequence of transmitters or with unusually reliable transmitters, people would be eager to say that they had learned hadith with him. In medieval Ibb, Yemen, Faqīh an-Nāhī (d. 566–7/1171) used to say, "Between me and the author [an eminent eleventh-century Baghdadi Shāfiʿī jurist, al-Shirāzī] are two men." In this way an-Nāhī established his reputation as a scholar in an intellectual universe where "the texts of knowledge were literally embodied."[67] Again, and this point needs to be stressed, there are qualitative differences between embodying books of intellectual knowledge, books of unwritten words comprising knowledge of the heart, and embodying the Prophet himself.[68]

Scripture-centered personal authority contrasts sharply with the authority of extraordinary sufis. Scripture-centered authority resides in books, personal authority in the most perfect of humans, the Prophet Muḥammad. By appropriating, indeed embodying, one of the central symbols of Islam, these living human authorities have in varying degrees achieved a position of superhuman status in Islamic societies. The accomplishment of this feat occurred over many centuries as sufis connected their activities to those of the Prophet, which enabled them adroitly to bask in the shadow of his extraordinary Prophetic charisma. In this process it was the directing-shaykhs among the sufis who were able to mobilize effectively, and in some cases even originate, sources of personal authority recognized by the Muslim community.

---

[67]Brinkley Messick, *The Calligraphic State: Textual Domination and History in a Muslim Society*, p. 15.

[68]Seyyid Hossein Nasr poetically describes these kinds of differences in his "Oral Transmission and the Book in Islamic Education: The Spoken and the Written Word."

CHAPTER 2

From Teaching-Shaykh to Directing-Shaykh

Sufism through verbal instruction [only] is like building [a house] on dung.
Abū Saʿīd-i Abū'l-Khayr

Any man who does not let himself be guided by a spiritual director is guilty of rebellion towards God. For without a guide he could not obtain access to the road of salvation, were he to possess by memory a thousand works of theology.
Shaykh ʿAbdulhādī b. Riḍwānī
(a nineteenth-century Algerian Shādhilī sufi)

As sufi practices became institutionalized in the ninth century, the respectful relationship between the teaching-shaykh and the student in both sufi and jurist circles began to change to a much more structured authoritarian master-disciple relationship.[1] As the sufi shaykh became endowed with the superhuman prophetic traits of a functionally infallible leader, he no longer acted as an informal guide or teaching-shaykh to an ad-hoc group of students. Instead he lived in his lodge among his community of disciples whose behavior he circumscribed by the rules set down in sufi manuals. This enlarging of both the scope and degree of the sufi's authority is expressed by the term "directing-shaykh."

This change came at a critical juncture in Islamic history, when

[1]The fluidity of the teaching-shaykh environment becoming relatively structured with the advent of the directing-shaykh paralleled similar kinds of developments in other Islamic institutions as Muslims grew from a minority Arab community to become a majority multiethnic community over four or five centuries. For these ninth- and tenth-century Muslims, "their God is a Persian shah, not an Arab king. His laws are not negotiated but decreed." Kevin Reinhart, *Before Revelation: The Boundaries of Muslim Moral Thought*, p. 179.

Islamic institutions, both juristic and sufi, were being established in increasingly Muslim multiethnic societies and the centralized caliphal empire was breaking up into a dynamic and expanding network of successor states ruled by independent rulers (beginning with the Buyids in 334/945). For much of the Islamic world in the ensuing six or more centuries directing-shaykhs were an integral part of the *aʿyān-amīr* social system through which the notables (*aʿyān*) legitimized and mediated the power of the local garrison commanders (*amīrs*).[2] In a social system where patronage and loyalty held the key to political power, many protégés of God supplied the resources for the needed mediatory expertise.[3] The inward "anti-structure" of sufi lodges transformed individuals while legitimizing the outer Islamic institutions that maintained landed families and supported commercial activities in cities.

A directing-shaykh, or someone like him, will always share an integral mediating role wherever there is an agrarian system with a weak central government. Islamicate herding/agrarian societies during this early period, based upon farming by horse and plow, operated with relatively scarce resources, most of which the urban minority (less than 10 percent of the population) drained off from the surrounding countryside.[4] This highly stratified society was composed of an aristocracy, officials, tradesmen, soldiers, ulama, sufis, peasants, and nomads. The authoritarian and hierarchical constructs of the Islamic religion kept this system from flying apart, not brute force. Such a situation resembled its counterparts in the premodern world, whether the mythological construct was Christian, Hindu, or Confucian-Buddhist. All these constructs had a system of doctrines and practices with an unquestioned universal claim that created a collective identity by relativizing prior ethnic and tribal identities.[5] The integrating power of this Muslim identity allowed a broad spectrum of views and practices that brought together many disparate (and potentially opposing) attitudes and interest groups. The social cohesion created by the shared set of Islamic symbolic resources

---

[2]Marshall Hodgson, *The Venture of Islam: Conscience and History in a World Civilization*, 3 vols., 2:64–69.

[3]Such a case parallels holy men in late Roman society (ca. 400–500 C.E.) eloquently described and analyzed by Peter Brown in his "The Rise and Function of the Holy Man in Late Antiquity." The centralized Persian government precluded the development of a parallel phenomenon of holy men in Persia.

[4]This synopsis of agrarian economies is based upon Gerhard Lenski, Jean Lenski, Patrick Nolan, *Human Societies: An Introduction to Macrosociology*, pp. 158–85.

[5]Jürgen Habermas, *Communication and the Evolution of Society*, pp. 110–16.

united these disparate parts into what Marshall Hodgson has aptly termed an "Islamicate" Civilization.

The authoritarian directing-shaykh was probably no more dictatorial than his peers in other domains of society. Sufis and other mediators were essential for the smooth operation of an agrarian society with no strong central authority, since they successfully embodied the central symbol of authority, Muḥammad, and the Islamic worldview while legitimizing the outer political structures of society.[6]

Ibn ʿAbbād ar-Rundī (d. 790/1388), a Moroccan sufi, explained the changes in the sufi's scope of authority by defining two kinds of sufi shaykhs in the teaching-shaykh (*shaykh al-taʿlīm*), who is required for guidance, and the directing-shaykh (*shaykh al-tarbiyya*), who, in his demand for unquestioning authority, is necessary only for those whose moral character and intellectual training are in some way defective.[7] Fritz Meier, following ar-Rundī's lead, determined that the transition between sufi teaching-shaykhs and directing-shaykhs began in Nishapur during the last quarter of the ninth century. From there the directing-shaykh model spread unabated along with other institutional developments throughout the Islamic world in the course of the eleventh century until it became the norm in sufism.[8]

Ar-Rundī explains that sufi teaching-shaykhs provided instruction in religious duties, morals (*akhlāq*), and theoretical sufism,

---

[6]In a Buddhist parallel, George Samuel has discovered a strikingly similar social structure with Tibetan lamas acting in a similar capacity as directing-shaykhs. He poses the question of why Tibet is unique among all other Buddhist societies in having lamas, i.e., Buddhist religious leaders who manipulate supernatural power, act as spiritual mentors to their disciples, and have a recognized spiritual lineage (the Buddhist equivalent of the three sources of authority associated with directing-shaykhs). George Samuel, "Tibet as a Stateless Society and Some Islamic Parallels." He also states that there is a partial but significant exception in the case of Burma.

[7]In practice this would mean everyone except the most talented and egoless seekers. *Fatwā Abī ʿAbdullāh Muḥammad b. Ibrāhīm b. ʿAbbād ar-Rundī,* in the appendix of ʿAbdurraḥmān Muḥammad Ibn Khaldūn, *Shifāʾ al-sāʾil, li-tahdhīb al-masāʾil* pp. 111–27. See also John Renard, trans., *Ibn ʿAbbād of Ronda: Letters on the Sūfī Path,* pp. 184–94. Ar-Rundi's *fatwā* answered a question posed by Andalusian sufis as to whether a sufi master is indispensable or not. An Andalusian Mālikī jurist, Abū'l-ʿAbbās al-Qabbāb (d. 777–78/1375), and Ibn Khaldūn were also involved in this discussion concerning whether one should learn from books or from a master. Muhsin Mahdi sums up the salient points in his article, "The Book and the Master as Poles of Cultural Change in Islam."

[8]Fritz Meier, "Ḫurāsān und das Ende der klassischen Ṣufik." See also Meier's "Qushayrī's Tartīb as-suluk," which might not be al-Qushayrī's. See ʿAbdulḥusayn Zarrīnkūb, "Justujū dar taṣawwuf-i Īrān (3)," p. 27 n. 113.

just as a teaching-shaykh in a madrasa did. Students traveled freely among sufi teaching shaykhs, sharing each other's companionship while learning and cultivating interior practices. Like other students in a conventional religious school, they had many teaching-shaykhs and no particular allegiance to any one of them.[9] But unlike ordinary religious-school students, these traveling sufis belonged to a spiritual, intellectual, and moral elite who already had their ego (*nafs*) under control before joining the small circles around the teaching-shaykhs.[10] Examples of such exceptional sufis were al-Ḥārith al-Muḥāsibī (d. 243/857) and Muḥammad Abū Ṭālib al-Makkī (d. 383/993 or 386/996), who apparently taught themselves independently and only went to teaching-shaykhs to refine and guide their learning.[11] But the student-teacher relationship was similar when the teacher was a religious scholar or a sufi.

Further research will likely refine ar-Rundī's idealistic picture of early sufism, but references in sufi literature do support his assertion that there was a category of directing-shaykh. By the eleventh century disciples conceived of their relationship as one of a willing slave, an orphan needing a father, or a sick person dependent upon the treatment of a physician.[12] In the twelfth century this last comparison was used to explain the trials to which Majduddīn Baghdādī (d. 616/1219) was subjected as a disciple: "When he entered the service of a sheikh, he was made to serve 'at the place of ablution,' i.e., to clean the latrines. His mother, a well-to-do lady physician, asked the master to exempt the tender boy from this work, and sent him twelve Turkish slaves to do the cleaning. But he replied: 'You are a physician—if your son had an inflammation of the gall bladder, should I give the medicine to a Turkish slave instead of giving it to him?' "[13]

Examples of the shift to directing-shaykh in Nishapur began with Abū Ḥafṣ al-Ḥaddād (d. ca. 265/879), who traveled with his

---

[9]Some allegedly had hundreds of teachers, e.g., Junayd (d. 297/910) had 200 masters and Abū Yazīd al-Bisṭāmī (d. 261/874) had 113 teachers; see Meier, "Qushayrī's Tartīb as-sulūk," p. 1.

[10]Renard, *Ibn ʿAbbād of Ronda,* p. 185.

[11]A good example of needing travel to deepen one's spiritual experiences is Muḥyīddīn Ibn al-ʿArabī (d. 638/1240). See Claude Addas, *Ibn ʿArabī ou la quête du soufre rouge,* translated by Peter Kingsley, *Quest for the Red Sulphur: The Life of Ibn ʿArabi.*

[12]Fritz Meier, "Ḫurāsān und das Ende der klassischen Ṣūfik," pp. 550–53; and J. L. Michon, "L'autobiographie *(Fahrasa)* du soufi marocain Aḥmad Ibn Ajība (1747–1809) (3me partie)," p. 120.

[13]Abū ʿAbdurraḥmān Jāmī, *Nafahāt al-uns,* p. 424, cited in Annemarie Schimmel, *Mystical Dimensions,* p. 101.

disciples to visit Junayd in Baghdad.[14] While there Junayd remarked that Abū Ḥafṣ seemed to drill his disciples like a sultan drilling his soldiers, to which Abū Ḥafṣ replied, "Outer discipline is the best sign of inner discipline." Mamshād ad-Dīnawarī (d. 299/911–12) stressed the need to venerate the shaykh, and Jaʿfar al-Khuldī (d. 348/959–60) the need not to hurt the shaykh's feelings or say unkind things about him. The extent of a disciple's unquestioning obedience determined his or her progress on the sufi path. Abū Sahl Muḥammad aṣ-Ṣuʿlukī (d. 369/980) remarked that a disciple who asked his spiritual mentor "Why?" would never progress (cf. Q. 21:23). When al-Qushayrī wrote his *Risāla* in 437–38/1046, for a disciple to contradict his master was a serious enough offense to sever the connection between them. With the advent of directing-shaykhs, each disciple was required to be under the supervision of only one shaykh. Carefree wandering between masters was henceforth prohibited; a novice had to ask the shaykh for permission to travel.

This concentration of authority in one person and the expectation of unquestioning obedience had its parallels in other concurrent Islamic institutional developments. By the tenth century the common people unquestioningly obeyed the teachings of one (and only one) imam of a school of jurisprudence in much the same way as the Imāmīs had obeyed the iman's legal advice a century earlier.[15] In sufi circles disciples were required to follow the directing-shaykh's school of jurisprudence, a natural corollary to the requirement that he behave and think in utter conformity with the master, a living heir of the Prophet.[16]

Having a single spiritual mentor meant that anyone who had not been properly initiated by a guide could no longer be considered a legitimate sufi: "There are many conditions for the master-disciple (*pīrī-murīdī*) relationship, the sufi robe, and companionship with the sufis (*ṣuḥbat*). Our group does not recognize

---

[14]For this paragraph I have relied on Meier, "Ḫurāsān und das Ende der klassischen Ṣūfik," pp. 548–59.

[15]The significant difference was that in practical terms an ordinary person could ask various jurists (who followed the same imam) and none were considered infallible like an Imāmī imam (although jurists' decisions were considered free from error). There were five hundred Sunnī schools of jurisprudence in the ninth century; the number by the thirteenth century had dwindled to four, the Ḥanbalī, Mālikī, Ḥanafī, and Shāfiʿī.

[16]Muḥammad b. Munawwar, *Asrār al-tawḥīd fī maqāmāt Shaykh Abī Saʿid*, pp. 20–21; translated by John O'Kane, *The Secrets of God's Mystical Oneness*, p. 83. Abū Saʿīd-i Abū'l-Khayr explains that Abū Yazīd al-Bisṭāmī followed Jaʿfar aṣ-Ṣādiq's school of law since he was Jaʿfar's disciple.

anyone who does not have a pir and who is not simultaneously following him. Even one who has had unseen things revealed to him [if he] does not have a guide, nothing [worthwhile] will come from his company."[17] Such a development indicates an institutionalization of the sufi shaykh involving a concentration of authority, both juridical and sufi, in the directing-shaykh. Only sufi masters having acknowledged connections with Muḥammad, e.g., a recognized spiritual genealogy, were considered valid sufi shaykhs.

These developments in sufi authority influenced practices in scholarly circles also. The shift from teaching- to directing-shaykh placed an unprecedented emphasis on correct behavior (*adab*). Before this time correct manners were already important and certainly acquired by the religious students, but sources do not indicate any systematic and conscious emphasis on behavior until the advent of the directing-shaykh. ʿAbdullāh b. al-Mubārak (d. 181/797) mentions the gnostic's (*ʿārif*) need for correct behavior. Sahl b. ʿAbdullāh at-Tustarī (d. 283/896) and later Abū ʿAbdurraḥmān as-Sulamī (d. 412/1021) mention correct behavior as a means to subdue the ego.[18] As-Sulamī advises those who are pursuing the sufi path to go "to an imam of the community whose sincere advice manifests [through his behavior] and [who] educates (*tuʾaddibu*) [on that basis]."[19] First one learns *adab* based upon the Prophetic model, which leads to the second station of *akhlāq*, realized by imitation of one's shaykh. On this basis one progresses to the third station, that of mystical states (*aḥwāl*).[20]

Using ar-Rundī's classification of shaykhs, where is the boundary between the teaching- and directing-shaykh? or a religious scholar and a sufi shaykh? A directing-shaykh requires unquestioning obedience to himself (typically sealed through an initiation ritual), but teaching correct behavior and acting as an exemplar for students were tasks that religious scholars could, and did, also perform. A person's status was to a significant extent determined by behavior, as Abū ʿAlī Muḥammad ath-Thaqafī (d. 328/939–940) relates, "[An educated person] can recognize the status/rank of people educated under a [sufi] shaykh, imam, or well-behaved teacher (*muʾaddib*). Someone who

---

[17]Ibid. p. 46 [additions mine] (trans. p. 119).

[18]Abū'l-Qāsim ʿAbdulkarīm b. Hawāzin al-Qushayrī, *Al-risāla al-qushayriyya fī ʿilm al-taṣawwuf*, 2:562, and Abū ʿAbdurraḥmān as-Sulamī, *Manāhij al-ʿārifīn*, p. 31.

[19]Here imam is used in the sense of a spiritual guide. See Sulami, *Manāhij al-ʿarifīn*, p. 25.

[20]Ibid., pp. 31, 38. Abū Saʿīd-i Abū'l-Khayr also underlines this threefold hierarchy. Muḥammad b. Munawwar, *Asrār al-tawḥīd*, p. 309 [trans. p. 479].

has not received an education from a teacher (*ustādh*) demonstrates [this] in his inappropriate behavior and exhibition of ego."[21] These examples confirm that the pedagogical developments occurring in the sufi environment were part of larger and widespread transformations in Islamic culture generally.[22] Part of the "sharʿī vision" involved appropriate behavior modeled on the Prophet. The religious elite directed their efforts particularly toward molding behavior, a task made easier by the unquestioned authority they had over their charges. At some point these Prophetic patterns became so widespread that fathers became directing-shaykhs of sorts to their sons. Life itself unconsciously expressed the sharʿī vision. The mythological ordering of society according to the Islamic sharʿī pattern had reached a self-replicating point as the twin trajectories of anti-structure (sufi activity) and structure (ulama/sufi activity) combined synergistically to undergird the politically decentralized agrarian societies encompassed by this same focused vision.

The ulama used every opportunity to acquire the kind of ritual power exercised by the sufis by associating religious knowledge with supernatural grace (*baraka*) and knowledge of the forbidden (*ḥarām*) and permitted (*ḥalāl*) with remembrance of God (*dhikr*).[23]

[21] Al-Qushayrī, *Al-risāla*, 1:164.

[22] One would expect that certain rituals of transmitting religious knowledge reported in medieval sources, e.g., unquestioning obedience to one's teacher and keeping a state of ritual purity when in the company of one's teacher, developed alongside the appearance of the directing-shaykh. For examples in medieval Damascus, see Michael Chamberlain, *Knowledge and Social Practice in Medieval Damascus, 1190–1350*, pp. 125–31. The famous sufi author al-Qushayrī (d. 465/1072) so revered his master that he fasted and made a complete ablution when he went to see him. See Margaret Malamud, "Sufi Organization and Structures of Authority in Medieval Nishapur," p. 435. Even a person following the dictates of a religious scholar who made an erroneous judgment following the leader *(imām)* of the school of jurisprudence was rewarded on the Last Day. One could always go to another scholar for an alternative legal opinion, which was not an option with a directing-shaykh. See Norman Calder, "Ikhtilâf and Ijmâʿ in Shâfiʿī's Risâla." Professor Muhammad Qasim Zaman kindly brought this latter article to my attention.

[23] This worked both ways—hence the justification of sufism in terms of another branch of knowledge. Many ulama were also sufis. Sufis specialized in channeling God's divine grace *(fayḍ)*, often facilitated by special individual and collective sessions, to recollect God. For ways ulama attempted to coopt sufi wonders and marvels, see Tarif Khalidi, *Arabic Historical Thought in the Classical Period*, p. 213. Jurists also had functional infallibility in their decisions, a position supported in part by interpreting ash-Shāfiʿī's discussion of *ijtihād*. Such reasoning concluded that all decisions made on the basis of *ijtihād* were equally valid, i.e., free from error *(kullu mujtahid muṣīb)*. Such a device conveniently allows for a diversity of legal opinion, aptly substantiated by a hadith, "Difference of opinion *(ikhtilāf)* in my community is a blessing." See Norman Calder, "Ikhtilâf and Ijmâʿ."

The net result of these developing patterns of authority and rituals of transmitting religious knowledge was to increase the prestige and status of sufis and ulama, both of whom considered themselves "heirs of the prophets." When discussing "those in authority" (*ūlū' al-amr*) in the Qur'ān, al-Qushayrī includes both the exemplary scholar (*imām*) and the shaykh in his group.[24] By the time of the directing-shaykh the Prophet had achieved supernatural status, the sufi pir with his functional infallibility had reached superhuman status, and the ulama were not far behind.

When spiritual journeying developed from ascetic practices the teaching-shaykh's role increasingly blended with that of the directing-shaykh. Unquestioning obedience to a spiritual mentor must always have been a requirement for intermediate and advanced disciples traveling in the spiritual heights; the dangers of solo travel were obvious. Conversely, a directing-shaykh's responsibilities would often include the teaching-shaykh's repertoire, especially when large numbers of people came to sufi lodges. Most of the aspirants who came to lodges never progressed beyond the most elementary stages of spiritual practice. Once initiated, technically the sufi pir was their directing-shaykh, but actual training for these novices would probably never go beyond instilling an outward *adab* in conformity with the sunna-based rules of the sufi lodge. The vast majority of people coming to the sufi lodge were impressed by the pir's exalted status and encompassing access to supernatural power, but they would probably not become formally initiated disciples.[25] For them the sufi pir was, at most, someone who could effectively act as a mediator between the divine and human worlds to assist them in their worldly difficulties. The awe that the pir inspired in his disciples might have impressed many visitors,[26] further enhancing sufi prestige in the wider—and increasingly Islamic—society.

[24]Abū'l-Qāsim al-Qushayrī, *Laṭā'if al-ishārāt*, 3 vols., 1:341. He is discussing Qur'ān, 4:59, in the context of God exhorting people to obey Muḥammad and those who are in authority.

[25]Hagiographers usually do not discuss the number of disciples in a shaykh's circle, and any numbers mentioned cannot be trusted. Some extremes are Ḥamīduddīn Nāgūrī Suhrawardī (d. 641–42/1244), who only had three disciples reaching perfection, and Ṣafīuddīn Ardabīlī (d. 735/1344), who allegedly facilitated twenty thousand to repent of their sins in one day. Of the earlier sufis, Sahl at-Tustarī (d. 283/896) was said to have had 400 disciples when he died; Abū Ḥāmid al-Ghazzālī (d. 505/1111) had 150 disciples; and Manṣūr al-Ḥallāj (martyred 309/922) had 400. See Muḥsin Kiyānī, *Tārīkh-i khānaqāh dar Īrān*, pp. 352–56.

[26]In 1936, Ṣibghatullāh II, the well-known Sindi sufi Pīr Pāgārō, was released from jail. In view of his envy of the Āghā Khān's worldwide respect and honor, Ṣibghatullāh II challenged, "I will produce for you ten Hurs [his most loyal disci-

As sufism became more institutionalized and thereby more prominent in the larger Muslim community, sufis became more involved in the community's devotional life and in a wide range of activities in addition to spiritual guidance. They cured diseases, averted calamities, and made amulets, functions that had been performed before by non-Muslims. By the eleventh century, when Muslims were in a majority, sufis performed these tasks and thus enlarged the scope of their authority. Since physical disease was believed to result from spiritual disease, efficacious cures depended on an unquestioning faith in the sufi master. This occasional psychological dependence on the shaykh had nothing to do with spiritual guidance along the path towards God; it simply reflected the increased mediatory functions of the directing-shaykh in Islamic society.

Still, the defining characteristic of the directing-shaykh was set within the sufi context of training others to approach God more closely and intimately. His role in the larger society, whether social, interpersonal, or political, rested upon his connection to the divine. His inner circle of initiated aspirants on the sufi path had claims upon him of vital dependence, "Just as the infant drinks milk at the breast of its mother or wetnurse, receiving from them the sustenance without which it would perish, so too the infant of the spirit drinks the milk of the Path and of Truth from the nipple of the mother of prophethood, or the wetnurse of sainthood [*wilāyat*], receiving from the prophet or the shaikh—who stands in place of the prophet—that sustenance without which it would perish."[27] Being in the company of a directing-shaykh often proved to be a qualitatively more intense experience than sitting at the feet of the teacher.

A common synonym for the shaykh or pir is a guide (*murshid*), which indicates the nature of his role. Few who enter his tutelage would think to doubt his spiritual authority any more than the average modern Westerner would question a surgeon about the

ples] who for my sake will confess to a murder they have not done and will gladly hang for it! Can the Agha Khan produce one such, even?" Cited in Peter Mayne, *Saints of Sind*, p. 121 [comments in brackets mine].

[27]Najmuddīn Rāzī, *Mirṣād al-ʿibād min al-mabdāʾ ilāʾl-maʿād*, translated by Ḥamid Algar, *The Path of God's Bondsmen from Origin to Return* (Delmar: Caravan Books, 1982), pp. 223–24 [additions in brackets mine]. Najmuddīn Rāzī's sobriquet *dāya* means wet nurse. Margaret Malamud's "Gender and Spiritual Self-Fashioning: The Master-Disciple Relationship in Classical Sufism," pp. 89–117, further explores these kind of relationships in sufism. Ṣadruddīn Qūnawī (d. 673/1274) declared that he had "drunk milk from the breasts of two mothers," i.e., his two shaykhs Ibn al-ʿArabī (d. 638/1240) and Awḥaduddīn Kirmānī (d. 635/1238). See Rāzī, *The Path of God's Bondsman*, p. 43.

procedures used in an operation or a commercial jet pilot about his skills in navigation. If serious misgivings arise one declines surgery or takes the train; correspondingly one would simply cease to associate with the sufi shaykh. Sufi practice requires an unquestioning demeanor. It is a rational response to a system based not only on psychological principles but also upon a sufi interpretation of how best to follow the Prophetic example. Sufis are qualified to monitor the manifold ego games that people play because they have gone on an inner mystical journey analogous to the Prophetic ascension. Abū Yazīd al-Bisṭāmī complained, " 'O God, with my egoism there is no way to You nor is there [any way] I can escape from egoism. What should I do?' God replied, 'O Abū Yazīd your deliverance from your ego [will result from] following My beloved [Muḥammad]. Anoint your eyes with the dust of his feet and follow him continually'. . . . Sufis call this Bāyazīd's ascension (*miʿrāj*), meaning [his] proximity [to God]. The ascension of prophets manifests outwardly with the [physical] body while that of the friends of God manifests as an inward journey of the spirit. The bodies of the prophets resemble the hearts of God's protégés in their purity and nearness [to God]."[28]

From a sufi point of view, a believer without a personal guide runs the risk of never progressing past the stage of belief (*īmān*) to become a *muslim*, i.e., a person who has submitted his or her ego to God.[29] The situation is similar to Iblīs, who, believing himself to be superior to a being of clay, refused to bow down to Adam (Q. 38:71–85). This would be equivalent to accepting the first half of the Muslim profession of faith, "There is no god but

---

[28] ʿAlī Ibn ʿUthmān al-Jullābī al-Hujwīrī, *Kashf al-maḥjūb*, p. 306; translated by Reynolds A. Nicholson, *The Kashf Al-Mahjūb: The Oldest Persian Treatise on Sufism*, p. 238. R. C. Zaehner notes the difference between al-Hujwīrī's rendition of Abū Yazīd's words and a similar quote preserved by Abū Naṣr as-Sarrāj (d. 378/988). See *Hindu and Muslim Mysticism*, p. 125.

[29] This section explains why many sufis place the stage of submission *(islām)* before the stage of faith *(īmān)* which then leads to the stage of perfection of worship *(iḥsān)*. Sufis declare that unless the ego *(nafs)* is tamed, belief and religious practice are meaningless. In other sufi interpretations, *islām* is compared to the starlight, *īmān* to moonlight, and *iḥsān* to sunlight. See Aḥmad b. ʿAjība al-Ḥasanī, *Īqāẓ al-himam fī sharḥ al-ḥikam*, pp. 80, 197–98, 278. In contrast, religious scholars and jurists require faith as a prerequisite to submission, which they define as correct performance of religious duties. Shariʿa-minded sufis, e.g., Naqshbandī-Mujaddidīs and the Shādhilīs, follow the order of faith before submission. See Aḥmad Sirhindī, *Maktūbāt-i imām-i rabbānī*, 3 vols., volume 1, Letter 71, pp. 52–53 [hereafter *Maktūbāt*, 1.71.52–53] and Vincent Cornell, "The Logic of Analogy and the Role of the Sufi Shaykh in Post-Marinid Morocco," p. 78.

God," without also fully accepting the second half, "and Muḥammad is His messenger." Identifying only with the transcendental aspect of Islam, as Iblīs did, makes one susceptible to the danger of pride. The human capacity for self-deception is such that people could easily think they were good Muslims on the basis of their love for an invisible, distant, and impersonal God and their fulfillment of ritual obligations. It is precisely this tendency, *Iblīsian Tawḥīd*,[30] of deviating from the teaching of the prophets, that eventually requires new prophets or heirs to the prophets to remind people of the "original" message.

Sufis assert their claim as specialists in the enterprise of rejuvenating religion since the last prophet, Muḥammad, has departed. Such a psychological emphasis on the Prophet reinforces the sociological concern for the particular community of Muslims. The original community of the Prophet and his Companions represents the ideal Muslim community, the re-creation of which is the goal of the sufi shaykh and his disciples.

Like the function of a prophet that of the sufi pir and other of God's protégés is to bring divine trials to those who have not submitted their egos to God.[31] Abū Yazīd, in the example above,

---

[30]*Tawḥid* is the declaration of God's oneness. The Sunnī consensus considers Iblīs's declaration of unity defective because of his failure to recognize the divine aspect in the human form. Minority views in the Muslim community have declared Iblīs to be the ultimate monotheist; see Peter Awn, *Satan's Tragedy and Redemption: Iblīs in Sufi Psychology*. "Muḥammadan Tawḥid" recognizes divine unity both in the human and in the transcendent, the human being potentially acting as a bridge between the material world and the divine. Such a human being, simultaneously in contact with the higher and lower spheres of existence, has been called the Perfect Human *(al-insān al-kāmil)* in later sufi treatises. See ʿAbdulkarīm al-Jīlī, *Kitāb al-insān al-kāmil*.

[31]Rūmī frequently groups prophets and friends of God *(awliyā')* together in one category. Although the sufi systematizers and jurists resolved religious dogmatic concerns by making clear existential boundaries between prophets and friends of God, sufis realized the functional similarity of both categories in guiding the spiritual development of humanity. There is a plausible argument linking the veneration of the sufi shaykh with the prior development of venerating the prophet. For details of this argument see Ignaz Goldziher, "The Veneration of Saints in Islam." For the historical development of Muslim veneration of Muḥammad, see Tor Andrae, *Die Person Muhammads in Lehre und Glaube seiner Gemeinde* and Annemarie Schimmel, *And Muhammad Is His Messenger: The Veneration of the Prophet in Islamic Piety*. Equally plausible is Bruce Lawrence's hypothesis that holy men became the exemplars by which Muḥammad was retrospectively portrayed. See his "The Chishtiya of Sultanate India: A Case Study of Biographical Complexities in South Asian Islam," p. 49. My argument is that, by Rūmī's time at least, Muḥammad and the pir were functionally equated, e.g., "God asserted that his (the pir's) hand is like His own [hand] as in God's hand is over their hands" (Q. 48:10) [referring to an oath of allegiance with Muḥammad]. See Jalāluddīn Rūmī, *Mathnawī-yi maʿnawī*, 6 vols., volume 1, verse 2972 [hereafter 1.2972]. The Prophet allegedly

was advised to follow the Prophetic path to escape from egoism. The personal authority of a shaykh, who himself follows the sunna, will continually utilize the skillful means at his disposal to challenge, entrap, and ultimately transform the egos of his disciples.[32] It is easy to be complacent and proud while worshiping a transcendent God, or even venerating the Prophet. But there is nowhere to hide under the piercing gaze of a sufi pir. People who proudly believe they are exemplary Muslims on the basis of memorization of the Qur'ān, hadith, and other knowledge obtained from books and who reject any need for personal guidance would from a sufi perspective be considered under the influence of *Iblīsian Tawḥid*. Through the master's example and guidance one learns how to tame the *nafs* and experience what it means to worship god in an unassuming fashion.

Maulānā Jalāluddīn Rūmī (d. 672/1273), whose compendium of mystical poetry in the *Mathnawī-yi ma'nawī* has been called "the Qur'ān in Persian," continually emphasizes the need for submitting one's ego to the directing-shaykh.[33] Underlining the functional equivalence of the Prophet and the intimate of God, he writes: "God made prophets intermediaries in order that envious feelings arise [in others] through anxiety [of the ego]. Since no one was shamed by God, no one was envious of God. [However] the person whom he considered like himself would be [the object

---

said, "A shaykh who has gone forward [to become near to God] is like a prophet among his own people." See *Mathnawī*, 3:1774. God brought friends of God to earth so that He may make them a mercy to the two worlds [refers to a hadith describing Muḥammad as the mercy to the jinn and humans]. See *Mathnawī*, 3:1804.

32Rūmī gives a masterful example of how humans must learn from other humans, i.e., the necessity of personal teaching, charismatic or otherwise. He first explains how parrots are taught to imitate human speech by putting them in front of a mirror. Although the unseen person behind the mirror is talking, the parrot thinks the parrot reflected in the mirror is speaking. The parrot, being totally ignorant of the actual situation, has little knowledge, if any, of human beings. In a similar fashion God holds the mirror of the shaykh in front of the disciple, who sees him- or herself reflected. Due to egoism the disciple cannot see the universal Reason *('aql-i kull)* behind the mirror and supposes a man is speaking. See Rūmī, *Mathnawī*, 5:1429–40. Note Rūmī's statement: As long as you view pious ones [prophets and intimates of God] as human beings, [know] this perception is an inheritance from Iblīs. See ibid., 1:3962.

33See Rūmī, *Mathnawī-yi ma'nawī*. It was the Naqshbandī 'Abdurraḥmān Jāmī (d. 898/1492) who declared Rūmī's masterful poetry to be the Persian equivalent of the Qur'ān (in the sense of a Persian commentary). Much of what has been commonly shared in the Persianate Islamic world (in this case the notion and justification of the directing-shaykh) has been facilitated by Rūmī's Persian poetry, which was much more accessible than an untranslated Arabic Qur'ān.

of his] envy—[precisely] for that reason. When the greatness of the Prophet became established, from [his] acceptance [by the Muslim community] no one became envious of him. Thus in every time a protégé of God (*walī*) exists to [act as] a continual test until the Day of Judgment."[34] Since God sent the Prophet to guide humanity personally, sufis believe there will always be heirs of the Prophet to guide succeeding generations.[35]

Naqshbandīs define a perfect and perfection-bestowing sufi master as a person who has arrived close to God (having *wilāyat*) by traveling along the Path and who has returned in a prophet-like way to assist others do the same. In this respect, the protégé of God is functionally equated with the Prophet. But how can the pirs demand so much authority that obedience to them appears to have priority over the worship of God as in the adage "Service [to the shaykh] is preferable to worship [of God]" (*al-khidma afḍal min al-ʿibāda*)?[36] When some travelers asked Abū'l-Hasan al-Kharaqānī (d. 425/1033) to pray for their safety, he advised them to set out on their journey in the name of God and call out Abū'l-Ḥasan's name if they ran into trouble. When highway robbers attacked the caravan, those who called on the shaykh were saved and those who called on God were robbed and killed. Abū'l-Ḥasan explained later that those who called on God directly petitioned someone they did not know and so received no aid. Those appealing to Abū'l-Ḥasan used the name of a person who knew God and who could then intercede and assist them.[37]

Even if one accepts the sufi contention that only a person with a controlled ego is truly a *muslim,* how does veneration and unquestioning obedience to the shaykh put a person in what sufis define as the correct relationship with the Divine? Abū Saʿīd-i Abū'l-Khayr's (d. 440/1049) hagiographer, Muḥammad b. Munawwar, relates this story:

> There was a certain Ibrāhīm Yanāl, who was the brother of the Sultan Ṭughril [Beg], coming down the road. When he saw our shaykh [Abū

[34]Rūmī, *Mathnawī,* 2:811–15.

[35]Twelver Shīʿīs declare that the world is never without an imam.

[36]See Louis Massignon, *Essai sur les origines du lexique technique de la mystique musulmane,* pp. 116–17.

[37]Mīr Khurd, *Siyar al-awliyā',* p. 338, cited in M. Mujeeb, *The Indian Muslims,* p. 125. Later, parallel ideas are reflected in ʿAbdulquddūs Gangōhī's (d. 944/1537) contention that, "a disciple worshipping [venerating] the *pir* was better than the worshipper of the Lord . . . for the latter was busy with the contemplation of his own self and therefore neglected God; one who adored the *pir* however, worshipped God through the contemplation of His creature." See *Maktūbāt-i quddūsiyya,* p. 125, cited in S. A. A. Rizvi, *A History of Sufism in India,* 2 volumes, 1:348.

Sa'īd-i Abū'l-Khayr] he got off his horse and came before our shaykh bowing his head and kissed his [Abū'l-Khayr's] hand. Our shaykh said, "Go lower," and he brought his head down lower. The shaykh said, "Go lower," and he lowered his head until it was almost touching the ground. [Then] the shaykh said, blessing him with a *bismillāh,* "OK, mount [your horse]." The shaykh rode off and returned to the sufi lodge (*khānaqāh*) .... [Explaining this event later to a dervish, the shaykh said,] "You do not know that whoever greets us does so for the sake of Him. Our body is the way for people to approach God. The goal, however, is Truth (J); we are not present. So the more humble each act of service that they do for the sake of Him, the more acceptable it is [to God]. Therefore I commanded Ibrāhīm Yanāl to serve God, not to serve us . . . The Ka'ba is regarded as the direction of prayer (*qibla*) by all Muslims so that people may bow down [to God], yet the Ka'ba itself is not even there. They reverence me as humanity's approach to God (*qibla-yi khalq*) but I am not there [either]."[38]

The sufi shaykh as the transparent intermediary between God and humanity has the same kind of authority as Muḥammad has in the Qur'ān, since obedience to the Prophet is synonymous with obedience to God.[39] For those who have submitted their egos to God, an equivalence between God and them exists; they have "taken on the color" of God. In Rūmī's words, "Whoever wants to sit with God should sit in the presence of the protégé of God."[40] When a prophet or friend of God is so absorbed in God, it is said that people's attitude toward either of them indicates their position toward God. This explains the alleged Divine saying from God (*ḥadīth qudsī*), "The person who harms a protégé of God makes war on me."[41]

Rūmī and other sufi commentators explain Manṣūr al-Ḥallāj's

---

[38]Muḥammad b. Munawwar, *Asrār al-tawḥīd,* p. 234 [trans. pp. 352–53]. The reigning Sultan was Ṭughril I (d. 429/1038).

[39]There are a dozen additional examples in the Qur'ān which equate obedience to God with obedience to the Prophet, e.g., "And obey God and the Messenger so that you may receive mercy" (Q. 3:132), or "If you obey God with His Messenger He will not withhold from you anything (you deserve) from your deeds" (Q. 49:14). Rūmī relates a story where a person asks why both Muḥammad and God are praised in the call to prayer (the profession of faith is repeated twice, mentioning that Muḥammad is the messenger of God) instead of just God. The answer is that praising Muḥammad is praising God. If God is compared to a king and Muḥammad is the man showing the way to the king then praising the man is, in reality, praising the king. See Jalāluddīn Rūmī, *Kitāb-i fīhi mā fīhi,* p. 227.

[40]Rūmī, *Mathnawī,* 2:2163.

[41]Al-Hujwīrī, *Kashf al-maḥjūb,* p. 268 [English trans. p. 212]. For variants, including a possible parallel Shī'ī hadith, see Badī'uzzamān Furūzānfar, *Aḥādīth-i mathnawī,* pp. 18, 185. One variant introduces the Divine saying (*ḥadīth qudsī*) cited above, "When I love a servant . . ."

utterance, "I am God" (*anā al-ḥaqq*), as meaning that he has annihilated himself and only God remains (*man fanā' gashtam ḥaqq mānad wa-bas*).[42] In sufi terminology this is annihilation of the ego in God (*fanā' fi'llāh*), bringing to mind the *ḥadīth qudsī* describing the condition of many pious Muslims: "They are not themselves, but in so far as they exist at all they exist in God. Their movements are caused by God, and their words are the words of God which are uttered by their tongues, and their sight is the sight of God, which has entered into their eyes. So God Most High has said: 'When I love a servant, I, the Lord, am his ear so that he hears by Me, I am his eye, so that he sees by Me, and I am his tongue so that he speaks by Me, and I am his hand so that he takes by Me.' "[43]

The prophets and the friends of God are not only vectors pointing to the Kaʿba (the "house of God") but are also referred to as the Kaʿba itself. Rūmī states, "The meaning of the Kaʿba is the heart of the prophets and friends of God and the dwelling place of God's revelation. The [physical] Kaʿba is a branch of that. If it were not for the heart what use would the Kaʿba be? The prophets and friends of God have totally abandoned their own desires and are following the desire of God. So whatever He commands, they do it."[44] According to sufis the real Kaʿba is, in fact, the light of God shining from the living protégé of God. This is a clear mandate for the primacy of a living, personal human guide who embodies prophet-like authority.

On what grounds did sufi directing-shaykhs accumulate the supernatural prestige needed to share with prophets the responsibility of subjecting human pride and ego to divine trials? Sufis explained that human conditions had deteriorated so much from the "Golden Age" of the Prophet's lifetime that sufi pirs were required to span the ever-increasing distance between humanity and God. Even to make such a claim indicates considerable sufi success in manipulating the Islamic symbolic universe. Yet one would have expected the ulama to have marginalized the sufis early in Islamic history. Memorized texts and the outward exemplary behavior of ulama manifested itself for all to behold. Sufi claims were much less visible, especially the claim that a sufi had arrived close enough to God to have become His protégé. Naqsh-

---

[42]Rūmī, *Fīhi mā fīhi*, p. 193.

[43]Margaret Smith, *Readings from the Mystics of Islam*, no. 20, cited in Annemarie Schimmel, *Mystical Dimensions*, p. 43. See also William A. Graham, *Divine Word and Prophetic Word in Early Islam: A Reconsideration of the Sources, with Special Reference to the Divine Saying or Hadîth Qudsî*, pp. 173–74.

[44]Rūmī, *Fīhi mā fīhi*, p. 165.

bandīs accused the ulama of only superficially imitating the Prophet and insisted that only sufis replicated both the outward and inward prophetic realities. The ulama easily countered these assertions by reminding doubters of their powerful connection to the sacred scriptures (a useless ploy when sufis had this knowledge also). Often in the Naqshbandī case a display of spiritual energy (or reports of such feats) more effectively influenced the average person than erudite ulama-sufi debates. The sufis also had the advantage of a larger repertoire of services, and these made their claims sufficiently forceful in Islamic societies. As a result, for many Muslims the sufi path became the means to reach God.

The Development of the Sufi Lodge

In their sufi lodges, the sufis tried to replicate the model community of the Prophet and his Companions. A set of rituals governed life in this new institution, including initiation, inculcation of special formulas to remember God (*dhikr*), the bestowal of sufi robes (sing. *khirqa*), and a set of elaborate behavioral injunctions governing every aspect of life—all justified on the basis of the Prophet's sunna. The concentration on ritual activities, in some lodges accompanied by ritual music (*samāʿ*) and regulated seclusion (*khalwa*), resulted in a new types of sufi identity and a new constellation of sufi relationships.[45] With the possible exception of seclusion and music, sufis really needed no special location to perform their religious practices when mosques could serve their purposes.

The development of the sufi lodge cannot be convincingly explained solely on the basis of a sudden upsurge of large sufi gatherings. Ibn al-Farajī (d. after 290/903) went with 120 sufis to visit Abū Turāb an-Nakhshabī (d. 245/859), and they stayed in mosques for the entire trip.[46] Aḥmad b. Khiḍrawayh (d. 240/854–

[45]Sufi lodges may have been necessary for those who performed exercises that would disturb others, e.g., vocal recollection of God. Yūsuf Hamadānī's (d. 535/1140) flourishing sufi lodge in Marv was known as "the Kaʿba of Khurasan." See Dawlatshāh Samarqandī, *Tadhkirat al-shuʿarā*ʾ, p. 76. His paramount successor, ʿAbdulkhāliq Ghujduvānī (d. 575/1179), was against constructing sufi lodges or even allowing his disciples to visit them because of vocal recollection practices. See Fakhruddīn ʿAlī Ṣafī Kāshifī, *Rashaḥāt-i ʿayn al-ḥayāt*, 1:37. Perhaps sufis like Yūsuf Hamadānī needed a separate building for vocal recollection practices or periods of seclusion *(khalwa)* while the silent recollection of ʿAbdulkhāliq Ghujduvānī could be performed in a mosque or anywhere else.

[46]Meier, *Abū Saʿīd-i Abū l-Ḫayr*, p. 296. For this paragraph on the history of sufi

855) allegedly came with a thousand students from Balkh to visit Abū Yazīd al-Bisṭāmī, who had a room for the storage of walking sticks; it was entirely filled. When in Nubadhan (near Herat) 62 sufis came to meet with the famous ʿAbdullāh Ansārī (d. 425/1034) for forty days; they lived as guests of a different person each day. Further east in Tirmidh, there were so many people in the house of al-Ḥakīm at-Tirmidhī in 269/883 that they had to move to the mosque. Reports indicate that sufis usually gathered in private houses, or if there were too many people, in a nearby mosque; the exact same practice is found in Muslim religious education of the time.[47] During the tenth century both activities slowly moved from the mosque to either a madrasa or a sufi lodge.[48] Makdisi has shown how the madrasa and pre-madrasa institution (mosque-inn complex) grew out of both philanthropic activity and the efforts of two great politician-statesmen, Badr b. Ḥasanawayh al-Kurdī (d. 405/1014) and Niẓām al-Mulk at-Tūsī (d. 485/1092), both of whom created vast networks of schools throughout the Islamic world.[49] Sufi lodges were sometimes attached to form a *madrasa-khānaqāh* complex and may have received their impetus from the spread of madrasas.[50] Often the

---

lodges I am relying on Fritz Meier's critical summary on pp. 292–312, unless otherwise noted. For a more complete but less critical history of the sufi lodge, see Kiyānī, *Tārīkh-i khānaqāh.*

[47]Often authors did not distinguish between madrasas and sufi lodges, e.g., one version of al-Muqaddasī's geographical account calls Karrāmī abodes *khānaqāhs* and another version calls them madrasas. See V. V. Bartol'd, "O Pogrebenii Timura," pp. 70–71. Bartol'd claims that the sufi lodge spread as an institution from west to east and the religious school from east to west.

[48]Just as the college in Islam developed from the mosque to mosque-inn complex to the college, the sufi lodge probably progressed from the mosque to a mosque-inn or frontier outpost *(ribāṭ)*-sufi lodge to a sufi lodge proper. See also Jacqueline Chabbi, "La fonction du ribat a Bagdad du Ve siècle au début du VIIe siècle." For the madrasa development, see George Makdisi, *The Rise of Colleges: Institutions of Learning in Islam and the West,* pp. 29–30. Contrary to Fritz Meier's skepticism concerning actual sufi lodges before the tenth century, Louis Massignon has Bishr al-Ḥāfī (d. 227/841) and al-Muḥāsibī (d. 243/857) building sufi lodges near Baghdad in Shuniz, imitating those already built at ʿAbbadan, Ramla, and Lukkam. See his *La Passion de Husayn Ibn Mansūr Hallāj,* 1:109–10, trans. Herbert Mason, *The Passion of Al-Hallaj: Mystic and Martyr of Islam,* 4 volumes, 1:68–69.

[49]Makdisi, *The Rise of Colleges,* pp. 28–32. This philanthropic activity had its practical agenda, viz., to distribute influence and control families of notables. How these forces operated through endowments in medieval Damascus is analyzed in Chamberlain's *Knowledge and Social Practice.*

[50]See Kiyānī, *Tārīkh-i khānaqāh,* pp. 311–22. In Khurasan the countryside became dotted with the tomb/sufi lodge complexes by the eleventh century. Thirty sufi lodges are mentioned in Muḥammad b. Munawwar's *Asrār al-tawḥīd.* The geographer al-Muqaddasī, traveling in Khurasan (and many other places) and writing in the period 375/985–380/990, describes the following Khurasani grave-shrines:

lodges belonged to a sufi and his family, for example, Abū ʿAbdurraḥmān Sulamī and his family or Abū Saʿīd-i Abū'l-Khayr and his descendants.[51]

Like the emergence of the directing-shaykh, the development of the sufi lodge began in Nishapur,[52] where sectarian strife between the Ḥanafīs and Shāfiʿīs had broken out. The Ḥanafī-Karrāmī old guard allied themselves against the Shāfiʿīs and sufis, the newer immigrants and converts. Since institutionalization of colleges or sufi lodges effectively allowed locally powerful men to control property and support their own faction, financial support channeled through colleges and sufi lodges enabled them to recruit new members and accumulate power and prestige. Perhaps the intense competition between conflicting groups (which eventually destroyed the city) acted as a catalyst to accelerate the development of both the college and sufi lodge. In any case, both prospered as institutions because they enabled notable families and governing groups (the *aʿyān-amīr* system) in other parts of the Islamic world to channel resources effectively in a decentralized agrarian economic system.[53]

The sufi lodge also functioned as a potent source of mediation in a society of continually shifting power structures. As a social integrator and a mediator the directing-shaykh needed to appear

---

that of ʿAlī al-Riḍa' at Tus, that of al-Riḍā's paternal uncle's son at Sarakhs, the head of Ḥusayn b. ʿAlī near Marv, and a grave of two Companions at Tabas. See al-Muqaddasī, *Aḥsan al-taqāsīm fī maʿrifat al-aqālīm*, translated by Basil Anthony Collins, *The Best Divisions for Knowledge of the Regions*, p. 294.

[51]Richard W. Bulliet, *The Patricians of Nishapur: A Study in Medieval Islamic Social History*, p. 299.

[52]Why this should be the case requires much more research on the Islamization of Khurasan and on the role of Karrāmiyya in this process. One can only speculate on the Karrāmī impetus in the development of sufi lodges and colleges—by the tenth century they had a network of quasimonastic institutions, which they called *khānaqāhs*, from Egypt to Samarqand. See Jacqueline Chabbi, "Remarques sur le développement historique des mouvements ascétiques et mystiques au Khurasan," p. 43. The Karrāmīs, named after Abū ʿAbdullāh Muḥammad b. Karrām, an Arab of Persian descent from Sijistan, was twice imprisoned by the Tahirids in Nishapur and finally exiled to Jerusalem, where he died in 255/869. Often considered a branch of the Ḥanafī school of jurisprudence, the Karrāmīs were notably successful in missionary work. From the remarkably little we know about the Karrāmiyya, they appear to have stressed mendicancy and renunciation of the world. See Wilferd Madelung, "Sufism and the Khurramiyya." As their movement disintegrated in the eleventh century, institutional sufism penetrated Muslim society. See the article by C. E. Bosworth, "Karrāmiyya," in the *Encyclopaedia of Islam*, 2d ed. In this article he notes Ribera y Tarragó's unsubstantiated theory that the madrasa system resulted from the Karrāmī network of lodges.

[53]For the *aʿyān-amīr* system, see Marshall Hodgson, *The Venture of Islam: Conscience and History in a World Civilization*, 3 volumes, 2:91–94.

aloof to any particular worldly faction. His exemplary connection to the Divine and his physical location in a lodge removed from the city allowed him to do that. The initiatory bond, a prerequisite for the transmission of special spiritual techniques, meant that as spiritual mentor he had connections with influential and powerful people from every class and political faction. Add to that actual observable manifestations of supernatural power, e.g., *himmat* or *taṣarruf,* both of which are associated with spiritual travel, and this bond would be taken very seriously indeed. In a society where rigid hierarchical power differentials were taken for granted, even required, the special behavioral norms of the master-disciple bond was no different from hierarchical relationships throughout society. Because sufis embodied the central personal figure of the Prophet, they could command even more obedience and psychological compliance. This gave the directing-shaykh the leverage he needed outside the lodge as others continually tested and contested his authority.

In the tenth century the combination of sufi manipulation of supernatural power and the ability to intercede with God on behalf of others motivated sultans and other wealthy figures to establish *waqf*s for the development of sufi lodges in return for which the donors stipulated that the sufis regularly offer prayers on the benefactors' behalf.[54] The conventional wisdom of the time—and still today in many parts of the Islamic world—was that the supplications of holy people could turn defeat into victory. Nūruddīn Zangī (d. 569/1174) responded typically (and angrily) when his nomad followers urged him to stop giving money to sufis and scholars (*fuqahā*ʾ, *fuqarā, ṣūfiyya, qurrā*ʾ) after he was defeated by the Crusaders, "By God, my only hope for victory lies in these people. Your very livelihood and your victories are only possible because of the weak among you. How can I stop my largesse to people who fight on my behalf as I lie on my bed asleep with arrows that do not miss their mark, and divert this largesse instead to others who do not fight for me unless they see me in person, and with arrows that may hit or miss?"[55] It is not

[54]For examples of reciting sacred texts for the founders in medieval Damascus, see Michael Chamberlain, *Knowledge and Social Practice in Medieval Damascus, 1190–1350,* p. 74.

[55]Ibn al-Athīr, *Al-tārīkh al-bāhir fi'l-dawla al-atābakiyya,* p. 118, cited in Khalidi, *Arabic Historical Thought,* p. 212. Note that scholars were included in this group of intercessors. Kings were known to verify the supernatural capabilities of shaykhs by a variety of strategems, including adminstering poison. See Monika Gronke, *Derwische im Vorhof der Macht: Social-und Wirtschaftsgeschichte Nordwestirans im 13. und 14. Jahrhundert,* pp. 133–34.

coincidental that Turkic nomads did not appreciate institutional sufis. In specific sociopolitical environments, (e.g., the agrarian), directing-shaykhs performed a necessary social role, and in others, (e.g., the nomadic), they were noticeably absent. Naqshbandī directing-shaykhs in Central Asia appealed to settled agrarian farmers and townspeople but not the nomadic tribes. In a parallel fashion, it was only when the nomadic Jat tribes in the Panjab settled to become farmers that institutional sufism developed. In the context of personal authority, the prestige of the sufi lodge reflected its profound symbolic role as it replicated the *communitas* of the Prophet and his Companions.

The relationship in the primordial Muslim community between the Prophet and his Companions permeates many types of authority relationships in Islamic societies. The ever-present example of the Prophet, like the *qibla* pointing to the Kaʿba, has guided pious Muslims: both the sufi pir and religious scholar patterned their behavior on the Prophetic model and taught others to do the same. A directing-shaykh, endowed with the highest possible spiritual prestige as the heir of the (supernatural) Prophet, intensified this behavioral model until it led eventually to the development of sufi communities.

In their lodges sufis attempted to pattern their micro-community on the sacred community of Muḥammad and his Companions,[56] and in this they succeeded beyond their wildest dreams; sufi lodges (often in combination with tomb-shrines) eventually spread throughout the Islamic world from Khurasan to North Africa, Turkey, Central Asia, and India. Although local conditions contributed to the success or failure of sufi lodges, as a general rule they flourished, because the ideals of the "original" Prophetic Islam contrasted so sharply with the day-to-day realities of the actual Islam four or more centuries later in places increasingly distant from Arabia.

The ideal community of the Prophet with his equally exem-

---

[56]The individual enacted the *sharʿī* vision both inside and outside sufi circles by consciously striving to imitate the Prophetic example. There is no evidence that sufi lodges were set up for this purpose since they merely institutionalized what already had existed on an ad-hoc basis. Fritz Meier indicates that when these lodges came under attack as "innovations" sufis began to justify them in terms of Prophetic antecedents by comparing them to the "People of the Porch" *(ahl al-ṣuffa)*. See his *Abū Saʿīd-i Abū l-Ḫayr*, p. 312. Examples of glorifying the People of the Porch and the establishment of the sufi lodge as sunna can be found in Aḥmad ʿAlī Rajāʾī Bukhārāʾī, *Farhang-i ashʿār-i Ḥāfiẓ*, pp. 162–63, 171. The Prophetic precedent of People of the Porch is used to explain the creation of sufi lodges in ʿIzzuddīn Maḥmūd Kāshānī (d. 735/1334), *Miṣbāḥ al-hidāya*, p. 153.

plary Companions necessarily diverged from social reality. Sunnī dogma represents the Companions collectively as the most exalted and pious generation of Muslims, impoverished and otherworldly. What strength they had came from God. Did not Muḥammad say, "My poverty is my pride"? In contrast, later Muslim rulers, the political counterparts to the Prophet, surrounded themselves with ostentatious wealth and strongarmed their subjects with military force to maintain their luxury. (Although some of the Companions became very rich as a result of the conquests, their wealth was not highlighted in the later tradition.) The light of ideal character, flawless religious knowledge, and continual remembrance and fear of God that later Sunnī dogma accords the Companions is reflected weakly, if at all, in the later Muslim community.

These contradictions are by no means limited to Islamic cultures; they are shared by any philosophy, ideology, mythology, or religion that tries to implement a system of ideals in an uncertain human social order. For the particular type of polarity represented by Islamic society (the actual community) and the sufi lodge (the ideal community), Victor Turner's notions of structure and *communitas* (anti-structure) fit particularly well.[57] According to Turner, structure is the dynamic configuration of patterned arrangements that are consciously recognized and operate regularly according to legal and political norms of a given society. Structure highlights and justifies economic, hierarchical, age, and sex differences. *Communitas* represents social reality as a homogeneous, undifferentiated whole, stressing the equality of individuals such as those going through "rites of passage."[58]

The homogeneous nature of *communitas* in the sufi lodge must have appealed to the masses. One found illiterate peasants sitting on the floor next to highly educated religious scholars, all presumably treated equally by the sufi master.[59] It was common

---

[57]For this section I am indebted to Victor Turner's *Dramas, Fields, and Metaphors: Symbolic Action in Human Society*, pp. 231–99; *From Ritual to Theatre*, pp. 20–59; and Gábor Klaniczay, *The Uses of Supernatural Power: The Transformation of Popular Religion in Medieval and Early-Modern Europe*, pp. 28–50.

[58]The *communitas* here is the circle of disciples, seekers, and others in the circle around the spiritual guide. The shaykh is hierarchically removed from the *communitas* due to his intimacy with God. As a threshold between God and humanity, he literally precipitates a liminal environment around him, which in turn is maintained by an elaborate system of rules and rituals in the sufi lodge.

[59]This sketch of sufi lodges tends toward an idealization of these communities, since many of those visiting sufi lodges probably had this impression. At the same time there were those who were well aware of the abuses of sufi authority. See Kāshānī, *Miṣbāḥ al-hidāya*, p. 151.

knowledge among the masses that when the sufi shaykh accepted donations it went to the community kitchen (*langar*) where the poor and travelers, Muslim or non-Muslim, could eat—the shaykhs themselves had the reputation of refusing honors and gifts. In this way the shaykh, not the wealthy patrons or the prominent members of the community who set up pious foundations, gained prestige in the community for charitable activity. The sufi lodge functioned as a refuge and asylum; in an emergency anyone could request assistance from the shaykh.[60] The atmosphere of the sufi lodge created a climate of trust in the sufi master. People who had received help from the divine intervention of the shaykh often returned to thank him. The word spread quickly, and, bolstered by legends and stories, sufis became integral and influential members of society.

The anti-structural aspect of the *communitas* reversed the normal order, giving the weak and inferior power while the strong and powerful were humiliated, since in a sufi environment, those who have minimized their *nafs* and outwardly appear weak have the highest status and those with exalted power are accorded lowest rank. This gives great symbolic value to poverty. Hagiographies explain how sufi masters were oblivious to the effects of poverty or riches in spite of the necessarily large quantity of resources often associated with their lodges. Their poverty was "liminal," the marginal condition associated with one who lives in *communitas*, instead of the literal poverty of everyday society. A sufi pir, like the Prophet, maintains a state of permanent liminality between heaven and earth, which gives him, like other permanently liminal individuals, supernatural power.

The sufi master differs from a prophet in that he needs more stringent rules and a more rigid hierarchical structure in order to maintain a normative, day-to-day *communitas* (as opposed to a short-lived, spontaneous *communitas*). The behavioral rituals and unquestioning obedience to the directing-shaykh facilitate the continuation of this normative *communitas*, as do the sufi manuals that dictate correct behavior. In the process of establishing the normative *communitas*, conflicting tensions arise as the anti-structure of the lodge meshes unevenly with the intruding structures of society—someone needs to provide the building and the food for the community on a regular basis. Many anecdotes in hagio-

[60]People used to call out the shaykh's name in emergencies. See Monika Gronke, *Derwische im Vorhof der Macht*, p. 113. There were even people who, though against sufis and sufism, even ended up calling on a sufi shaykh when in a tight spot. See ibid., p. 118.

graphies are illustrations of how these inevitable contradictions are resolved.[61]

Abū Saʿīd-i Abū'l-Khayr established one of the first manuals for the sufi lodge, based on the practices of the "Companions of the Porch" (*ahl al-ṣuffa*), the Qur'ān, and the practices of Muḥammad.[62] The first group of injunctions focuses on a constant recollection of God. All inhabitants must maintain ritual purity and have clean clothing, so that they can pray or recite the Qur'ān at any time. As long as they reside in the sufi lodge they should supplicate God for forgiveness after the dawn prayer, recite the Qur'ān at daybreak, not talk to anyone until the sun rises, recite litanies between the last two ritual prayers, and perform supererogatory prayers (*tahajjud*) at night. Nonhierarchical notions of equality, in keeping with the Prophetic ideal, demand that residents receive the poor and weak and ease their burdens, always eat in the company of others (usually a very basic fare of bread dipped in soup broth [*tharīd*]), and not leave each other's presence without mutual consent. Free time was devoted to religious study, earning a livelihood, or giving comfort to another person.

Such a circumscribed life was not suitable for the vast majority of sufi aspirants, nor was it meant to be. Of the 120 residents noted at Abū Saʿīd's sufi lodge in the eleventh century, 80 were temporary residents ("travelers"). Of the other 40 at least half

---

[61]One common theme is the sufi lodge running up debts and one of the sufis asking a wealthy patron for financial assistance. If he refuses, the shaykh sends the messenger back with a clairvoyant message or a reminder of death and the Day of Judgment (when material wealth will be of no use). Almost always the person supplies the money; if not he risks dying soon after. See Muḥammad b. Munawwar, *Asrār al-tawḥīd*, pp. 181–82; 270–71 [trans. 284–85; 410–11].

[62]The Companions of the Porch are invoked as the ascetic and poor Companions who slept in Muḥammad's porch in Medina and from whom the word *ṣūfī* is derived. Al-Qushayrī, a contemporary of Abū Saʿīd-i Abū'l-Khayr, correctly refutes such contrived derivations (from *ṣuffa*, porch or bench; or *ṣāfī*, pure) on the basis of grammatical impossibility. See W. Montgomery Watt, "Ahl al-ṣuffa," in the *Encyclopaedia of Islam*, 2d. ed. For the architectural use of *ṣuffa* in Central Asian tomb-shrines, see Bartol'd, "The Burial of Tīmūr," pp. 78–79. A short compilation of hadiths referring to the Companions of the Porch is in Maḥmūd Abū al-Fayd al-Manūfī, *Jamharat al-awliyā'*, 2 volumes, 2:32–36. When Abū Saʿd, a disciple of Abū Saʿīd-i Abū'l-Khayr, founded a sufi lodge in Baghdad, the large assembly room was called the *ṣuffa*. See Muḥammad b. Munawwar, *Asrār al-tawḥīd*, p. 357 [trans. p. 544]. By this time sufis were distancing themselves from practices of asceticism that included wearing woolen clothes, which might have been the motive behind looking for an alternate derivation for the word *ṣūfī*. Abū Saʿīd criticized someone for following the path of asceticism since it involved undertaking action on one's own rather than following one's shaykh. See ibid., p. 166 [English trans., p. 267].

would stay for three years or less.[63] One advantage of the sufi lodge system was precisely that it did allow short visits, with the aspirant then continuing sufi training when he left the lodge and returned to ordinary society. Only the most advanced seekers resided there for long periods. For them overexposure to the sufi lodge could cause it to lose its extraordinary quality, allowing the more tedious aspects of group living among ordinary people to emerge.

The ritual structure in the sufi lodge re-enacted the sacred history of the Prophet and his Companions in its punctilious performance of activities that God mandated through Muḥammad for all Muslims: the five daily prayers; supererogatory rituals performed by Muḥammad (additional sunna prayers before and after ritual prayer); and finally recommended ritual (*mustaḥabb*) practices, e.g., evening *taḥajjud* prayers and recitation of litanies, for those who wanted to go beyond the minimum requirements. This degree of ritual could be followed by any pious Muslim living in an Islamic society. The intricate ritual behavior expected in the company of the sufi master could otherwise be duplicated outside the sufi lodge, in any mosque or private home, and to some extent overlapped the kind of ritual behavior expected in the company of any notable religious scholar.

A third aspect of the ritual, however, involved specific sufi customs limited to the lodge; these included initiation (*bayʿa*), inculcating a formula to recollect God (*dhikr*), and eventually the bestowal of a sufi robe (*khirqa*). The initiation ritual imitating the oath between the Prophet and his Companions at Hudaybiya formally sealed the master-disciple relationship. The formula for recollecting God retrospectively was fashioned to duplicate the transmission from Muḥammad to either Abū Bakr (silent recollection) or ʿAlī (vocal recollection) and closely resembled the Imāmī notion of esoteric transmission (*naṣṣ*). The patched sufi robe hearkened back to the Prophet giving a cloak (*burda*) to Kaʿb b. Zubayr, allegedly purchased by the Umayyad caliph, Muʿāwiyya; by the ninth century it was worn out and patched.[64] Not all

---

[63]The time to progress along the path and receive permission to teach varies considerably from a few weeks to decades. For the length of training required for seekers, see Kiyānī, *Tārīkh-i khānaqāh*, pp. 425–27.

[64]The sufi robe is mentioned as early as the ninth century by al-Ḥārith al-Muḥāsibī (d. 243/857). See L. Massignon, *Essai*, p. 128. Ibn Qutayba (d. 276/889) states that the Umayyad caliph Muʿāwiya purchased the robe for twenty thousand dirhams and was subsequently worn by the caliphs on the two major Muslim holidays at the end of Ramaḍān and the tenth of Dhū'l-ḥijja. See David S. Margoliouth, "The Relics of the Prophet Muhammad," p. 21. The caliphal heirloom might very well have come from the Christians of Ayla, near modern

visitors to the sufi lodge would participate in these rituals, but all could at least observe them.

A fourth aspect of ritual involved an intricate set of rules governing every aspect of behavior in the lodge. As these are re-enacted and performed ritually in the *communitas*, the cumulative effect of this experience resulted in a powerful but subtle inculcation of the *sharʿī* ideal. Symbols took on a life of their own. At the center of this ritual universe was the Prophet, the human Kaʿba. The effect of the overlapping rules governing behavior in the sufi lodge is described by Abū Saʿīd-i Abūʾl-Khayr as follows: "At first a rule is something people adopt with difficulty, but then it becomes a habit. Then that habit becomes second nature and finally, what is second nature becomes reality."[65]

The sufi construction of *communitas* made sufis prime agents for the Islamization of society. As Victor Turner maintains, "Man grows through anti-structure and conserves through structure."[66] The veneration of Muḥammad and his central place in the hearts of Muslims influenced the sufi community when it re-created its version of the early charismatic community. In a reciprocal fashion the sufi lodge became a vehicle for incorporating popular local culture into Islamic society while Muslims became connected to the mythical golden age of Islam. Both the myth of the Prophetic Golden Age and the "enchanted universe" of local culture met in the *communitas* of the sufi lodge.[67] Within popular culture was a common field of religion shared by both the subordinate classes and the elite. It did not completely overlap, since some of the literate shariʿa-minded Muslims strived to impose their religious values, and the masses, not typically drawn to theological nuances or rational analysis, often expected their religious figures simply to manipulate reality through intercession. But the lodge accommodated these divergent religious tendencies by exposing visitors to an intensified shariʿa-oriented ritual environment where the sufi master harnessed supernatural power for the benefit of his guests.

Over time this interaction resulted in the regulation by ritual means of the entire rhythm of individual and family life. Scholars have emphasized the fundamental nomocratic basis of Islamic society but have not recognized the "inward" and charismatic anti-

---

ʿAqaba. See M. Zwettler, "The Poet and the Prophet: Towards Understanding the Evolution of a Narrative," pp. 348–49.

[65]Muḥammad b. Munawwar, p. 316 [trans. p. 493].

[66]Turner, *Dreams*, p. 298.

[67]A Weberian term employed by Harjot Oberoi in *The Construction of Religious Boundaries: Culture, Identity and Diversity in the Sikh Tradition*, p. 141.

structure which allowed this imposed structure to evolve and give meaning to their lives. The charismatic authority of the sufi shaykh reinforced the communal ritual center of Islam: the charismatic community of the Prophet surrounded by his Companions located in the sacred geographical center, Mecca.

Some of the ideological and symbolic methods harmonizing *communitas* and structure in Islamic society involved the tensions between the ulama and sufis. These two groups of religious specialists put the Prophet at the center of their symbolic universe by ritually and symbolically replicating the Prophet and his circle—the scholar with his students replicated the Prophetic model just as the sufi pir with his disciples did. The difference was only one of degree.

The scholar's circle did not have four degrees of ritual; its tendency was to keep activity near the center and keep it well structured and historically under control. Hence the ulama's image of the Prophet was narrowly defined by validated hadith. The sufis, on the other hand, expanded their notions of Prophetic identity and took more liberty in their interpretations of sacred history, formulating their expanded notion of *communitas* by incorporating non-Islamic elements of popular culture into it. In this centrifugal mode entirely new elements were added to the Islamic repertoire, for example, the practice of visualizing the shaykh, listening to ecstasy-producing music (*samāʿ*), extended periods of seclusion (even upside down), and holding the breath while meditating.

Structure requires a conservative and limiting mode. Anti-structure implies an exaggeration, an expansion, as the growth of new possibilities constantly pulls outward to encompass new cultures. The crucial point is that these centripetal and centrifugal forces were constantly in tension. The framework that held them together was the sacred history of Muḥammad and the potent symbol that developed in the Muslim imagination with each religious scholar and sufi pir. Yet the memory of Muḥammad, the original charismatic impulse, however embellished and selective it had become in the first four centuries, was preserved. The sufi shaykhs succeeded in satisfying the communal demand for personal charismatic authority. To the extent that Muḥammad's charisma was renewed by sufis, sufism would remain a reality—with a name.[68]

[68]For those who saw sufism as an innovation in Islam, sufis responded by repeating Abū'l-Ḥasan Būshanja's maxim, "Sufism started as a reality without a name and now is a name without a reality." See al-Hujwīrī, *Kashf al-maḥjūb*, p. 49 [trans., p. 44]. Such an aphorism also assumes a progressive decline in the number of people becoming close to God as a result of sufi practice.

CHAPTER 3

The Naqshbandiyya in India from Their Foundation to the Colonial Period

A Naqshband is one whose glance forms an imprint [of God] on the mirror of the heart which remains until the Day of Judgment.

Muhammad Hāshimī Kishmī, *Nasamāt al-Quds*

Imagine a museum of Sufism,[1] each wing housing an exhibition of a major sufi lineage. At the entrance of the Naqshbandī wing you pick up a small brochure describing the history of the Naqshbandiyya which emphasizes the founder-figure, Bahā'-uddīn Naqshband (d. 791/1389), with an accompanying picture of his tomb in Qaṣr-i'Ārifān,[2] located twelve kilometers from Bukhara, in present-day Uzbekistan. A small box on the first page explains the origin of "Naqshband" (*naqsh* as a design; *band* as etching or affixing). According to legend, it stems from Bahā'-uddīn's family livelihood as weavers of embroidery cloth. Later, Bahā'uddīn, with God's name woven or engraved on his heart, began to imprint or impress the name of God on others' hearts.

The historical sketch continues, describing the worldwide spread of the Naqshbandiyya, pausing briefly to underline the importance of Shaykh Aḥmad Sirhindī (d. 1034/1624) of India and Maulānā Khālid Baghdādī (d. 1242/1827), a Kurdish Naqsh-

[1]To do so requires a certain degree of reification, since practices and knowledge are difficult to put in a museum—hence a capitalized Sufism.

[2]Before being renamed "Gnostics' Castle" in Bahā'uddīn's honor, it was known as the "Hindus' Castle" or Qaṣr-i Hinduwān. For Central Asian Muslims it is a leading pilgrimage site.

bandī buried in Damascus. A short explanation then lists the distinctive characteristics of the Naqshbandiyya: strict adherence to the practices of the Prophet (*sunna*), a spiritual lineage traced back to Abū Bakr aṣ-Ṣiddīq (d. 13/634), the first caliph, and the silent repetition of God's name (*dhikr*). On the last page of the pamphlet is a photograph of a letter with the original seal imprints written by the last great Mughal emperor of India, Aurangzīb (r. 1068–69/1658–1118/1707) to an Indian Naqshbandī, Khwāja Sayfuddīn Sirhindī (d. 1095/1684).[3]

When you enter the Naqshbandī exhibition, your eye is immediately attracted to a textile display. Coming closer you see some threadbare examples of sufi robes (sing. *khirqa*) of the type worn by Naqshbandī notables, some drawings of sufis wearing these robes and distinctive turbans, and an array of canes, some with intricate wood and ivory carving. A glass case displays old prayer rugs, faded but intricately woven, with designs indicating the side that is pointed toward the Kaʿba. There are no clues as to how many prostrations were needed to wear the places on some of these faded pieces. A placard explains that they are believed to be laden with blessing and auspiciousness (*baraka*) and that they are still symbols of authority to contemporary Naqshbandīs.

To demonstrate the geographic spread of the Naqshbandiyya, a large world map is equipped with lights to show the location of Naqshbandī centers, controlled by six buttons, each representing a century. Press the fifteenth-century button and you see many lights in Transoxiana (particularly around Samarqand and Bukhara), Herat, Qazvin, Tabriz, and Istanbul; the sixteenth-century lamp lights up Kashgar, Kabul, Surat (Gujarat), Medina, Mecca, and Damascus. Representing the twentieth century, a collage of lights is needed to show Naqshbandī activity all over the world (except Iran and parts of Africa), including North America and Europe.

The last exhibit conveys the same information in a different way: an entire wall is filled with an intricate genealogical chart of the Naqshbandiyya with Muḥammad, the Prophet of Islam, at the top; it spreads out century by century with myriad branches at the bottom indicating prominent Naqshbandīs of the late nineteenth century. You would be unable to find the genealogical particulars of a contemporary Naqshbandī group in Concord,

[3]The anglicized Tīmūrī, "Timurid," is used for Tīmūrī rulers from Central Asia up to Bābur. Beginning with Humāyūn, "Mughal" is used for the Indian Tīmūrī lineage ("Mughal" is a Turkicized version of "Mongol") until the last Mughal emperor in 1857.

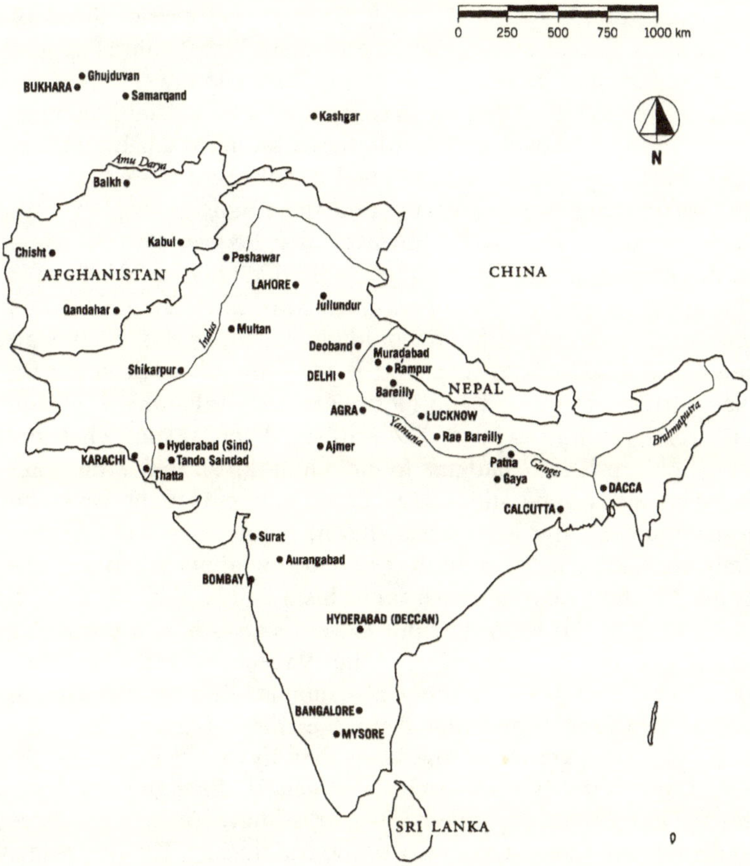

Central and South Asia

California, but the international nature of the Naqshbandiyya would be obvious.

Sufis would describe this diagram in terms of many chains (sing. *silsila*), each shaykh being a link in a chain of loosely united common spiritual practices believed to have originated with the founder. At the bottom of the final exhibit you read "Naqshbandī *ṭarīqa*":[4] this is the Naqshbandī path whose lineage designation "Naqshbandiyya" is defined as the aggregate of all lineages coming from Bahā'uddīn Naqshband. While you are pondering the display, the curator arrives to explain the absence of the usual video booth in the Naqshbandī section; there is nothing to show

[4]In Persian and Urdu sufi literature, *silsila* and *ṭarīqa* are often used interchangeably. See figure 4 for the Naqshbandī *silsila*. Note the vertical aspect of authority up and down the *silsila*. There are few cross-linkages.

that corresponds to the singing, dancing, and exotic rituals of other sufis. Except for occasional outbursts, Naqshbandīs appear just to sit around in a circle and to meditate silently.

Now imagine that you are accompanying a Pakistani member of one of these Naqshbandī meditation sessions to this hypothetical exhibit.[5] He can tell you in great detail about the robe, cane, and prayer rug of his own pir and the rituals associated with each. It would be unlikely, however, that he ever saw the same *baraka*-impregnated objects (*tabarrukāt*) which his grandfather pir (his spiritual mentor's pir) had given him, carefully guarded as any other priceless heirloom would be. Playing with the lights on the world map he is as surprised as you might have been to find Naqshbandīs in Europe and North America. When he discovers his great-grandfather pir on the wall-sized genealogical chart his eyes light up as if he had just found a long-lost friend. After tracing it up a few generations to ascertain its accuracy, however, he loses interest. Later he remarks that he is impressed that Americans are taking such an interest in learning about Islam and sufism. Privately, he reminisces about his own Naqshbandī master.

Another of the lessons of our exhibit shows how a particular lineage of the Naqshbandiyya, the Naqshbandiyya-Mujaddidiyya, predominates over other Naqshbandī lineages worldwide within two generations after Aḥmad Sirhindī's death. The spiritual path now known as the Naqshbandiyya can in fact be divided into three stages, each of which is distinguished by a pivotal charismatic figure who developed new spiritual practices and even redefined the identity of the sufi lineage. The first stage, called "the way of the masters" (*ṭarīqa-yi khwājagān*), begins with Khwāja ʿAbdulkhāliq Ghujduwānī (d. 575/1179) and spans the "prehistoric" stage originating with the Prophet Muḥammad.[6] The second historical stage starts with Bahā'uddīn Naqshband (d. 791/1389), the founder-figure, after whom the spiritual path

---

[5]Shortly after I first wrote this in early 1992, a museum very similar to the one I have just described was opened at the tomb of Bahā'uddīn Naqshband (personal communication, Professor Jo Ann Gross).

[6]Indo-Muslim sources give Ghujduwānī's death date as 575/1179 while Saʿīd Nafīsī and Hamid Algar use 617/1220; Fritz Meier and others use the first date. As the book was going to press Devin Deweese informed me that both Ghujdūvānī and Aḥmad Yasawī probably lived into the early thirteenth century. See the discussion in Fritz Meier, *Zwei Abhandlung-en über die Naqšbandiyya*, p. 25, n. 2. At least a few earlier sufis were named "Khwāja," e.g., Khwāja Yūsuf Hamadānī (d. 535/1140) who was Khwāja Ghujduwānī's spiritual guide *(murshid)*, in addition to Khwāja Aḥmad Yasawī (d. 562/1166–67) and Khwāja Abū Muḥammad al-Ḥasan b. al-Ḥusayn al-Andāqī (d. 522/1157) who were Khwāja Ghujduwānī's fellow disciples. For other uses of *khwāja* and *khwājagān* see ibid., pp. 190–92.

(*ṭarīqa*) is named the Naqshbandiyya.[7] The third historical stage begins with Aḥmad Sirhindī (d. 1034/1624) and includes those applying his teachings and spiritual techniques.[8] It is with Sirhindī that the movement changes its name to Naqshbandiyya-Mujaddidiyya or simply Mujaddidiyya.

In fourteenth-century Central Asia the Naqshbandiyya gave organized assistance and religious sanction to influential landlords. Tughluq Tīmūr (r. 748/1347–763/1362) propagated Islam by example;[9] when he converted he had himself circumcised and required all his followers to convert. The sufis and wandering Muslim holy men (sing. *darvīsh*) spread Islam among the people while legitimizing Tīmūr's rule.[10] In return the rulers respected and patronized sufis, building them mausoleums and providing *waqfs*. Even the names of Tughluq Tīmūr's successors in eastern Turkestan and Transoxiana reveal dervish influence: Ilyās Khwāja (r. 763/1362–767/1366), Khiḍr Khwāja (r. 791/1389–801/1399), and Uways (r. 821/1418–831/1428).

---

[7]Dina Le Gall states, on the basis of hagiographical sources, that the *ṭarīqa* was not named after Bahā'uddīn Naqshband until roughly one hundred years after his death. See Dina Le Gall, "The Ottoman Naqshbandiyya in the Pre-Mujaddidī Phase: A Study in Islamic Religious Culture and Its Transmission," pp. 12–13. Note the title of ʿAbdurraḥmān Jāmī's (d. 898/1492) treatise, *Sarrishta-yi ṭarīqa-yi khwājagān,* whose title confirms Le Gall's statement. This treatise discusses the first hundred-year history of what was later called the Naqshbandiyya.

[8]A fourth stage, the Naqshbandiyya-Khālidiyya named after Maulānā Khālid Kurdī/Baghdādī (d. 1242/1827), may also be included. The spread of this lineage has been largely limited to Turkey, the Arab world, and Indonesia. See Mahīndokht Muʿtamadī, *Maulānā Khālid Naqshband.* Some modern Naqshbandī writers include two additional stages, from Abū Bakr aṣ-Ṣiddīq (d. 13/634) to Ṭayfūr b. ʿĪsā Abū Yazīd al-Bisṭāmī (d. 261/874) called the Ṣiddīqiyya and from Abū Yazīd al-Bisṭāmī to Khwāja ʿAbdulkhāliq Ghujduwānī called the Ṭayfūriyya. See Muḥammad Nūr Bakhsh Tawakkulī, *Tadhkira-yi mashā'ikh-i naqshband* with additions by Muḥammad Ṣādiq Quṣūrī', p. 488. The Ṭayfūriyya are first discussed by al-Hujwīrī, *Kashf al-maḥjūb,* ed. Zhukovski, pp. 228–35; [English trans., pp. 184–89]. Later, Aḥmad b. Muḥammad al-Qushshāshī (d. 1071/1660) discusses a Madārī lineage through the Ṭayfūriyya and Abū Bakr aṣ-Ṣiddīq in his *Al-simṭ al-majīd fī shā'n al-bayʿat wa'l-dhikr wa-talqīnihi wa-salāsil ahl al-tawḥīd,* p. 74. This typology has been duplicated by various later Arab Naqshbandī authors. See Muḥammad Pārsā, *Qudsiyya: Kalimāt-i Bahā'uddīn Naqshband,* p. 28 (introduction). There is no historical evidence that any sufis identified themselves as members of the Ṣiddīqiyya or Ṭayfūriyya.

[9]Here I am using the western, Persianized version of Tughlug Temür's name (Turkish-Mongol *temür* meaning "iron") instead of the eastern, Chaghatai Turkish spelling. This is the ruler of the Eastern Chaghatayids, not to be confused with the later Tīmūr (d. 807/1405) from whom the Timurids are named.

[10]I am indebted to the archives in the Harvard University Archives, Cambridge, Massachusetts, [hereafter Archives] of the late Joseph Fletcher for this Central Asian historical sketch. See box 13: "Khojas: Chapter 1."

Generally the sufis in Central Asia represented the voices of the sedentary middle and lower classes; sufi economic interests therefore centered on the oasis populations—all of which contributed to the ultimate collapse of the nomadic hegemony in Central Asia.[11] Later, Tīmūr (d. 807/1405), the "founding ruler" of the Timurids, ordered the building of a spectacular tomb complex for the sufi Aḥmad Yasawī (d. 562/1166–1167) and in his earlier years honored one of Bahā'uddīn Naqshband's sufi guides, Amīr Kulāl (d. 772/1370), next to whom the Timurid ruler chose to be buried.[12]

In the sixteenth century Aḥmad Khwājagī b. Jalāluddīn Kāsānī (d. 949/1542–43 in Dahbid) and other Naqshbandīs linked many groups in Central Asian society, including the artisan guilds of the towns and the peasant population of the villages. Given this broad following, Aḥmad Kāsānī obtained patronage from Uzbek rulers to build a sufi lodge in Bukhara. His assistance paid off when Aḥmad Kāsānī persuaded Baraq Khān to lift the siege of Bukhara.[13] Naqshbandīs followed Timurid patronage and provided valuable services both as mediators between the people and rulers and between the people and God.[14] This pattern of patronage was only intermittently replicated in India; Naqshbandīs did not automatically receive favor from Mughal rulers.

The most significant person behind the Naqshbandiyya's subsequent influence was Khwāja Naṣīruddīn 'Ubaydullāh Aḥrār (d. 895/1490), whose lineal and spiritual descendants dominated the Indian Naqshbandiyya.[15] Aḥrār's remarkably powerful spiri-

---

[11]This happened by the seventeenth century when *boza* a drink made of barley (an agricultural product), replaces *kumiss*, the drink of the nomads. See Archives, box 12, untitled mss., p. 27.

[12]See J. M. Rogers, trans., "V. V. Bartol'd's Article *O Pogrebenii Timura* ('The Burial of Tīmūr')."

[13]Joseph Fletcher, "Aḥmad Kāsānī," in *Encyclopaedia Iranica*. Aḥmad Kāsānī's descendants dominated the history of eastern Turkestan in the seventeenth and eighteenth centuries. A disciple of Muḥammad Qāḍī (d. 903/1497–98 or 921/1515 in Samarqand), a famous successor of Aḥrār, Aḥmad Kāsānī is also known as Makhdūm-i 'Aẓam, Khwājagī Aḥmad, and Maulānā Khwājagī Aḥmad b. Jalāluddīn. See Muḥammad Ghawthī Manḍawī, *Gulzār-i abrār*, p. 259, who gives his death date as 950/1543–44.

[14]Tīmūr transferred the body of his father, Ṭarāgāī, to be near the grave of Shamsuddīn Kulāl. This is not Bahā'uddīn Naqshband's spiritual mentor, as I once believed. See Jürgen Paul, "Scheiche und Herrscher." Devin Deweese kindly informed me of this article.

[15]There is a note in the Persian *Hidāyat nāma*, written by Mīr Khāluddīn Kātib b. Maulānā Qāḍī Shāh Kūchak al-Yārkandī, ca. 1100/1700 (British Museum mss. Oriental 8162), folio 1r, stating that Khwājagī Muḥammad Amkanagī (d. 1008/1600) established the Naqshbandiyya in India. For voweling of Amkanagī, see

tual personality attracted large numbers of influential disciples who spread out over India, Turkey, Iran, and Arabia. As one of the largest landowners in Transoxiana and the de facto ruler of much of the eastern Timurid kingdom, Aḥrār continued the precedent for Naqshbandīs to cultivate close relationships with ruling dynasties.[16] The Naqshbandī political agenda, among their other goals, was to influence political leaders to establish and enforce Islamic practices. Aḥrār set the precedent for Naqshbandī relationships with temporal rulers: "[The ruler] should be like a royal falcon (*shāhīn*) so that whatever [his instructor] makes him pounce upon, whether his strength is equal [to the task] or not, [the ruler] will hold it fast, and he will not care what will happen and what will not happen."[17]

Aḥrār attempted to rid Transoxiana of Turko-Mongol customs and laws contrary to Islamic practice while protecting the Muslim community.[18] Political means were critical in this enterprise. "We have been charged with another task: that we should preserve Muslims from the wickedness of oppressors. Because of this it is necessary to associate with emperors and to bring [them] under control and by means of this work to fulfill the purpose of the Muslims."[19]

Ẓahīruddīn Muḥammad Bābur (d. 937/1530) continued these close ties with the Naqshbandīs.[20] Khwāja Aḥrār's descendants

---

Fritz Meier's discussion in *Zwei Abhandlungen*, p. 38, n. 7. In addition to Bāqībillāh we know about two other of his disciples, Khwāja Aḥmad (also known as Khwāja 'Amal), who died in 1020/1611–12 in Gujarat and 'Abdulazīz, who died in 1041/1631–32 in Burhanpur, neither of whose lineages became widely established in India. See Kishmī, *Nasamat al-quds*, pp. 288–92. Studies on Aḥrār include Jürgen Paul, *Die politische und sociale Bedeutung der Naqšbandiyya in Mittelasien in 15. Jahrhundert;* Jo-Ann Gross, "Khoja Aḥrār: A Study of the Perceptions of Religious Power and Prestige in the Late Timurid period"; and Muḥammad Taqī Anwar 'Alawī Kākūrī, *Ḥaḍrat Sulṭān al-awliyā' Khwāja 'Ubaydullāh Aḥrār Naqshbandī.*

16See Hamid Algar, "A Brief History of the Naqshbandī Order," in *Naqshbandis: Historical Development and Present Situation of a Muslim Mystical Order*, pp. 13–15. In addition, Bahā'uddīn Naqshband continued the tradition by serving Qaḍān Khān, as did Muḥammad Pārsā, who helped Tīmūr's son Shāhrukh overpower Khalīl Sulṭān, Tīmūr's grandson.

17Dughlat, "Tārīkh-i Rashīdī," British Museum Oriental 157, fol. 167r–v and mss. add. 24,090, fol. 147r, cited and translated by Joseph Fletcher, Archives, Box 20, p. 37 [additions in brackets are Fletcher's].

18Hamid Algar, "Political Aspects of Naqshbandī History," p. 126.

19Quoted from Kāshifī's *Rashaḥāt*, cited and translated by Fletcher, Archives, box 20, pp. 37–38.

20Bābur's father, his paternal uncle Sulṭān Aḥmad Mīrzā, as well as Bābur himself respected Khwāja Aḥrār but were not formally Aḥrār's disciples. Naqshbandī sources sometimes exaggerate Timurid connections to the Naqshbandiyya, e.g., Khurshīd Ḥasan Bukhārī, "Mughal siyāsat par awliyā'-i naqshband kā athar,"

were already established in Kabul when Bābur captured the city in 909–910/1504.[21] As he moved on to conquer portions of northern India in 932–933/1526, the Naqshbandīs continued to find a receptive climate to spread their teaching. Aḥrār's third son, Muḥammad Amīn, accompanied Bābur when he conquered Kabul and India.[22] In battle against the forces of the Lōdhī King Sulṭān Ibrāhīm in Delhi, Bābur is said to have "[first] visualized Aḥrār and [soon after] a man came dressed in white on a white horse who fought fiercely. After the Gurgānīs [Bābur's forces] won the battle, this man was later identified as Khwājagī Aḥmad [Aḥmad Kāsānī] and was rewarded by Mīr Qāḍī."[23]

When Bābur's cousin Ḥaydar Mīrzā Muḥammad described the unrespectful treatment accorded to Aḥmad Kāsānī by the Mughal emperor Humāyūn (r. 937/1530–947/1539; 962/1555–963/1556) and his entourage, he noted, "Khwāja Nūrā . . . had an hereditary claim to their veneration."[24] Just as his grandfather Aḥrār had foreseen Bābur's son, Mīrzā Kāmrān, would take the

p. 138. In his memoirs, Bābur recounts a dream in which Aḥrār predicted his successful victory taking Samarqand. See Bābur, *Bābur nāma*, 2 volumes, translated by Annette S. Beveridge, *The Memoirs of Babur*, p. 132. A more recent translation is by Wheeler Thackson Jr., *The Baburnama: Memoirs of Babur, Prince and Emperor*. In addition, Bābur relates having especially honored a visiting grandson of Aḥrār, Khwāja ʿAbdushshahīd (d. 983/1575); see Beveridge, *The Memoirs of Babur*, p. 631. Khwāja ʿAbdushshahīd later spent fifteen years in India (966/1558–59 to 982/1574–75) where he reportedly had a following of twelve thousand people before returning to Samarqand in 983/1575; see Kishmī, *Nasamāt*, pp. 168–69.

[21]Stephen Dale describes Aḥrār's extensive pious endowments (sing. *waqf*) probably obtained in cooperation with Bābur's uncle Ulugh Bēg Kābulī. One endowment was a madrasa, Qur'ān school *(maktab)*, and a mosque, all of which provided a base for education and patronage that could have been one of Bāqībillāh's (d. 1012/1603) institutional affiliations when he was in Kabul before migrating to Delhi in 1007–08/1599. Dale, revising earlier studies by S. Athar Abbas Rizvi, *Muslim Revival Movements in the 16th and 17th Centuries*, pp. 179–83, has shown the close interrelationship of the Naqshbandiyya and Mughal dynasty in India, particularly in marriage ties between the Aḥrārīs and the Mughals ruling India. See Stephen Dale, "The Legacy of the Timurids." I am particularly grateful for Stephen Dale making this unpublished manuscript available and giving me permission to cite it. See also Bukhārī, "Mughal siyāsat," pp. 140–41.

[22]Kishmī, *Nasamāt*, pp. 153–54.

[23]It was a common practice of the time to have holy men accompany armies as "spiritual artillery" to assist in gaining victory. Bābā Palangposh (d. 1110–11/1699), originally from Ghujduwan, was a Naqshbandī military pir who accompanied Ghāzī'uddīn Khān, a Timurid general fighting India. See Simon Digby, "The Naqshbandīs in the Deccan in the Late Seventeenth and Early Eighteenth Century A.D.: Bābā Palangposh, Bābā Musāfir and Their Adherents."

[24]Mīrzā Muḥammad Haydar, *A History of the Mughals in Central Asia Being the Tarikh-i Rashidi of Mirza Muḥammad Haidar Dughlát*, p. 399.

city of Qandahar.[25] Conversely, after being treated brusquely by Humāyūn, who was a devotee of Shaykh Bahlūl, the elder brother of Shaṭṭārī Muḥammad Ghawth Gwaliorī (d. 970/1562), Aḥmad Kāsānī is said to have predicted Humāyūn's defeat by Shēr Shāh. Sufi anecdotes such as these perpetuated the belief that there was a causal relationship between Naqshbandī-Aḥrārī spiritual intercession and Mughal military success. A shaykh's authority was thought to be based on his ability to affect mundane affairs through intercession with the Divine in addition to genealogical factors.

The Naqshbandī-Timurid partnership had many dimensions. There were master-disciple ties; for example, Muʿīnuddīn ʿAbdulḥaqq (d. 956/1549–50 or 962/1554–55), the brother of Aḥmad Kāsānī, acted as Mīrzā Kāmrān's spiritual mentor.[26] Bairam Khān, the Emperor Akbar's tutor, was the disciple of Iranian Naqshbandī Maulānā Zaynuddīn Kamankar.[27] Other Naqshbandīs, particularly descendants of Aḥrār such as his great-grandsons Khwāja ʿAbdulkāfī and Khwāja Qāsim, held governmental posts during Humāyūn's reign. Sulṭān Khwāja Naqshbandī, a disciple of Khwāja ʿAbdushshahīd, was appointed the *ṣadr* in charge of religious endowments and land grants from 985–86/1578 to 992/1584 by Akbar.[28] Muḥammad Yaḥyā (d. 999/1590–1591 in Agra), the principal successor to his father, Abū Fayḍ, a grandson of Aḥrār, was appointed *mīr-i ḥajj* for the year 986/1578, also by Akbar; the previous *ḥajj* had been led by a lineal descendant of Aḥrār, Sulṭān Khwāja.[29] Timurid/Mughal respect and veneration of Naqshbandīs reflected a more widespread public recognition of Naqshbandīs. It was a reciprocal relationship; the Timurids and the Mughals acquired religious legitimacy and access to divine power from the Naqshbandīs, and the Naqshbandīs secured patronage and an elevated sociopolitical status in their association with the rulers.

Aḥrārīs also intermarried within the top echelons of Timurid

---

[25]Kishmī, *Nasamāt*, p. 161. Both of these forecasts were interpreted as divine assistance mediated by the Naqshbandīs.

[26]Ibid., p. 163. ʿAbdulḥaqq parted ways with Humāyūn due to some unspecified animosity between them.

[27]Dale, "Legacy of the Timurids."

[28]Ibid.

[29]ʿAbdulqādir Badāʾūnī *Muntakhab al-tawārīkh*, pp. 246, 275. According to Badāʾūnī, Sulṭān Khwāja was the son of Khwāja Khāwand Maḥmūd. See ibid., p. 246. Others say he was a disciple of Khwāja Dōst whose shaykh was a disciple of Khwāja ʿAbdushshahīd. See Abū Faḍl ʿAllāmī, *Akbar nāma: History of the Reign of Akbar Including an Account of His Predecessors*, 3 vols., 3:192, 271.

ruling families. Bābur's daughter was married to Nūruddīn Muḥammad Naqshbandī; a daughter of this marriage married Akbar's tutor, Bairam Khān, and later became one of Akbar's wives after her first husband's death. Humāyūn's daughter was given in marriage to Khwāja Ḥasan Naqshbandī by Akbar's half-brother, Mīrzā Muḥammad Ḥakīm (d. 993/1585), the governor of Kabul.[30] The intermarriage of Mughal families with Aḥrārīs, combined with a hereditary discipleship and government patronage of the Aḥrārīs, made northern India fertile ground for the spread of Naqshbandiyya.

Stephen Dale notes that Naqshbandī-Timurid associations continued to exist between Naqshbandīs and both Turko-Mongol and Afghan nobles in South Asia until the nineteenth century.[31] These liaisons were most numerous when Naqshbandīs emigrating from Afghanistan or Central Asia to northern India were most likely to receive some kind of Mughal patronage. In later times the descendants of Sirhindī had strong ties with Afghani notables, which in the eighteenth century facilitated their migration to Afghanistan after the Sikhs razed Sirhind in 1177/1764, the home and base of Sirhindī and his descendants.[32] Later yet, Naqshbandī Shāh Abū'l-Khayr (d. 1341/1924) of Delhi had many important links with top-ranking figures in the Afghani government in the twentieth century, including the king, Amānullāh Khān.[33]

Not all Naqshbandīs in early Mughal India were Aḥrār's lineal descendants, nor did every Naqshbandī have a government affiliation. Non-Aḥrārī Naqshbandīs, like other Muslims emigrating from Transoxiana, sometimes settled in one of the major centers—Balkh, Kabul, Lahore, Agra, or Surat—on the pilgrimage route to the Hijaz. Often they would stay in the port of Surat

[30]Dale, "Legacy of the Timurids."

[31]Ibid.

[32]Sirhindī's name is derived from his birthplace, Sirhind. The ties between Sirhindī's descendants and Afghani affairs is an intriguing subject that requires further research. See ʿAzīzuddīn Wakīl Fūfalzā'ī, *Tīmūr Shāh Durrānī,* 2 vols., 2:677–88.

[33]Abū'l-Ḥasan Zayd Fārūqī, *Maqāmāt-i khayr* p. 344. The powerful Ḥaḍrats, descendants of Aḥmad Sirhindī living in Afghanistan who had a large Pashtun following among the Sulaymān Khēl, forced Amānullāh Khān to leave Afghanistan in 1929. See Joseph Fletcher's unpublished manuscript, "The Naqshbandiyya in Afghanistan," Archives, box 5, pp. 2–3. Members of the Mujaddidī family, e.g., Ṣibghatullāh Mujaddidī, are still prominent in the contemporary (early 1990s) Afghani political scene. For further examples of Afghan-Naqshbandī affinities, see Juan Cole, *Roots of North Indian Shīʿīsm in Iran and Iraq: Religion and State in Awadh, 1722–1859*, pp. 230–39.

when the pilgrimage was over. For example, Jamāluddīn b. Badshāh Pardah Pūsh Khwarzmī (d. 1015–16/1606–7), commonly known as Khwāja Dānā in later hagiographies, became the disciple of Khwāja Muḥammad Islām Juybārī (d. 971/1563–64 in Bukhara) in Balkh and then went to Thatta and Agra before settling down in Surat.[34]

Bāqībillāh (d. 1012/1603) is the other key figure (along with Khwāja Aḥrār) in the second stage of Naqshbandī history,[35] the most significant Naqshbandī in sixteenth-century India.[36] He was probably exposed to the Naqshbandiyya from an early age: his grandfather received spiritual guidance from Khwāja Muḥammad Zakariyā, one of Aḥrār's grandsons, and the two families had begun to intermarry.[37] It is likely that Bāqībillāh associated with Naqshbandīs in Kabul such as Khwāja 'Ubayd Kābulī before setting out for India in quest of the perfect pir. After spending

[34]Shāh Ẓuhūr al-Ḥasan Shārib, *Tārīkh-i ṣūfīyā-i Gujarāt*, pp. 97–113. His sobriquet is also Khwāja Dīvāna; see 'Abdulḥayy b. Fakhruddīn al-Ḥasanī, *Nuzhat al-khawāṭir wa-bahjat al-masāmi' wa'l-nawāẓir*, 9 volumes, 5:115. The shift in sobriquet reflects a preference of sobriety over intoxication in sufi identity (*dānā* = wise and *dīvāna* = ecstatic). His son, Abū'l-Ḥasan b. al-Jamāl (d. 1054/1644–45) and Abū'l-Ḥasan's son Muḥammad (d. 1078/1667–68) continued his teaching in Surat. See ibid., 5:15, 337.

[35]For more information on Bāqībillāh, see Muḥammad Hāshim Kishmī, *Zubdat al-maqāmāt*, and Muḥammad Ṣādiq Dihlawī Kashmīrī Hamadānī, *Kalimāt al-ṣādiqīn*, pp. 161–96. Muḥammad Ṣādiq, in his *Ṭabaqāt-i Shāhjahānī*, states that he introduced Aḥmad Sirhindī to Bāqībillāh (personal communication from Professor Iqbāl Mujaddidī, Lahore, January 1995). All of Bāqībillāh's writing has been collected in Bāqībillāh, *Kulliyāt-i Bāqībillāh*. In one of the few biographical compendiums detailing Muslim religious personages of the seventeenth century, *Nuzhat al-khawāṭir*, 32 are prominent Naqshbandīs from Bāqībillāh's lineage, 26 are Naqshbandī-Mujaddidīs, and 5 are with Central Asian shaykhs; see 'Abdulḥayy, *Nuzhat al-khawāṭir*, vol. 3.

[36]A common misperception among historians of Indian sufism has been that Bāqībillāh was the first Naqshbandī in India, e.g., Abdul Haqq Ansari, *Sufism and Shari'ah: A Study of Shaykh Aḥmad Sirhindi's Efforts to Reform Sufism*, p. 13. Bāqībillāh was not the first spiritual descendant of Aḥrār outside of Aḥrār's bloodline to arrive in India (contrary to Algar, cf. Algar, "A Brief History," p. 19). Non-Aḥrārī Naqshbandī, i.e., those not of Aḥrārī lineal descent, had been arriving and initiating disciples long before Bāqībillāh arrived in India. The biographical sources mention many spiritual descendants of Muḥammad Qāḍī, one of Aḥrār's important successors, who came to India spreading the Naqshbandiyya, e.g., Maulānā Tarsūn Qāḍī (d. 1013/1604–05 in Mecca) with disciples in Lahore and Fatehpur; Ḥamīduddīn Harawī, son of Muḥammad Qādi, who died in Surat; and Khāwand Maḥmūd (d. 1052/1642 in Lahore), who came to India the same year as Bāqībillāh. See Kishmī, *Nasamāt*, pp. 226, 265–66, 242. For more specific information on Khāwand Maḥmūd, see David Damrel, "Forgotten Grace: Khwāja Khāwand Mahmūd Naqshbandī in Central Asia and Mughal India."

[37]Kishmī, *Nasamāt*, pp. 153–54.

time with Bābā Walī (d. 1011/1602–3), a Kubrawī shaykh residing in Kashmir, he went to Samarqand to reach intimacy with God (*wilāya*) under the tutelage of Muḥammad Khwājagī Amkanagī (d. 1008/1600 in Bukhara). After Amkanagī's death, Bāqībillāh stayed about a year in Lahore and later set up his sufi lodge near Delhi in the Firuzi fort supported by one of Akbar's viziers, Shaykh Farīd Bukhārī.[38]

By the time Bāqībillāh arrived in Delhi, however, Akbar, the Mughal emperor, had become attached to Chishtī holy men and had visited Muʿīnuddīn Chishtī's (d. 633/1236) tomb many times. He had performed his first pilgrimage on foot to the mausoleum in 971–72/1564; therefore, like his father, Humāyūn, Akbar gave no special patronage to the Naqshbandiyya. Instead he visited another Chishtī, Salīm Chishtī (d. 978–79/1571), whose holy intercession and prayer Akbar believed had expedited the birth of his first surviving son. Akbar's Chishtī affiliation especially aggravated the Naqshbandīs, because not only were they politically marginalized, but the Chishtīs at court engaged in practices such as sufi music concerts (*samāʿ*) that the Naqshbandīs considered forbidden by Islamic law.

Observing the precedent set by Khwāja Aḥrār, the Naqshbandī-Mughal partnership in India bolstered the Islamic identity of the Mughal regime while facilitating the spread of Naqshbandī teachings among the Indian Muslim community. The Naqshbandī-Mughal alliance had established the precedent of social and religious ties between Naqshbandīs and Afghans and the potential political role of the Naqshbandī pir as a shaykh-intimate to the ruler. Not only did Naqshbandī shaykhs advise and mediate Mughal administrative affairs, but they were also expected to focus divine favor to the ruler's advantage. This Central Asian legacy had a lasting impression on Indian Islam.

Ahmad Sirhindī: The Advent of the Mujaddidiyya

Shaykh Aḥmad Sirhindī (971/1564–1034/1624) initiated the third stage of Naqshbandī history, when the Naqshbandiyya became an Indian lineage. Known as "the renewer of the second millennium" (*mujaddid-i alf-i thānī*), he was the most famous of Bāqībillāh's disciples and exhibited his extraordinary spiritual aptitude by becoming a successor to Bāqībillāh in less than three

[38]Māndawī, *Gulzār-i abrār*, Urdu trans., p. 477. He is also known as Mīr Murtaḍā Khān.

A calendar depicting the tomb of Aḥmad Sirhindī at Sirhind produced by the current successor of Shēr Muḥammad Sharaqpūrī, Miyān Jamīl

months. More than any other Indian Naqshbandī after Bahā'-uddīn, both redefined the role of sufi practice in society and elaborated Naqshbandī mystical exercises. The renaming of the path to Mujaddidiyya reflects the significance of Sirhindī's influence; he is regarded as a co-founder by the later Naqshbandiyya.[39]

With the goal of implementing a universal set of Islamic symbols, Islamic law, and the Prophetic model, Sirhindī's enterprise ran counter to Akbar, who regarded himself as having unified diverse religious groups through his person, legitimized by precedents in Central Asia and India. To unify the Indian Muslim community, Sirhindī defined its boundaries according to the Sunnī dogma (*'aqā'id*) to counteract the universalizing of all religious communities through Mughal political structures. Many members of Akbar's court were among Sirhindī's large circle of disciples. After Akbar's death, Muslim self-identity in the subcontinent became progressively more clearly defined, in part due to Mujaddidī political influence and alliances, even though the patronage of non-Muslim religious institutions was continued under Aurangzīb (d. 1118/1707) and later rulers. Shortly before his death, Sirhindī was imprisoned for a year by Akbar's successor, Jahāngīr, for his controversial claim to have reached a higher spiritual rank than Abū Bakr, the first caliph.[40] Indian Naqshbandīs continued to advise rulers until the breakup of the Indian Mughal empire.

In 1032–33/1623 Sirhindī declared his middle son, Muḥammad Ma'ṣūm (d. 1079/1668), to be his principal successor and the next *qayyūm* (or *quṭb al-aqṭab*), the living person considered to have the highest spiritual rank of all sufis on earth. Through the mediation of the *qayyūm* God grants existence to all people; thus, the *qayyūm*

---

[39]David Damrel suggests that Sirhindī's enterprise was more a result of Chishtī-Ṣābirī influences through his father than Central Asian Naqshbandi influences. See " 'The Naqshbandî Reaction' Reconsidered."

[40]Naqshbandīs claim that Sirhindī was imprisoned because of the Shī'ī intrigues initiated by Nūrjahān, Jahāngīr's Shī'ī wife. Supposedly this measure was precipitated by Sirhindī's failing to perform the necessary obeisance mandated by court protocol. This controversy was one of many which has involved Sirhindī from his lifetime to the present. Yohanan Friedmann, in his *Shaykh Aḥmad Sirhindī: An Outline of His Thought and a Study of His Image in the Eyes of Posterity,* discusses Sirhindī's image, the perceptions of his contemporaries, and how critics and supporters up to the present have interpreted him. From a pro-Sirhindī perspective, Muḥammad Iqbāl Mujaddidī in his *Aḥwāl wa-āthār-i 'Abdullāh Khūshagī Quṣūrī* analyzes critically many of the seventeenth-century sources used by Friedmann in addition to adding data from sources not available to Friedmann. The most complete scholarly treatments of Sirhindī are Zawwār Ḥusayn, *Haḍrat mujaddid-i alf-i thānī,* and Muḥammad Mas'ūd Aḥmad, *Sīrat-i mujaddid-i alf-i thānī.*

supports creation.[41] Like his father,[42] Muḥammad Maʿṣūm wrote letters to the royal family encouraging them to promote and implement Islamic policies throughout India.[43] It is said that Aurangzīb, Dārā Shikūh's younger brother, visited Muḥammad Maʿṣūm in Sirhind after Shāh Jahān's death in 1076/1666 and became his formal disciple there.[44] Further evidence in the collected letters of Muḥammad Maʿṣūm and his son, Ḥujjatullāh Naqshband (d. 1114/1702), suggest that Aurangzīb was even himself a practicing Naqshbandī at one time.[45]

When Shāh Jahān died and war for succession between Aurangzīb and Dārā Shikūh broke out, Aurangzīb is said to have looked to the Naqshbandīs for support. The sufis were the specialists to mediate and focus divine grace and energy on the ruler's behalf. Muḥammad Maʿṣūm ordered his nephew Shaykh Saʿduddīn, the son of Muḥammad Saʿīd, and his own son Muḥammad Ashraf, both of whom were preparing to go on pilgrimage, to go immediately to Aurangzīb; the latter supposedly had

[41]See J. G. J. ter Haar, *Follower and Heir of the Prophet: Shaykh Aḥmad Sirhindī (1564–1624) as Mystic*, pp. 153–55. After Muḥammad Maʿṣūm, the next two *qayyūms* were Ḥujjatullāh Naqshband (d. 1114/1702) and Muḥammad Zubayr (d. 1152/1740), both lineal descendants of Muḥammad Maʿṣūm.

[42]Sirhindī wrote many letters to persons holding governmental posts during the reigns of Akbar and Jahāngīr. For an analysis of these letters, most of which were written requesting help on behalf of a third person, see Haar, *Follower and Heir*, pp. 16–17.

[43]Five letters to Aurangzīb are collected in Muḥammad Maʿṣūm, *Maktūbāt-i maʿṣūmiyya*, 3 volumes. Letter 64 in volume 1 (henceforth written 1.64) was written before Aurangzīb became emperor, and 2.5, 3.6, 3.122, 3.221, 3.227 were all written before Aurangzīb became emperor. A discussion of letters written by Aḥmad Sirhindī's descendants to Aurangzīb, his family members, and members of the Mughal Court are collected in S. Athar Abbas Rizvi, *A History of Sufism in India*, 2 volumes, 2:482–91. Because Shāhjahān and Crown Prince Dārā Shikūh (d. 1069–70/1659) were devotees of Mullā Shāh, a Qādirī shaykh in Srinagar, Muḥammad Maʿṣūm had no reason to write any letters to them.

[44]Sayfuddīn, *Maktūbāt-i sayfiyya*, letter 83, pp. 123–24, cited in Muḥammad Maʿṣūm, *Ḥasanāt al-ḥaramayn*, p. 112. Aurangzīb was in Muḥammad Maʿṣūm's presence three times according to Muḥammad Maʿṣūm's grandson and successor, Sayfuddīn. See Sayfuddīn, *Maktūbāt*, letter 84, p. 123, cited in Muḥammad Maʿṣūm, *Ḥasanāt*, p. 112. Aurangzīb's Naqshbandī connection should not be exaggerated; he visited Burhānuddīn Shaṭṭārī Burhānpūrī a few times for spiritual blessing. His request to be buried near Zaynuddīn Shīrāzī Chishtī's tomb indicates that there was no particular Naqshbandī affinity toward the latter part of his reign. Carl Ernst perceptively details the biases of sufi historiography in his *Eternal Garden: Mysticism, History, and Politics at a South Asian Sufi Center*, pp. 38–61.

[45]Muḥammad Maʿṣūm, *Maktūbāt*, letters 6, 122, 194, 220, 221, 227. Ḥujjatullāh Naqshband, *Wasīlat al-qabūl ilā Allāh wa'l-rasūl*, p. 139, cited in Khaliq Ahmad Nizami, "Naqshbandi Influence on Mughal Rulers and Politics," pp. 49–50.

orders to stay by Aurangzīb's side,[46] while Muḥammad Maʿṣūm went to Mecca to mobilize the spiritual support of the ulama and sufis in the holy city and pray for Aurangzīb's victory. His eldest son, Sibghatullāh, was dispatched to Baghdad to appeal to ʿAbdulqādir al-Jīlānī, the founder-figure of the Qādiriyya, to abandon support for Dārā Shikūh, since the Naqshbandīs no longer considered him worthy of being in the Qādiriyya because he had stopped writing *ḥanafī* and *qādirī* after his name.[47] The loss of ʿAbdulqādir's spiritual assistance would have isolated Dārā from the flow of divine energy (*fayḍ*) and rendered him powerless. Whether or not the Naqshbandīs actually performed this barrage of prayer and spiritual lobbying is not the point. They shared the popular assumption that Shāh Jahān's succession would be decided in the heavenly sphere and that the sufis had the most power to influence this decision and effect changes in this world. The Mujaddidīs wanted to be the sufi lineage that wielded both supernatural and worldly power just as their spiritual ancestors had done in Central Asia.

With the victory of Aurangzīb, Mughal support of a universalist idea that all religions had equal validity came to an end as the Indo-Muslim community opted for stricter definitions of Muslim identity. Sirhindī's descendants and disciples still found employment in the Mughal administration as long as it lasted,[48] but it is debatable how much influence the Naqshbandīs actually had over Aurangzīb's subsequent policies. Naqshbandīs believed they could encourage the Islam of those following the Prophetic model and the mainstream Sunnī community (*ahl al-sunna wa'l-jamāʿa*) by influencing the leaders of the community in the manner of Aḥrār and his descendants. At the same time these shaykhs and their senior successors had thousands of disciples who were being taught to adhere assiduously to Islamic law and the Pro-

---

[46]Iḥsān Sirhindī, *Rawḍat al-qayyūmiyya*, 2:91, cited in Muḥammad Maʿṣūm, *Ḥasanāt*, p. 126. Muḥammad Ashraf, by performing supplications (sing. *duʿā*) for divine intervention on the battlefield, was supposed to help Aurangzīb emerge victorious. Dārā Shikūh took tantrics and Hindu holy men in addition to sufis on his Qandahar campaign in 1063/1653 (he lost the battle). See S. A. A. Rizvi, *A History of Sufism in India*, 2:414.

[47]Muḥammad Maʿṣūm, *Ḥasanāt*, pp. 126–27. Professor Mujaddidī lists the numerous contemporary sources (without page references) that mention this all-important intervention by Ṣibghatullāh. If this actually occurred, the Naqshbandīs probably assumed that he had renounced both ritually acting in accordance with Ḥanafī jurisprudence, a marker of Indian Sunnī identity, and his spiritual connection with ʿAbdulqādir al-Jīlānī.

[48]See Muḥammad Maʿṣūm, *Ḥasanāt*, pp. 126–59, for an analysis of the *maktūbāt* literature between Aurangzīb and the Naqshbandīs of the time.

phetic model as they progressed along the sufi path. Political expedience, on the other hand, dictated a legitimate government supported by religious notables. The Mughals expected all religious shrines receiving land grants to pray "for the prosperity of the government."[49]

From these government landgrants the worldly fortunes of many sufis were enhanced. Even Mughal emperors like Humāyūn and Shāh Jahān, who did not utilize the services and protection of the Naqshbandīs, supported their own sufis through land grants in their all-important tasks of intercession; political considerations reigned supreme in all Mughal-sufi relationships. Jahāngīr took action against Aḥmad Sirhindī because he needed to minimize discord in his realm. Similarly, Shāh Jahān immediately banished Sayyid Ādam Banūrī (d. 1053/1644), an influential successor of Aḥmad Sirhindī, to the Hijaz in 1052/1642–43 when the emperor's messengers in Lahore reported to him that ten thousand threatening Afghans had joined his entourage.[50] Aurangzīb's proscription of Sirhindī's collected letters is not inconsistent with his previous association with the Naqshbandīs. Political issues required political responses, and spiritual issues spiritual responses. The sufis were useful to the Mughals but were not considered invincible; when the boundaries of political acceptability were transgressed, they were still the emperor's subjects.

After Aurangzīb: Shāh Walīullāh and Mīr Dard

In the eighteenth century a new era in Indo-Muslim history began; the Mughal empire disintegrated after Aurangzīb's death in 1118/1707, and the spiritual descendants of Aḥmad Sirhindī became the most prominent Naqshbandīs, overshadowing other

---

[49]A statement noted in a late-Mughal land grant to the shrine of Bahawal Haq at Multan and part of a translated abstract of a copy of a Chaknama dated 25th Rabī II, 1141 A.H. (Board of Revenue, file 131/1575), cited in David Gilmartin, *Empire and Islam,* p. 45. Counter to "praying for prosperity" an alternative is a shaykh praying for ruin. In modern Pakistani politics, legal proceedings were brought against the pir of Manki Sharif after he had "tried to restrain the Members of the Electoral College from the free exercise of their right to vote by invoking divine wrath against those who do not support President Ayub." See *Pakistan Times,* 21 December 1964, cited in Adrian C. Mayer, "Pir and Murshid: An Aspect of Religious Leadership in West Pakistan," p. 166. Later, presidential election rules were revised to include a clause prohibiting the threatening of electors with divine displeasure. See *Pakistan Times,* 12 January 1965, cited in ibid., p. 169, n. 15.

[50]Although not explicitly stated, many of these Afghans were probably armed. Ghulām Sarvar Lāhūrī, *Khazīnat al-aṣfiyā',* 2 volumes, 1:630–31.

lineages. Shāh Walīullāh Dihlawī (d. 1176/1762), the most famous Indian Muslim of the period, continued the reform tradition of Aḥmad Sirhindī and became known internationally for his erudite scholarship in Qur'ān exegesis (*tafsīr*), hadith, jurisprudence (*fiqh*), and sufism (*taṣawwuf*). His best-known work, *Ḥujjat Allāh al-bāligha*,[51] was used for a long time in the course of study at Al-Azhar University in Cairo.[52] Through his original syntheses of Islamic religious subjects, Shāh Walīullāh demonstrated his genius, whether by formulating unprecedented legal decisions on the basis of original hadith scholarship or by showing that the so-called *shuhūdī* (subjective witnessing the oneness of God and Creation) and *wujūdī* (the objective declaration that God and Creation were identical) positions had complementary functions in sufism. His own talents harmonized the best of sufi experience and scholarly attainment, making Shāh Walīullāh an ideal religious leader. In striving to eliminate practices of Indian Muslims that did not conform to the Prophetic sunna, he not only followed the reform tradition of Aḥmad Sirhindī but provided an example for nineteenth-and twentieth-century sufis later on.

Shāh Walīullāh's Naqshbandī contemporary, Mīr Dard (d. 1199/1785), also lived in Delhi. Mīr Dard's father, Muḥammad Nāṣir ʿAndalīb (d. 1172/1759), successor of Shāh Gulshan (d. 1170/1757), was the first Indian to call his sufi path the "Muḥammadan path" (*ṭarīqa Muḥammadiyya*), a designation first used in a sufi context by Moroccan Abū ʿAbdullāh Muḥammad Jazūlī (d. 869/1465) and subsequently by various sufi lineages, including the nineteenth-century North African Idrīsiyya and Sanūsiyya sufis and the Indian Sayyid Aḥmad Shahīd Barēlwī (d. 1246/1831) of Rai Bareilly. When Mīr Dard asked his father how to name this new path, he replied: "If my intention had been so, I would have named the *ṭarīqa* after my own name, as the others do. But all of us are children, lost in the sea of identity and drowned in one ocean. Our name is the name of Muhammad, and our sign is the sign of Muhammad. Our love is the love of Muhammad and our claim is the claim of Muhammad. One must call this order the *ṭarīqa Muḥammadiyya*, the Muhammadan path. It is exactly the path of Muhammad, and we have not added anything to it. Our conduct is the conduct of the Prophet, and our way the Muhammadan way."[53]

---

[51]This has been recently translated by Marcia Hermansen as *The Conclusive Argument from God: Shah Waliullah of Delhi's Hujjat Allah al-Baligha.*

[52]For further information see J. M. S. Baljon, *Religion and Thought of Shāh Walī Allāh Dihlawī, 1703–1762.*

[53]Annemarie Schimmel, *Pain and Grace: A Study of Two Mystical Writers of Eighteenth-Century Muslim India*, p. 42.

Both Mīr Dard and Shāh Walīullāh identified two ways to God: the higher path of prophethood (*ṭarīq-i nubūwat*) and the lower path of intimates of God (*ṭarīq-i wilāyat*). Like Shāh Walīullāh, Mīr Dard's emphasis on the Prophet influenced concepts of Muslim identity in nineteenth-century India.

Shāh Walīullāh brought together all the eight major sublineages of the Indian Naqshbandiyya,[54] though of them he preferred the Naqshbandiyya-Mujaddidiyya, describing it as "the most illustrious and pure and the least heretical *ṭarīqa*."[55] The reformist sufi path was to live according to a strict interpretation of Islamic law and model one's actions after those of the Prophet. Other Naqshbandī sublineages, such as those following Abū'l-ʿUlā's and Bāqībillāh's teachings, listened to *samāʿ* to produce spiritual ecstasy, an activity not considered permissible by shariʿa-minded Naqshbandī-Mujaddidīs. Abū'l-ʿUlā's sublineage combined Chishtī practices of singing and *samāʿ* with Aḥrārī *dhikr*, but it never became widespread in South Asia.[56] Even be-

[54]He was first initiated into the Naqshbandiyya by his father, Shaykh ʿAbdurraḥīm (d. 1131–32/1719), who had received instruction from four different Naqshbandī shaykhs: (1) Sayyid ʿAbdullāh Akbarābādī, a spiritual great-grandson of Aḥmad Sirhindī through Ādam Banūrī (d. 1053/1644); (2) Amīr Abū Qāsim Akbarābādī, the spiritual grandson of Abū'l-ʿUlā Akbarābādī (d. 1061/1651), a lineal descendant of ʿUbaydullāh Aḥrār; (3) Khwāja Khurd, the son of Bāqībillāh; and (4) Amīr Nūrulʿulā (d. 1081/1671), the son of Abū'l-ʿUlā Akbarābādī. See Shāh Walīullāh, *Intibāh fī salāsil awliyā' Allāh*, p. 31. In *Anfās al-ʿārifīn* Shāh Walīullāh describes his father and his other teachers. For more information on the non-Mujaddidī lineage of an Indian Aḥrārī, Abū'l-ʿUlā, see Abū'l-ʿUlā'ī Aḥrārī, *Iṣrār-i Abū'l-ʿUlā*, pp. 5–8. This non-Mujaddidī lineage still has functioning sufi lodges in Gaya, Bihar, and Agra. At least through the nineteenth century, descendants of Khwāja Aḥrār were *sajjādanishīns* at the sufi lodge in Agra (contrary to Algar's assertion that the descendants of Aḥrār in India "died out in the seventeenth century"—"A Brief History," p. 19). Initiation from his father involved no Naqshbandī-Mujaddidī spiritual practices; Shāh Walīullāh mentions that he learned these practices from Mullā Dalīl Kakyānī, a spiritual grandson of Muḥammad Maʿṣūm. The scholar/mystic Abū Ṭāhir Muḥammad (d. 1145–46/1733) initiated Shāh Walīullāh into the Naqshbandiyya, Shādhiliyya, Shaṭṭāriyya, Suhrawardiyya, and Kubrawiyya in Medina. See Baljon, *Religion and Thought*, pp. 5–6. Abū Ṭāhir had three Naqshbandī affiliations: (1) His father, Ibrāhīm al-Kūrānī, (d. 1101–2/1690), who was a non-Aḥrārī spiritual descendant in ʿAbdurraḥmān Jāmī's (d. 898/1492) lineage; (2) Aḥmad an-Nakhlī (d. 1130/1717–18 Mecca) of Aḥrārī lineage; and (3) ʿAbdullāh al-Baṣrī, the spiritual grandson of Tājuddīn Sanbhalī, a senior *khalīfa* of Bāqībillāh.

[55]Baljon, *Religion and Thought*, p. 85. Later he makes favorable, inclusive comments about other Indian sufi lineages, e.g., the Chishtiyya, Suhrawardiyya, and Qādiriyya.

[56]ʿAbdulḥayy, *Nuzhat*, 5:22; Shāh Amīr Abū'l-ʿUlā'ī Aḥrārī, *Isrār*, p. 21. Jī Ḥālī Abū'l-ʿUlā'ī (d. 1250/1834–35) had many disciples in Hyderabad, Deccan. See ʿAṭā' Ḥusayn, *Kayfiyat al-ʿārifīn*, pp. 105–06. Successors of ʿAṭā' Ḥusayn (d. 1311/

fore the early eighteenth century, Bāqībillāh's non-Mujaddidī sublineage had apparently withered away in India, subsumed by the vigorous Mujaddidīs.[57] In addition, other non-Mujaddidī Naqshbandī sublineages, represented by Khwāja Khāwand Maḥmūd (d. 1052/1642 in Lahore) and by a Central Asian sublineage of Bāhā Shāh Muḥammad Musāfir (d. 1126/1714 in Aurangabad), failed to attract disciples and perpetuate their teachings.[58] Within a century of Aḥmad Sirhindī's death, the Naqshbandiyya-Mujaddidiyya reigned supreme among the Naqshbandīs in India.

The end of Naqshbandī influence over the rulers of India came with the advent of British rule. In 1803 the British ousted the Marathas from Delhi and became the new protectors of the titular Muslim king; by 1849 the Panjab was under British control. After the Indian rebellion of 1857, the British exiled the last Mughal ruler, Bahādur Shāh, to Rangoon and singled out the Muslim community as the scapegoat for the uprising. The British closed the great mosque of Delhi for five years after the revolt; as late as 1899 Europeans still considered entering the Delhi mosque with their shoes on to be a "right of conquest."[59]

Naqshbandī activity in Delhi was disrupted. Aḥmad Saʿīd's Naqshbandī sufi lodge in Chatli Qabr, housing the graves of Mīrzā Maẓhar Jān-i jānān (assassinated in 1195/1781) and Ghulām ʿAlī Shāh (d. 1240/1824), was entrusted to a Panjabi disciple of Dōst Muḥammad (d. 1284/1868) after Aḥmad Saʿīd (d. 1277/1860) fled with his family to the Hijaz in 1858. Thirty years later, his grandson Shāh Abū'l-Khayr reorganized the sufi lodge and the Naqshbandīs renewed their religious activity in the capi-

---

1893–94 in Gaya), e.g., Mīr Ashrafʿ Alī, transmitted the teachings to Dacca, Bombay, and Hyderabad.

[57]Khwāja Khurd, Bāqībillāh's younger son, studied with Aḥmad Sirhindī: see Shāh Walīullāh, *Intibāh*, p. 31. ʿAbdulḥaqq Muḥaddith Dihlawī's son, Nūrulḥaqq Mashraqī (d. 1073/1662), instead of following Bāqībillāh's senior disciples, became a disciple of Muḥammad Maʿṣūm. See Raḥmān ʿAli, *Tadhkira-yi ʿulamā'-i Hind*, p. 246.

[58]For further information on Khāwand Maḥmūd, see David Damrel, "Forgotten Grace." For additional information on the Deccan Naqshbandī, Bābā Musāfir, see Digby, "The Naqshbandīs in the Deccan."

[59]Home political proceedings, cited in Warren Fusfeld, "The Shaping of Sufi Leadership in Delhi: The Naqshbandiyya-Mujaddidiyya, 1750–1920," p. 53. Wearing of European foot-covering was charged with symbolic meaning. Before the issuing of a 1867 Bengal Circular Order, the British had allowed Christian Indians to wear English shoes or boots while forbidding the same privileges to non-Christian Indians. Equally charged symbolic issues involved kinds of head covering. For the original documents detailing these issues, see J. S. Jha, ed., *Imperial Honeymoon with Indian Aristocracy*, pp. 425–36.

tal,[60] but Naqshbandī political influence became a memory, as the status of Muslims in India steadily declined. In eighteenth-century India, rulers generally ignored well-intentioned Naqshbandī advice. By the end of the nineteenth century, the British government had become hostile to any hint of potential Muslim political involvement, Naqshbandī or otherwise, in the cities. Thereafter the Panjab became the major center of Naqshbandī activity in India, perhaps even surpassing its influence in Ottoman Turkey.

Mujaddidī Influence: From India to the World

By the eighteenth century, Mujaddidīs lodges were located throughout the subcontinent, neighboring Afghanistan, and places in Central Asia where Bahā'uddīn and his successors had established Naqshbandī practices. Hamid Algar notes that Central Asia remained closed to external influence, both in sufi matters and in general, but the Mujaddidīyya nonetheless established itself in places like Bukhara, Tashkent, and Yarkand, thus indicating its compatibility with the original Naqshbandī impulse that remained dominant in the area.[61] This compatibility was based on the conscious and successful replication of Prophetic authority, symbolically, experientially, intellectually, and even politically in the person of the sufi shaykh.

Mujaddidī authority was comprehensive: the Mujaddidiyya influenced both politics and Islamic practices at the same time, first by urging the Mughal government to unify the Indian Muslim community by imposing universal symbols of Islamic law and following the Prophetic sunna throughout India (which also gave the Mujaddidīs special patronage privileges in the process). Second, seekers on the Mujaddidī sufi path were first briefed in correct practices and correct credal dogma that differentiated a Muslim from a non-Muslim. Only then were they taught the spiritual techniques leading them closer to God. After counseling a ruler about his own individual Islamic practices, the Mujaddidīs expected to guide the development of Islamic social institutions for the Indian Muslim community.[62]

[60] Fusfeld, "The Shaping of Sufi Leadership," pp. 243–48. In addition, Fakhruddīn Jahān Chishtī Dihlawī's (d. 1199/1785) sufi lodge was also forced to close. See Ghulām Muḥyīddīn Quṣūrī, *Malfūẓāt-i sharīf*, p. 12.

[61] Algar, "Brief History," p. 24.

[62] One should not uncritically assume, as one might from reading Naqshbandī sources, that the rulers usually listened to sufi advice. There is evidence that they did not. See Irfan M. Habib, "The Political Role of Shaikh Ahmad Sirhindi and Shah Waliullah."

Figure 3. Mujaddidī genealogy

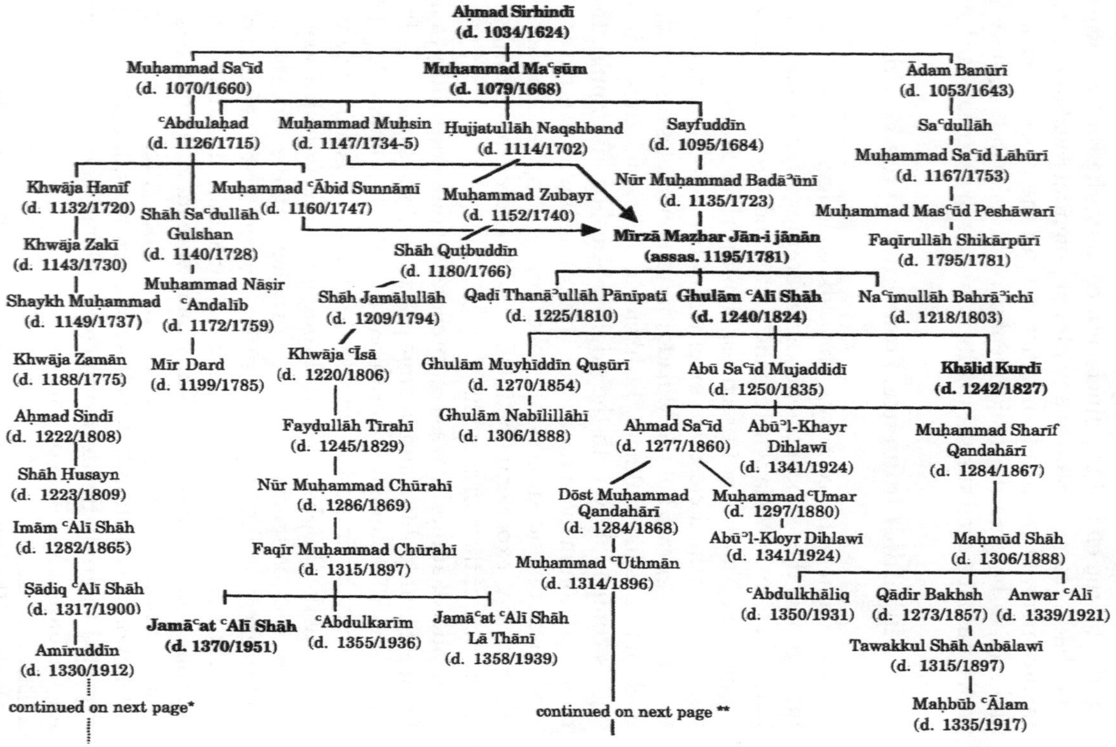

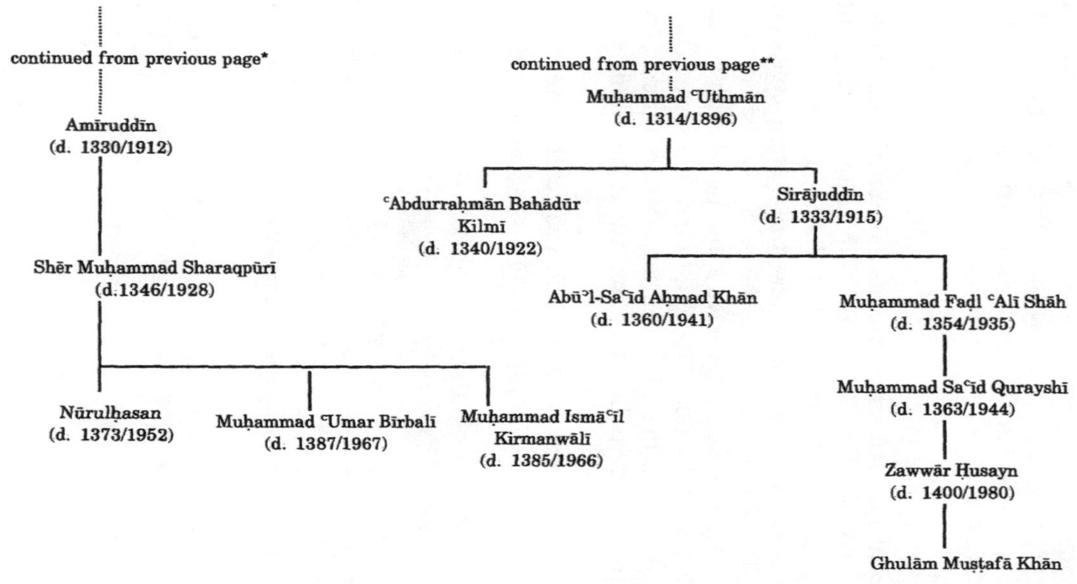
continued from previous page*
Amīruddīn
(d. 1330/1912)
Shēr Muḥammad Sharaqpūrī
(d.1346/1928)
Nūrulḥasan
(d. 1373/1952)
Muḥammad ᶜUmar Bīrbalī
(d. 1387/1967)
Muḥammad Ismāᶜīl
Kirmanwālī
(d. 1385/1966)
continued from previous page**
Muḥammad ᶜUthmān
(d. 1314/1896)
ᶜAbdurraḥmān Bahādūr
Kilmī
(d. 1340/1922)
Sirājuddīn
(d. 1333/1915)
Abūᵓl-Saᶜīd Aḥmad Khān
(d. 1360/1941)
Muḥammad Faḍl ᶜAlī Shāh
(d. 1354/1935)
Muḥammad Saᶜīd Qurayshī
(d. 1363/1944)
Zawwār Ḥusayn
(d. 1400/1980)
Ghulām Muṣṭafā Khān

The combined efforts of sufi jurists, of whom the Mujaddidīs were the most important, contributed to the political reshaping of Islam in South Asia. In a span of fifty-eight years Mujaddidī political influence, supported by favorably inclined elites such as the *manṣabdārs* and ulama, helped reverse Akbar's universal religious policy and replace it with Islamic universal symbols. Even if one assumes that the Mujaddidīs had little political influence, one cannot deny that a more formally defined and necessarily closed Muslim community became the norm in subsequent years.[63]

Naqshbandī efforts to influence the ineffectual Mughal rulers who followed Aurangzīb met with failure. Shāh Walīullāh, for example, naively trusted Aḥmad Shāh Durrānī, a rampaging Afghan, who then wantonly sacked numerous cities in northern India. The days of counseling the ruling elite had clearly passed.[64] Sayyid Aḥmad Shahīd Barēlwī, a disciple of Shāh Walīullāh's son ʿAbdulʿazīz, was killed fighting to restore Muslim rule in northern India. With the advent of British rule, Indian Naqshbandīs withdrew from political action altogether until the Pakistan movement began in the 1930s.[65]

The activities of the Mujaddidiyya consolidated the authority of ulama and sufis in the subcontinent. The Mujaddidīs insisted

[63]To what degree Sirhindī and later Mujaddidī shaykhs directly contributed to a new conception of Muslim community is hotly debated, since much scholarship reflects the twentieth-century developments of the Indo-Pakistan subcontinent. See ter Haar, *Follower and Heir*, pp. ix–x, 4, 16–19. In India the development of a more narrowly defined Muslim community coincides with the growth of the Mujaddidiyya. Until Mujaddidī emphasis on credal dogma and developments in other Indian sufi lineages, especially the Chishtiyya, are studied in more detail, one cannot necessarily assume a direct cause and effect relationship between these two processes.

[64]Shāh Faqīrullāh (d. 1195/1781) and Shāh Walīullāh were among the last Naqshbandīs in northern India to continue the Naqshbandī practice of advising rules. For additional information concerning Shāh Walīullāh's letters, see Khalīq Aḥmad Niẓāmī, ed., *Shāh Walīullāh Dihlawī kē siyāsī maktūbāt.* For letters by Faqīrullāh to Shāh Abdālī, see Faqīrullāh Shikārpūrī, *Maktūbāt-i Faqīrullāh,* letters 18, 29, 57, 66; for communications with Shāh Abdālī's chief minister, Shāh Walī Khān, letters 56, 69; for letters to Qāḍī Idrīs, a grandson of Aḥmad Sirhindī and Shāh Abdālī's chief mufti, letter 19. As far as Indian Muslims were concerned, these letters were of little avail in preventing the pillaging by Shāh Abdālī's armies.

[65]Although it is risky to retrospectively project nationalistic concerns, there is a possibility that Pakistan might very well be the twentieth-century political outcome of a religious crystallization process initiated 350 years previously. See Wilfred Cantwell Smith, "The Crystallization of Religious Communities in Mughal India," p. 178. In Pakistan the efforts directed against the Ahmadis are an example of a crystallization process still in operation.

that adherence to Islamic law be a prerequisite to mystical practice under the guidance of a shaykh and considered a religious scholar's (*ʿālim*) knowledge to be only partly valid if it did not partake of the inner light of divine grace. They emphasized the shariʿa and jurisprudence (*fiqh*) in the mystical path and that attracted many ulama to the Naqshbandiyya.[66]

Under the British, without any Islamic polity to support Islamic institutions financially and to provide an identity so necessary for the minority Indian Muslim community, Naqshbandī pirs stressed the personal nature of Muslim identity. From their rural sufi lodges, they proclaimed the essentials of correct Islamic credal dogma (*ʿaqīda*) and behavior modeled on the Prophet as prerequisites to the performance of mystical practices.[67] For thousands of Indian Muslims an intimate relationship with a spiritual mentor established and confirmed one's identity as a Muslim.[68] Religious authority and communal identity were transferred from sociopolitical symbols to the personal and approachable figure embodied in a *living*, perfect, and perfection-bestowing sufi shaykh.[69]

---

[66]That over 60 percent of the prominent ulama in nineteenth- and twentieth-century Panjab are sufis (and most of these sufis are Mujaddidīs) suggests a significant Mujaddidī contribution. This is based on a two-volume biographical dictionary of 307 Panjabi non-Barelwi ulama from 1200/1786–1400/1980, Safīr Akhtar's *Tadhkira-yi ʿulamāʾ-i Panjāb*. Another biographical compendium, a Barelwi survey of 179 ulama in the present-day boundaries of Pakistan from ca. 1297/1880–1400/1980, indicates that 77 percent had sufi affiliation. See Muḥammad ʿAbdulḥakīm Sharaf, *Tadhkira-yi akābir-i ahl-i sunnat (Pākistān)*.

[67]Credal affirmations *(ʿaqāʾid)*, often written in numbered lists, are the beliefs that Muslims are expected to accept as true. These lists vary from time to time, between Sunnī and Shīʿī, and between the various Shīʿī groups. For the early Sunnī formulations of credal dogma, see A. J. Wensinck, *The Muslim Creed: Its Genesis and Historical Development*. The goal of these affirmations is to make one's inner faith *(īmān)*, the quality of religiousness, outwardly tangible.

[68]Muslims chose other avenues to individualize Islamic identity which also allowed them to participate in the larger geographical and historical Islamic community. One alternative was to identify Islam totally on the basis of Islamic scriptural norms, i.e., the Qurʾān and hadith. Although considerably less popular in Muslim India, these scripturalist-minded groups, pejoratively termed "Wahhābīs," have had an influence on the religious life of Indian Muslims. Their definition of Sunnī orthodoxy based only on scripture and a totally transcendent God is a much narrower vision of Islam than that of sufis who value the scriptural dimensions of their religion in addition to appreciating a mediational paradigm involving the personal guidance of pirs with or without the practice of a contemplative discipline. See my "Charismatic Versus Scriptural Authority: Naqshbandī Response to Deniers of Mediational Sufism in British India."

[69]The late Fazlur Rahman noted that many contemporary Indo-Pakistani Muslims come close to equating a person without a pir *(bē pīrā)* to a "godless person";

Mujaddidī charismatic authority, like that of other sufi lineages, had gradually consolidated religious authority in the living shaykh, a tendency that had accelerated in India after the seventeenth century. Not only was the pir expected to exemplify the Prophetic sunna and to be conversant in correct Islamic practices, but in the Mujaddidī case he was expected to teach special spiritual practices to qualified aspirants. There were to be no conflicts of interest between the living spiritual guide and spirits of deceased shaykhs; the living shaykh was the supreme guide, even superior to Khiḍr. Deceased pirs were used only to buttress the institution of the living shaykh through their letters, upon which the living pir was free to comment. In the nineteenth century, the Barelwi school of ulama, stressing a mediating sufi authority and unquestioning obedience to the sufi guide, institutionally manifested this consolidation of religious authority.

Mujaddidīs were literary people who utilized the popular genre of collected sufi letters;[70] the living Mujaddidī shaykh was thought to have in his hands a coherent and authoritative body of teaching that effectively assisted an aspirant's progress on the sufi path. These letters, especially the letters of Sirhindī, discussed religious matters in detail that only an educated Muslim could comprehend. Unlike sufi discourses, which were essentially recorded oral histories, sufi letters required the commentary of a shaykh possessing a background in jurisprudence and mystical experience. Collections of sufi letters, by establishing a scriptural Naqshbandī identity, served also to concentrate greater authority in the figure of the living shaykh.

The Mujaddidīs, who guided religious sentiments since the be-

---

see his *Islam,* p. 154. In Urdu the adjective *bē pīr* (literally, without pir) means pitiless, cruel, or vicious.

[70]There were at least eleven pre-Mughal (1206–1526) Indian sufis who wrote collections of letters. The most popular collection has been Sharafuddīn Manērī's *Maktūbāt-i sadī,* recently translated by Paul Jackson as *The Hundred Letters.* As Bruce Lawrence explains in the foreword to Jackson's translation, Sharafuddīn's (d. 782/1381) letters are broadly descriptive of theoretical sufism in the same fashion as al-Hujwīrī's *Kashf Al-Maḥjūb.* The impersonal style of *The Hundred Letters* makes it suitable for use in medieval religious schools and for consultation by the Indian Mughal emperors Akbar and Aurangzīb. See Manērī, *The Hundred Letters,* pp. xii–xiii. In contrast, Sirhindī's collected letters have had an entirely different international audience, having been translated into Arabic, Turkish, and Urdu. As Bruce Lawrence notes, the personal nature of Sirhindī's letters contrasts sharply with Manērī's detached style. This dimension of Sirhindī's literary legacy has contributed to make Sirhindī a controversial figure, whether he writes about his own individual spiritual experience, his controversies with contemporaries, or his own spiritual eminence; see ibid., pp. xviii–xix.

ginning of the seventeenth century, were over time endorsed by significant numbers of the Indian Muslim elite and ended up profoundly altering the nature of normative Indian Islam. The same Mujaddidī systematization that limited Indian expressions of Islam managed successfully to persuade large numbers of influential Muslims that the boundaries of the Muslim community should be clearly defined. This new formulation of Islam, in Wilfred Cantwell Smith's words, was a "formalist closed-system reified interpretation."[71] For those Muslims who became convinced of the new orthodoxy, it was anything but a closed, reified expression of Islam. On the contrary, the Mujaddidiyya enclosed and nurtured an unparalleled inner vitality which has continued to this day to sustain the lineage throughout the world.

[71] W. C. Smith, "The Crystallization of Religious Communities," p. 190. As recently as 1992 Fritz Meier said the [so-called] stagnation of Sufism begins in the seventeenth century with the Mujaddidiyya and the Shīʿī scholastic-ʿ*irfān* tradition. See his "Nachtrag des Verfassers," p. 130.

CHAPTER 4

Genealogy as a Source of Authority

There are as many ways to God as there are souls.
A sufi saying attributed to Bahā'uddīn Naqshband

The science of the isnād *is part of religion; therefore, scrutinize those from whom you learn your religion.*
Muslim, *Ṣaḥīḥ Muslim*

The sufi directing-shaykh and his authority could not have developed merely as a result of local historical conditions. The spiritual connection to the Prophet Muḥammad, the most potent pan-Islamic symbol, authenticated the figure of the sufi shaykh and made him a compelling figure in popular religion.[1] The importance of continuous links to the Prophet was nothing new, of course, but the Naqshbandīs expanded the principle to include a heart-to-heart transmission of divine grace that enabled their disciples to feel as if they were actually in the presence of the Prophet.

In technical sufi terminology each Naqshbandī disciple has *nisba* (Persian *nisbat*) with the Prophet, derived from the formal spiritual connection to his or her spiritual mentor; the mentor has the same type of connection with his spiritual guide.[2] This series of spiritual links forms a chain (*silsila*) that ultimately leads back to the Prophet and transmits divine grace or auspiciousness (*fayḍ*,

[1]Muslim apologists have continually used the figure of Muḥammad to underpin their authority by employing Prophetic hadith in sufi apologetics and by emphasizing the Prophetic sunna as a model of orthoprax behavior.

[2]This sufi *nisba* overrides all other *nisbas* such as place of birth or blood ties. For an overview of *nisbas* referring to place of birth, residence or origin, see Annemarie Schimmel, *Islamic Names*, p. 10.

baraka) from God. Since there are varying degrees of connectedness to the Prophet, even non-sufis can receive some divine energy (*fayḍ*), but without a shaykh there is seldom enough divine grace to make spiritual progress.[3] For the Naqshbandīs a "proper connection" (*nisbat-i durust*) assumes formal initiation (*bayʿa*) and participation in Naqshbandī mystical practices (*sulūk*).[4]

In many respects these sufi genealogical chains resemble *isnāds* (sing. *sanad*, literally support, backing), which have been used to certify that a specific hadith transmission actually originated with the Prophet or a Companion. Muslim scholars consider a hadith authentic (*ṣaḥīḥ*) if all the transmitters of the *isnād* are reputable and if their lifetimes sufficiently overlap. In Islam this *isnād* principle also applies to the transmission of knowledge in general, Qurʾān recitation, the religious sciences (*tafsīr, ḥadīth, fiqh*), and history (*tāʾrīkh, sīra, maghāzī*).[5] As a general principle, the *isnād*

---

[3]Of the various categories of sufi initiates, two are represented by the type of robes *(khirqas)* bestowed, e.g., a *khirqa-yi irāda* for initiates performing mystical exercises and a *khirqa-yi tabarruk* for those who simply desire blessing from the shaykh. See Spencer Trimingham, *The Sufi Orders in Islam,* pp. 36, 181–85, and Richard Gramlich, *Die schiitischen Derwischorden Persiens,* 3 volumes, 2:171–75.

[4]ʿAbdurraḥmān Jāmī, *Nafahāt al-uns min hadarāt al-quds,* ed. M. Tawḥīdīpūr, p. 614, cited in Muḥammad b. Muḥammad Pārsā, *Qudsiyya: Kalimāt-i Bahāʾuddīn Naqshband,* ed. Aḥmad Ṭāhirī ʿIrāqī, p. 119. Naʿīmullāh Bahrāʾichī, a disciple of Mīrzā Maẓhar Jān-i jānān writing four centuries later, describes this as *nisbat-i ṣaḥīḥ* in his *Maʿmūlāt-i maẓharī,* p. 16. ʿIrāqī discusses the various usages of *nisba* in Kāshifī's *Rashaḥāt-i ʿayn al-hayāt* and in his edition of *Qudsiyya.* He states that the more common meaning for the Naqshbandīs is the equation of *nisba* and *ṭarīqa.* Sometimes *nisba* describes the condition of God's attributes overpowering the one moving along the Path *(sālik)* to the point that the *sālik* loses all sense of ego, i.e., takes on the quality of *bē khudī* and is drowned in God's attributes; see Pārsā, *Qudsiyya,* pp. 118–20. It is this latter meaning of *nisba* that is equated with *wilāya, qurb,* and *ḥuḍūr* (all meaning being close to God) in Zawwār Ḥusayn, *ʿUmdat al-sulūk,* p. 306. It is described by Ghulām ʿAlī Shāh in *Maqāmāt-i Maẓharī,* p. 478, as *nisbat-i kashifī,* a quality which, in his opinion, few of his contemporaries possessed. All Muslims are considered to have some residual *nisba* although only someone who has a pir can be properly called *ṣāḥib-i nisbat;* see Zawwār Ḥusayn, *ʿUmdat al-sulūk,* p. 306.

[5]Traditionally, any knowledge acquired without a valid *isnād* has not been recognized by the community of ulama. Detractors of Abūʾl-ʿAlāʾ Mawdūdī (d. 1979), a Pakistani ideologue who has, among his numerous other works, published a lengthy Qurʾān commentary, dismiss anything he says about Islam because they consider it to be based on personal opinion *(rāʾy).* This is in sharp contrast to knowledge that is *mustanad,* i.e., validated by an *isnād.* In terms of authority in Islam, knowledge with an *isnād* is knowledge that has been validated by the community over centuries; it bears the stamp of community consensus *(ijmāʿ)* in its unquestioning acceptance *(taqlīd)* of knowledge narrated by devout predecessors. From this frame of reference, independent *rāʾy* is not valued, sometimes even considered a threat to the cohesion of the community. The discussion of William A. Graham concerning the fundamental nature of the *isnād* paradigm

mechanism is an Islamic knowledge-validation principle designed to guarantee connection to the Prophet and his Companions.

Both *isnāds* and sufi genealogical chains are based on a more encompassing principle: the personal encounter between two reliable transmitters. In Islam, religious knowledge (*ʿilm*) is much more than just factual information that can be either read or written down. According to an alleged Prophetic hadith, it is divided in two "modes": knowledge of the heart (*ʿilm al-qalb*) and oral knowledge (*ʿilm al-lisān*).[6] These two categories can overlap: for example, the profession of faith (*shahāda*) is spoken but must be affirmed in the heart (*taṣdīq bi-qalb*). Both modes are communicated through personal contact and, whether verbal or nonverbal, are expected to touch the believer's heart to some degree. In a comprehensive discussion of the oral aspects of scripture, William A. Graham states, "It is a vastly different thing to read and revere a text as an authoritative *document* than to *internalize* it in memory and meditation until it permeates the sensual as well as the intellectual sphere of consciousness. This [is] internalization, or 'having the text by heart. . . .' "[7]

Naqshbandī genealogy chains indicate the path of continuous heart-to-heart transmission of divinely emanating power and grace from God via Muḥammad to the Muslim community. Great emphasis is placed upon the involvement of the believer's heart, the locus of God's immanence. The student "above all should have companionship (*ṣuḥbat*) with those who are perfected spiritually and who are adorned with both inner and outer exemplary deeds. From these perfected individuals [the students] should learn religious sciences which are connected to shariʿa, e.g., *fiqh*, *ḥadīth*, *tafsīr*, so that through this knowledge one may desire God Almighty's friendship and so that one's heart (*dil*) may proceed on the path of virtue."[8]

The key pedagogical factor is the process of *ṣuḥbat*, which is an intimate spiritual communication between human hearts.[9] From

in Islamic culture in "Traditionalism in Islam: An Essay in Interpretation" has stimulated my thinking along these lines.

[6]Bahā'uddīn cites a hadith not found in the standard collections in Yaʿqūb Charkhī, *Risāla-yi unsiyya*, p. 12.

[7]William A. Graham Jr., *Beyond the Written Word: Oral Aspects of Scripture in the History of Religion*, p. 165.

[8]Zawwār Ḥusayn, *ʿUmdat al-suluk*, p. 179.

[9]Naqshbandīs are aware that practically speaking it is not easy to find a scholar of religious sciences who can simultaneously engage students in *ṣuḥbat*, but when it does occur, it is "light upon light" (Q. 24:25).

a Naqshbandī point of view at least, the heart is the proper receptacle or medium for religious knowledge. Only when it is linked with the companionship (*ṣuḥbat*) of a spiritual mentor can this knowledge be transformed into a religious wisdom inherited from the prophets.[10] This is qualitatively different from any notion of intellectual knowledge. Companionship with the shaykh, even when teaching hadith, is ideally experienced as actually being in the presence of the Prophet himself.[11]

Written documents—and in modern times radio broadcasts, television, and fax communications—all lack this connection to Muḥammad and are not considered to be authoritative media for religious knowledge. This is not to say religious knowledge cannot be communicated and stored in them, but they lack a necessary "potency of the heart."[12] Naqshbandī definitions of connectedness to Muḥammad encompass the general criteria for valid Islamic knowledge while emphasizing the necessity of divine energy and grace. What exactly comprises a valid connection to the Prophet, however, is another matter. Sufis and hadith scholars have used radically differing paradigms to validate their positions.

The Naqshbandī spiritual pedigree differs from a proper hadith *isnād* in its age discrepancies between transmitters. Qāsim b. Muḥammad b. Muḥammad b. Abī Bakr (d. 107/725) could only have met Salmān al-Fārisī (d. 36/656) as a small child. And how could Abū Yazīd al-Bisṭāmī (d. 261/875) have met Jaʿfar aṣ-Ṣādiq

---

[10]This is said to be in accordance with the hadith, "The ulama are to my people as the prophets were to the sons of Israel" (*ʿulamāʾ ummatī k-ʾanbiyāʾi banī isrāʾīl).* For Naqshbandīs, the true ulama are those who have both the outer religious knowledge of the religious scholars and the inner knowledge of sufis. As a technical term in Islam, *ʿulama'* (sing. *ʿālim*) usually means religious specialists who have studied the "outer" religious sciences, specializing in Islamic jurisprudence *(fiqh).*

[11]See the quotation by Mīrzā Maẓhar Jān-i jānān on pages 16–17 above.

[12]One example is a well-known invocatory prayer, *Ḥizb al-baḥr,* which is believed to have special protective power and often recited by seafarers. In *ṣuḥbat* a Naqshbandī shaykh communicates this invocatory prayer to individual disciples, giving them "permission" *(ijāza)* to use the invocatory prayer. The preceptor has activated it. Supported by an authoritative *isnād* going directly back to the Prophet via Abū'l-Ḥasan ʿAlī ash-Shādhilī (d. 656/1258), the *Ḥizb al-baḥr* now is connected. Maḥbūb ʿĀlam (d. 1335/1917), a Panjabi Naqshbandī pir, explicitly states that it would be insolent and presumptuous to recite the *Ḥizb al-baḥr* before receiving permission from a spiritual guide; disregarding such measures would result in certain harm and ruin; see his *Dhikr-i kathīr: maḥbūb al-sulūk,* p. 41. For another interchange involving a disciple asking a shaykh for permission to use *Ḥizb al-baḥr,* see Abū'l-Ḥasan Zayd Fārūqī, *Manāhij al-sayr,* p. 79, and ʿAbdullāh Jān, *Mu'nis al-mukhlisīn,* pp. 141–43.

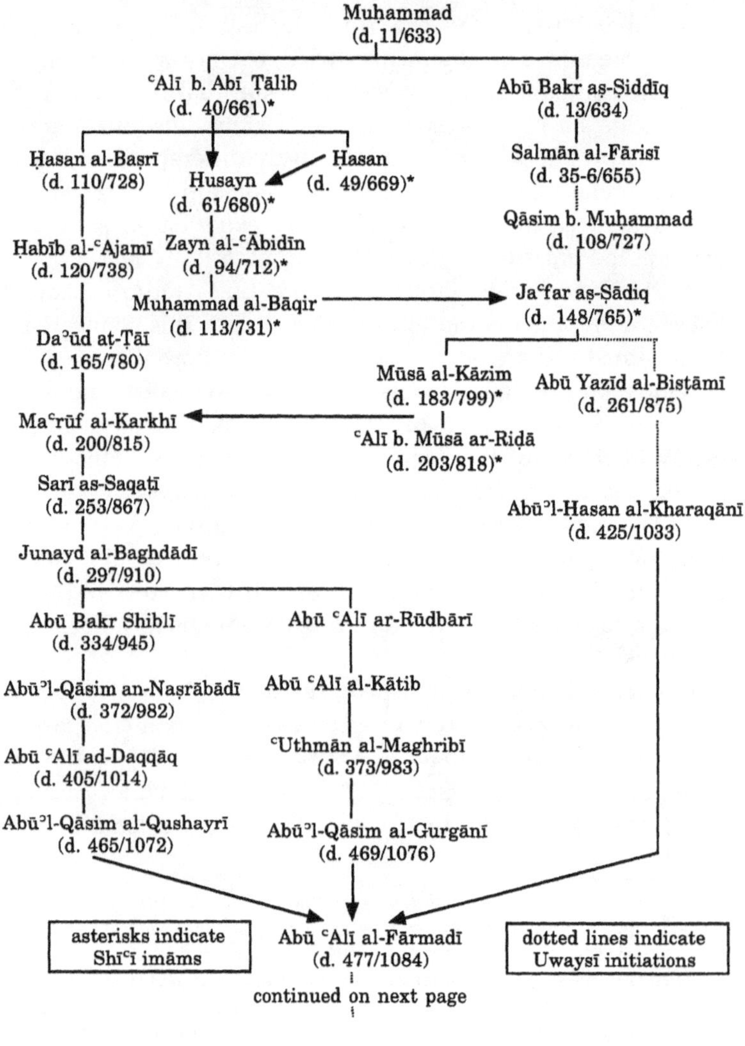

Figure 4. Naqshbandī genealogy

(d. 148/765) or Abū'l-Ḥasan al-Kharaqānī (d. 425/1033) have met Abū Yazīd al-Bisṭāmī?[13]

Historical evidence suggests that the earliest links of sufi chains were fabricated. In the Naqshbandī case, three of the first

[13]According to Shāh Walīullāh, a recognized hadith scholar and eminent Indian Naqshbandī, the biographical literature unequivocally states that Qāsim b. Muḥammad b. Muḥammad b. Abī Bakr could not have met Salmān al-Fārisī. Shāh Walīullāh's response is that God knows best. As for the link between Ḥasan al-Baṣrī (d. 110/728) and ʿAlī b. Abī Ṭālib (d. 41/661), Shāh Walīullāh states that the sufis are convinced this is a valid link even though it cannot be proven by hadith

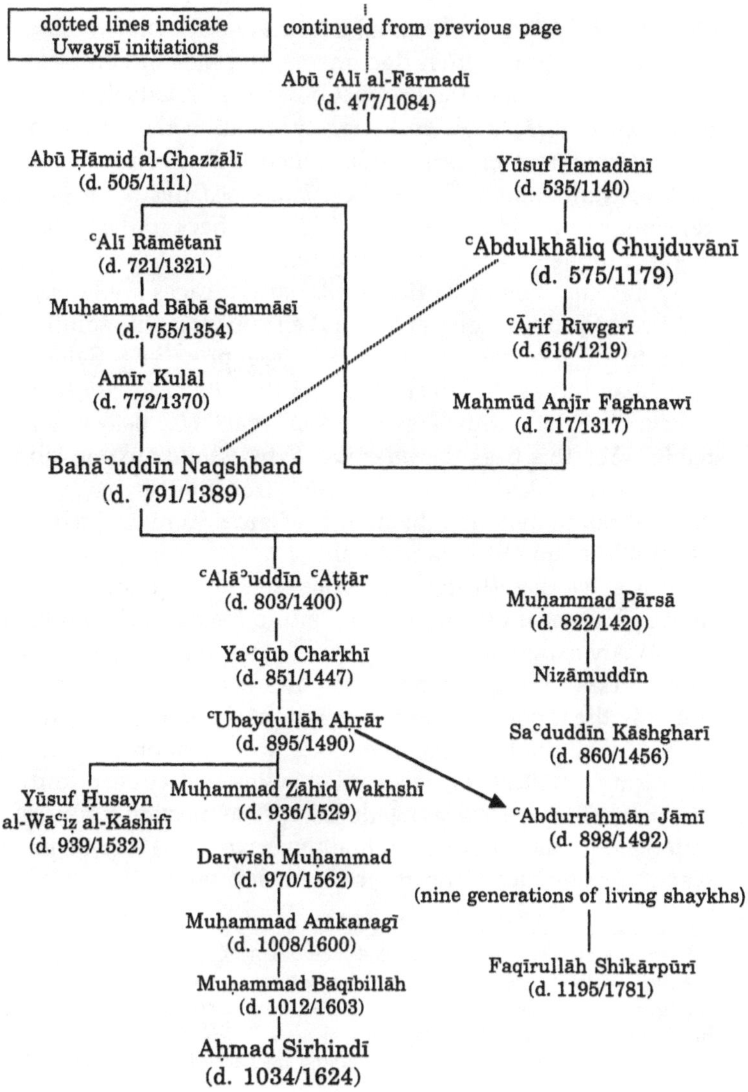

scholars. See Shāh Walīullāh, *Intibāh fī salāsil awliyā' Allāh*, p. 34. Later, Shāh Walīullāh states that Abū ʿAlī al-Fārmadī (d. 477/1084) has *nisbat-i jadhba* and *ṣuḥbat* from Abū'l-Ḥasan al-Kharaqānī (d. 425/1033). In addition, Shāh Walīullāh states that Abū'l-Ḥasan al-Kharaqānī and Abū Yazīd are spiritually connected even though the link between Abū Yazīd and Jaʿfar Ṣādiq is not valid (*ṣaḥīḥ*). Any Bakrī affiliation for Naqshbandīs depends upon the validity of this latter connection. See ibid., pp. 38–39, and also Fakhruddīn ʿAlī Ṣafī Kāshifī, *Rashahāt-i ʿayn al-hayāt*, pp. 51–63 (introduction).

six links of the Bakrī *silsila* are historically impossible.[14] Based on information from written documents, the idea of complete sufi chains linked back to the Prophet developed relatively late in the tradition. Biographical works rarely mention the names of the spiritual mentors of early sufis, much less a complete lineage back to Muḥammad. The earliest sufi *isnād* traces the spiritual genealogy of Jaʿfar al-Khuldī (d. 348/959) back to the Successors of the Prophet (*ṭābiʿūn*).[15] In the tenth century, paralleling the early development of hadith *isnāds*, sufi lineages are "raised" to ʿAlī b. Abī Ṭālib, a Companion of the Prophet.[16] One solution has been to declare the spiritual pedigree preceding Bahā'uddīn Naqshband to be "pre-historical" and only consider subsequent links from Bahā'uddīn Naqshband as "real," i.e., historically verifiable.[17] Yet, this begs the question: Why would anyone fabricating an *isnād* decide to separate two transmitters by 164 lunar years—especially when the hadith sciences were well developed by Abū'l-Ḥasan al-Kharaqānī's time?

Sufis solve these historical inconsistencies by citing the precedent of Uways al-Qaranī, who is said to have met the Prophet in a visionary experience without ever having seen him in corporeal form.[18] This "Uwaysī connection" has become, in sufi practice, not only the model for the transmission of divine energy directly from Muḥammad but also the model for initiation by the imaginal form (*rūḥānīyāt*) of deceased shaykhs that appears during a visionary experience. Having an Uwaysī connection is like having independent use of power, while the established sufi chains represent dependence upon the relationship with a living pir. Al-

---

[14]The Bakrī *silsila* is the lineage that includes Abū Bakr aṣ-Ṣiddīq. In general, the early parts of *silsilas* are not historically tenable. See Louis Massignon, *Essai sur les origines du lexique technique de la mystique musulmane,* pp. 128–32, and Kāshifī, *Rashaḥāt,* pp. 50–51 (introduction).

[15]Massignon, *Essai,* pp. 128–30; Gramlich, *Die schiitischen Derwischorden,* 2:171–72.

[16]Ibid., 2:171–73.

[17]Algar, "Brief History," p. 6; according to extant sources, Bahā'uddīn Naqshband is anything but a historically coherent figure. For historical ambiguities concerning Bahā'uddīn; see Pārsā, *Qudsiyya,* ed. ʿIrāqī, p. 10, and Algar's article "Bahā al-Dīn Naqshband," in *Encyclopaedia Iranica.*

[18]There is a small shrine near Zabid, Yemen, where it is said Uways is entombed. Allegedly he died in 37/657 at the battle of Siffin. See Annemarie Schimmel, *Mystical Dimensions of Islam,* pp. 28–29, and A. S. Husaini, "Uways al-Qaranī and the Uwaysī Sufis." The Uwaysī tradition, representing an unaffiliated non-*ṭarīqa* sufi organization, went through a particularly intensive development in Central Asia. See Devin Deweese, *An "Uvaysi" Sufi in Timurid Mawarannahr: Notes on Hagiography and Taxonomy of Sanctity in the Religious History of Central Asia.*

though the Uwaysī model poses problems for historicist models it has been a crucial part of Naqshbandī life.

Bahā'uddīn Naqshband cites Farīduddīn 'Aṭṭār's (d. 617/1220) discussion of Uwaysīs, who remarks that those who are sustained directly by Muḥammad have a very exalted spiritual status. 'Aṭṭār also mentions the Kubrawī shaykh Abū Qāsim al-Gurgānī (d. 469/1077), who used to say "Uways, Uways" before beginning the practice of recollecting God (*dhikr*).[19] Relating his own experiences, Bahā'uddīn, himself an Uwaysī, explains that he no longer had a relationship with the spirit of Uways al-Qaranī but had extended contact with al-Ḥakīm at-Tirmidhī (d. ca. 298/910), whose spiritual presence (*tawajjuh*) appeared without attributes.[20] Bahā'uddīn's best-known Uwaysī pir, 'Abdulkhāliq Ghujduwānī (d. 575/1179), instructed Bahā'uddīn in silent *dhikr* and the necessity of strictly following the sunna.[21] Although Bahā'uddīn Naqshband met his first sufi shaykh, Bābā Muḥammad Sammāsī (d. 755/1354), as a youth and later remained under the guidance of Sammāsī's successor, Amīr Kulāl (d. 772/1370), he considered his primary spiritual mentor to be 'Abdulkhāliq Ghujduwānī.[22] This precedence of an Uwaysī guide was typical of the early Naqshbandiyya; an Uwaysī connection (*nisbat-i ruḥānī*) was considered stronger and was preferred over a connection with a living shaykh (*nisbat-i jismānī*).[23] In a certain sense a hadith scholar would agree, since an Uwaysī connection makes the chain shorter and brings the *isnād* closer to Muḥammad.

All sufis include one or more of the first eight Shī'ī imams

---

[19]Pārsā, *Qudsiyya*, ed. 'Irāqī, p. 15 (introduction).

[20]According to Bahā'uddīn and later Naqshbandīs, spiritual journeying *(sayr)* without experiencing any attributes is a high stage of those who experience continual revelation *(kashf)* of Reality *(ahl-i tamkīn);* See ibid. (text), pp. 25–26, 139. For references to experiences at al-Hakīm at-Tirmidhī's grave see ibid. (text), pp. 140–41. Before being cut off from Uways's companionship, Bahā'uddīn experienced the attributes of Uways al-Qaranī's spirit, i.e., he saw Uways's form. In contrast, for the 22 years he had followed the path of al-Ḥakīm at-Tirmidhī, al-Ḥakīm had remained formless. Muḥammad Ḥasan, *Ḥālāt-i mashā'ikh-i Naqshbandiyya-Mujaddidiyya*, p. 66.

[21]Pārsā, *Qudsiyya*, ed. 'Irāqī, p. 8 (text).

[22]Bahā'uddīn acknowledges his *nisbat-i irādat, ṣuḥbat,* acquiring correct behavior in spiritual exercises *(adāb-i sulūk),* and learning *dhikr* from his living spiritual preceptor, Amīr Kulāl. In spiritual exercises pertaining to Reality *(sulūk bi-ḥaqīqat)* his Uwaysī guide, 'Abdulkhāliq Ghujduwānī, is his foremost guide. Bahā'uddīn always refers to his Uwaysī pir as "our master" *(khwāja-yi mā)* or as "the grand master" *(khwāja-yi buzurg)* in ibid. (text), pp. 8–10. Bahā'uddīn separated himself from Amīr Kulāl's group when they did vocal *dhikr;* see Kāshifī, *Rashaḥāt,* pp. 95–96.

[23]Pārsā, *Qudsiyya*, ed. 'Irāqī, p. 32 (introduction).

among their spiritual ancestors,[24] because these eight imams were the "golden chain" linking subsequent generations to the Prophet. Like Jaʿfar aṣ-Ṣādiq, ʿAlī ar-Riḍā (d. 203/818), the eighth imam, was considered a learned and pious leader by many of his contemporaries—even to the point that the Caliph al-Maʾmūn (d. 218/833) attempted to appoint him as his successor.[25] ʿAlī ar-Riḍā taught Maʿrūf al-Karkhī (d. 200/815), who then brought sufism to Baghdad.[26] Naqshbandī genealogies include at least one of the Shīʿī imams: Jaʿfar aṣ-Ṣādiq, ʿAlī ar-Riḍā, or ʿAlī b. Abī Ṭālib. This part of the Naqshbandī lineage was ignored in later Mujaddidī constructs of self-identity.

Mujaddidī Redefinitions

Aḥmad Sirhindī reformulated the genealogical interpretations of Naqshbandī authority by emphasizing the line of spiritual transmission from Abū Bakr. In this fashion the Naqshbandiyya-Mujaddidiyya declared its superiority over other sufis, since Ḥanafī Sunnī credal dogma presumed Abū Bakr to be the most laudable human after the prophets.[27] It was believed that the sobriety of the Naqshbandiyya, silent recollection of God (*dhikr*), and strict adherence to the shariʿa and to sunna were ultimately inherited from Abū Bakr.[28] This Bakrī emphasis was accompanied by a pronounced hostility of the Naqshbandiyya toward

[24]An important confluence between Shīʿīs and sufis is the shared spiritual lineage, which in the Naqshbandī case is called the "Golden Chain."

[25]Wilferd Madelung shows how the ninth century was one of great uncertainty and apocalyptic prophecies which might have influenced the caliph to appoint the imam as his successor to usher in the Mahdī. The Mahdī is believed to be the person who brings justice to the world immediately before the Day of Judgment. See "New Documents Concerning Al-Maʾmūn, al-Faḍl b. Sahl, and ʿAlī al-Riḍā," pp. 345–46. Al-Maʾmūn very likely had practical political motives behind this decision; see Patricia Crone and Martin Hinds, *God's Caliph: Religious Authority in the First Centuries of Islam*, pp. 94–96.

[26]There are reports stating that ʿAlī ar-Riḍā was responsible for Maʿrūf al-Karkhī's conversion to Islam. ʿAlī b. ʿUthmān al-Jullābī Hujwīrī, *Kashf al-maḥjūb*, p. 141; trans. Reynold A. Nicholson, *The Kashf Al-Maḥjūb: The Oldest Persian Treatise on Sufism*, p. 114.

[27]Aḥmad Sirhindī, *Maktūbāt-i imām-i rabbānī*, 3 volumes, vol. 1, letter 221, p. 3 [hereafter 1.221.3].

[28]Some Turkish Naqshbandīs emphasized a distinctive Sunnī identity by professing Bakrī origins; "more often, however, Naqshbandī *silsilas* of the sixteenth and seventeenth centuries consist of several parallel derivations, Bakrī as well as ʿAlid." See Dina Le Gall, "The Ottoman Naqshbandiyya in the Pre-Mujaddidī Phase: A Study in Islamic Religious Culture and Its Transmission," p. 137.

A genealogical tree with the Naqshbandī lineage as the trunk and the other lineages as flowers. The original version was probably produced by a disciple of Naqshbandī shaykh Shāh Abū Saʿīd (d. 250/1835) or by one of his successors in the Musa Zai sublineage before 1911. There is a more ornate version in Muḥammad Amīr Ḥasan, *Tadhkirat al-muttaqīn,* 2d ed., part 1 (Kanpur: Qayyūmī Press, 1911), a hagiography of the Madārī lineage, with two Madārī shaykhs on the trunk instead of Aḥmad Saʿīd and Dōst Muḥammad. The genealogical tree shown here is an even later version of these, having two generations of Musa Zai shaykhs added at the top of the trunk after Sirājuddīn.

Shīʿīs, a characteristic shared by few other Indian sufi lineages.[29] In sharp contrast with Bahāʾuddīn's perception of the Naqshbandī spiritual pedigree, Sirhindī disregarded the two other lines from Muḥammad's cousin and son-in-law, ʿAlī b. Abī Ṭālib (d. 40/661).[30] The issue for Bahāʾuddīn was not which Companion transmitted God's divine grace through Muḥammad but that each connection (*nisba*) to the Prophet had its own unique blessing.[31]

The Mujaddidī preoccupation with the Bakrī heritage and sobriety meant a marked deemphasis of spiritual ecstasy and Uwaysī initiations. The tension between sufis valuing ecstatic spiritual intoxication and those advocating the superiority of sobriety had existed since the early history of sufism. Typically, the exhibition of mystical intoxication had been considered evidence of an advanced adept on the Path. Junayd's (d. 297/910) well-known answer to the intoxicated enthusiasm of an-Nūrī (d. 295/908), who chastised Junayd's sitting calmly while the sufis performed their whirling dance, was "You see the mountains—you think them firm, yet they move like clouds" (Q. 27:90).[32]

The Mujaddidīs would concur; the Prophetic sobriety exemplified by Abū Bakr represented the mode of an advanced spiritual guide. It was the sobriety of a sufi who, having subdued his carnal nature, experienced intoxication, and traversed various stages of the Path, returned to the world outwardly behaving like any ordinary pious person. He had become extraordinarily ordinary.

---

[29]During the rise of the Safavid empire in the sixteenth century, Bakrī origins were emphasized politically to distinguish the Naqshbandiyya (as Sunnīs) from the Shīʿīs. See Dina Le Gall, "The Ottoman Naqshbandiyya," pp. 137–47. From Sirhindī's time the objection to Shīʿīs has been largely based on credal dogma. Many Naqshbandīs have considered those not recognizing Abū Bakr as the first rightly-guided caliph and ʿAlī b. Abī Ṭālib as the fourth caliph to be outside the fold of Islam (Shīʿīs assert that Abū Bakr unjustly usurped the caliphate from ʿAlī.).

[30]Explaining the various lines of his own spiritual genealogy, Bahāʾuddīn first stresses the preeminence of the Golden Chain *(silsilat al-dhahāb)* of the imams of Muḥammad's family *(āʾimmat-i ahl-i bayt)* because of the distinction they make between inner and outer knowledge. Lest he be accused of Shīʿī tendencies, he then mentions his spiritual descent from Abū Bakr and how it is the consensus of the Sunnī community that Abū Bakr is the closest to God after the prophets; see Pārsā, *Qudsiyya*, ed. ʿIrāqī, pp. 11–15 (text).

[31]When Bahāʾuddīn was asked where his sufi chain *(silsila)* arrived at, he responded "No one arrives anywhere on the basis of a *silsila* alone"; see ibid., p. 10 (introduction). I would extend this dictum to say that almost no one arrives on the basis of one source of personal authority alone.

[32]Cited in Schimmel, *Mystical Dimensions*, p. 181.

Sobriety, in addition, fit in conveniently with the Naqshbandī emphasis on strict adherence to Islamic law and on imitating the way of the Prophet.[33]

Uwaysī pirs were associated with intoxication. In Bahā'uddīn's first encounters with his Uwaysī shaykh, 'Abdulkhāliq Ghujduwānī, he was in such an unstable state, overpowered by *jadhba* (often characterized by uncontrollable shaking and involuntary utterances), that he could do nothing but walk around the outskirts of Bukhara at night.[34] This is hardly the sober model that the Mujaddidīs would have their disciples imitate. It is not surprising, therefore, that Sirhindī did not consider Uways to have reached the stage of the lowest Companion of the Prophet, but declared him to be the best of the Successors, i.e., the best of those who had embraced Islam from a person who had met the Prophet.[35] By denying Uways al-Qaranī's *ṣuḥbat* with the Prophet, Sirhindī negated the general phenomenon of Uwaysī initiation and affirmed the requirement for guidance from a living Naqshbandī shaykh.

An apocryphal narrative by Bahā'uddīn illustrates this shift in emphasis to a living pir: "Khiḍr, wearing a kulah hat, approached me with a shepherd's staff in his hand. Speaking in Turkish he accused me of seeing some horses and beating him with the staff he was now carrying. I did not say anything. He blocked my path a few times which caused me to worry. I said that I knew him to be Khiḍr as he followed me to Qarāwwul Ribāṭ. He said to sit down for awhile, but I did not turn around. When I reached Amīr Kulāl's, he [Amīr Kulāl] asked me if I had met Khiḍr on the road and if I had not turned around. I answered

[33]This does not imply that intoxication is nonexistent in Mujaddidī practice. First-hand accounts of beginning Mujaddidī disciples in the company of a practicing shaykh often give examples of *jadhba* (literally, attraction), the widespread technical term used throughout Naqshbandī and Naqshbandī-Mujaddidī literature to describe the phenomenon of intoxication, a state of overpowering attraction by God. One characteristic of spiritual intoxication is that it can affect a person at any time, which can cause potential difficulties in situations such as communal ritual prayer. The Prophet never exhibited signs of *jadhba*.

[34]Pārsā, *Qudsiyya*, ed. 'Irāqī, p. 116 (text). For the relationship between *jadhba* and types of traveling (*sayr-i anfusī* and *sayr-i āfāqī*), see ter Haar, *Follower and Heir*, pp. 108–09, and Aḥmad Sirhindī, *Mukāshafa-yi 'ayniyya*, pp. 21–23. According to Bahā'uddīn, the special aspect of the "path of attraction" *(tarīq-i jadhba)* was that there was its lack of intermediaries, effectively eliminating any initiatory chain between the person and Muḥammad. This path shortcut the much longer way of traversing the path *(tarīq-i sulūk)* which did not involve *jadhba*.

[35]Sirhindī, *Maktūbāt*, 1.58.35.

yes because I had been going in your direction and therefore did not turn around. Amīr Kulāl said that the *nisbat* of the Khwājagān is from four people, the first of which is Khiḍr."[36]

In the narrative, not only did Amīr Kulāl become Bahā'uddīn's primary spiritual mentor instead of Ghujduwānī, but Amīr Kulāl, his living guide, even outranked Khiḍr. The enigmatic figure of Khiḍr was said in later sources to have taught Ghujduwānī silent repetition of God's name (*dhikr-i khafī*) and *nafy wa-ithbāt*,[37] making Khiḍr Bahā'uddīn's grandfather pir, in addition to being one of the four principal connections for the Naqshbandiyya.

This didactic story illustrates how a disciple should obediently focus on one's living spiritual master, subordinating all other shaykhs, even Khiḍr, if need be. In addition, it indicates the potential conflict of authority between the spirit of a deceased shaykh and one's living spiritual guide. Logically, the devaluation of Uwaysī initiations goes hand-in-hand with an emphasis on outward sobriety. In a reformist, shari'a-minded sufi lineage like the Naqshbandiyya-Mujaddidiyya, difficulties with out-of-control sufis would be minimized.[38]

After Abū'l-Ḥasan al-Kharaqānī, Uwaysī connections are erased from the formal Naqshbandī genealogies. The pivotal figure of Khiḍr is no longer even mentioned in spiritual genealo-

---

[36]Muḥammad Ḥasan, *Ḥālāt-i mashā'ikh-i naqshband*, p. 108. Khiḍr is often identified with the companion of Moses of Qur'ān sūra 18 in addition to being identified as a prophet, one of the three heavenly *awtād*, the seventh *abdāl*, and being associated with the water of life. See Aḥmad Sharāfat Naushāhī, *Sharīf al-tawārīkh*, 3 volumes, 1:55, 74, 89, 176, and Massignon, *Essai*, pp. 131–32. Khiḍr is also the first of the four "salt of the elders" *(namak-i mashā'ikh)* in Muḥammad Pārsā, *Risāla-yi qudsiyya*, ed. M. Iqbāl, p. 197. The issue of turning around here is significant because it is considered extremely disrespectful to turn one's back to one's shaykh.

[37]Kāshifī, *Rashaḥāt*, pp. 34–35. Hamid Algar conflates these two practices in Algar, "A Brief History," p. 8. *Dhikr-i khafī*, more correctly, *dhikr-i qalbī*, is the repetition of God's name, "Allāh." *Nafy wa-ithbāt*, meaning "negation and affirmation," involves counting the number of times one says *La ilāha illā Allāh* "There is no god" (the negation) and "but God" (the affirmation)] while holding the breath. According to tradition, Khiḍr taught Ghujduwānī this exercise while the latter was submerged under water. A Kubrawī shaykh, 'Alā'uddawla Simnānī (d. 736/1336) practiced a similar exercise, allegedly communicated via Ma'rūf al-Karkhī (d. 200/815). See Jamal Elias, *The Throne Carrier of God*, pp. 126–28.

[38]Intoxicated behavior has often clashed with orthopraxic norms in Islam. Sufis who consistently exhibit intoxicated behavior (sing. *majdhūb*) by rending clothes, dancing, and ecstatic utterances have usually had a somewhat marginal existence in the established *ṭarīqas* in spite of the following they may have had among common people. The so-called sober Naqshbandiyya-Mujaddidiyya includes such Lahori *majdhūbs* as Pīr Zuhdī (d. 1139–40/1727), Sayyid Maḥmūd Āghā (d. 1299/1882), and Muḥammad Ṣādiq (d. 1404–5/1984).

gies, nor are Bahā'uddīn's Uwaysī pirs considered in his formal spiritual pedigree. Except for the early links in the Naqshbandiyya, Uwaysīs do not have formal genealogical connections to Muḥammad; they stand apart from established sufi genealogies.[39]

In later Indo-Pakistani biographical compendiums, no Naqshbandī Uwaysīs are mentioned after the time of Sirhindī,[40] although the Uwaysī status of Bahā'uddīn and Ghujduwānī is not ignored in modern Naqshbandī hagiographies.[41] This does not necessarily mean that Naqshbandīs no longer had Uwaysī experiences; Muḥammad Amīn Lāhūrī (d. 1391–92/1972) and Maulānā Allāh Yār Khān (d. 1404–5/1984) are two examples of modern Naqshbandī Uwaysīs. Yet Allāh Yār Khān's strong apologetics defending the legitimacy of the Uwaysī phenomena is an unequivocal indication that established sufi pedigrees of living shaykhs have by now become the norm in South Asia.[42]

Naqshbandīs and other sufis have defined links to the Prophetic source in such a way that anyone desiring to transmit religious knowledge must be a sufi; without a spiritual connection to the Prophet, a hadith scholar can only transmit the literal aspect of Muḥammad utterance. For this knowledge to be considered an inheritance of the Prophet, the actual conditions between the Prophet and his Companions must be simulated, and for that the transmission of divine power is required. A pir with an impeccable spiritual lineage is the best qualified to transmit this power.

Historically, there has never been a consensus among Naqshbandīs specifying what the parameters of a valid connection to the Prophet might be. Even if there had been, people would not have become attracted to the Mujaddidiyya for intellectual reasons. In any tradition religious sentiment is rarely governed only by the intellect. Mujaddidī personal authority attracted many people because it allowed aspirants to taste mystical experience

[39]Pārsā, *Qudsiyya*, ed. 'Irāqī, p. 29 (introduction).

[40]In sufi biographical compendiums organizing sufis by *ṭarīqa*, there is often a miscellaneous section which includes Uwaysīs and others whose spiritual guidance does not fit into the established *ṭarīqa* format; a small percentage are Uwaysīs.

[41]Yet even Aḥmad Sirhindī identifies himself as an Uwaysī in his *Maktūbāt*, volume 3, letter 87, and is recognized in later tradition, e.g., Aḥmad Sirhindī Naqshbandī Uwaysi Raḥmānī. See Muḥammad 'Abdullāh, "I'lān" (dated 1918), in Aḥmad Sirhindī, *Maktūbāt-i Imām Rabbānī*, ed. Nūr Aḥmad (Amristar: Maṭba'-i Mujaddidī, n.d.), 2d part, 1st section, p. 124a.

[42]Allāh Yār Khān, *Dalā'il al-sulūk*, translated by Abu Talha as *An Objective Appraisal of the Sublime Sufi Path*, pp. 286–92.

or to have contact with those who had. We know from numerous accounts of disciples that a heart-to-heart communication was associated with a shaykh's spiritual power (*tawajjuh*), which often caused others to manifest the phenomenon of *jadhba* (literally, attraction) in Naqshbandī assemblies. Spiritual attraction would affect certain sensitive people by causing them to shake uncontrollably and even writhe on the floor in the shaykh's presence. Within the sufi assembly, this *jadhba* was interpreted as being attracted to God. Any shaykh who could demonstrate his spiritual power in such a fashion did not have to rely on sweet words or intellectual prowess to attract disciples. If the aspirant felt a special affinity toward the shaykh he or she would often become initiated and perhaps, in the initiation process itself, have a personal experience of spiritual attraction. Although few would go on to advanced levels of contemplative practice, all who came into the master's presence would have the opportunity to learn how to become better Muslims.

After beginning the Path the new disciple would learn the Mujaddidī methods of activating the subtle centers (*laṭā'if*) and performing the guided meditations (*murāqabāt*). The Mujaddidiyya, like other lineages, had an organized system of mystical practice, a spiritual road map. Commentary on Sirhindī's *Maktūbāt* often was intended to provide a spiritual travel guide at various stages along the Path, assisting disciples to model their every action on the Prophet's behavior. To actualize the symbols of Islam was the goal, both in one's heart and in society. The prospect of mystical experience or an association with those who had such a capacity must have exercised a powerful effect on some who were drawn to Naqshbandī circles—in addition to the experience of being in a charismatic community modeled after the Prophet and his Companions.

When an effective method of spiritual practice is accompanied by the extraordinary caliber of a spiritual mentor, the combination enables numbers of seekers to encounter something beyond, to be a little closer to God. They are experiencing the personal charismatic presence of the shaykh. For Mujaddidīs, the path outlined by Sirhindī is nothing more nor less than the path of Muḥammad; any spiritual greatness attributed to the Naqshbandiyya is only a shadow of the Prophet's. From a historian's perspective, the collective authority of the Naqshbandiyya-Mujaddidiyya is represented by its ability not only to survive and predominate over other lineages of the *ṭarīqa* in India, but also to become a thriving worldwide sufi lineage.[43] To a large extent this expansion of the Mujaddidiyya resulted from their peculiar ability to use recognized sources of authority in Islam that mesh effectively and connect with the symbol of authority par excellence, Muḥammad.

Naqshbandī collective personal authority is a concept; in human experience it manifests itself through individual Naqshbandī shaykhs. Without their convincing spiritual accomplishments in replicating and, indeed, embodying prophetic symbols, Naqshbandī ideas and consolidation of religious authority would not have been accepted by the Indian Muslim community. Prominent Mujaddidī shaykhs were first and foremost sufis, regardless of their expertise in the religious sciences. In spite of the many factors contributing to the success of the Naqshbandiyya throughout their long history, for example, revivalist programs, political influence, social prestige of ulama, or use of collected letters, all would have been insignificant, if not nonexistent, without the essential ingredient: the directing-shaykh's inner experiential connection to the Prophet. Mujaddidīs went about following the "inner sunna" of the Prophet through the performance of well-defined spiritual practices (*sulūk*), the "system" which enabled each disciple to develop and refine his or her connection to the Prophet.

---

[43]Often *ṭarīqa* is translated as "order," i.e., a group of persons living under a religious rule, as in a Christian monastic order, e.g., the order of St. Benedict. Defining a *ṭarīqa* as an "order" fails to communicate the sufi ad-hoc organizational style based on initiatic chains *(silsilas)* which, in turn, are based on a succession of pirs who have guided disciples according to defined spiritual methods. The use of "brotherhood" to describe a sufi lineage ignores the many women participants in sufi *ṭarīqas*.

CHAPTER 5

Spiritual Travel as a Source of Authority

One who believes that God can be reached by human exertion will encounter endless torment; and one who believes nearness to God can be attained without exertions will encounter an endless wishful dream.

Abū Saʿīd al-Kharrāz (d. 286/899)

As in the case of Muḥammad's heavenly journey (*miʿrāj*), the metaphysical and mystical experiences of founder-figures have been an impetus for the development of religious traditions throughout history.[1] Naqshbandīs, as heirs of the Prophet, attempt to duplicate Muḥammad's mystical journey towards God. The inner transformation and resulting access to supernatural power, believed to derive from spiritual travel towards God, has provided Naqshbandīs with a potent source of spiritual and temporal authority in society.

Not everyone reaching closeness or intimacy with God (*wilāya*) had the ability to manifest this holy power.[2] We know from the

[1]Annemarie Schimmel discusses the Ascension and related literature in *And Muhammad Is His Messenger: The Veneration of the Prophet in Islamic Piety*, pp. 159–75. Some other worthwhile works on the Ascension include Nadhīr al-ʿAẓma, *al-Miʿrāj wa'l-ramz al-ṣūfī*, and Abū ʿAlī Sīnā, *Miʿrājnāma*.

[2]For Sirhindī, the station *(maqām)* of being near to God, a relatively preliminary stage on the path *(wilāyat-i ṣughrā)* achieved by negating human attributes, indicates that one still remains in the realm of duality. See Aḥmad Sirhindī, *Maktūbāt-i imām-i rabbānī*, 3 vols., vol. 1, letter 302, p. 144 [hereafter 1.302.144]. Beyond is the station of the credal formula *(maqām-i shahādat)* reached by many illustrious Naqshbandīs of the past, including ʿAbdulkhāliq Ghujduwānī (d. 575/1179) and Bahā'uddīn Naqshband (d. 791/1389). See J. G. J. ter Haar, *Follower and Heir of the Prophet: Shaykh Aḥmad Sirhindī (1564–1624) as Mystic*, p. 37, n. 47. Then is the station of veracity *(maqām-i ṣiddīqīyat)*, probably the station of Abū Bakr aṣ-Ṣiddīq,

letters of notable Naqshbandī shaykhs that they displayed supernatural power (*taṣarruf, himmat,* or *tawajjuh,* a concentration of this power) through a special bond with their disciples (*rābiṭa*) in order to further the progress of their disciples. To what extent this supernatural power allowed them to intervene in extraordinary ways is less certain, because the sources attribute formulaic non-prophetic miracles to almost all deceased sufis.[3] People have generally expected sufis to function as brokers of supernatural power to help them—whether to cure illness, to influence rulers, or to act as spiritual artillery in battle. Rather than explaining these powers on the basis of physical or psychological laws (or dismissing them altogether), Muslims have used a religious paradigm to account for what they perceive to be divine interventions. According to this paradigm, all authority originates with God, who channels divine energy through a spiritual hierarchy of intimate protégés who in their capacity as brokers of supernatural power then mediate this divinely emanating grace (*fayḍ*) to humanity. Within each sufi lineage specific methods developed for disciples to draw near to God, some of whom arrived close enough to become power-wielding friends of God themselves. Fortunately Naqshbandīs discuss their path to God and the methods used to traverse it in considerable detail.

Aḥmad Sirhindī extended the Naqshbandī spiritual path far beyond what his predecessors had taught, pioneering a critical analysis of the structure and hierarchy of mystical experience in his claim to have traveled far beyond other mystics.[4] Not only was Sirhindī's elaboration more extensive, but it was profusely more detailed in its description of specific methods and stages

---

followed by the station of prophethood *(maqām-i nubūwat),* also called the station of greater intimacy *(wilāyat-i kubrā).*

[3]It is rare to find the distinction made between *wilāya* and *walāya* in Naqshbandī writings, since short vowels are written neither in Persian nor in Urdu. There is one mention in Muḥammad Hāshim Kishmī, *Zubdat al-maqāmāt,* p. 60, cited in ter Haar, *Follower and Heir,* pp. 87–88, but this does not further a nuanced understanding of significant differences between these two terms. Despite occasional technical discussions of this kind (which seek to demonstrate differences), Naqshbandī sources acknowledge supernatural power resulting from the *wilāya* of a legitimate sufi to be a result of his close intimacy with God, i.e., which presumes *walāya.* Such a situation indicates a partially functional conflation of these terms. See also Michel Chodkiewicz's extended linguistic discussion of these two terms in *Le sceau des saints: Prophétie et sainteté dans la doctrine d'Ibn Arabî,* pp. 35–39; trans. Liadain Sherrard, *Seal of the Saints: Prophethood and Sainthood in the Doctrine of Ibn ʿArabī,* pp. 17–25.

[4]Sirhindī formulated twenty-five of the twenty-six contemplations of the Mujaddidī path. See appendixes 1 and 2.

(*sayr wa-sulūk*). Before him, sufi theoreticians of the ninth to eleventh centuries had only discussed the spiritual path in general terms, e.g., stations (*maqāmāt*) and various temporary states. Earlier Naqshbandīs outlined eleven guiding principles.[5] But Sirhindī claimed to have discovered many higher degrees of perfection in a well-articulated hierarchy of mystical experience.

This was just part of his agenda. Sirhindī's formulations extended beyond sufis to encompass the rest of the Muslim community, declaring the Prophetic ideal, associated with the mundane sphere, to be the model for Muslim practice. Since spiritual perfection was manifested in the material world, the practices of the general Muslim community (and even to a greater degree of sufis) were to conform strictly to the sharīʿa and Prophetic sunna. Sirhindī reserved the highest spiritual rank for the mystic who, having shared in the Prophetic perfections, returned to the ordinary world with a transformed perception. Beginners for him included those who had merely annihilated the ego of the ocean of Unity.[6] It is this aspect of return combined with a beginning where other sufis finish that caused Mujaddidīs to describe their path as the "end in the beginning."[7]

Perfect performance of religious requirements and emulation of Prophetic behavior became the Mujaddidī touchstone of legitimacy for a person who had returned from the spiritual heights/depths. Underpinning this comprehensive program of ritual performance (following the dictates of Ḥanafī *fiqh*) and mystical ex-

---

[5] For a discussion of the stations see Annemarie Schimmel, *Mystical Dimensions of Islam*, pp. 117–30, and for the eleven principles see appendix 1. In the ninth to eleventh centuries the formative sufi theoreticians began to write the first treatises on stations and states. See Abū Naṣr as-Sarrāj, *Kitāb al-lumaʿ fī'l-taṣawwuf*, Abū Bakr Muḥammad Kalābadhī, *Kitāb al-taʿarruf li-madhab ahl al-taṣawwuf*, and Abū Ṭālib al-Makkī, *Qūt al-qulūb fī muʿāmalāt al-maḥbūb wa-waṣf ṭarīq al-murīd ilā maqām al-tawḥīd*.

[6] This annihilation (*fanāʾ*) in early sufi theory meant the loss of consciousness of self or I-ness so that only the awareness of God remained. This subsequent state of remaining in God (*baqāʾ*) is often contrasted with *fanāʾ*. It is said that Abū Saʿīd al-Kharrāz (d. 286/899) was the first to elaborate the theory of *fanāʾ*. Later, especially in the Indian Naqshbandī tradition, this model reached its most developed form. Khwāja Mīr Dard (d. 1199/1785) discussed three consecutive annihilations: in the shaykh (*fanāʾ fī'l-shaykh*), in the Messenger (*fanāʾ fī'l-rasūl*), and in God (*fanāʾ fī'llāh*) while returning to the world involved three consecutive types of remaining: in God (*baqāʾ billāh*), in the Messenger (*baqāʾ fī'l-rasūl*), and in the shaykh (*baqāʾ fī'l-shaykh*). The latter two *baqāʾ*'s are new formulations by Mīr Dard. See Annemarie Schimmel, *Pain and Grace: A Study of Two Mystical Writers of Eighteenth-Century Muslim India*, pp. 70–71.

[7] Shādhilīs also describe their path in a similar fashion, e.g., as "Our beginning is their end." See ʿAbdullāh Nūr ad-Dīn Durkee, *Orisons*, p. 22.

ercises (*sulūk*) was correct credal dogma (*ʿaqīda*), which Sirhindī repeatedly stressed as necessary even before the performance of the ritual duties common to all Muslims. Such a synthesis of dogma, ritual, and mystical experience not only altered the concept of South Asian Muslim self-identity but, in retrospect, has had an impact on Muslim life in numerous other Islamic countries as well. Thus Aḥmad Sirhindī is still recognized by many as "the renewer of the second millennium."

Spiritual journeying in the Naqshbandī context involves an intensely close master-disciple relationship. Aspirants usually spend years performing devotional exercises meant to change sociopsychological habit patterns before embarking on such journeys. When embarking on the first spiritual journeys the spiritual mentor repeatedly instructs the novices to ignore visions or voices in order to proceed to an experience without attributes,[8] though the markers on the Path and the conceptual requisites remain clearly Islamic. The Naqshbandī does not become a religiocultural blank before embarking on the mystical quest. The Islamic prerequisites, creed and ritual, combine with the Mujaddidī cosmological paradigm to facilitate travel along the path and minimize the dangers confronting the unprepared traveler. For Naqshbandīs, this travel in more subtle ontological realms duplicates the path trodden by former prophets and advanced intimates of God; it is a return to the experiential sources of Islam. Culture influencing mystical experience is only part of the story;[9] Naqshbandī paradigms and Islamic culture have been significantly informed by mystical experience also.[10]

Unlike many other mystics, Naqshbandīs have not concerned themselves with a description of their mystical experiences per se.[11] Instead they have described the structure of the Mujaddidī universe and principles for travel on the Mujaddidī spiritual path as a paradigm or cognitive map for would-be travelers.

---

[8]Bahāʾuddīn Naqshband characterizes the very high stage of those who do spiritual journeying *(sayr)* without experiencing any attributes as the continual revelation *(kashf)* of Reality. See Muḥammad Pārsā, *Qudsiyya: Kalimāt-i Bahāʾuddīn Naqshband,* ed. Aḥmad Ṭāhirī ʿIrāqī, pp. 25–26, 139.

[9]Reports of mystical experiences generally reflect the mystic's previously acquired paradigms and cognitive patterns. For a discussion of these issues, see Steven T. Katz, "Language, Epistemology, and Mysticism." A sophisticated refutation of this constructivist approach is Donald Rothberg, "Contemporary Epistemology and the Study of Mysticism."

[10]See Carl Ernst, "Mystical Language and the Teaching Context in the Early Lexicons of Sufism."

[11]For philosophical attempts see Wayne Proudfoot, *Religious Experience,* and Huston Smith, "Is There a Perennial Philosophy?"

Mujaddidī literature, in the British Indian colonial period at least, is more concerned with introducing the concept of spiritual travel and elucidating how each aspirant can proceed on the Path. Although some scripture-centered non-sufi Muslims claim that Naqshbandī doctrine and practice deviate from the Islam of the Qur'ān and hadith,[12] Naqshbandīs assert that their practices most faithfully replicate the path of the Prophet's companions.

The direction Naqshbandīs travel in their inner journeys depends on which paradigm of God one uses. God is both transcendent and immanent. If God is perceived as a transcendent entity in the highest "heaven," then Plato's ontology applies in the Naqshbandī universe; in other words, something higher is subtler and closer to God, and what is lower is coarser and farther from God. If God is perceived as immanent—"We are nearer to him than his jugular vein" (Q. 50:16)—then Naqshbandīs supply a parallel model of concentric circles to represent spiritual travel where going towards the center means moving closer to God.[13] Sometimes Naqshbandīs combine these up-down and inner-outer concepts, visualizing the human microcosm as a series of sheaths or "bodies," the outer being the coarse physical body and the five other bodies as becoming progressively subtler. Naqshbandī spiritual journeying can be conceptualized either as upward-downward or as inward-outward.[14]

Exactly where Naqshbandīs go in their mystical travel is more difficult to determine.[15] They describe two kinds of traveling: one

---

[12]The necessity for a shaykh to mediate between God and the believer *(tawassul)* has been an issue of contention for centuries. See my "Charismatic Versus Scriptural Authority: Naqshbandī Response to Deniers of Mediational Sufism in British India."

[13]For diagrams depicting the Naqshbandī path by means of concentric circles, see Faqīrullāh Shikārpūrī, *Futūḥāt al-ghaybiyya*, pp. 195, 211, 224. Sufi levels of existence are represented in the same fashion in Muḥammad Dhawqī, *Sirr-i dilbarān*, p. 343.

[14]I prefer to represent Naqshbandī spiritual travel as a gyre going up the outside of a circular cone in a spiral fashion; as one goes upward, one goes inward at the same time.

[15]The journeying discussed here is "ascent and descent," imitating the Prophet who, like other prophets before him, is believed by Naqshbandīs to have traveled to higher realities and to have transmitted the revelatory message to his companions in addition to teaching them how to perform similar journeys. This is to be differentiated from equally inexplicable otherworldly revelatory journeys and the Platonic ascent/descent of the soul. See Ioan Culianu, *Psychanodia I: A Survey of the Evidence Concerning the Ascension of the Soul and Its Relevance*, p. 5. An overview of supramundane traveling is the late Ioan Culianu's *Out of This World: Otherworldly Journeys from Gilgamesh to Albert Einstein*, a collection of secondary literature on this subject.

in the outside world (*sayr-i āfāqī*) and the other inside oneself (*sayr-i anfusī*), although the latter includes the former.[16] For the Naqshbandīs, the inner world encompasses a much vaster realm than the outer—the outside world has eight stages and the inner world seventeen.[17] Wherever this journey takes place it is certainly not in the normal waking mind. Naqshbandīs, like many other mystics, do not even begin to travel until the mind is rendered completely free from thought.[18] Abandoning the three-dimensional Cartesian mind is a prerequisite for traveling in the fourth and higher dimensions.[19]

What part of the human being actually travels in these higher dimensions? Naqshbandīs and other sufis have developed a notion of a *laṭīfa* which has been variously translated as "subtle substance," "subtle body," and "subtle center." Functionally it can have all these meanings depending on context, but for spiritual travel "subtle body" works best as a model.[20] The corporeal body is the vehicle for travel in this world, but more subtle vehicles can be used in other worlds. For inner travel, there are five such vehicles, each progressively more subtle. The further one goes in toward the center and/or upward, the more subtle the vehicle one needs. Picture a ferry carrying a car with people in it. For traveling in water the boat is the vehicle for the medium of water, and upon landing the car becomes the vehicle for the medium of land. To enter a building the physical body is the vehicle and in dreams the astral vehicle operates. Whether this succession of subtle bodies described by Naqshbandīs is literal or metaphorical is unclear, but it nonetheless serves as a convenient model.

---

[16]Qādī Thanā'ullāh Pānīpatī, *Irshād al-ṭālibīn*, pp. 40–41; and Dhawqī, *Sirr-i dilbarān*, pp. 65–66.

[17]See the section on the contemplations in appendixes 2 and 3.

[18]One is reminded of Śri Ramana Maharshi's comment on the mind: "The mind is only a bundle of thoughts. The thoughts arise because there is the thinker. The thinker is the ego. The ego if sought will vanish automatically"; see *Talks With Sri Ramana Maharshi*, p. 160. Culianu continually describes out-of-this-world experiences as mental universes, their reality being in the mind of the explorer. See *Out of This World*, pp. 3–5. Surely this is true when they come back from certain travels and report their experiences. However, the "three-dimensional" mind as we know it does not exist in these "further" universes, which only are described as ineffable. Culianu's argument and conclusions are limited by not taking into account the spiritual methods used to achieve supramundane travels, so often designed to bypass the mind completely.

[19]For an informative discussion pertaining to the fourth dimension and the history of the concept, see Culianu, *Out of This World*, pp. 12–32.

[20]Note the discussion of "The Astral Body in Neoplatonism" in Proclus, *The Elements of Theology: A Revised Text*, pp. 313–21. Professor Carl Ernst kindly supplied this reference.

One does not casually undertake such a journey towards God. The beginning recollection exercise (*dhikr*) does not demand much from the aspirant and can be performed anywhere, but the advanced recollection exercises (*nafy wa-ithbāt*) and contemplations (*murāqabāt*) require near total solitude for an hour or two in the early morning or late evening. Not all adepts take the time or have the discipline to perform these advanced exercises in addition to the two hours or so involved in going to the mosque five times each day to perform ritual prayers.[21] Non-sufi Muslims have asked why the performance of ritual duties is not sufficient. Sufis through the ages have answered that ritual performance suffices for happiness in the next world, but a sufi desires to please God in order to become an intimate friend of God (*walī*) in this world. Intimacy requires additional effort.

Diligent performance of ritual duties provides the foundation for all other sufi practice, since it is believed to assist in transforming the ego or carnal soul (*nafs*), which has many different stages of perfection. Islamic ritual practices function to control the ego in its everyday fallen state, described as "the soul which incites to evil" (*al-nafs al-ammāra*). Yet sufis only consider ritual practice as a preparatory stage for those intending to turn continually toward God and concentrate totally on God. For those desiring spiritual perfection the soul must first become "the soul which blames itself for its own limitations" (*al-nafs al-lawwāma*), finally attaining perfection in a tranquil and obedient condition as the "tranquil soul" (*al-nafs al-muṭma'inna*).[22] Naqshbandīs assert that ritual performance may have eliminated the outward idol (*maʿbūd-i āfāqī*) like Lāt or ʿAzza, (the two well-known pre-Islamic gods worshipped by Arabs), but the desires of an uncontrolled *nafs* cause one to worship other than God within oneself (*maʿbūd-i anfusī*).[23] Anyone wanting to control the ego and presuming to achieve inner perfection, such as the Naqshbandīs, will learn about the subtle centers (*laṭā'if*, plural of *laṭīfa;* hereafter *laṭīfas*) and the sphere of contingent existence (*dā'ira-yi imkān*).[24]

---

[21]Naqshbandīs emphasized the need for each of the daily five prayers to be communal. Sirhindī, for example, stated that two cycles *(rakʿa)* of communal prayer are better than spending an entire night performing supererogatory prayer. See Sirhindī, *Maktūbāt*, 1.52.25. See also Zawwār Ḥusayn, *'Umdat al-sulūk*, p. 16. For Muslim men, communal prayer is normally only required once a week for Friday noon prayer.

[22]The Qur'ān mentions the *al-nafs al-ammāra* (Q. 12:53), *al-nafs al-lawwāma* (Q. 75:2), and *al-nafs al-muṭma 'inna* (Q. 89:27).

[23]Muḥammad 'Ināyatullāh, *Maqāmāt-i irshādiyya*, translated by Muḥammad Allāh Khān, *Maʿārif-i ʿ ināyatiyya*, pp. 223–24. Page numbers refer to the Urdu translation which includes valuable explanatory footnotes.

[24]Ibid., p. 238.

The Naqshbandī-Mujaddidī Universe

The entire Naqshbandī paradigm of spiritual travel is based upon the sufi development of a mystical physiology involving subtle centers, which in turn correspond with both Prophetic realities and distinct levels of the cosmos.[25] From the moment of initiation, the spiritual guide begins to activate each disciple's subtle entities, beginning a lifelong process of assisting the aspirant to attract divine grace/energy. Since no mystical experiences can occur without a suitable vehicle, the shaykh, by enlivening the disciple's *laṭīfas,* assists him or her to create the means for the journey.

Human beings, the most comprehensive beings of creation, contain the essence (*khulāṣa*) of the macrocosm in combination with the four elements of earth, air, water, and fire. Because they perceive these latter elements as real and necessary, humans imprison themselves in earthly matters and end up isolating themselves from God.[26] To correct this situation Naqshbandī shaykhs first teach newly initiated disciples about *laṭīfas.*

Disciples learn that spiritual centers correspond to defined places in the human body yet are not part of it because their noncorporeal nature is more subtle than the physical body.[27] The subtle centers of the soul (*nafs*) and the physical frame (*qālab*) are located in the world of creation (*ʿālam al-khalq*) below the throne (*ʿarsh*), while the world of divine command (*ʿālam al-amr*) above the throne contains the five jewels (*al-jawāhir al-khamsa*) or the five *laṭīfas:* the heart (*qalb*), spirit (*rūḥ*), mystery (*sirr*), arcanum (*khafī*),

---

[25]In the following discussion "Mujaddidī" refers to those practices and ideals originating with Sirhindī; "Naqshbandī" to practices before Sirhindī and ideals shared by Naqshbandīs whether before or after Sirhindī.

[26]Ibid., p. 223.

[27]These seven subtle centers from "coarse" to "fine" are the physical body *(qālab),* soul *(nafs),* heart, spirit, mystery, arcanum, and super-arcanum. Often the seven subtle centers are described in ten parts (see figure 9) with the four elements and *nafs* in the world of creation and the five subtle centers in the world of divine command. The four elements are contained in the *qālab.* According to the Naqshbandiyya-Mujaddidiyya of the nineteenth and twentieth centuries, the *qalb laṭīfa* is roughly three centimeters below the left nipple and a yellow light emanates from it; the *rūḥ laṭīfa* is the same distance below the right nipple with red light; the *sirr* is roughly three centimeters above the left nipple and toward the center of the chest emanating a white light; the *khafī* is in the same place on the right side with a black light; the *akhfā* emits green light from an area of the sternum; the *nafs* is located in the middle of the forehead; and the *qālab,* often considered to be the entire physical body, is centered on the top of the head. See ibid., pp. 244–45, and Abū'l-Ḥasan Zayd Fārūqī, *Manāhij al-sayr,* translated by Muḥammad Naʿīmullāh Khiyālī, *Madārij al-khayr,* pp. 32–33.

and super-arcanum (*akhfā*) (see figure 5). These latter five *laṭīfas*, considered to be lights pervading the body and receptors emanating divine energy (*fayḍ*), constitute the interior of the human being (*bāṭin-i insānī*), an inner body.[28] The specific correspondences between the human *laṭīfas* and God's names and attributes (*al-asmā' wa'l-ṣifāt*) allow divine emanations to reach human beings through the channels of *laṭīfas*.[29] Although this is a conceptual summary of what Naqshbandī shaykhs consider necessary for beginning disciples to know, it is not the whole story. *Laṭīfas* are not really subtle centers at all, but instead are subtle fields or subtle bodies.

The origin of the idea of subtle centers and cosmological correspondences in sufism comes from Junayd (d. 297/910), who apparently first cultivated *laṭīfas* in the human body,[30] and Junayd's contemporaries, such as Sahl at-Tustarī (d. 283/896), ʿAmr b. ʿUthmān al-Makkī (d. 297/909), and Ḥusayn b. Manṣūr al-Ḥallāj (martyred 309/922).[31] Abū ʿAbdurraḥmān as-Sulamī (d. 412/1021), Abū Ḥāmid al-Ghazzālī (d. 505/1111), and Shihābuddīn Abū Ḥafṣ ʿUmar as-Suhrawardī (d. 632/1234) further elaborated the concept of subtle entities.[32] From these brief descriptions the

[28]Ibid. See also Abū Saʿīd Dihlawī, *Hidāyat al-tālibīn*, translated by Ghulām Muṣṭafā Khān, *Jawāhir-i maẓhariyya wa-maẓāhir-i zawwāriyya*, p. 28.

[29]Muḥammad ʿInāyatullāh, *Maqāmāt-i irshādiyya*, p. 243. For these correspondences between the *laṭīfas* and the origins of *fayḍ*, see figure 6.

[30]The Shādhilīs, whose spiritual anatomy consists of seven *laṭīfas*, also count Junayd in their spiritual pedigree. For diagrams and bodily locations of these subtle centers in the Shādhilī lineage, see Durkee, *Orisons*, pp. 234, 322.

[31]Shāh Walīullāh confirms this in his *Alṭāf al-quds*, p. 72, cited in Marcia Hermansen, "Shāh Walī Allāh's Theory of the Subtle Centers *(laṭā'if)*: A Sufi Model of Personhood and Self-Transformation," p. 20. At-Tustarī mentions a subtle substance *(laṭīf)* giving life to the dense natural self and another subtle substance associated with the spiritual self. The latter subtle substance is from recollection of God *(dhikr)*. See Gerhard Böwering, *The Mystical Vision of Existence in Classical Islam: The Qur'ānic Hermeneutics of the Sūfī Sahl at-Tustarī (d. 283/896)*, pp. 244–45. ʿAmr al-Makkī conceived of the *laṭīfas* to be like veils wrapped in one another, e.g., the *nafs* in *qalb*, *qalb* in *rūḥ*, and *rūḥ* in *sirr*, which would be removed successively as one got closer to God. Louis Massignon, *La Passion de Husayn Ibn Mansūr Hallāj*, 4 volumes, 3:24; trans. Herbert Mason, *The Passion of Al-Hallaj: Mystic and Martyr of Islam*, 4 volumes, 3:17. Al-Ḥallāj has Muḥammad in the heavenly journey *(miʿrāj)* leaving one subtle covering *(laṭīfa)* of his soul for each heaven he passed through. See ibid., 1:54, n. 13 [English trans. 1:14, n. 78]. These latter interpretations would conceive of *laṭīfas* as subtle bodies or sheaths. Given the variety of interpretations of *laṭīfas* in various situations, I will use the term "subtle entity" as a generic term when the context is not more specific.

[32]Sulamī discusses (in ascending order) *nafs*, *qalb*, *sirr*, and *rūh*. See Roger Deladrière, "Les premiers Malâmatiyya: les gardiens du secret." Al-Ghazzālī discusses subtle entities of the *qalb*, *rūh*, and *nafs*. See his *Iḥyā' ʿulūm al-dīn* 3.3–5. Shihābuddīn Abū Ḥafṣ ʿUmar Suhrawardī discusses the subtle entities of *qalb*,

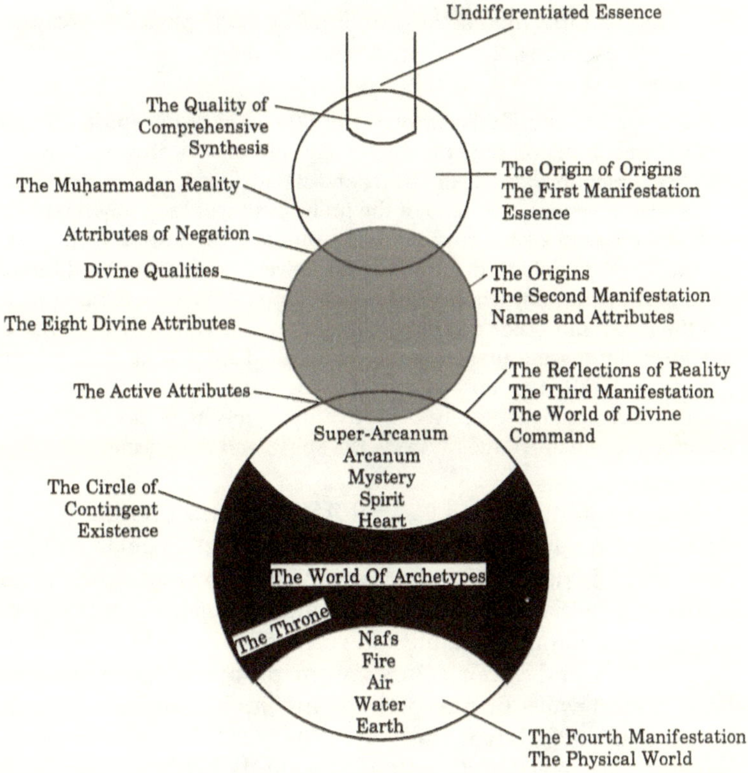

Figure 5. A model of Naqshbandī cosmology

idea of *laṭīfa* began in the ninth century as a generic subtle substance before being defined functionally as a subtle body. Two centuries later *laṭīfa* became a more localized subtle entity or organ associated with the human body.

The major conceptual development of *laṭīfas*, however, grows out of a Central Asian sufi lineage, the Kubrawiyya, whose founder-figure, Najmuddīn Kubrā (d. 618/1221), analyzed the inner morphology of the human body in terms of three subtle fields: the heart, spirit, and mystery.[33] Najmuddīn Rāzī (d. 654/1256), a disciple of Kubrā's, created a fivefold structure by adding

rūh, sirr, and *nafs* in his *Kitāb ʿawārif al-maʿārif*, pp. 443–57. Aḥmad al-Ghazzālī (d. 520/1126) discussed three worlds or stages (sing. *manzil*), *dil*, *rūḥ*, and *sirr*, through which the wayfarer passed; see Naṣrullāh Pūrjawādī, *Ṣulṭān-i ṭarīqat: sawānih zindagī wa-sharḥ-i athār-i Khwāja Aḥmad Ghazzālī*, p. 208. Some thinkers by that time had begun to associate these subtle entities with the world of divine command, although there was no consensus on their locations or relative subtleness.

[33]Najmuddīn Kubrā, *Die Fawā'ih al-ǧamāl wa-fawātiḥ al-ǧalāl des Naǧm ud-dīn al-Kubrā*, pp. 168–74. See the Arabic text, ibid., pp. 24, 27–28. The Kubrawiyya only

two other subtle fields: the intelligence (*'aql*) and the arcanum (*khafī*).[34] Describing this schema, Rāzī writes,

> . . . the tree of the body has grown from the seed of the spirit, and put forth in one direction the branches of the soul and its attributes, and in another direction those of the heart and its attributes. The leaves of the outer senses appear; the roots of the inner faculties reach down into the soil; the blossom of the mystery [*sirr*] unfolds; the unripe fruit of the arcane [*khafī*] sprints forth. . . . Thus the spirit . . . has acquired different tools and instruments that it did not previously possess. Among these are the inner and outer means of perception. . . . That which cannot be perceived by these [outer] five senses is called the World of Dominion [*'ālam-i malakūt*], the unseen world with its numerous degrees and stages. This world is perceived by five inner means of perception: the intelligence, the heart, the mystery, the spirit, and the arcane.[35]

As a transmitter of the Central Asian Kubrawī tradition, 'Alā'-uddawla Simnānī (d. 736/1336) extended Rāzī's pentad of inner perceptual fields to a sevenfold arrangement by adding the physical frame (*qālab*) and the super-arcanum (*akhfā*). Equipped with this schema, Simnānī established correspondences between these seven *laṭīfas* and seven colors, seven prophets, seven spiritual types, seven ways of interpreting the Qur'ān, and seven levels of the cosmos.[36] Muḥammad Pārsā (d. 822/1420), a successor of Bahā'uddīn Naqshband, defined the subtle fields in exactly the

---

associates the *laṭīfas* with the human body. From the limited material in the *Fawā'iḥ* it would be tenuous to define these as either subtle bodies or subtle centers.

[34]Marcia Hermansen notes that the fivefold structure of the *laṭīfas* parallels the Islamic adaptation of Greek medical theory *(ṭibb yunānī)* with its five inner and five outer senses. See her "Shāh Walī Allāh's Theory of the Subtle Centers," p. 7, where she analyzes Shāh Walīullāh's new theoretical synthesis of *laṭīfas*. Shāh Walīullāh in his *Tafhīmāt al-ilāhiyya* explains that the development of *laṭīfas* began with Adam when there were three spiritual centers: the heart, intelligence, and lower soul. In Muḥammad's time the higher *laṭīfas* of the spirit and mystery were awakened in the ideal human form. At the time of Ibn al-'Arabī (d. 638/1240) the potential of the arcanum *laṭīfa* was available to the human species. Finally, Shāh Walīullāh was selected by God to reveal two additional subtle centers: "the Philosopher's stone" *(ḥajar-i baht)* and "selfhood" *(anāniyya)*. See Hermansen, "Shāh Walī Allāh's Theory," p. 24. The *ḥajar-i baht* was already described by Ibn al-'Arabī as an essential point in the heart emanating a marvelous and perplexing light. See H.S. Nyberg, *Kleinere Schriften des Ibn al-'Arabī*, pp. 216–17, cited in Hermansen, "Shāh Walī Allāh's Theory," p. 15. To date no subsequent Naqshbandī writing indicates the use, theoretical or practical, of either of these last two subtle centers after Shāh Walīullāh's response to them.

[35]Najmuddīn Rāzī, *The Path of God's Bondsmen from Origin to Return*, p. 138 [additions mine].

[36]Henry Corbin, *En Islam Iranien*, 4 volumes, 3:275–355.

same order and with the same corresponding prophets as Simnānī had done.[37]

The Mujaddidīs then created their own synthesis of the sevenfold nature of the inner human being, but this was not a completely standardized system, in India at least, until the nineteenth century.[38] By that time each *laṭīfa* had become associated with a certain part of the body, and in sufi training, *laṭīfas* had become conceptualized as subtle centers. Some Mujaddidī shaykhs described the *laṭīfas* as a six-fold structure, with different positions for the *sirr, khafī, akhfā,* and *nafs* than those described by Mujaddidī shaykhs writing in the nineteenth century.[39]

---

[37]Compare ibid., p. 339, and Muḥammad Pārsā, *Tuḥfat al-sālikīn: taḥqīqāt Khwāja Muḥammad Pārsā,* p. 377. From lowest to highest: *qālab*/Adam, *nafs*/Noah, *qalb*/Abraham, *sirr*/Moses, *rūḥ*/David, *khafī*/Jesus, and *ḥaqqī*/Muḥammad. Each day of the week was also correlated to a subtle center. The "unity of witnessing" *(waḥdat al-shuhūd),* later emphasized by Aḥmad Sirhindī, is originally Simnānī's formulation. The early Kubrawiyya appears to share many ideas and practices with the Naqshbandiyya. Who developed these concepts and practices in Central Asia will remain an open question until more detailed research is done on the early history of these lineages. One preliminary study in this direction is Jamal Elias, *The Throne Carrier of God: The Life and Thought of ʿAlā' ad-dawla as-Simnānī.*

[38]Bāqībillāh discusses the seven subtle centers from *qālab* to *akhfā,* suggesting that the seven-*laṭīfa* system detailed by Sirhindī and standardized in the nineteenth century might not have originated with Aḥmad Sirhindī. See Bāqībillāh, *Kulliyāt-i Bāqībillāh,* p. 111.

[39]Faqīrullāh Shikārpūrī (d. 1195/1781), in the spiritual lineage of Ādam Banūrī, describes various six-*laṭīfa* systems. See Faqīrullāh's *Quṭb al-irshād,* pp. 565–66 and his *Futuḥāt al-ghaybiyya,* pp. 171–72. There is no mention of the *qālab.* Other shaykhs, including Faqīrullāh Shikārpūrī and other Naqshbandīs of Ādam Banūrī's lineage, located the *qalb* and *rūḥ* below the left and right nipples respectively, the *sirr* at the sternum, the *khafī* in the middle of the forehead between the eyes, the *nafs* under the *sirr* (under the navel), and the *akhfā* at the crown of the head. This sixfold system is described in Dhawqī, *Sirr-i dilbarān,* pp. 298–99, but not attributed to any particular sufi lineage. There is evidence that these locations of the *laṭīfas* were the ones Sirhindī used. See Nūr Aḥmad's note in *Maktūbāt-i Imām-i Rabbānī,* 1.34.95, n. 1, and Mīr Nuʿmān, *Risāla-yi sulūk,* p. 9. In the Mujaddidī system of *laṭīfas* often the *qālab,* representing the physical body composed of four elements, was not mentioned and classified instead as the four elements. Thus, in the same Mujaddidī system the terminology could indicate seven *laṭīfas,* six *laṭīfas* (and four elements), or ten *laṭīfas,* five in the world of creation (the four elements and the *nafs*) and five in the world of command. Occasionally there are references to the *nafs laṭīfa* being located below the navel where the Chinese Taoists locate the *tan t'ien.* See Muḥammad ʿUmar Bīrbalī, *Inqilāb al-ḥaqīqat,* p. 71. By the beginning of the twentieth century Abū'l-ʿUlā's lineage, a non-Mujaddidī Naqshbandī lineage incorporating Chishtī practices, designated the subnavel position as the location of the *nafs laṭīfa.* They had also designated a seventh subtle center as *naṣīrān-i Mahmūd.* See ʿAṭā' Ḥusayn, *Daqīqat al-sālikīn,* pp. 108–09. For this reference I am indebted to ʿAtā' Khurshīd, librarian at Aligarh University.

Although Mujaddidīs agree upon the correspondences between prophets and the individual *laṭīfas*, almost every shaykh ascribe different colors to each subtle center.[40] Sufis examining these different configurations of *laṭīfas* among Mujaddidīs stress that each shaykh describes what is revealed to him. All seemingly contradictory results are valid, just as the process of divergent independent legal judgments (*ijtihād*) of qualified jurisprudents are equally valid in the interpretation of Islamic law: all of these paths lead to the goal.[41] Until more Naqshbandī manuscripts concerning spiritual practices are discovered, it will be impossible to determine which shaykhs developed the present Mujaddidī system of subtle centers.

By the latter half of the eighteenth century two things are certain. First, the position and colors of *laṭīfas* were already in the process of being standardized, and, second, the overall Mujaddidī version of the human spiritual morphology had become firmly established.[42] This meant that each of the seven *laṭīfas*, which are receptors for divine energy that comes from more subtle cosmic realms, not only coincides with the human microcosm, but also corresponds to a prophet, a colored light, and (except for the *nafs* and *qālab*) a specific cosmic emanation (see figure 6).[43]

Compared to the established mystical physiology of Indian *chakra* systems and Chinese "elixir fields," the Mujaddidī system has a transitory, even experimental quality.[44] It is logical to think that the system of correspondences established and used by nine-

---

[40]The only constants were the colors themselves: red, yellow, green, black, white, and blue. For the Mujaddidī correspondences, which were standardized by the nineteenth century, see figure 6.

[41]Dhawqī, *Sirr-i dilbarān*, p. 299, and Faqīrullāh Shikārpūrī, *Quṭb al-irshād*, p. 566.

[42]Shikārpūrī, *Quṭb al-irshād*, p. 565, and Ghulām ʿAlī Shāh, *Maqāmāt-i maẓharī*, pp. 522–25.

[43]See also Henry Corbin, *L'homme de lumière dans le Soufism iranien;* translated by Nancy Pearson, *The Man of Light in Iranian Sufism.*

[44]The Hindu Yoga equivalent of *laṭīfas* is seven *chakras* (literally, wheels) located at the base of the spinal column, sacral plexus, navel, heart, throat, between the eyebrows, and the crown of the head. The Buddhists use the top four. See Mircea Eliade, *Yoga: Immortality and Freedom*, pp. 241–44. Contemporary Taoists, in addition to using a very intricate physiological system which maps the three currents of seed *(ching)*, breath *(ch'i)*, and spirit *(shēn)*, also distinguish an upper elixir field in the forehead, a middle one in the region of the heart *(chung tan t'ien)* and a lower elixir field below the navel *(chēng tan t'ien)*. See Erwin Rousselle, "Spiritual Guidance in Contemporary Taoism." Contemporary Naqshbandīs say that these chakras and elixir fields are related to the body. Only the *laṭīfas*, which are related to the spirit *(rūḥ)*, can effectively refine the carnal soul *(nafs)*.

<table>
<tr><th colspan="2">Laṭīfa</th><th colspan="2">Origin of fayḍ</th><th>Prophet</th><th>Color</th><th>Location</th></tr>
<tr><td colspan="2">super-arcanum (akhfā)</td><td colspan="2">the quality of comprehensive synthesis (shaʾn-i jamʿ)</td><td>Muḥammad</td><td>green</td><td>sternum</td></tr>
<tr><td colspan="2">arcanum (khafī)</td><td colspan="2">attributes of negation (ṣifāt-i salbiyya)</td><td>Jesus</td><td>black</td><td>above right breast</td></tr>
<tr><td colspan="2">mystery (sirr)</td><td colspan="2">divine qualities (shuʾūn-i dhatiyya)</td><td>Moses</td><td>white</td><td>above left breast</td></tr>
<tr><td colspan="2">spirit (rūḥ)</td><td colspan="2">the eight immutable divine attributes (ṣifāt-i thubūtiyya dhātiyya)</td><td>Abraham
Noah</td><td>red</td><td>below right breast</td></tr>
<tr><td colspan="2">heart (qalb)</td><td colspan="2">active attributes (ṣifāt-i fiʿliyya)</td><td>Adam</td><td>yellow</td><td>below left breast</td></tr>
<tr><td colspan="2">soul (nafs)</td><td rowspan="5">Origin in world of divine command</td><td>heart</td><td>-</td><td>-</td><td>middle of forehead</td></tr>
<tr><td rowspan="4">Physical frame (qalab)</td><td>fire</td><td>arcanum</td><td>-</td><td>-</td><td rowspan="4">crown of head</td></tr>
<tr><td>air</td><td>spirit</td><td>-</td><td>-</td></tr>
<tr><td>water</td><td>mystery</td><td>-</td><td>-</td></tr>
<tr><td>earth</td><td>super-arcanum</td><td>-</td><td>-</td></tr>
</table>

Figure 6. Nineteenth- and twentieth-century Mujaddidī correspondences of *laṭīfas*

teenth-century Indian Naqshbandīs is the result of generations of mystical activity over centuries of experimentation with subtle fields of the body. This might have been the case. But Faqīrullāh Shikārpūrī, explaining the different interpretations of the subtle centers' color and location, says, "Some say the five subtle centers of the world of command are not in the body nor outside of it; neither are they connected to it nor are they separate from it. The subtle centers envelop the entire body . . . their appearance depends on the differing capacities of those traveling on the path (*sālikīn*). Therefore, to make it easy for those traveling on the path some shaykhs established the *qalb* under the left breast, the *rūḥ* under the right breast, the *sirr* is above the *qalb* by a distance of four fingers' width toward the center of the chest . . . the *khafī* is above the *rūḥ* by a distance of four fingers' width, the *akhfā* is in the middle of the chest . . . and the *nafs* is in the head (*dimāgh*)."[45]

[45]Faqīrullāh Shikārpūrī, *Quṭb al-irshād*, p. 565. He does not mention which shaykhs first standardized the locations of the *laṭīfas*. Mīr Nuʿmān explains that in reality the *laṭīfas* have no exact places corresponding to specific places in the body; see *Risāla-yi sulūk*, p. 9.

From this report, it is clear that the concept of *laṭīfa* depends on the functional context.[46] In the Mujaddidī teaching environment the schema of *laṭīfas* as subtle centers is a heuristic device for the disciple to develop a subtle body or a subtle field with which to travel in the nonmaterial realms.[47] Simnānī has mentioned an acquired body (*al-badan al-muktasab*) which would fit this description.[48] In many respects it is analogous to the Buddhist tantric "diamond body" (Skr. *vajrakāya*). Simnānī described the acquired body composed of light as that which comes into being by partaking in divine effusions (*fuyūḍ*), just as the Naqshbandī subtle fields develop by receiving divine energy (*fayḍ*).[49]

Once the function of *laṭīfas* is ascertained, the next problem is deciding whether a *laṭīfa* is a "place" or a "subtle body." Mujaddidīs sometimes mention traveling in a certain *laṭīfa*. Simnānī postulated ten *laṭīfas* emanating from the Essence while discussing the subtle, acquired body moving through these *laṭīfas*.[50] Does this mean traveling in the vehicle of a subtle body or passing through subtle worlds beyond the material one, or both?[51] Given

[46]Relying only on the nineteenth- and twentieth-century *ma'mūlāt* literature and occasional discussions of *laṭīfas* in other contexts, which are oriented toward outsiders or novices, a reader would never know that a *laṭīfa* is anything but a subtle center with a specific, determined place in the human body.

[47]This concept is consistent with the advanced stage of *dhikr-i sulṭānī* necessary before traveling in the world of command and beyond, i.e., before beginning the *murāqabāt*. 'Abdulquddūs Gangōhī (d. 944/1537) of the Chishtī-Ṣabirī lineage also mentions *dhikr sultānī*. See Simon Digby, "'Abd al-Quddus Gangohi (1456–1537 A.D.): The Personality and Attitudes of a Medieval Indian Sufi," pp. 21–23. The concept of a subtle body is also implicit in the *hay'at-i waḥdānī*, a consolidation of all the *laṭīfas* formed in the advanced stages of *sulūk*, i.e., *kamālāt-i risāla*. Mujaddidīs do not explicitly mention a subtle body *(jism-i laṭīf)* but instead discuss progressively subtler sheaths. See Mīr Nu'mān, *Risāla-yi sulūk*, p. 118. In light of this ambiguity I translate a *laṭīfa* enveloping the body as a "subtle field."

[48]Corbin, *En Islam iranien*, 3.279, and Elias, *Throne Carrier*, p. 81.

[49]See 'Alā'uddawla Simnānī, "Khitām al-misk," p. 73.

[50]Such a situation indicates the necessity functionally to define the term *laṭīfa* as thoroughly as possible. Jamal Elias's consistent translation of *laṭīfa* as "subtle substance" becomes strained when a "subtle bodily substance" is traveling through other "subtle substances," e.g., Elias, *Throne Carrier*, p. 89. Given that *laṭīfas* do not have mass or occupy three-dimensional space it is even more problematic to define *laṭīfa* as a type of "substance."

[51]Faqīrullāh Shikārpūrī mentions traveling in all five *laṭīfas* in the world of divine command and then going to their origins. See his *Maktūbāt-i Faqīrullāh*, pp. 241–42. For the Mujaddidīs the evidence supports the concept of subtle body as static concept, i.e., as the disciple eliminates veils to receive more light, he or she enters an enlightened existence *(wujūd-i nūrānī)*, presumably closer to God. See ibid., p. 236. As a dynamic concept, i.e., body as vehicle, two clear transitions in spiritual exercises indicate a subtler body has been formed: when one can per-

no consistent answers to this question in sufi sources, a working hypothesis might be that the body or sheath a human being occupies at a given moment determines the corresponding ontological reality. By progressively developing these bodies and/or learning how to move between them at will, a person can experience different ontological realities. In this way access to various levels of the cosmos are inside each human being; a person visits them at will by transferring "inside" from subtle body to subtle body: a person in a third-dimensional physical body travels in the third-dimensional physical world as a person in a fourth-dimensional body would travel in the fourth-dimensional world.

Such a model of subtle bodies could explain many other phenomena not explicable by existing paradigms. A well-developed subtle body could be the prerequisite for an Uwaysī experience, i.e., the meeting of the subtle body (*ruḥāniyat*) of a deceased shaykh and the still-embodied sufi with well-developed *laṭīfas*.[52] Indeed, the special connection between the disciple and shaykh (*rābiṭa*), often confirmed by the disciple seeing the shaykh in dreams, could be explained as another instance of an interaction between subtle bodies.

Whether these *laṭīfas* are conceived as a collective subtle body or as individual subtle centers, they not only act as interfaces between the created world and more refined ontological stages, but they are themselves manifestations of these more rarefied cosmological realms. It is through these subtle fields associated with the human body that the human microcosm can be said to contain the macrocosm.

Muslim philosophers have started from the assumption that before creation there was only God in His absolute, undifferentiated existence.[53] Then, according to the hadith, "I was a hidden

---

form *sulṭān-i dhikr*, and when one has consolidated the *laṭīfas* in the *hay'at-i waḥdānī*.

[52]There also may be a relationship between this subtle body and Simnānī's "invisible teacher" *(ustād-i ghaybī)*. See Corbin, *En Islam Iranien*, 3.290–308. Uwaysī phenomena would also be included in this category.

[53]Much of the terminology and cosmological structure for Naqshbandī cosmology has been derived from the school of Ibn al-ʿArabī. See Fakhruddīn ʿIrāqī, *Divine Flashes*, pp. 6–17; and William C. Chittick, "The Five Divine Presences: From al-Qūnawī to al-Qayṣarī." In Persian this undifferentiated existence is described by such terms as *ʿayn-i wujūd-i muṭlaq*, *wājib-i wujūd*, *ʿayn-i dhāt*, *aḥadiyat*, and *wujūd-i ʿamm*. See Faqīrullāh Shikārpūrī, *Maktūbāt-i Faqīrullāh*, pp. 27–30. Faqīrullāh also includes *lāhūt* in this category (some authors place it in the circle of the first manifestation), citing the origin of the word in an enigmatic expression "Not Him, You" *(Lā huwa, anta)*; see ibid., p. 30. In Naqshbandī literature, the

treasure wanting to be known, so I created the world"—God metaphorically created a reflection of His manifestations through His divine breath, the *nafas al-Raḥmān*.[54] Annemarie Schimmel writes, "The pure Essence was as if it had held its 'breath' until it could no longer do so—and the world appeared as *nafas al-Raḥmān*."[55] Aḥmad Sirhindī, following the philosophy of ʿAlāʾuddawla Simnānī, declared an existential difference between the "Breather" and the exhaled breath, defining creation as that "present outside God" (*mawjūd fī khārij*). For this school of thought, everything humans can perceive and understand is from God and outside Him; the originating agency is hidden (*makhfī*).[56]

The primary manifestation (*taʿayyun-i awwal*) of the Essence, the most subtle of all created realms, is the source of divine energy for the super-arcanum, arcanum, mystery, and spirit *laṭīfas*.[57] Functioning as a bridge (*barzakh*) between the absolute, undifferentiated Essence and creation is the "quality of comprehensive synthesis" (*shaʾn-i jāmiʿ*).[58] All divine energy from God emanates via this portal in the cosmic order to the rest of creation. In addition, the super-arcanum *laṭīfa*, associated with Muḥammad, receives its divine grace directly from the quality of comprehensive synthesis. This circle of the first manifestation also contains the

---

undifferentiated Essence is associated with *lā taʿayyun, dhāt-i baht, ḥubb-i ṣirf,* and *ghayb-i muṭlaq*. The most complete and concise discussion of the ranks of existence in the *wujūdī* sufi macrocosm, originally elaborated by Ibn al-ʿArabī, is Dhawqī's *Sirr-i dilbarān*, pp. 340–57. For the Naqshbandī nuances to this system, see Zawwār Ḥusayn, *ʿUmdat al-sulūk*, pp. 231–343, in addition to the more scholarly treatment in *Maktūbāt-i Faqīrullāh* cited above.

[54]Note the hadith: "I feel the breath of the Merciful coming from Yemen." See Badīʿuzzamān Furūzānfar, *Aḥādīth-i mathnawī*, p. 83. This hadith has often been interpreted as Muḥammad recognizing Uways al-Qaranī's presence, although the two had never physically met.

[55]Annemarie Schimmel, *Mystical Dimensions*, p. 268.

[56]Faqīrullāh Shikārpūrī, *Maktūbāt-i Faqīrullāh*, pp. 27–30. This philosophy is often described as testimonial unity *(tawḥīd-i shuhūdī)* or unity of vision *(waḥdat al-shuhūd)* as distinct from what Ibn al-ʿArabī's interpreters term "existential unity" *(tawḥīd-i wujūdī)* or "unity of existence" *(waḥdat al-wujūd)*. These philosophies can be correlated with spiritual practice and types of mystical experience.

[57]This primary manifestation is also known as the "exalted pen" *(qalam-i ʿalā)*, the spirit of Muḥammad *(rūḥ-i Muḥammadī)*, and the first Intellect *(ʿaql al-awwal)* with its primary aspect *(ʿitibār)* being love *(ḥubb)*. See Dhawqī, *Sirr-i dilbarān*, pp. 282–83, and Zawwār Ḥusayn, *ʿUmdat al-sulūk*, p. 207. Naqshbandīs refer to travel in this first manifestation as traveling in the essence *(dhāt)*, i.e., the relative essence which is distinct from the Absolute, undifferentiated Essence.

[58]It is also called the "quality of exalted knowledge," *(shaʾn al-ʿilm)* which is associated with Muḥammad. See Sirhindī, *Maktūbāt*, 1.260.75. See also 1.287.62, where the "quality of comprehensive synthesis" takes on the "color" of the quality of exalted knowledge.

"Muḥammadan reality" (*ḥaqīqat-i Muḥammadī*), the attributes of negation (*ṣifāt-i salbiyya* or *ṣifāt-i tanzīhiyya*) transmitting divine energy to the arcanum *laṭīfa* associated with Jesus, the "essential qualities" (*shu'ūn-i dhātiyya*) which channel divinely emanating grace to the mystery *laṭīfa* under the auspices of the prophet Moses, and the eight immutable divine attributes (*ṣifāt-i thubūtiyya dhātiyya*) that transmit divine energy to the subtle center of the spirit associated with Abraham and Noah.[59] Divinely emanating grace is distributed to creation via the primary manifestation of the Essence. In creation the source of this blessing is believed to be mediated through Muḥammad; indeed all other prophets receive their divine energy and grace through him.[60]

The second manifestation (*ta'ayyun-i thānī*) contains God's names and attributes (*al-asmā' wa'l-ṣifāt*) in addition to the active attributes (*ṣifāt-i fi'liyya*) which direct divine energy to the subtle center of the heart associated with the prophet Adam. Naqshbandīs refer to travel in this manifestation as travel in the names and attributes. In the third manifestation, commonly called the "world of divine command" (*'ālam al-amr*), shapes of essences with corresponding attributes begin to arise. This is also called the world of angels (*'ālam-i malā'ika*) or the world of sovereignty (*'ālam-i malakūt*). Five *laṭīfa*s are located in this realm. The lower limit of this third manifestation is the world of image-exemplars (*'alam-i mithāl*) which serves as an intermediary zone between the world of divine command and the world of corporeal bodies (*'ālam-i ajsām*), the fourth manifestation. The upper limit of the corporeal world is the Throne (*'arsh*) below which are the subtle center of the *nafs*, the elements, and the world of humans, animals, plants, and minerals.[61]

The composite nature of the human being is represented by the circle of contingent existence (*dā'ira-yi imkān*), which includes the world of divine command, the world of image-exemplars, the

---

[59]See figures 5 and 7. The eight divine attributes are knowledge *('ilm)*, life *(ḥayāt)*, power *(qudrat)*, will *(irāda)*, speech *(kalām)*, hearing *(sam')*, sight *(baṣar)*, and origination *(takwīn)*. See Muḥammad 'Ināyatullāh, *Maqāmāt-i irshādiyya*, p. 252, n. 1. These correspond to Alā'uddawla Simnānī's conception of essential attributes, except for origination, which Simnāni replaced with wisdom *(ḥikma)*. See Elias, *Throne Carrier*, p. 65.

[60]See appendixes 2 and 3.

[61]See figure 7. In Qur'ān commentaries, e.g., that of aṭ-Ṭabarī, the *'arsh* and *kursī* are related to the *qalb* and *sirr*. See Muḥammad Ali Amir-Moezzi, *Le Guide Divine dans le Shi'isme Originel* trans. David Streight, *The Divine Guide in Early Shi'ism: The Sources of Esotericism in Islam*, p. 177, n. 261. Dārā Shikūh describes the four worlds of the spiritual wayfarer; see Bikrama Jit Hasrat, *Dārā Shikūh: Life and Works*, pp. 125–28.

Throne, and the upper reaches of the corporeal world, i.e., the heavens. In this realm of contingent existence there is no end or zenith, since a circle has no limits. Here the immediacy of God's command operates and is separated from the corporeal world by a world of image-exemplars. The world of divine command refers to God's creation, i.e., "If God decrees something He just says 'Be!' and it is" (Q. 3:47). It is in this circle of contingent existence that most sufi activity takes place. Few reach the upper realms beyond the world of divine command.

Mujaddidīs begin by activating the five *laṭīfas* of the world of divine command and complete the advanced stages of their journey in the world of corporeal bodies. In this fashion, Mujaddidīs follow the path of the prophets who have passed beyond the sphere of lesser intimacy to God (*wilāyat-i ṣughrā*) and beyond the names and divine attributes to greater intimacy with God (*wilāyat-i kubrā*). After this "climb" (*ʿurūj*) they return to the corporeal world for the propagation of their prophetic message. Paradoxical as it might first appear, prophethood is associated with the perfections of the corporeal world instead of being purely a function of intimacy with God.[62]

Mujaddidīs say other sufis begin their spiritual journey in the created world and finish the journey in the world of divine command, experiencing only lesser intimacy with God (*wilāyat-i ṣughrā*). Even though Mujaddidīs define further stages beyond the world of divine command, these domains still exist far from the reality of the first manifestation. Associating *wilāyat-i kubrā* and the prophetic path with the path of the Companions, Mujaddidīs distinguish themselves from other sufis who are said to have stopped traveling long before achieving this greater intimacy with God. Careful to acknowledge the ontological difference between advanced seekers and prophetic perfection, Mujaddidīs emphasize following the path of the Companions, thereby conforming to Sunnī credal dogma which affirms that prophets are qualitatively superior to non-prophets.

In this way, Naqshbandīs define a hierarchy of mystical experience. Think of a paradoxical M. C. Escher picture. The apparently "higher" activities of the world of divine command are "the

[62]Muḥammad ʿInāyatullāh, *Maqāmāt-i irshādiyya*, pp. 147–48. According to the Naqshbandīs, other sufis not following the prophetic path remain relatively close to God and never return to communicate their experiences except in the form of ecstatic utterances. Their way, the way of the mystics, is approaching God through supererogatory practices *(qurb al-nawāfil)* while the much higher state for the Naqshbandīs is achieving proximity by performing legally prescribed actions *(qurb al-farāʾid)*, the way of the Prophet; see Schimmel, *Pain and Grace*, pp. 74–75.

stairs," leading ontologically upward toward the perfections of the (apparently lower) created world. Following the path of the prophets, the sufi on the spiritual path (*ṭarīqa*) realizes the reality (*ḥaqīqa*) of the Essence in the primary manifestation of the Essence and continues onward to the realm of the shariʿa, the corporeal world. From their definition of prophethood, Naqshbandīs ontologically subordinate both the sufi path and realization of Reality to complete fulfillment of the shariʿa. Cosmologically this is a Naqshbandī expression of Sunnī credal dogma: any prophet is by definition more intimate, and therefore superior, to any non-prophet who is only relatively intimate with God.[63] Thus, Naqshbandīs, even perfected shaykhs, are always ontologically distinct from prophets, endeavoring to follow the Prophetic path as the Companions had done.

Divinely emanating grace (*fayḍ*) is the "enabling energy" sufis utilize to connect the human microcosm through the *laṭīfas* to other parts of the macrocosm and actually travel.[64] Electricity provides an appropriate metaphor for this divine energy, for just as the modern world could not function without an abundant supply of energy, Naqshbandīs declare that divine grace from God sustains all earthly life.[65] Naqshbandīs can account for this divine energy to about the same extent as physicists can tell us what electricity really is.[66] Both electricity and *fayḍ* have been described having the properties of light. As electricity has been "explained" as a flow of electrons, *fayḍ* has been experienced as rain or as subtle rays.[67] In the same fashion that physicists give approximate

---

[63]For a discussion of the early formulations differentiating *awliyā*ʾ and prophets, see Michel Chodkiewicz, *Sceau de Prophets: Prophétie et sainteté dans la doctrine d'Ibn Arabī.*

[64]The Neoplatonic background of *fayḍ* is discussed in the article "Faiḍ," in Tj. de Boer, *Supplement to the Encyclopaedia of Islam.* In the Hindu tradition there is a similar phenomenon, *shaktipāt,* transmitted during initiation where "the guru's vibrational substance is said to enter the disciple." See Elizabeth Lassell Hallstrom, "My Mother, My God: Ānandamayī Mā (1896–1982)," p. 292. Occasionally the word *fayḍ* is supplemented with the Persian *barakat* (Arabic *baraka*) in such phrases as *fayḍ wa-barakat. Baraka* usually has a meaning of "auspiciousness" or "well being." See Joseph Chelhod, "La baraka chez les Arabes ou l'influence bienfaisante du sacré."

[65]Abū Saʿīd Dihlawī, *Hidāyat-i ṭālibīn,* p. 52.

[66]Twentieth-century Naqshbandīs often explained aspects of their practice in terms of modern science and technology. Agehananda Bharati notices how "gadgetry language is now part of the religious homiletic," citing a Ramakrishna monk who declared "Swamiji is an electric powerhouse." See "The Hindu Renaissance and Its Apologetic Patterns," p. 282.

[67]It also has been described as the descending of lights. See Bīrbalī, *Inqilāb al-ḥaqīqat,* p. 19. Words using the verbal root "f = y = d" are found nine times in

(and paradoxical) models to explain electricity, Naqshbandīs account for the "spiritual electricity" they experience. Theoretical understanding is not necessary to benefit from either electricity or *fayḍ*. Engineers concentrate on the generation and manipulation of electricity just as Naqshbandī shaykhs focus their interest on the practicalities of attracting and transmitting divine energy. Naqshbandī spiritual methods and the spiritual path itself have been formulated and elaborated according to the concept and phenomenon of divinely emanating grace.

Mujaddidīs say divine energy originates with God and has diverse forms emanating from God's names and attributes. Sirhindī describes two kinds of *fayḍ*, general and particular. General *fayḍ* comes from the attributes (*ṣifāt*) and is responsible for created life, while special *fayḍ* deals with faith (*īmān*), gnosis (*maʿrifa*), intimacy with God (*wilāya*), and prophethood (*nubūwa*).[68] The difference between these two types of divine grace is that only those Muslims who are intimate with God, namely the *awliyāʾ*, receive the special, particular *fayḍ*. This is a significant difference. As Sirhindī puts it, "the arrival of *fayḍ* to the Presence (S) [Muḥammad] having the rank of perfect intimacy (*wilāyat*) to God is from the Essence (*dhāt*). It is not by means of anything else, whether essential qualities (*shuʾūnāt*) or any other entity outside of the Essence. Therefore the Essence's emanation (*tajallī-yi dhātī*) has become special to him [Muḥammad] and all his [Muḥammad's] followers. When they take *fayḍ* from his way, they also profit from this [Muḥammad's] station (*maqām*). Others, having intermediate links of the attributes (*ṣifāt*) . . . [which are like] an impregnable barrier falling between [them and *fayḍ* from the Essence]. [Receiving *fayḍ* from] the manifestation of attributes becomes their appointed lot."[69]

---

the Qurʾān with the general meaning of God's "pouring forth" or "giving." The root "f = y = d" has a meaning of "pouring water." Grand unified theories of the universe of the 1980s propose that electricity be interpreted as a force from the fourth dimension, that higher dimensions of space can be wrapped in tiny particles, and that electromagnetism be conceived as four-dimensional gravity. Here we have some scientific parallels to what Naqshbandīs call *fayḍ*. See Paul Davies, *Superforce: The Search for the Grand Unified Theory of Nature,* cited in Ioan Culianu, *Out of This World: Other Worldly Journeys from Gilgamesh to Albert Einstein,* p. 22.

[68]Sirhindī, *Maktūbāt*, 1.287.61. Nūr Aḥmad, the editor and commentator of this edition of the *Maktūbāt*, states that the substitutes (*abdāl*) mediate general *fayḍ* and the pole of guidance (*quṭb al-irshād*) mediates special *fayḍ*. See ibid., n. 4 and 5. Much of this discussion of *fayḍ* is reproduced in Urdu. See Zawwār Ḥusayn, *ʿUmdat al-sulūk*, pp. 204–06.

[69]Sirhindī, *Maktūbāt*, 1.287.63.

In Naqshbandī discourse, this "impregnable barrier" is expressed in terms of the Prophetic hadith describing seventy thousand veils of light and darkness separating humans from God.[70] These veils act as a medium enabling God's grace to reach creation. Naqshbandīs believe that if these veils did not exist, created beings would be destroyed by the intensity of God's "face."[71] Mujaddidīs say that only for non-Muslims are these veils "impregnable"; for them the veils of darkness are manifested in one of God's names, "the one leading astray" (*al-muḍill*). Muslims, on the other hand, are veiled by light expressed in another name of God, "the guide" (*al-hādī*).[72] This is one more example of cosmology reflecting credal dogma, which Sirhindī and his followers apply strictly to define the Muslim community in India.[73] Correct dogmatic affirmations remain a prerequisite to embarking on the Naqshbandī-Mujaddidī path; divine grace (*nūr-i baṭinī*) is blocked if one's credal affirmations do not correspond point by point to the creed of Abū Ḥanīfa.[74]

For the aspirant on the path, special divine energy is received via human *laṭīfa*s. The shaykh reflects and focuses this emanating grace to hasten the disciple's progress.[75] Starting with the subtle center of the heart, the disciple concentrates on receiving divine

---

[70]Furūzānfar, *Aḥādīth-i mathnawī*, pp. 50–51, 142.

[71]Zawwār Ḥusayn, *'Umdat al-sulūk*, pp. 204–06.

[72]Ibid. Note the hadith, "First God created my light which was created from God's light and the believers *(mu'minūn)* are from my light," cited in Sirhindī, *Maktūbāt*, 3.122.127, and Furūzānfar, *Aḥādīth-i mathnawī*, pp. 113–14.

[73]The supremacy of Muḥammad and (by extension) Islam is clearly stated by Sirhindī, who, after declaring Muḥammad to be the first appearance in creation and the reality of realities, says, "This meaning is that other realities, whether the realities of the blessed prophets or realities of the great angels, are just reflections [of Muḥammad's reality] . . . For a person to arrive at the goal, [having traversed the distance] between the rest of the realities [other than Muḥammad's reality] and God the most exalted and sublime, is impossible without the mediation of Muḥammad (S)"; see Sirhindī, *Maktūbāt*, 3.122.127.

[74]Jaipūrī, *Mi'yār al-sulūk*, p. 172. Note also Najmuddīn Rāzī's explanation of how spiritual light can be blocked by certain actions of the body, hence the necessity to act in accordance with the shari'a. See Herman Landoldt's introduction to Nūruddīn 'Abdurraḥmān Isfarāyanī's *Kashf al-asrār*, trans. Hermann Landolt, *Le révélateur des mystères*, p. 59. For a western historical analysis of the early development of Muslim credal dogmatics, see A. J. Wensinck, *The Muslim Creed: Its Genesis and Historical Development*, and Josef van Ess, *Theologie und Gesellschaft im 2. und 3. Jahrhundert Hidschra: Eine Geschichte des religiösen Denken im frühen Islam*. See also 'Abdulḥaqq Dihlawi's *Takmīl al-īmān*. A study incorporating an analysis of credal dogma and modern conflicting Sunnī orthodoxies is a desiratum for Islamic studies.

[75]When the shaykh focuses this *fayḍ* to benefit others it is called *tawajjuh* (literally concentration) or *taṣarruf*.

energy in each *laṭīfa* in turn: spirit, mystery, arcanum, super-arcanum, carnal soul, and physical frame. As Muḥammad is "seal of the prophets," so the subtle center associated with Muḥammad, the *akhfā*, is the most sublime and most inclusive. In the Mujaddidī system a prophet governs each subtle center and mediates divine energy from a certain reality (*ḥaqīqa*) in the cosmos. A disciple's station (*maqām*) exists under the foot of a certain prophet, so a beginner working on the heart is "under the foot of Adam," that is, the disciple receives special divinely emanating grace from Adam.[76]

Muḥammad mediates divine energy to all other prophets. Likewise, the disciple's goal is to go far enough along the path to receive the direct connection of divine grace from Muḥammad.[77] For example, when the disciple waits for divine energy to go into the *akhfā*, the shaykh instructs the disciple to visualize all the Naqshbandī shaykhs of the chain going back to Muḥammad as if they were in front of this subtle center.[78] In this fashion, there is a correspondence between the human microcosm, the spiritual genealogy, and cosmology—all of which coincide on one vital point: the supremacy of Muḥammad in the created world.

Naqshbandī-Mujaddidī Spiritual Practices

Naqshbandīs, like other sufis, realize that there are many paths to God but have declared their path (*ṭarīqa*) to be the "closest."[79] More than most other sufi lineages, Naqshbandīs acknowledge

[76]Muḥammad 'Ināyatullāh, *Maqāmāt-i irshādiyya*, pp. 241–43. See figure 6 for the correspondences between prophets and the other *laṭīfas*. When someone is under the foot of a prophet, according to Faqīrullāh Shikārpūrī, it means that "the person intimate with God *(walī)* will receive the inner and outer knowledge, occurrences, visions, and states that are special to that prophet by means of his [the Prophet's] help and cooperation." See Faqīrullāh, *Maktūbāt-i Faqīrullāh*, p. 239.

[77]Zawwār Ḥusayn, *'Umdat al-sulūk*, pp. 205–09.

[78]Ibid., p. 288.

[79]Sirhindī, *Maktūbāt*, 1.131.9–10. Najmuddīn Kubrā uses the same words to describe the Kubrawī *ṭarīqa*. See Kubrā, *Fawā'iḥ*, p. 285. The spiritual path, the way of proceeding along the path, and the methods for this journey are conveniently expressed in the term *sayr wa-sulūk*, which has been amply described in Naqshbandī literature. One of the earliest summaries in a Western language is Heinrich Fleischer's "Über die farbigen Lichterscheinungen der Sufi's." Michel Chodkiewicz provides a brief summary of Naqshbandī spiritual techniques in his "Quelques aspects des techniques spirituelles dans la *ṭarīqa* Naqshbandiyya," pp. 69–82. Qādirī practices in India have many parallels with those of the Naqshbandīs; see Hasrat, *Dārā Shikūh*, pp. 72–74, where he mentions *sulṭān al-adhkār*.

the necessity of following the shariʿa, but they also claim that merely piously following the outward dictates of the shariʿa by itself rarely allows one to arrive near God. There are occasional accounts of a shaykh who, upon meeting such a pious person, immediately takes him close to God, but almost always the person ends up being so divinely inspired (*majdhūb*, literally, attracted by God) that he is unable to function in society.[80] The second path, the path of asceticism, characterized by extensive fasting, performance of spiritual exercises, and solitary retreats, enabled many to purify the heart and subdue the *nafs*. These methods, particularly exemplified by ascetics and sufis during the first three centuries of Islam, enabled more aspirants to arrive close to God than did the path of piety, but still very few achieved their goal. Najmuddīn Kubrā describes the limitations of this method: "Ibn Manṣūr [al-Ḥallāj] once asked Ibrāhīm al-Khawwāṣ in which stage (*maqām*) of mystical practice he was. Ibrāhīm answered, 'For thirty years I have been in the station of complete trust in God' (*tawakkul*). Ibn Manṣūr replied, 'You have spent your life in the edifice of the inner self; where are you with respect to annihilation (*fanā*ʾ) in God?' "[81]

From a Naqshbandī perspective, other sufis spend their time on the sufi path traveling in the created world (*sayr-i āfāqī*) to end up finally in the world of divine command. In contrast, Naqshbandīs, in the process of activating the *laṭīfas*, begin in the world of divine command where *sayr-i āfāqī* ends. By God's attraction (*jadhba*) they proceed to travel within themselves (*sayr-i anfusī*) on the path, again demonstrating the Naqshbandī practice of "including the end in the beginning" (*indirāj al-nihāya fi'l-bidāya*).[82]

---

[80]Jaipūrī, *Miʿyār al-sulūk*, p. 128. One behavioral pattern they share in common is being subject to unpredictable, epileptic-like seizures.

[81]Kubrā, *Fawāʾiḥ*, p. 285 [comments mine]. *Tawakkul* was the eighth of ten stations on the classical sufi path. See Annemarie Schimmel *Mystical Dimensions*, pp. 109–30. The most detailed exposition of *tawakkul* is Benedikt Reinert, *Die Lehre vom Tawakkul in der klassischen Sufik*. The Naqshbandīs put all the stations except the last (contentment or *riḍā*) in the realm of the created world. The path through the stations is appropriate for a certain type of traveler who is attracted by God, *sālik-i majdhūb*, who has to purify his or her *laṭīfas* in the created world before proceeding to the world of divine command. This is the common disciple (*murīd*, literally, one desiring) on the path. The Naqshbandīs, who start in the world of divine command, bypass these ten stations completely. Naqshbandīs call this type of aspirant "an attracted one who is traveling" (*majdhūb-i sālik*).

[82]Pānīpatī, *Irshād al-ṭālibīn*, pp. 40–41. The concept of the end being included in the beginning is often used to describe the uniqueness of the Naqshbandī path. The concept of *jadhba* at the beginning of the path being a quicker way to the goal is also expressed by Najmuddīn Kubrā. See Kubrā, *Fawāʾiḥ*, p. 285.

Naqshbandīs say this third path is not only safe but allows more people to arrive near God than any other path.

A few spiritually gifted people travel on the quickest path, the "path of attraction" (*ṭarīq-i jadhba*) through the intermediary of an Uwaysī guide. This path shortcuts the much longer way of traversing the path (*ṭarīq-i sulūk*) without *jadhba* and effectively eliminates any initiatory chain between the person and Muḥammad. A promising disciple who has a tendency to experience *jadhba* easily, however, usually does not have an Uwaysī guide but travels along the sufi path very quickly compared to others. Such a person is designated by Naqshbandīs as "an attracted one who is traveling" (*majdhūb-i sālik*).[83] Naqshbandīs define those exceptionally talented individuals in the spiritual fast lane who only need a very short time to arrive close to God as "those desired by God" (sing. *murād*).[84] Carl Vett interviewed one of these people, asking him what he experienced when he went into ecstasy. Answering that he could not describe it, he said, "It is as if I were seized with a fever. It goes through me like fire. The power of the sheikh seizes me. The farther away I am from the *tekké* [Turkish word for sufi lodge] the more powerfully I feel it. Once I was sent to Smyrna, but I had to come back very soon. At that distance I felt his power so strongly that I could not endure it. [These sensations] cannot be called pleasant, neither can they be called unpleasant. It is a though I were taken possession of by stronger powers that streak through my body like fire and move it without asking the permission of my will. It is as though I were carried into the heights."[85]

There are two kinds of intimacy with God on the Naqshbandī path: lesser and greater. The first portion of the cyclical fourfold Mujaddidī path is "going to God" (*sayr ila'llāh*), which describes the entry into the world of divine command or the reflections of God's names and attributes (*ẓilāl-i asma' wa-ṣifāt*) and is associated with "lesser intimacy" (*wilāyat-i ṣughrā*). Mujaddidīs would place most sufi shaykhs at this stage of intimacy with God. Naqshbandī disciples are often given permission to teach at this

[83]ʿIzzuddīn Maḥmūd Kāshānī (d. 735/1335) and Abū Ḥafṣ as-Suhrawardī (d. 632/1234) both discuss the terms *majdhūb-i sālik*, one who starts out in *jadhba* as a beloved of God and then traverses the stages of the path, and *sālik-i majdhūb*, one who starts out traversing the path as a lover of God before experiencing *jadhba*. See Naṣrullāh Pūrjawādī, *Sulṭān-i ṭarīqat*, p. 231.

[84]This is in contrast to an ordinary disciple (*murīd*) who desires God. Some individuals become intimate with God after only one meeting with the shaykh. See Abū'l-Asfār ʿAlī Muḥammad al-Balkhī, *Maʿmūlāt-i sayfī*, pp. 79–80.

[85]Carl Vett, *Dervish Diary*, pp. 141–42 [additions mine].

point even though it is the station of intoxication and the domain of *waḥdat al-wujūd*.[86]

Leaving the circle of contingent existence, the aspirant proceeds to the second segment of the cyclical Mujaddidī path and enters the circle of names and attributes. Called "traveling in God" (*sayr fi'llāh*), this part of the journey is associated with "greater intimacy" (*wilāyat-i kubrā*).[87] This is the second "remaining in God" (*baqā'*) described by Junayd and the domain of *waḥdat al-shuhūd* emphasized by Aḥmad Sirhindī.[88] In the company of an exceptionally spiritually gifted individual such as Muḥammad, the Companions were able to proceed on the path without the need of "lesser intimacy" and the intoxication associated with it.[89] Such a spiritual boon is one more reason why Muslims believe the Companions to be the most preferred group of Muslims. Hidāyat ʿAlī Jaipūrī says, "If an intimate of God (*walī*) intensely exerts himself doing spiritual exercises for one hundred thousand years, he will never be able to approach the great Companions' (R) nearness to God, inner pureness, strength of faith, or high rank. [This is true by analogy] because one hour in the company (*ṣuḥbat*) of a *walī* is better than hundreds of years of sincere obedience and worship."[90]

God calls on prophets and those who follow them perfectly to proselytize. These chosen individuals begin the third portion of the journey, "returning to the world of creation for God and by means of God" (*sayr ʿan Allāh billāh*). At this point they complete the fourth and last cycle in their travels by returning to live as an apparently ordinary person in the created world (*sayr fi'l-ashyā'*). Only at this last stage does a traveler return with a transformed understanding of the phenomenal world, having acquired the knowledge of corporeal things as things.[91] Naqshbandīs claim

---

[86]See Zawwār Ḥusayn, *ʿUmdat al-sulūk*, p. 168.

[87]There are differing interpretations concerning where in the cosmological order this greater intimacy is located because of the overlap of circles of manifestation. It begins in the names and attributes of the second manifestation and goes through the divine qualities of the first manifestation, an area roughly approximating the overlap between the circles; see ibid., p. 195 and figure 5 in this chapter. Those entering the first manifestation near the reality of Muḥammad enter the realm of "greatest intimacy" (*wilāyat-i ʿulyā*) which is reserved for a very few travelers on the way, prophets, and angels.

[88]The first *baqā'* is the ordinary mundane human consciousness of someone who has never had any mystical experiences.

[89]Jaipūrī, *Miʿyār al-sulūk*, p. 130. This is how Naqshbandīs respond to critics who ask how the Naqshbandī path can be the way of the Companions when the Companions did not experience *jadhba*.

[90]Ibid.

[91]Muḥammad ʿInāyatullāh, *Maqāmāt-i irshādiyya*, p. 290.

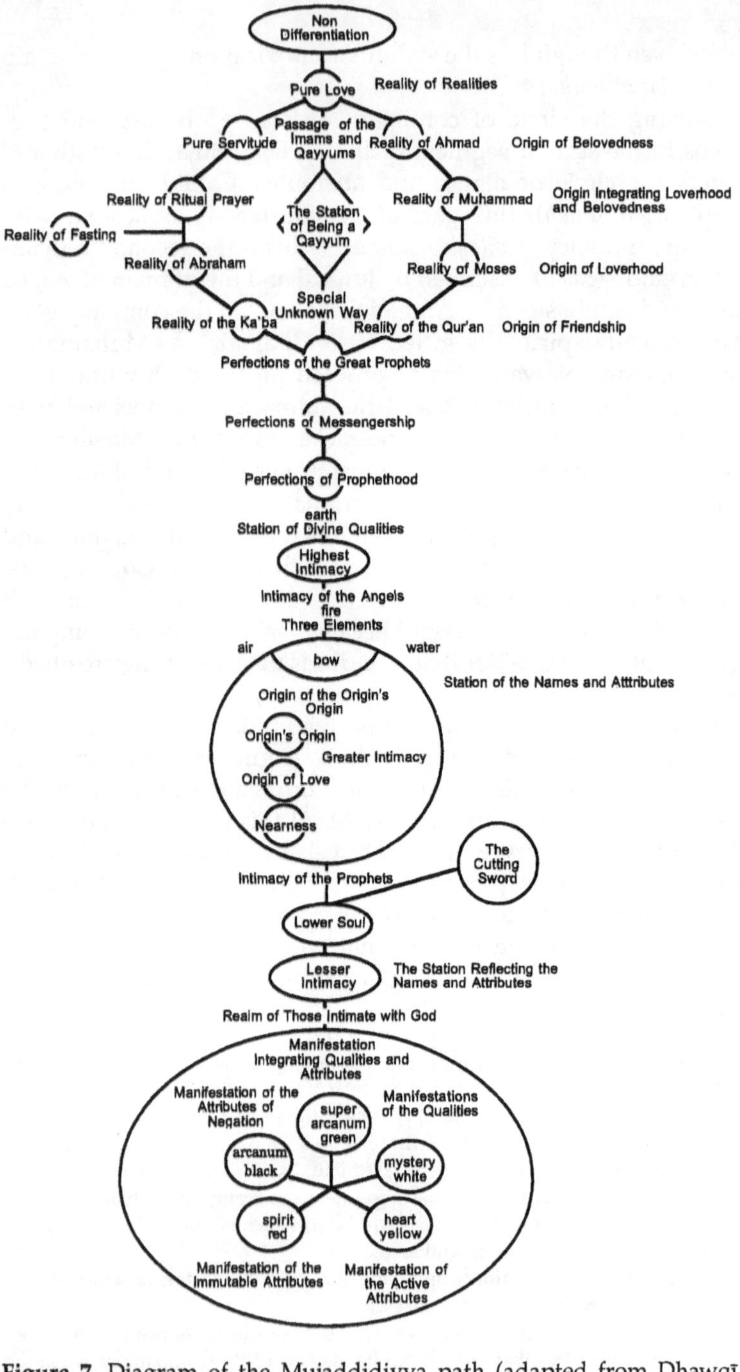

Figure 7. Diagram of the Mujaddidiyya path (adapted from Dhawqī, *Sirr-i dilbarān*, p. 201a)

this fourfold cycle is the path of the prophets and the Companions, which they attempt to imitate as closely as possible.

To proceed on the fourfold Naqshbandī path, three methods are employed to cultivate the *laṭīfas* of the world of divine command: recollection of God (*dhikr*), the exercise of negation and affirmation (*nafy wa-ithbāt*), and contemplation (*murāqaba*).[92] By activating the *laṭīfas* through the recollection of God one is functionally creating a subtle body and then subsequently energizing it by the practice of *nafy wa-ithbāt* before traveling via the contemplations toward the Essence.

Recollecting God

The literal meaning of *islām*, submission to God, cannot but involve the remembrance of God.[93] This submission, formally defined by the religion of Islam, involves ritual prayer five times a day in which the believer is enjoined to pray "as if one were in the direct presence of God." The other pillars of Islam, in addition to ritual prayer, i.e., giving of alms, fasting during the month of Ramaḍān, and the pilgrimage to Mecca, are all practical enactments designed to remind Muslims continually of the first pillar of Islam, "There is no god but God and Muḥammad is His messenger." The design for remembering God, according to Muslim faith, is contained in the Qur'ān and the hadith of the Prophet. By following this divine Law by which God has graced humanity, Muslims come to be in harmony with God's universal design, individually, socially, and spiritually.

Elements of recollecting God have been incorporated into diverse aspects of Islamic culture and languages by Muslims intentionally imitating the practices of the Prophet.[94] The linguistic aspects of recollecting God were first incorporated into the Arabic language and then transmitted to other languages spoken by Muslims. Before beginning any activity, Muslims are enjoined to repeat "in the name of God" (*bismillāh*). Any future action is always deferred to God's will, and it is considered spiritually arrogant to speak of doing something in the future without qualifying it with "if God wills" (*in shā' Allāh*). It is virtually the Arabic future-tense marker. When asked how one is doing, no matter

[92]The special bond between the shaykh and the disciple (*rābiṭa*) is a crucial component throughout these stages.

[93]For *dhikr* in a Shīʿī environment see Muḥammad Gunābādī, *Walāyat nāma*, pp. 176–82.

[94]See M. Piamenta, *Islam in Everyday Speech.*

how bad the situation may be, one first replies "May God be praised" (*al-ḥamdu lillāh*). In the linguistic sphere of Islamic culture God is mentioned relatively often in everyday conversation. Islamic calligraphic art reinforces a remembrance of God on a visual level, the world "Allāh" being one of the most common and recognizable words in ornate calligraphic designs.

Sufis, while wholeheartedly supporting outward religio-cultural structure and symbols, still emphasize the limitations of such symbols without the proper inner foundations. In spite of the myriad linguistic, artistic, and religious means to remember God, sufis note that humans are all too prone to forget Him. If they are heedless, for example, a *bismillāh* at the beginning of a meal can become a *bon appétit* rather than an occasion to remember God. Sufis have repeatedly stressed that the foundation of any remembrance of God rests in the heart, just as the profession of faith involves the tongue and the heart simultaneously. To activate the heart and lift the veils of heedlessness sufis have developed the formal exercises to remember God known as *dhikr*.[95]

The heart is the starting point for *dhikr* exercises. Naqshbandīs conceive of the heart as the bridge between the Creator and the human being, the locus of an inner catalyst that enables other subtle centers to become active.[96] In cosmic terms Naqshbandīs define the heart as the interface between the created world and the world of divine command and the bridge between the spirit (*rūḥ*) and the body.[97] The hadiths, "My heaven and earth cannot contain Me," and "There is not a person whose heart is not between the two fingers of God" reflect this way of understanding the heart in Muslim tradition.[98]

A Naqshbandī shaykh activates the subtle center of the heart

[95]For Naqshbandīs the heart means the heart *laṭīfa* (not the physical heart of the human body). Often the "real" heart, the heart *laṭīfa*, is associated with the physical pineal heart *(qalb ṣanawbarī)* since the latter resembles an inverted pine cone. See ʿAbdulaḥad Sirhindī, *Gulshan-i waḥdat*, p. 119. For the benefits and hadith support for the practice of *dhikr*, see Zawwār Ḥusayn, *ʿUmdat al-sulūk*, pp. 17–25. The development of *dhikr* and the types of *dhikr* of major sufi lineages has yet to be researched in detail.

[96]Jaipūrī, *Miʿyār al-sulūk*, p. 93.

[97]Fārūqī, *Madārij al-khayr*, pp. 30–31, and Faqīrullāh Shikārpūrī, *Maktūbāt-i Faqīrullāh*, p. 234.

[98]Furūzānfar, *Aḥādīth-i mathnawī*, p. 26, and A. J. Wensinck, *Concordance et indices de la tradition musulmane*, 8 volumes, 5:454. Concerning this latter hadith contemporary Pakistani Naqshbandīs have interpreted these two fingers to be the Compassionate *(al-raḥmān)* and the Merciful *(al-raḥīm)*; the former attribute is for all of humanity and the latter for Muslims, a similar dichotomy to that between general and special *fayḍ*.

by putting his four fingers in the place of the heart *laṭīfa.* Putting pressure on this place (sometimes called the "mouth of the heart"), he says "Allāh" three times while giving a burst of spiritual energy (*tawajjuh*) to the disciple's heart.[99] In this fashion, "remembering the name of the Essence" (*dhikr-i ism-i dhāt*) is imparted to the disciple. Naqshbandī shaykhs have explained to their disciples that by imparting this *dhikr* (*talqīn-i dhikr*) they are establishing God's imprint (*naqsh*), one that is sufficiently potent to be unaffected by ordinary events.[100] Similarly, Muḥammad Maʿṣūm (d. 1079/1668), son of Aḥmad Sirhindī, is reported to have said that the disciple should concentrate on the heart so that the *naqsh* of everything other than God would be effaced.[101] The spiritual guide then instructs the disciple to spend time each day in ritual purity sitting with his or her face toward Mecca with total mental concentration on the heart, mentally picturing the heart saying "Allāh, Allāh."[102] The goal is a receptive heart, undistracted by thoughts, which is continually turned to the source of divinely emanating energy. Such a condition is defined as recollection of the heart (*dhikr-i qalbī*).[103] Although Naqshbandīs perform this recollection of God silently, properly speaking it is known as recollection of the heart (*dhikr-i qalbī*), not silent recollection (*dhikr-i khafī*).[104]

---

[99]Zawwār Ḥusayn, *'Umdat al-sulūk,* p. 280.

[100]Muḥammad Hāshim Kishmī, *Nasamāt al-quds,* p. 31.

[101]Fārūqī, *Madārij al-khayr,* p. 62. One explanation of Bahā'uddīn's name "Naqshband" is "the person whose heart is impressed with God's name Allāh." Other explanations are summarized in 'Iraqī's introduction to Muḥammad Pārsā's *Qudsiyya,* pp. 46–47. One apocryphal story relates how Bahā'uddīn was unable to receive the *dhikr* from his living pir, Amīr Kulāl, so he went into the desert, where Khiḍr informed him that 'Abdulqādir al-Jīlānī would impart the *dhikr-i ism-i dhāt* to him in a dream; he proceeded to do so that very evening; see Shikārpūrī, *Maktūbāt-i Faqīrullāh,* p. 211.

[102]Zawwār Ḥusayn, *'Umdat al-sulūk,* p. 280.

[103]Fārūqī, *Madārij al-khayr,* p. 60. *Dhikr-i qalbī* is also called *wuqūf-i qalbī.* In Naqshbandī technical vocabulary *wuqūf* means "concentration" when discussing the *laṭīfas* and "understanding" in the context of contemplation *(murāqabāt).*

[104]There is a substantial conceptual difference between these two kinds of *dhikr. Dhikr* of the heart is contrasted with *dhikr* of the tongue *(dhikr-i lisānī),* while silent *dhikr* is contrasted with audible *dhikr.* By definition, *dhikr* of the heart is silent but silent *dhikr* can also be performed by members of sufi lineages who normally have loud *dhikr,* e.g., the Shādhiliyya practice silent *dhikr* of the tongue when in public places. See also ʿAlā'uddawla Simnānī's *Dhikr al-lisānī al-qawī al-khafī,* mentioned in Elias, *Throne Carrier,* p. 131. In an otherwise insightful presentation of *dhikr,* Hamid Algar confuses silent *dhikr* with *dhikr* of the heart. See his "Silent and Vocal *dhikr* in the Naqshbandī order." By conflating silent *dhikr* and *dhikr-i qalbī* he confuses two different Naqshbandī practices: the heart's silent repetition of "Allāh" *(dhikr-i qalbī)* and the silent repetition of *lā ilāh illā Allāh* while holding the

The advantage of recollection of the heart is that one can perform it continuously in any circumstance. Although silent recollection of God enables the adept to remember God in both waking and sleeping states, recollection of the heart is superior to silent recollection of the tongue since an action focused in the heart allows one to continue remembering God whether speaking, eating, drinking, or anything else.[105] Naqshbandīs explain the rarity of the practice of heart *dhikr* among other sufi lineages by the lack of spiritual guides who can activate the heart, in addition to the relatively greater difficulty of performing recollection of the heart. Many other sufi lineages consider recollection of the heart to be an advanced sufi exercise at the end of the path, while Naqshbandīs begin practicing heart *dhikr* from the time of initiation. Naqshbandīs have explained that in recollection of the heart they begin receiving divine grace from the Essence, while other sufis only receive divine emanations from the Essence at the end of the path.[106] Naqshbandī pirs expect high standards of performance from seekers recollecting God in the heart. The disciple should feel nothing else but the presence of God in the heart, so that one is like "a breast-fed baby who always stays near its mother; if it is separated [from its mother] for even an instant, [the baby] cries and becomes agitated."[107] From this strict definition of recollecting God in the heart Naqshbandīs have declared it sinful for the elect to forget God for even an instant.[108]

When the heart of the disciple is established in recollecting God, the shaykh activates the other subtle centers of the body in turn,[109] until eventually the entire body, even the individual hairs,

---

breath *(nafy wa-ithbāt)*, which Khiḍr was supposed to have taught ʿAbdulkhāliq Ghujduwānī. The latter is the *dhikr-i khafī* which Yaʿqūb Charkhī is discussing in his *Risāla-yi unsiyya*, cited by Algar.

The most vocal of all *dhikr* activities is *samāʿ*, involving instrumental music and singing of devotional poetry, causing many to experience ecstasy. Shariʿa-minded sufis like the Naqshbandīs have declared *samāʿ* to be a forbidden activity. Indeed, sufi singing *(qawwālī)* has become a distinctive activity which some interpret as setting the participants apart from the rest of the Muslim community. For a detailed ethnomusical study, see Regula A. Qureshi, *Sufi Music of India and Pakistan: Sound, Context, and Meaning in Qawwali.*

105 Silent recollection is one of many examples of practices and attitudes in the Naqshbandiyya that could have been transmitted from the early Malāmatiyya originating in Nishapur. See Hamid Algar, "Elements de provenance Malāmatī dans la tradition primitive Naqshbandī." This and many of the other papers are to be edited by Roger Deladrière and published by l'Institut Français.

106 Muḥammad Ṣādiq Quṣūrī, *Tadhkira-yi Naqshbandiyya-Khayriyya*, p. 177.

107 Zawwār Ḥusayn, *ʿUmdat al-sulūk*, p. 167.

108 Ibid., p. 168.

109 The usual order for nineteenth- and twentieth-century Indian Naqshbandī-

become one *laṭīfa* continually remembering God, a stage called *dhikr-i sulṭānī*.[110] It is at this point that the one engaged in recollecting God can begin to become conscious of God's entire creation, remembering God according to the Qur'ānic dictum, "There is nothing in creation that does not praise Him" (Q. 17:44).[111] With respect to the Naqshbandī path, the disciple has created a luminous vehicle, a subtle body of light, with which to travel towards God.

If recollection of the heart creates the vehicle for the traveler, the next level of *dhikr* and the second of the three methods used by the Naqshbandīs, "recollection of negation and affirmation" (*nafy wa-ithbāt*), is like developing an accelerator for the vehicle. (The negation is "There is no god" and the affirmation is "but God.") The disciple is taught an exercise involving the silent mental repetition of the first half of the Muslim profession of faith, there is no god but God (*lā ilāh illā Allāh*) while holding the breath.[112] Naqshbandīs assert that this exercise was taught to ʿAbdulkhāliq Ghujduwānī (d. 575/1179) by Khiḍr as the former was submerged in water. Adepts begin the three-movement exercise by first holding the breath below the navel and then mentally bringing up the word *lā* from below the navel to the middle of the forehead.[113]

The second movement (*ḍarb*) is mentally conveying the word *ilāh* from the middle of the forehead to the right shoulder, ending with the final forceful mental motion "hitting" the heart from the right shoulder with *illā Allāh*. Disciples are required to do one additional task of counting how many times they say *tahlīl* in one breath (*wuqūf-i ʿadadī*) in order to finish with an odd number. A short supplication (*duʿā*ʾ) follows each exhalation, "Muḥammad is the messenger of God" (the second half of the Muslim profes-

---

Mujaddidīs is *qalb, rūḥ, sirr, khafī, akhfā, nafs, qālab*. Muḥammad Maʿṣūm, performing a "sufi *ijtihād*," started with the *qalb* and then activated the *nafs, rūḥ, akhfā, sirr,* and *khafī*; see Jaipūrī, *Miʿyār al-sulūk*, p. 104.

[110]Bīrbalī, *Inqilāb al-ḥaqīqat*, p. 17, and Zawwār Ḥusayn, *ʿUmdat al-sulūk*, p. 283. The point of *dhikr-i sulṭānī*, coincides with "annihilation" of the coarse material body (*fanāʾ-i jasadī*), implying one can leave the coarse body now that a subtle body has been formed.

[111]Jaipūrī, *Miʿyār al-sulūk*, p. 103.

[112]The repetition of *lā ilāh illā Allāh* is also called *tahlīl*, and some Naqshbandī manuals mention an alternative, loud repetition of this phrase called *dhikr-i tahlīl-i lisāni*. See Zawwār Ḥusayn, *ʿUmdat al-sulūk*, pp. 283–85. This *dhikr* formula of twelve letters was also the most popular *dhikr* formula used by early Imāmīs; see Amir-Moezzi, *The Divine Guide*, pp. 107; 217, n. 574.

[113]Some seventeenth-century Naqshbandīs located the *nafs laṭīfa* below the navel and the *akhfā laṭīfa* in the middle of the forehead.

sion of faith), and "[To arrive near] God is my purpose (*maqṣūdī*) and my desire (*maṭlūbī*) is His pleasure. Give me knowledge and love of Him."[114] Such a supplication reminds the disciple that his or her own actions alone cannot guarantee success; the disciple must ultimately rely on God's merciful grace to reach the goal. When proficient in *nafy wa-ithbāt* the disciple has a vehicle that is "warmed up" and ready to travel towards God through the contemplations (*murāqabāt*).[115] Throughout this entire process one's spiritual achievements depend upon a well-developed psycho-emotional tie with the shaykh. Indeed, this intimate bond forms the basis for subsequent transformation and spiritual travel.

[114]See Muḥammad 'Ināyatullāh, *Maqāmāt-i irshādiyya*, p. 249 in the note, and Zawwār Ḥusayn, *'Umdat al-sulūk*, p. 284. Both these sources mention the necessity to repeat the *tahlīl* twenty-one times in a breath but Naqshbandīs have told me that advanced practitioners in this exercise can repeat the *tahlīl* over one thousand times in one breath.

[115]Appendixes 2 and 3 explain these in detail.

CHAPTER 6

Bonding the Heart with the Shaykh

In our path [the Naqshbandiyya] arriving at the degree of perfection is related to a loving bond (rābiṭa) *with the exemplary shaykh. The sincere disciple, through his love of the shaykh, receives divine energy* (fayḍ) *from the inner being* (bāṭin) *of the shaykh and becomes colored with the color of the shaykh, having an essential connection to the shaykh. . . . They call this annihilation in the shaykh, the beginning of true annihilation [in God]. [Anyone doing]* dhikr *without bonding his heart with the master* (rābiṭa) *and without achieving annihilation in the shaykh will not arrive.*

Khwāja Muḥammad Maʿṣum, *Maktubāt*

In terms of the spiritual practices described here, namely, recollection of God *(dhikr)* and contemplation of God *(murāqaba)*, the most efficacious method for spiritual development arises from the bond *(rābiṭa)* with the mentor that enables the seeker to benefit from the focused energy of the shaykh's spiritual attention *(tawajjuh)*.[1] The success of spiritual travel depends on cultivating

[1]Aḥmad Saʿīd, *Arbaʿ anhar*, p. 2, and Zawwār Ḥusayn, *ʿUmdat al-sulūk*, p. 279. Naqshbandīs refer to the three "ways to God" as *dhikr*, *fikr*, and *rābiṭa*. See Hidāyat ʿAlī Jaipūrī, *Miʿyār al-sulūk, wa-dāfiʿ al-awhām wa'l-shukūk*, p. 69. In another triad, Mujaddidīs define three types of religious education: (1) learning the religious sciences governing outward behavior, which is the most basic; (2) practical training in recollection of God; and (3) *tawajjuh*; see Muḥammad ʿUmar Bīrbalī, *Inqilāb al-ḥaqīqat*, pp. 26–27. Such an emphasis on the connection to the shaykh had Naqshbandī precedents. For ʿAbdurraḥmān Jāmī (d. 898/1492) *rābiṭa* was the nearest, i.e., fastest, means to arrive at the goal. See *Sarrishta-yi ṭarīqa-yi khwājagān*, p. 15. ʿUbaydullāh Aḥrār (d. 895/1490), a contemporary of Jāmī, outlined three possibilities: (1) doing good deeds and spiritual exercises; (2) realizing one's weakness and surrendering to God; and (3) depending on the influence of a master's spiritual power *(himmat)*. The third method is the fastest and most sure, for a seeker realizing his weakness can use the means *(wasīla)* of his pir's spiritual power to arrive near God. Kāshifī, *Rashaḥāt*, pp. 500–01, cited in Fritz Meier, *Zwei Abhandlungen über die Naqšbandiyya*, p. 256.

this relationship with the spiritual guide; solitary recollection without this bond will make the goal extremely difficult, if not impossible, to reach.[2] The need for this bond grows out of the principle that the sufi genealogical chain conducts the divine energy *(fayḍ)* mediated by Muḥammad. Without a sound connection to the shaykh one remains disconnected from God.[3] The spiritual tie *(rābiṭa)* determines the disciple's progress.[4]

ʿAbdurraḥmān Jāmī (d. 898/1492) gives one of the earliest and most complete descriptions of *rābiṭa* for the Naqshbandiyya. Being with the spiritual guide is equivalent to being in the company with one of the protégés of God, since they both have the highest degree of perfection in contemplating the divine essence *(maqām-i mushāhada)* and also cause tears to flow when imparting the recollection of God.[5] A contemporary of Jāmī, ʿUbaydullāh Aḥrār, wrote in his *Fiqarāt*, "The shadow of the master is better than the recollection of God *(dhikr)*," which Sirhindī later interpreted as the superiority of *rābiṭa* over *dhikr*, because without a complete connection to the shaykh the seeker will not be able to derive full benefit from recollection of God.[6]

Historically *rābiṭa* was an essential component of both companionship with the shaykh *(ṣuḥbat)* and ability to receive his transmission of spiritual energy *(tawajjuh)*. Fritz Meier[7] in a monograph on this bonding, traces the concept to the writings of Najmuddīn Kubrā (d. 618/1221) and Abū Ḥafṣ as-Suhrawardī (d. 632/1234).[8] A century later ʿAlā'uddawla Simnānī (d. 736/

[2]See Aḥmad Sirhindī, *Maktūbāt-i imām-i rabbānī*, 3 volumes, vol. 1, letter 61, p. 39 [hereafter 1.61.39]; Muḥammad Maʿṣūm, *Maktūbāt-i maʿṣūmiyya*, 3 volumes, vol. 1, letter 78, p. 196 [Hereafter 1.78.196]; and ʿAbdullāh Shāh, *Sulūk-i mujaddidiyya*, p. 17.

[3]There are always exceptions, for example, "When one cannot have companionship *(ṣuḥbat)* with God then enter companionship with those who do"; see Zawwār Ḥusayn, *ʿUmdat al-sulūk*, p. 99. Evidently very few people are able to have companionship with God without the intermediary of the shaykh.

[4]"Any benefit [for the disciple] is because of the shaykh." See Sirhindī, *Maktūbāt*, 1.187.74.

[5]Jāmī, *Sarrishta-yi ṭarīqa-yi khwājagān*, p. 15. Jāmī explains that a person who has reached the *maqām-i mushāhada* has become a verifier of the manifestations of the divine essence *(bih tajalliyāt-i dhātiyya muḥaqqiq gashtah)*.

[6]This quote is cited in Aḥmad Saʿīd, *Bi'l-fawā'id al-ḍābiṭa*, p. 35. See also Muḥammad Maʿṣūm, *Maktūbāt-i maʿṣūmiyya*, 1.50.165.

[7]See Meier, *Zwei Abhandlungen*, in particular, "Die Herzensbindung an den Meister."

[8]Suhrawardī, in his *ʿAwārif al-maʿārif*, mentions how ʿAbdulqādir al-Jīlānī used the presence of the bond of hearts between master and disciple *(rābiṭa qalbiyya)* to account for his refraining from customary exchanges of polite expressions. Kubrā attributed the bonding of the heart with the shaykh *(rabṭ al-qalb bi'l-shaykh)* to Junayd (d. 298/910). See ibid., pp. 17–18.

1336), from whom the Naqshbandīs most likely developed their schema of colors and subtle centers, mentions how the tie of the heart with the master *(rābiṭa-yi shaykhī)* determines the quality of bonding with the Prophet *(rābiṭa-yi nabawī)*.[9] Later sufis describe the disciple's ego as dissolving in the shaykh *(fanā' fī'l-shaykh)* before becoming annihilated in the Prophet and eventually God. The bond with the shaykh *(rābiṭa)* in the sufi path corresponds to the Kaʿba in the shariʿa; both are means of worship between the Creator and the created, since God's light had been confirmed both in the Kaʿba (the house of God) and in the heart of God's slave.[10]

This intentional flow of *fayḍ* from the pir is often described as spiritual attention *(tawajjuh, taṣarruf, himma)* which hastens the disciple's inner transformation as a profound bond develops with the shaykh.[11] When a disciple becomes psychologically and emotionally attuned with the guide, the shaykh's spiritual attention can work effectively. Whether this divine grace actually exists at all or whether a particular master is capable of channeling this energy is not the primary concern. The concept of divinely emanating power in the larger paradigm of protégés of God acting as mediators between humans and God explains how a shaykh can positively influence a disciple's behavior or cure others of undesirable conditions and illnesses. It was Indian Shēr Muḥammad's (d. 1346–47/1928) multidimensional spiritual attention, for example, that allegedly changed common people's worldly situation through lectures and discussions. Depending on a disciple's capacity, he would transmit this divine grace through physical contact, with a handshake or touching their forehead or places on their chest.[12] Physical distance does not impair the transmission of divine energy when "hearts are near," i.e., when there is

[9]ʿAlā'uddawla Simnānī, "Khitām al-misk," p. 123.

[10]Jaipūrī, *Miʿyār al-sulūk*, p. 71.

[11]When giving *tawajjuh* the shaykh thinks, "I focus God's light by means of the blessed shaykhs on this disciple." The disciple thinks, "The pir is the access of divine grace and is the means for the divine energy which is coming to my heart." See ʿAbdullāh Shāh, *Sulūk-i mujaddidiyya*, p. 21. There are many parallels with a disciple's performance of the contemplative exercises—See appendixes 2 and 3. Before Sirhindī, ʿUbaydullāh Aḥrār explained that when the shaykh puts his spiritual attention on the heart of the seeker there develops a connection and affinity between the hearts until they are one. See Kāshifī, *Rashaḥāt*, p. 464. Jāmī defined *tawajjuh* as the process of the disciple concentrating on the heart *laṭīfa*, presumably while doing *dhikr*. See ʿAbdurraḥmān Jāmī, *Sarrishta-yi ṭarīqa-yi khwājagān*, pp. 14–15.

[12]Bīrbalī, *Inqilāb al-ḥaqīqat*, pp. 50–53. Touching points on the chest is how shaykhs activate a disciple's subtle entities *(laṭīfas)*.

a close bond between the shaykh and disciple.[13] Rūmī attributes a similar type of silent companionship and wordless transmission to the third Caliph, ʿUthmān.

When ʿUthmān (R) became Caliph he went to the pulpit *(minbar)* [to give a sermon]. People waited for him to say something, [but] he did not say anything. He [just] kept looking intently at the people, causing [such] a state of ecstasy to descend upon the people that they could not leave nor have any idea where each other were sitting. Never with a hundred admonishments, preachings, and sermons would they have had such an excellent state. [Nor] would they have received [such] benefits and have [had such] secrets revealed with so much effort and preaching. Until the end of the session he kept looking at them like this without uttering a word. When he wanted to descend from the pulpit he said "It is better that you have an effective imam [leader] rather than a prattling imam."[14]

Perfect *rābiṭa,* however, is not only a function of *tawajjuh,* but is achieved from the simultaneous efforts of both the master and disciple in a reciprocal process. While the disciple receives the shaykh's focused spiritual attention the disciple continuously visualizes the shaykh's face.

Visualizing the Shaykh (*taṣawwur-i shaykh*)

The bond with the spiritual mentor, first experienced by disciples and later institutionalized in the sufi practice of *taṣawwur-i shaykh,* developed into one of the most heated points of contention between sufis and their opponents in the reformist environment of nineteenth- and twentieth-century India.[15] Sufi apologists for this visualization activity cited the elaborate description of the

[13]Ibid., p. 60.

[14]Jalāluddīn Rūmī, *Kitāb-i fīhi mā fīhi,* p. 129. Badīʿuzzamān Furūzānfar documents how this story related by Rūmī changed considerably from the shorter version he had located in the hadith literature. See ibid., 316–17.

[15]In addition to Aḥmad Saʿīd's (d. 1277/1860) detailed apologetic work cited above, many other shorter treatises appeared justifying visualizing the shaykh. See Aḥmad Riḍā Khān Barēlwī, *Al-yāqūtat al-wāsiṭa,* and Muḥammad Amīn, *Ithbāt-i taṣawwur-i shaykh.* There are in addition many articles in Jamāʿat ʿAlī Shāh's monthly sufi magazine, *Risāla-yi anwār al-ṣūfiyya,* e.g., Shaykh Ghulām Naqshband, "Ḥaqīqat-i taṣawwur," 13.6.9–20; Nūr Muḥammad, "Taṣawwur-i Shaykh," 16.5.11–16; and 16.6.17–24; Muḥammad Sharīf, "Taṣawwur-i Shaykh," 18.1.17–24; 18.2.17–24; 18.3.9–15; 19.2.14–15. Mujaddidīs agreed that making pictures of Muḥammad was forbidden by the shariʿa, but argued that visualization of the shaykh differed entirely from pictures in books. They considered visualization as a process occurring in the imagination, the same process by which one used to acquire acknowledge; see Aḥmad Saʿid, *Bi'l-fawā'id al-ḍābiṭa,* p. 58.

Prophet *(ḥilyat an-nabī)*.[16] Referring to the Arabic adage, "Choose your companions carefully before traveling" *(ar-rafīq qabl aṭ-ṭarīq)*, Aḥmad Saʿīd (d. 1277/1860) notes the precedent of Bahā'uddīn Naqshband guarding the image of his shaykh's face in his imagination when traveling to the Hijaz.[17] A disciple of Khwāja Ḥasan ʿAṭṭār, the eldest son of ʿAlā'uddīn ʿAṭṭār (d. 803/1400), showed signs of spiritual attraction *(jadhba)* when visualizing the face of his shaykh.[18] If the disciple could not be in the presence of the master, ʿAbdurraḥmān Jāmī recommended that the disciple visualize the pir's face in the heart while eliminating any distracting thoughts.[19] ʿUbaydullāh Aḥrār, interpreting the Qur'ānic verse "Be with those who are sincere and true" *(kūnū maʿ aṣ-ṣādiqīn* [9:119]), indicated that one should outwardly be in the guide's physical presence and inwardly have a bond with him *(rābiṭa)*.[20] One unites sincerely with the shaykh's face to develop continuous companionship with "the lights of his lofty attributes and beautiful character,"[21] creating continual *rābiṭa*, independent of physical proximity. In this way a person can develop an affinity *(munāsabat)* with the mentor and arrive at the goal.[22]

Sirhindī incorporated this practice of visualization into the Mujaddidī system, especially when he perceived that persons had not controlled their egos sufficiently. He would order them to engage in *rābiṭa* and visualize his face in their hearts, causing some of them to show visible signs of spiritual attraction: "Khwāja Burhān, one of the shaykhs of Dahbid who had already been initiated and received permission to teach *(ijāzat)* from the notables of his locale, asked Sirhindī for spiritual guidance. Burhān was surprised when Sirhindī said for him to visualize his [Sirhindī's] blessed face. His trusted companion informed him [Khwāja Burhān] that this exercise is suitable for beginners so that they can be taught the advanced contemplations *(murāqabāt)*. . . . After being convinced, he practiced this exercise for a day and became overpowered with a connection *(nisba)* with God to the

[16]Ibid., p. 50.

[17]Pārsā, *Risāla-yi Qudsiyya*, cited in Aḥmad Saʿīd, *Bi'l-fawā'id al-ḍābiṭa*, pp. 41–42. Evidently Bahā'uddīn, on his second trip to the Hijaz, ordered his companion and disciple, Muḥammad Pārsā, to fix his face in his imagination; see ibid., p. 42.

[18]Ibid., p. 44.

[19]Jāmī, *Sarrishta-yi ṭarīqa-yi khwājagān*, p. 15.

[20]Kāshifī, *Rashaḥāt-i ʿayn al-ḥayāt*, cited in Aḥmad Saʿīd, *Bi'l-fawā'id al-ḍābiṭa*, p. 47. Later reformist sufis would justify visualization of the shaykh on the basis of numerous Qur'ānic and hadith passages.

[21]Ibid.

[22]Ibid., pp. 47–48.

point that he showed signs of extreme spiritual intoxication *(jadhba)*."[23]

Naqshbandīs have praised visualization of the shaykh as an effective technique for concentration, since humans cannot follow two directions at once or meditate with distracting thoughts. "Keeping the picture of the shaykh in the state of recollection of God *(dhikr)* is the essence of causing recollection *(tadhkīr)* because the remembered One exists in the presence of one [the shaykh] who does not heedlessly leave God—may He be blessed—for an instant."[24]

It is much easier for beginners to concentrate on the face of the shaykh than on God. There is a synergistic effect between the visualization of the shaykh and love of the shaykh which allows the seeker to open him- or herself to a transformative process activated by the pir's character and actions. This in turn strengthens the seeker's connection to God. Eventually the pir's astral body *(jism-i mithālī)* can be summoned.[25]

One common technique of visualization involves completely emptying the mind of all thoughts while feeling love for the shaykh and for God as one receives divinely emanating energy *(fayḍ)* from the pir. Keeping the eyes either open or closed, one should begin to gaze steadfastly at a point in between the shaykh's eyes. Even if the shaykh is not present one can still keep lovingly imagining the shaykh between the eyes, which produces an effect like physical companionship *(ṣuḥbat)*.[26] More advanced techniques involve visualizing the shaykh progressively, in front of the heart, actually in the heart, and finally visualizing one's own face as being the shaykh's.[27] One essential component of this practice is that it be done in a loving and sincere manner. As love of the pir should arise spontaneously, visualization of the pir should be a natural process without struggle.[28]

Success in this endeavor means that a strong, firm connection has been formed and that whatever the seeker looks at he or she

---

[23]Muḥammad Hāshim Kishmī, *Zubdat al-maqāmāt*, cited by Aḥmad Saʿīd, *Bi'l-fawā'id al-ḍābiṭa*, pp. 32–33.

[24]Aḥmad Saʿīd, *Bi'l-fawā 'id al-ḍābiṭa*, p. 58.

[25]ʿAbdullāh Shāh, *Sulūk-i mujaddidiyya*, p. 16. This is also mentioned by Muḥammad ʿUmar Bīrbalī. When a person reaches a certain station, people's astral bodies can appear. Someone with a connection to the Prophet *(nisba)*, e.g., a protégé of God, can supposedly manifest as if he were physically present. See Bīrbalī, *Inqilāb al-ḥaqīqat*, p. 219 n. 1.

[26]Zawwār Ḥusayn, *ʿUmdat al-sulūk*, p. 99.

[27]Abū'l-Ḥasan Zayd Fārūqī, *Manāhij al-sayr*, translated by Muḥammad Naʿīmullāh Khān, *Madārij al-khayr*, p. 64, and Jaipūrī, *Miʿyār al-sulūk*, p. 70.

[28]Bīrbalī, *Inqilāb al-ḥaqīqat*, p. 44 n. 3, p. 68 n. 5.

will see the shaykh, an essential condition for annihilation in the shaykh *(fanā' fi'l-shaykh)*.[29] Aḥmad Riḍā Khān Barēlwī (d. 1340/ 1921) relates the following story: "Hafiz ul-Hadis Sayyid Aḥmad Sujalmasi <as-Sijilmasī> was going somewhere. Suddenly his eyes lifted from the ground, and he saw a beautiful woman. The glance had been inadvertent [and so no blame attached to him]. But then he looked up again. This time he saw his pir and murshid, Sayyid Ghaus ul-Waqt ʿAbd al-ʿAziz Dabagh <ad-Dabbāgh>."[30] ʿAbdulḥaqq Dihlawī (d. 1052/1642) utilizes these principles for other applications. Having his heart "extended" in recollection of God by the spiritual power of his shaykh, he declares that it is religiously permitted to call out to one's shaykh for help.[31]

In the Naqshbandī tradition it is generally difficult to achieve annihilation in God *(fanā' fi'llāh)* without prior annihilation in the shaykh *(fana' fi'l-shaykh)*.[32] Muḥammad Maʿṣūm, says, "As long as there is not an intermediary *(wāsiṭa)* how can one find the way to the goal? . . . The will of the disciple must follow the will of the shaykh. . . . In his companionship he should be like a corpse in the hands of the washer. This principle, valid for all sufi groups, is especially true for ours [the Naqshbandiyya] where . . . [the practice is based on] reciprocal action and centered on companionship."[33]

Not all Mujaddidīs enthusiastically endorsed visualization of the shaykh. Shēr Muḥammad, perhaps to avoid reformist criticism, advised against intentionally visualizing the shaykh (he never encouraged or requested his disciples to perform visualization). He did not object to their forming a *rābiṭa* with the shaykh, since this comes by itself if there is a connection with the spiritual mentor.[34] Shēr Muḥammad did, however, prohibit even spontaneous visualization of the shaykh when one praised the

---

[29]See Sirhindī, *Maktūbāt*, 1.61.39, and Muḥammad Maʿṣūm, *Maktūbāt-i maʿṣūmiyya*, 1.78.197.

[30]From Aḥmad Riḍā Khān, *Malfūẓāt*, 2:45, cited in Usha Sanyal, *Devotional Islam and Politics in British India: Ahmad Riza Khan Barelwi and His Movement, 1870–1920* [Comments in brackets are Sanyal's; my additions are in angle brackets.] ʿAbdul ʿazīz ad-Dabbāgh (d. 1131/1718–19) was the North African founder-figure of the Khiḍriyya sufi lineage.

[31]Aḥmad Saʿīd, *Bi'l-fawā'id al-ḍābiṭa*, p. 59. The Sunnī consensus and many sufis stressed the need for depending only on God *(tawakkul)* for one's needs in this and the next world.

[32]See Muḥammad Maʿṣūm, *Maktūbāt-i maʿṣūmiyya*, 1.50.164.

[33]Ibid.

[34]Muḥammad Ibrāhīm Quṣūrī, *Khazīna-yi maʿrifat*, pp. 257–58. The author mentions that sometimes the *rābiṭa* affected him while praying.

Prophet.[35] Instead, Shēr Muḥammad had disciples visualize the written forms of "Allāh" and "Hu," which he drew with his fingers.[36] Although the principal goal of visualization is establishing and maintaining a connection with God, for the disciple the awesome figure of the shaykh looms in the behavioral, psychological, and emotional foreground. At first, when the seeker begins recollecting God, the form of the shaykh appears in the heart to assist the seeker. Later, the shaykh's heart spurs the seeker's heart via the chain of masters leading to the Prophet's presence. The novice, having the picture of his shaykh's face in his heart at this point, is assisted by Muḥammad to arrive at God. Divine grace is then transmitted from Muḥammad's heart via the chain of masters ending at the seeker's guide, which in the last link is communicated from the shaykh's heart to the seeker's heart.[37] It is the pivotal role of the disciple's shaykh that makes the entire transformative process possible.

The Necessity of the Directing-Shaykh

Pedagogically, the shaykh instructs through example and personal contact; much of a seeker's learning involves conscious behavioral modification and unconscious modeling (and subsequent internalization) of one's spiritual guide.[38] Such an environment implies close supervision in the controlled environment of the sufi lodge. Within this context, the rapport between shaykh and disciple mirrors a myriad of other types of relationships, including father-son, master-slave, guide-traveler, physician-patient, teacher-student, and beloved-lover.

If the metaphor of a disciple's spiritual growth is a journey, then the shaykh functions as both the guide for the perilous trip through unknown territory and as the teacher of the exercises necessary to proceed on that voyage. Using the metaphor of transformation for the disciple's spiritual journey implies other relationships which involve both father-son, physician-patient, and beloved-lover roles. In actual practice, each spiritual director

---

[35]Muḥammad ʿUmar Bīrbalī used to visualize his shaykh in front of him as if he were Muḥammad; see his *Inqilāb al-haqīqat*, p. 236. Such a practice is also regularly performed in the contemplations. See appendix 3.

[36]Bīrbalī, *Inqilāb al-ḥaqīqat*, pp. 69, 44 n. 3.

[37]ʿAbdulḥaqq Dihlawī, *Maktūbāt*, letter 4, cited in Aḥmad Saʿīd, *Bi'l-fawā'id al-ḍābiṭa*, pp. 59–60.

[38]The holy person's role as exemplar has been discussed by Peter Brown, "The Saint as Exemplar in Late Antiquity"; and by Steven T. Katz, "Models, Modeling, and Mystical Training."

uses a comprehensive array of behavioral and psychological strategies to enact these changes.

The directing-shaykh, as the heir of the Prophet, represents the living archetype of the Prophetic ideal. Psychologically the master has to be perceived as an infallible guide for the disciple since both the ego and the discursive mind constantly attempt to convince the reader that they know better than the master. To overcome these two usurpers, skillful and apparently ruthless means are used. To many modern (or even not so modern) observers such practices often appear to be tantamount to brainwashing or worse.[39] Sufis view things differently. Sufi training performed by a friend of God subdues the ego while purifying the mind, emotions, and heart. The seeker should not only allow him or herself to be a corpse in the hands of the washer, but also to love the corpsewasher.

Even though the repertoire of Naqshbandī spiritual methods appears relatively uniform in the literature, there have been creative variations not only between individual shaykhs but in the techniques each individual master used for each person. Bāqībillāh, for example, used to teach the way of bonding with the shaykh *(ṭarīq-i rābiṭa)* to novices having an inclination for love. One particularly adept disciple reportedly achieved such an intense connection to God *(nisbat-i ʿaẓīm)* after two days of visualizing Bāqībillāh that, in spite of his advanced age, he would spring two arm-lengths off the ground from the intense uncontrollable intoxication that resulted.[40] For most seekers, however, Bāqībillāh would teach remembrance of the heart. ʿUbaydullāh Aḥrār, on the other hand, was so occupied with worldly activities in Tashkent, Herat, and Samarqand that he had little time to train his

---

[39]There have been many modern examples of people unquestioningly following unscrupulous persons. In an Islamic context this situation, often called "pirism," has done much to give sufism a bad reputation. The psychological processes unfolding in the master-disciple relationship, like instruments of technology, can be used equally for beneficial or destructive purposes. For example, a disciple of Charles Manson says, "Following Manson, trying to become Manson, brought the disciples subjectively near what was imagined the ultimate source of power. And, indeed, the closest converts who imitated Manson most avidly—who became empty mirrors—felt themselves to be acquiring his magical abilities. . . . Susan Atkins [one of Manson's senior disciples] found herself able to read their thoughts and to manipulate them, just as she believed Manson did." See Charles Lindholm, *Charisma*, p. 132. Charles Manson was an ex-convict before becoming a charismatic leader in the 1970s whose grandiose and paranoiac fantasies of domination involved his group in many illegal activities.

[40]Kishmī, *Zubdat al-maqāmāt*, p. 17, cited in Meier, *Zwei Abhandlungen*, pp. 169–70.

students in recollection of God *(nafy wa-ithbāt)* or the contemplations *(murāqabāt)*. Instead, he relied mostly on creating a *rābiṭa* with them.[41]

Busy schedules aside, many Naqshbandī shaykhs have declared the visualization of the shaykh to be more efficacious than the remembrance of God (especially for the beginner). Historically this situation literally and symbolically represents the increasing tendency over time for authority to be more and more concentrated in the person of the sufi shaykh. This visual focus on the spiritual guide involves both an emotional tie of love and a specific psychological tie of modeling.

The tradition of loving the shaykh had already been established by Bahā'uddīn Naqshband's time.[42] For Aḥrār the *rābiṭa* with the master entailed a perfect connection of love *(kamāl-i nisbat-i ḥubbī)* whose Prophetic origin began with Abū Bakr's love for the Prophet and subsequently was transmitted through the spiritual links of the Naqshbandī lineage.[43] Consequently Aḥrār sanctioned "loveplay" *('ishqbāzī)*, inspired by Joseph's legendary beauty,

> Open the window facing Joseph. Begin happiness from this breakthrough. Loveplay is opening that window. The eye is luminous from the beauty of the beloved.[44]

Loveplay adds an intriguing twist in the discussion of love in the master-disciple relationship because it indicates a reciprocal sharing of love. For the early Naqshbandīs the starting point of any meaningful connection to God begins by loving the master who in turn must make himself worthy of being loved.[45] When someone suggested to Aḥrār that looking at beardless youths was

---

[41]Kāshifī, *Rashaḥāt*, p. 601, cited in Meier, *Zwei Abhandlungen*, p. 76. Presumably this involved visualization, since we have Nūruddīn Tashkandī having only one wish to request of 'Ubaydullāh Aḥrār—to see his face from time to time; see Kāshifī, *Rashaḥāt*, p. 636, cited in Meier, *Zwei Abhandlungen*, p. 64.

[42]See ibid., p. 157.

[43]Aḥrār mentions how Muḥammad, during his last illness, closed all the doors in the Medina Mosque except that of Abū Bakr; see Kāshifī, *Rashaḥāt*, p. 442, cited in Meier, *Zwei Abhandlungen*, p. 108. Bāqībillāh reinforced this concept by representing the shaykh as a burning mirror with God as the sun and the disciple burning up like dry cotton; see Kishmī, *Zubdat al-maqāmāt*, p. 42, cited in Meier, *Zwei Abhandlungen*, p. 109.

[44]Kāshifī, *Rashaḥāt*, p. 442, cited in Meier, *Zwei Abhandlungen*, p. 156. This loosely translated verse uses a word play on one of the words found in the hadith used to substantiate Abū Bakr's love of Muḥammad. Jāmī often mentioned loveplay; see ibid, pp. 156–57.

[45]See ibid., p. 161.

not against the shariʿa as long as one's desire was chaste *(shawat-i pāk)*, Aḥrār responded, "I cannot look without lust so where are you coming from so that you gaze [at beardless youths] without lust?"[46] Due to its controversial nature, loveplay appears rarely in sufi literature and even more rarely in the writings of the self-consciously shariʿa-minded Naqshbandiyya.[47] Although loveplay was a relatively limited practice among the Naqshbandiyya, it is one more example of the skillful means sufis have to harness human emotions to accelerate their disciples' voyage toward God.

Later, Mujaddidīs attributed Shīʿīs' extreme love for the Prophet's family (sometimes expressed through corporeal flagellation during Muḥarram celebrations) and the Christian attribution of divine ontological status to the prophet Jesus as examples of excessive love.[48] Since the love of God is obligatory *(mūjib)* for Muslims, it is a religious obligation *(farḍ)* to love both the Prophet and an intimate of God since both have happily arrived *(muwaṣṣil)* at God.[49] Yet this cannot be forced; instead the disciple should spontaneously love the shaykh.[50] Naturally a true lover never finds fault with the beloved.

Psychological Methods

The behavioral and psychological dynamics involved in sufi training are complex. There is a strict behavioral code governing anyone visiting the shaykh; in addition, initiates must learn to imitate the spiritual mentor as the living archetype of the Prophetic ideal, the "symbolizer" who embodies Muḥammad and who is empowered to transform the disciple's existence. Like the Prophet the shaykh has to be unconditionally obeyed; only then can the disciple expect to change his behavior in a way that produces the psychological attitude necessary for spiritual transformation.

In actual practice obedience means that even the most learned religious scholar must as a disciple recognize that his shaykh

[46]Kāshifī, *Rashaḥāt*, p. 559, cited in Meier, *Zwei Abhandlungen*, p. 162.

[47]Peter Lamborn Wilson discusses loveplay in his *Scandal: Essays in Islamic Heresy*, pp. 93–121.

[48]See Jaipūrī, *Miʿyār al-sulūk*, p. 37 [taken from Qāḍī Thanāʾullāh Pānīpatī, *Irshād al-ṭālibīn*, p. 27]. In the reformist environment of British India love took on a much larger role in Naqshbandī practice.

[49]Pānīpatī, *Irshād al-ṭālibīn*, p. 26. The functional equation of the shaykh and the Prophet is common in sufi literature.

[50]Jaipūrī, *Miʿyār al-sulūk*, p. 38.

knows best. In Indian sufism a well-known example is that of Niẓāmuddīn Awliyā' (d. 725/1325), who suggested that his master, Farīduddīn, was reading from a faulty manuscript and should use another, better one. This implication that the master could not correct the copy he was using was enough to banish him from the master's presence. Only the quick intervention of Farīduddīn's son enabled the anguished Niẓāmuddīn to return again to his mentor's circle. The same principle applies even before initiation.[51] Ghulām Nabīlillāhī (d. 1306/1888) was said to have thought that Muḥyīddīn Quṣūrī (d. 1270/1854) was not a qualified shaykh because he did not keep his feet apart at the optimal *(mustaḥabb)* distance during ritual prayer. Allegedly Muḥyīddīn read Ghulām Nabīlillāhī's thoughts and told him after the prayer that as a shaykh he was aware of these nuances.[52]

To derive benefit from the shaykh, the visitor or disciple must believe in the pir's ability to heal, counsel, and act as a spiritual guide. A disciple who hears of any inappropriate saying or action attributed to his or her spiritual mentor is asked either to discover its inner meaning, consider it as a faulty understanding, or dismiss it as the pir's involuntary intoxication *(jadhba)*.[53] A shaykh's deeds are always performed with God's permission, so a person objecting to them can receive no divine energy:[54] "A thought against the shaykh is like an enemy, and an enemy cannot receive any benefit."[55]

The Qur'ānic precedent validating the pir's seemingly inexplicable actions comes from Qur'ān 18:65–82, where Moses is unable to see the deeper meaning in his guide Khiḍr's apparently illicit behavior, and Moses's lack of trust in Khiḍr causes the shaykh to dismiss him.[56] God guides the shaykh through inspiration *(ilhām)*.

---

[51]At this stage one is supposed to be more critical—making sure that the pir follows the shari'a is one more mechanism to insure against gross abuses of authority.

[52]Muḥammad Maṭlūb ar-Rasūl, *Anwār-i Haḍrat Lillāhī*, pp. 16–17. It is reported that Ghulām Nabīlillāhī asked for and was granted initiation immediately afterward.

[53]Muḥammad 'Ināyatullāh, *Maqāmāt-i irshādiyya*, pp. 227–28. There are limits to this unquestioning acceptance. If a shaykh continually acts contrary to the sunna then the disciple should go to another shaykh. The pir is not considered absolutely infallible since he could do something against the shari'a as a result of human nature just as the Companions had done.

[54]Pānīpatī, *Irshād al-ṭālibīn*, p. 26.

[55]Qā'imuddīn Qānūngū'ī, *Dhikr-i mubārak: masha'ikh-i sādāt-i Makān Sharīf*, p. 161.

[56]Khiḍr, soon after sinking the ship in which they were traveling, killed a boy whom they met on the way for no apparent reason. Later Khiḍr explained that a king was seizing all ships and that by sinking the ship he had saved it for the poor

Unlike prophetic revelation *(waḥy)*, inspirations can be mistaken. Sufis justify this idea by comparing shaykhs to those who are qualified to give independent legal judgments *(mujtahids)*. Like them, the intimates of God are not punished for their mistakes, and criticism is not allowed.[57] Abū Ḥāmid al-Ghazzālī (d. 505/1111) states, "Let him know that the advantage he [the disciple] gains from the error of his Shaykh, if he [the shaykh] should err, is greater than the advantage he [the disciple] gains from his own rightness if he should be right."[58]

The psychological and emotional bond with the spiritual mentor should be complete so that a *rābiṭa* can be developed and the aspirant can be connected to Muḥammad. The disciple, like a child imitating its parents, should follow the shaykh in everything he does—eating, drinking, dress, tying his turban, sleeping, and worship.[59] The shaykh is self-consciously the exemplar of Muḥammad. The disciple should consult with the spiritual guide concerning any out-of-the-ordinary event or significant dreams, concealing nothing, as one would with a parent (or today a psychoanalyst).[60]

The shaykh's inner connection with Muḥammad makes his rights over the disciple greater than any other human being's, because his rights over others are equivalent to Muḥammad's. Sufis contrast biological birth leading to earthly life, which lasts (figuratively) a few days, to one's spiritual birth at the feet of a pir, which lasts forever.[61] Sufis state that all the disciple's goals both in this world and the next are built upon the shaykh's contentment with the seeker. Disciples who forget to perform to their pirs' satisfaction will be cut off from *fayḍ* and will receive none of God's rewards.[62] Muḥammad ʿAlī Jaipūrī relates, "When the pir's disposition is content then God will be content because the pir's happiness and unhappiness are [directly] related to God's happiness and unhappiness."[63]

If the disciple is in the company of an intimate of God other than his or her own guide, he should behave toward this other

owners. The boy was a tyrant who would have caused his parents undeserved afflictions, leading them unwittingly to commit serious sins themselves.

[57]Muḥammad ʿInāyatullāh, *Maqāmāt-i irshādiyya*, pp. 229–30.

[58]H. A. R. Gibb, *Mohammedanism: An Historical Survey*, pp. 102–03.

[59]Muḥammad ʿInāyatullāh, *Maqāmāt-i irshādiyya*, p. 230.

[60]Ibid., p. 231.

[61]Jaipūrī, *Miʿyār al-sulūk*, p. 36.

[62]Zawwār Ḥusayn, *ʿUmdat al-sulūk*, p. 48.

[63]Jaipūrī, *Miʿyār al-sulūk*, p. 172. Bāqībillāh was so happy with a blind man that he arrived close to God in one sitting; see ibid., p. 173.

pir just as if he were his own spiritual guide, and any *fayḍ* received should be regarded as coming from his or her own mentor.[64] When one's shaykh is perceived as preferable to all others, then an outpouring of love for the pir ensues, resulting in an inner affinity *(munāsabat)* with the pir. As love for the mentor develops it becomes egoless. An extreme example of this principle is exemplified in the story of a faithful disciple who became closer to God than his spiritual mentor had. Later the shaykh even lost his intimacy with God *(wilāya)* by committing a grave sin, but this loyal disciple was the only one who did not abandon him.[65] Rūmī asks, ". . . [How do you expect] to attain endless and everlasting life, which is the station of the prophets and the intimates of God *(awliyā')*, and nothing disagreeable happens to you, and you never give up anything? . . . [You should consider] how a person, when he loves a youth or a woman, will pretend, grovel, and sacrifice all belongings, going to the greatest pains to trick her so that he may soothe her heart night and day, unflagging in this [activity] and wearying of all else. Is the love of the shaykh and the love of God less than this? . . . He who abandons the shaykh . . . it is known that he is no lover or seeker. If he were a [true] lover and seeker, he would put up with much more than what we have presented."[66]

In addition to the emotional bonding of love, another parallel process in the master-disciple relationship is consciously modeling oneself on the spiritual guide. This too requires an unquestioning attitude toward the shaykh and a loving desire to be like him. For those unacquainted with the process, the degree to which a person can undergo an inner transformation through modeling can be astonishing.[67]

---

[64]Muḥammad 'Ināyatullāh, *Maqāmāt-i irshādiyya*, p. 232. Zawwār Ḥusayn says that everyone has to perceive his or her own pir as better than all others. See *'Umdat al-sulūk*, p. 59.

[65]Qā'imuddīn Qānūngū'ī, *Dhikr-i mubārak*, p. 115. Rūmī cites the exceptional case of a disciple putting such faith in an impostor that he progresses far beyond the impostor spiritually. See Jalāluddīn Rūmī, *Mathnawī-yi ma'nawī*, 6 volumes, vol. 1, verse 2283–85 [hereafter 1.2283–85].

[66]Rūmī, *Fīhi mā fīhi*, p. 96.

[67]"A number of people several years ago, for instance, spent some time modeling Milton Erickson. He was pretty much *the* medical hypnotist of the twentieth century. A number of people went down to visit Erickson in Phoenix, Arizona, and spent a great deal of time studying his nonverbal behavior. They took videotapes of him and invested themselves in an experiment whereby they went around imitating Milton. He was in his mid-seventies and a lot of these people were young men. Milton also had a number of medical problems. He was in a wheel chair, a purple wheel chair, because he was color blind and this was the main color he could see. So we had several young men riding around in purple

By itself the modeling process has extraordinary potential for individual transformation, especially when practiced in conjunction with the other methods used by directing-shaykhs. The appropriate symbols defining the Prophetic ideal are transmitted culturally, especially through the living sufi master who embodies them. In turn his disciples do their utmost to follow in every detail the model of his inner and outer behavior. Their experience of the prophetic realities results in the reinforcement of their Islamic beliefs and paradigms which they in turn transmit to others. For skeptics—Muslim or non-Muslim—it is difficult to accept that the modeling of the Prophet now—or even two hundred years after his death—would correspond to the actual historical Muḥammad because of the dramatic changes in Muslim conceptions of Muḥammad over time. On the other hand, for those either modeling the Prophet themselves or meeting someone who exhibits recognizable prophetic traits, the transformational experience of what they perceive the presence of the Prophet to be overshadows all other considerations.

In retrospect the nineteenth-century training repertoire of directing-shaykhs goes far beyond his tenth-century counterpart. The early consolidation of authority in the directing-shaykh underscores his infallibility in disciplining the recalcitrant ego of an unquestioning aspirant. In the early Naqshbandī context this taming of the ego involved surrender to the spiritual guide both behaviorally and psychologically, as the novice persevered in disciplined performance of recollection and contemplation exercises. By the fifteenth century cultivating the *rābiṭa* between the master and disciple became a spiritual method in its own right, potentially independent of other spiritual exercises. It was yet another addition to the Naqshbandī repertoire; directing-shaykhs like Aḥrār would train novices using a combination of some or all of these methods.

In stark contrast to the teaching-shaykh, the directing-shaykh created a bond which, along with modeling and visualizing him, consciously cultivated a transformative psychological climate.

wheel chairs acting like a very old man who had no teeth, who mumbled and put everyone in trance that he met. They did this for six months or so. One guy got so good and so much like Milton Erickson, that people who knew Milton Erickson were very spooked by this guy's behavior and presence. In addition, he began to take on Milton Erickson's physical limitations. Erickson's left side was in pretty bad shape and paralysed. After six months or so, this nineteen-year-old man's left side started to paralyse. At that point, he abandoned the experiment. . . ." "Panel comments" by Tom Condon in Ruth-Inge Heinze, *Proceedings of the International Conference on the Study of Shamanism*, p. 77.

The emotional dimension of this relationship is heightened in the bonding process as the natural respect and veneration that used to develop spontaneously into love of the shaykh was now deliberately made an integral part of the spiritual tie. One common factor in both the cultivation of the spiritual bond and the performance of spiritual exercises is the necessity of the shaykh's directed spiritual energy.

Available Naqshbandī sources are not detailed enough to compare various Naqshbandī shaykhs and determine the extent to which the emphasis on the spiritual bond dominated Sufi training. The collected letters of notable Indian Naqshbandī shaykhs supply ample evidence of directing-shaykhs at work through their activation of subtle centers and the resultant uncontrolled responses of spiritual attraction to spiritual energy. There is every reason to suppose that visualization exercises and love of the shaykh complemented the teaching of recollection and contemplation. The *communitas* of the sufi lodge provided an ideal setting for simultaneous transmission of these practices.

CHAPTER 7

From Initiation to Shaykhdom

A few believers founded a sufi lodge that was just like the bench in the Prophet's mosque; subsequently over the centuries it has become perfected.
Jalāluddīn Humā'ī, *Taṣawwuf dar Islām*

Anyone who does not have a shaykh has Satan for a shaykh.
A saying attributed to Abū Yazīd al-Bisṭāmī

Guiding others in the "inner sunna" of the Prophet, i.e., spiritual travel, was the exclusive domain of the directing-shaykh, who often lived in the *communitas* of the sufi lodge, where correct outward behavior was the preliminary stage of obedience. When the inner transformation involving the inculcation of an unquestioning and uncritical attitude toward the shaykh and his actions had been achieved and a spontaneous love for the master had developed, the disciple would be in harmony with the shaykh and ready to achieve a direct connection to Muḥammad and God.

In the sufi community the disciple was continually under scrutiny, which from the outset could be intensely, even uncomfortably, personal. Like a psychiatrist,[1] the shaykh advised and counseled individuals in addition to seeing through the ruses of the ego. Unlike a psychiatrist, however, he would prescribe de-

[1]In an article synthesizing the essence of psychotherapy, Judd Marmor writes, "There are at least seven different major factors that take place in the psychotherapeutic process. The most basic of these is the patient-therapist relationship. Other factors are the release of emotional tension in the context of expectancy and hope, the acquisition of cognitive insight, operant conditioning (including corrective emotional experiences), identification with the therapist, suggestion and persuasion, and finally, rehearsal and working-through of the new adaptive patterns of behavior and thought." See "Common Denominators in Diverse Approaches," p. 270. The sufi master in his lodge performs quite similar functions.

meaning tasks or other chores as a corrective to any pretentious tendencies. No book or intellectual achievement could substitute for a personal relationship with the spiritual mentor. This authority, based on his divine mandate as heir to the Prophet, enabled the guide to wield supernatural power as God's mediator. In addition to the sufi shaykhs' role as intermediary between God and humans, sufis could also be called upon to mediate worldly concerns. The sufi shaykh became the living pointer to God, the embodied Kaʿba showing the Way, and for many, the primary approach to God. For these reasons when visiting the sufi lodge one behaved in an appropriate fashion just as one behaved in a certain way when in the presence of a king in his court.

Ritual in the sufi lodge involves behavioral codes just as if one were in the presence of a king. In both cases a lapse in protocol could have dire consequences. Sufi literature indicates that at minimum a person would be cut off from the *fayḍ* of the shaykh. There are innumerable examples in both sufi and non-sufi literature of cases involving a shaykh's retaliation for treating him with anything but the utmost respect.[2] The three goals of properly observed sufi etiquette are to improve morals, to assist the student to control his or her ego, and finally, to facilitate spiritual wayfaring. Without correct attitudes toward the pir and appropriate behavior in his presence the aspirant can go nowhere; everything depends on these basics *(aṭ-ṭarīq kulluhu adab)*.[3]

In nineteenth- and twentieth-century India, some rules applied to everyone coming into the presence of a sufi master. Usually people sat on the floor, for example, because no one would dare sit on a seat higher than that of the shaykh—whether in elevation

---

[2]The examples used in this chapter are drawn largely from Indian Naqshbandī material from the British colonial period. For a Central Asian comparison, see Abū'l-Mufākhir Yaḥyā Bākharzī (d. 723–4/1323–4), *Awrād al-aḥbāb wa-fuṣūṣ al-ādāb*, 2 vols., 2:64–76. A large literature has accumulated on correct behavior in the sufi environment. Fritz Meier has comprehensively reviewed the early literature on sufi rules for disciples in addition to translating an early manual of sufi etiquette by Najmuddīn Kubrā, *Ādāb al-murīdīn*. See Fritz Meier, "Ein Knigge für Sufis." For a brief summary of sufi etiquette in English, see Caesar E. Farah, "Rules Governing the Shaykh-Murshid's Conduct." A later compilation (ca. 712/1314) of appropriate sufi conduct can be found in Shamsuddīn Ibrāhīm Abarquhī, *Majmaʿ al-baḥrayn*, pp. 292–319.

[3]Meier, "Ḫurāsān und das Ende der klassischen Ṣūfik," p. 556, quoting the ninth-century sufi Abū Ḥafṣ Nīshāpūrī al-Ḥaddād. In recent times an Indian Naqshbandī shaykh, Imām ʿAlī Shāh (d. 1282/1865), wrote, "Sufism is completely perfect behavior *(adab)*" and "Disciples with improper behavior *(bē adab)* are blocked from worldly benefits"; see Qāʾimuddīn Qānūngūʾī, *Dhikr-i mubārak: mashāʾikh-i sādāt-i Makān Sharīf*, p. 161.

or in positioning within the room.[4] In an empty room the shaykh sat on cushions, like the throne of a king, to ensure he had the higher seat. In addition no one could use the pir's special receptacle for carrying water, perform ablutions at his special place, step on his special place of prayer, talk to him in a loud voice, and look him straight in the face.[5]

Protocol required that everyone stand when the shaykh came in to or left an assembly.[6] No person's shadow was supposed to touch the pir's clothing or body, nor was anyone to spit toward him. The soles of the feet could never face in his direction, nor could one turn one's back on him.[7] One left the presence of a shaykh, whether living or deceased, by backing up, until one reached the door and put one's shoes on.

The sufis had taken many of these rules of etiquette from the Persian court at least as long ago as the thirteenth century.[8] Sufi shrines and the seat of a sufi master in Indo-Pakistan are also often called the "king's court" *(dargāh* or *darbār).* Maulānā Rūmī (d. 672/1273) relates:

There was a shaykh who used to leave his disciples standing with their hands folded in service. Others [seeing this situation] asked him, "O

---

[4]With the advent of the British and the European custom of sitting on chairs, sitting on the floor was considered sunna. See Maḥbūbilāhī, *Tuḥfa-yi sa'diyya,* p. 169.

[5]Muḥammad 'Ināyatullāh, *Maqāmāt-i irshādiyya,* p. 229, and Zawwār Ḥusayn, *'Umdat al-sulūk,* p. 57. There is a Qur'ānic admonition (49:2) against speaking in a louder voice than Muḥammad.

[6]Muḥammad 'Umar Bīrbalī, *Inqilāb al-ḥaqīqat,* p. 13.

[7]Ibid.; see also Hidāyat 'Alī Jaipūrī, *Mi'yār al-sulūk wa-dāfi' al-awhām wa'l-shukūk,* p. 241, where it is said that Imām 'Alī Shāh (d. 1282/1865) never turned his back or spat in the direction of his pir's village. In ordinary social situations it is considered extremely impolite to point the sole of the foot in anyone's direction or to have one's back toward someone. Children are reprimanded in the mosque for pointing the soles of their feet in the direction of prayer *(qibla);* this explains why Muslims sleeping in the mosque invariably sleep with their heads pointing toward the *qibla.* I have yet to find anyone to supply a textual justification for such a rule and can only assume that it is another example of community consensus *(ijmā').* The shaykh assumes the same status as the *qibla,* as the disciple is admonished not to extend his leg in the pir's direction when he is absent; see Na'īmullāh Bahrā'ichī, *Ma'mūlāt-i Maẓhariyya,* p. 58.

[8]It is common for writers to explain correct sufi etiquette in terms of a king and his subjects; see Muḥammad 'Ināyatullāh, *Maqāmāt-i irshādiyya,* p. 229. Although not a Naqshbandī custom, there are cases of Indo-Muslim pirs justifying ritual prostration, a direct adaptation from the Persian kingship paradigm. See Paul Jackson, *The Way of a Sufi: Sharafuddin Maneri,* p. 142, and Niẓāmuddīn Awliyā', *Morals for the Heart,* pp. 321–22. For a discussion of Persian kingship and the Indo-Muslim state, see Carl Ernst, *Eternal Garden: Mysticism, History, and Politics at a*

> Shaykh! Why do you not let this group sit down? This is not the practice of dervishes; this is the custom of princes and kings." He replied, "No. Be quiet. I want them to respect this way [of behavior], so that they may enjoy full benefit. Although veneration is in the heart, 'the outward is the title page of the inward'. . . . The meaning of the title page is that from it [people] know for whom and to whom the treatise [is written] . . . and may know what chapters and sections there are. From outward veneration *(taʿẓīm)*, bowing the head and standing on the feet, it becomes evident what inward reverence *(taʿẓīm)* they have, and in what manner they honor God. If they do not show outward respect, it becomes known that inwardly they are impudent and do not venerate the men of God."[9]

One possible consequence of adapting the Persian court model was that it might have discouraged the meeting of kings and sufis. When the court of man and the court of God share overlapping rules of etiquette, it is no wonder that kings and sufis might have avoided meeting each other, lest one or the other feel the need to insist on ceremony.[10]

One basis of the pir's authority rested on his ability to move between subtle worlds and help others do the same. In practice, however, many white-bearded, outwardly pious Muslims, generally recognized as shaykhs, accepted thousands of eager aspirants in the name of sufism without having even a minimum of spiritual qualifications by Naqshbandī standards. Finding a perfect and perfection-bestowing master under these conditions was the first and perhaps the most difficult task of all for the aspirant desiring to embark on the spiritual path.

A twentieth-century Naqshbandī poignantly described the difficulty of finding a suitable spiritual mentor as more difficult than locating pure flour, milk, or ghee.[11] Considering the adulterated food supply in South Asia, that is tantamount to indicating a difficulty that borders on the impossible. In the nineteenth century, revivalist Naqshbandīs observed that most people calling themselves shaykhs conformed neither to the shariʿa nor to the practices of the Prophet, citing their infrequent performance of ritual prayer, a shaved or trimmed beard, long mustaches, and the

---

South Asian Sufi Center, pp. 38–47; and Ann K. Lambton, "Quis Custodiet Custodes: Some Reflections on the Persian Theory of Government."

[9]Jalāluddīn Rūmī, *Kitāb-i fīhi mā fīhi*, p. 149.

[10]One common theme in sufi stories is how the shaykh avoids meeting the king or how the shaykh treats him ordinarily if a meeting occurs. In practice there were many instances of sufi-ruler interactions in India and Central Asia.

[11]Ṣiddīq Aḥmad, *Dhikr-i maḥbūb*, p. 11.

wearing of long trousers.[12] In addition, Naqshbandīs warned against the family custom of going to hereditary pirs; though their ancestors may have been qualified pirs at one time and these hereditary pirs could often counsel people in their mundane problems, they were not qualified to be spiritual guides.[13] They had no inner connection *(nisbat)* to the Prophet, nor had they ever traveled along the sufi path.[14]

Muḥammad ʿUmar Bīrbalī (d. 1387/1967), in talking about his grandfather Ghulām Murtaḍā (d. 1321/1903), succinctly describes the revivalist Naqshbandī ideal of a spiritual guide who embodies both inner and outer knowledge: "On one the hand he was a comprehensive religious scholar *(ʿālim)* who used to convey subtly nuanced points of sufism in simple and common language. On the other hand, he used to enliven dead hearts with one glance. . . . He was a lover and exemplary follower of the [Prophetic] *sunnat* . . . yet would perform miracles *(kharq wa-karāmāt)*. . . . Like the Prophet's (S) assemblies, the young and the old and the lowest and highest would receive divine grace [in his presence] . . . [and he] would speak to each according to each individual's understanding."[15]

---

[12]Jaipūrī, *Miʿyār al-sulūk*, p. 29. Certain Muslim groups in British colonial India observed the following sunna practices: a beard that was only trimmed in excess of one fist length, a mustache that was trimmed above the upper lip or preferably shaved, a turban, trousers whose length was above the ankle bone, and for women, *parda* ensuring that women would not have any contact with men outside their immediate family. Naqshbandīs interpreted *parda* as an unambiguous religious duty *(farḍ)* and expected disciples to practice total *parda*. The reasoning was that the sunna action of *bayʿa* is useless unless one performed *farḍ* obligations first. The Naqshbandīs (and later the Tablīghī Jamāʿat group) expected these norms to be strictly observed by their members. How these aspects of the Prophet's dress and behavior (as opposed to others) came to define correct nineteenth-century Islamic norms would be a worthwhile study.

[13]In contemporary studies, there is evidence of strong family pressure for all family members to give allegiance to the same pir, and family ties are often reinforced this way. In Delhi and Lucknow, most interviewees state that their ancestors are disciples of the ancestors of their respective pirs. Census of India, "Beliefs and Practices Associated with Muslim Pirs in Two Cities of India (Delhi and Lucknow)," pp. 23, 33. Turk's study shows that 41 percent of the villagers surveyed had the same shaykh as their fathers; the corresponding figure for the urban population was 15 percent. See G. M. S. Turk, "Attitudes of 'Mureeds' Towards 'Pirs' in Two Selected Samples," cited by Adrian C. Mayer, "Pir and Murshid: An Aspect of Religious Leadership in West Pakistan," p. 164.

[14]Jaipūrī, *Miʿyār al-sulūk*, p. 31; Ṣiddīq Aḥmad, *Dhikr-i maḥbūb*, p. 48. For examples of finding and choosing a shaykh according to Abū Madyan (d. 594/1198) and his followers, see Vincent Cornell, "Mirrors of Prophethood: The Evolving Image of the Spiritual Master in the Western Maghrib from the Origins of Sufism to the End of the Sixteenth Century," pp. 327–29.

[15]Bīrbalī, *Inqilāb al-ḥaqīqat*, p. 6 [comments mine].

Shāh Walīullāh (d. 1176/1762) specified seven criteria for a spiritual guide which also set the standards for the revivalist milieu of the nineteenth and twentieth centuries: (1) The pir should have studied the Qur'ānic exegesis of either the *Jalālayn* or the *Madārik* with a qualified scholar.[16] In hadith studies he should have studied either the *Mishkat al-maṣābīḥ* or the *Mashāriq al-anwār*.[17] (2) The pir should have abandoned desire for this world and the next world and demonstrate this by obediently acting in accordance with what has been transmitted from the Prophet and the early generations of Islam. 3) The shaykh should exhibit piety *(taqwā)*, completely avoid major sins, and hold minor sins in check. (4) The shaykh should abstain from prohibited things and order others to act in a permissible manner. (5) The pir should have purified his nature by companionship *(ṣuḥbat)* with a perfected pir and, having continual presence of God in his heart, the pir should have formal permission to teach *(ijāza)*. (6) The shaykh should not feel the need to perform miracles. (7) Finally, companionship with the pir should affect others in such a way as to make their heart cold to the world and instill a love of God, the Prophet, and intimates of God *(awliyā')*.[18]

This combination of qualifications in a spiritual guide is rare enough; rarer still is the ability of a seeker to recognize it. A minority of especially sensitive seekers involuntarily react to a shaykh's spiritual power *(tawajjuh)*. Dōst Muḥammad (d. 1284/1868), for example, first met Ghulām ʿAlī Shāh (d. 1240/1824) in the Prophet's Mosque in Medina. Ghulām ʿAlī's *fayḍ* was so strong that it caused Dōst Muḥammad to become restless and disturbed *(bē qarār)*, so that he could hardly move from one corner of the mosque to another for an entire day. Ghulām ʿAlī passed away before Dōst Muḥammad could become his disciple. The latter kept having fits of ecstasy, however, some of which lasted weeks on end. After much traveling and inner turmoil, he became the disciple of Aḥmad Saʿīd (d. 1277/1860), the son of

[16]Jalāluddīn as-Suyūṭī and Jalāluddīn Muḥammad b. Aḥmad al-Maḥallī, *Tafsīr al-qur'ān al-karīm, tafsīr al-jalālayn*, and Ḥāfiẓuddīn ʿAbdullāh b. Aḥmad an-Nasafī, *Madārik al-tanzīl wa-ḥaqā'iq al-tā'wīl*.

[17]The *Mishkat al-maṣābīḥ*, written by Muḥammad b. ʿAbdullāh al-Khaṭīb at-Tabrīzī (d. 743/1342), is a revised version of Abū Muḥammad al-Ḥusayn b. Masʿūd al-Baghawī's (d. ca. 516/1122) *Maṣābīḥ al-sunna*. *Mashāriq al-anwār* was written by Raḍīuddīn al-Ḥasan b. al-Ḥasan Ṣaghānī and translated into Urdu as *Tuḥfat al-akhyār* (Lucknow: Nawal Kishōr, 1920).

[18]See Shāh Walīullāh, *Al-qawl al-jamīl*, Urdu trans. Khurram ʿAlī, *Shifā' al-ʿalīl*, 2d ed., pp. 22–26, Ṣiddīq Aḥmad, *Dhikr-i mahbūb*, pp. 46–47, and Zawwār Ḥusayn, *ʿUmdat al-sulūk*, pp. 43–45.

Ghulām ʿAlī Shāh's successor, Abū Saʿīd (d. 1250/1835), in Delhi.[19] This example illustrates another principle: if one cannot have the great fortune to be a disciple of a shaykh who is permanently in the Essence *(dhāt)*, then the next best alternative is to follow one of his disciples.[20]

Seekers without these unmistakable indications need more careful guidance. One alternative for aspirants without a background in the religious sciences is to ask knowledgeable ulama about a shaykh's qualifications.[21] Since most people do not feel the effects of a pir's spiritual power in the beginning, it is recommended that seekers investigate the effects of a pir's companionship *(ṣuḥbat)* upon his disciples. The seeker is supposed to confer with respectable members of the community to ascertain that the behavior of the shaykh's disciples is upright and that his disciples have no desire for high position or for worldly gain.[22] The sons of pirs and people displaying ecstatic behavior are particularly to be avoided.[23]

At minimum the shaykh should be outwardly pious and follow the dictates of the shariʿa. A spiritual guide sits in the company of ulama and, in addition to mastering practical jurisprudence *(fiqh)*, he exhibits perfected correct behavior *(ādāb)*, the sum total of which he demonstrates in behavior conforming with the Qurʾān and the Prophetic sunna.[24] If, in addition, the pir has respectable ulama in his company and impresses the seeker favorably, then this exemplary spiritual mentor is "red sulfur" *(kibrīt aḥmar)*, a special and precious human being.[25] Such a perfect pir, *ṣāḥib-i qāl wa-ḥāl*, represents one having an inner connection to Muḥammad through the oral transmission *(qāl)* of knowledge, e.g., hadith study, and a person whose inner connection to Muḥammad manifests itself outwardly in a spiritual state *(ḥāl)*.[26]

---

[19]Muḥammad Ismāʿīl, *Mawāhib raḥmāniyya fī fawāʾiḍ wa-fuyūḍāt ḥaḍarāt thalātha dāmāniyya: al-tajalliyāt al-dōstiyya* [hereafter *Al-tajalliyāt al-dōstiyya*], pp. 24–32.

[20]Muḥammad ʿInāyatullāh, *Maqāmāt-i irshādiyya*, p. 227.

[21]Ibid., p. 227.

[22]Qāḍī Thanāʾullāh Pānīpatī, *Irshād al-ṭālibīn*, pp. 23–24.

[23]Ibid., p. 23. Intoxicated behavior was acceptable for an aspirant, but not considered by Mujaddidīs as a sign of spiritual advancement.

[24]Ibid. p. 44.

[25]Bahrāʾichī, *Maʿmūlāt-i maẓhariyya*, p. 31. The effect of a pir's spiritual energy *(tawajjuh)* should override all other considerations except shariʿa-mindedness. Shēr Muḥammad expected his spiritual guide to be older than the youthful Amīruddīn, but having felt Amīruddīn's spiritual power, Shēr Muḥammad had no choice but to ask him for initiation. See Muḥammad Ibrāhīm Quṣūrī, *Khazīna-yi maʿrifat*, p. 155.

[26]Bīrbalī, *Inqilāb al-ḥaqīqat*, p. 6 n. 2.

Many other avenues leading to a spiritual guide bypass the checklist approach of revivalist sufi literature. Some find their guide after seeing him in a dream. Budd'han Shāh (d. 1272/1855–56), for example, became extremely agitated in the presence of Shāh Ḥusayn (d. 1225/1809) when requesting initiation. Shāh Ḥusayn suggested he do *istikhāra* first, but Budd'han Shāh said he already had confirmation that Shāh Ḥusayn was the correct person from a dream.[27]

For Muḥammad 'Umar Bīrbalī matters were not so straight forward. Although he was the son of a hereditary shaykh, he felt cut off from any inner heritage and deprived of an "inner education," both of which kindled a desire for a spiritual guide in his heart.[28] He first made a supplication to God *(du'ā')* in order to find a spiritual guide before visiting the graves of his grandfather Ghulām Murtaḍā and of other shaykhs, including Niẓāmuddīn Awilyā' (d. 725/1325), Quṭbuddīn Bakhtiyār Kākī (d. 633/1235), and Bāqībillāh (d. 1012/1603). While in Delhi, he was able to talk with Shāh Abū'l-Khayr (d. 1341/1924). Eventually he found his spiritual guide after some people in Lahore told him about Shēr Muḥammad (d. 1345/1928). In Hidāyat 'Alī Jaipūrī's case, he thought his life was at an end because of a four-month bout of fever. After visiting Muḥammad 'Alī Shēr Khān (d. 1328/1910) his fever was cured in a day. Hidāyat 'Alī became his disciple and remained in his service for eighteen years.[29]

When a seeker finds the perfect spiritual mentor there is no guarantee that the shaykh will agree to accept the potential disciple. Muḥammad 'Uthmān (d. 1314/1896), represented in hagiographical literature as being so overcome with the love of God *(istighrāq)* that he could no longer continue his religious studies, decided to go into the service of a shaykh. After crossing the river near Dōst Muḥammad's residence at Musa Zai, such a strong heat swelled up in him (he attributed this condition to his inner connection to Dōst Muḥammad) that he was forced to stay in the

---

[27]Qā'imuddīn Qānūngū'ī, *Dhikr-i mubārak,* pp. 116–17. *Istikhāra* is trusting God to make a decision between one or more alternatives. Muḥammad is said to have taught Muslims to pray two *rak'as* followed by a supplication referring to the matter to be decided. Muḥammad Sa'īd Qurayshī also saw his future pir in a dream. See Zawwār Ḥusayn, *Ḥayāt-i sa'diyya,* p. 17.

[28]Bīrbalī, *Inqilāb al-ḥaqīqat,* p. 3.

[29]Jaipūrī, *Mi'yār al-sulūk,* p. 265. This kind of affiliation process, i.e., becoming initiated after a spectacular cure, occurs with contemporary pirs, although it does not necessarily result in a disciple following the sufi path; i.e., one can become a nonpracticing disciple. See P. Lewis, *Pirs, Shrines and Pakistani Islam,* pp. 12–13.

river to cool down. Upon arrival at Musa Zai he kissed Dōst Muḥammad's feet and indicated his intention to become initiated. Dōst Muḥammad refused to initiate him, saying, "It is a very difficult business to choose spiritual poverty." Muḥammad 'Uthmān responded, "O Qibla I have become absolutely ready for this work. [Although] I have tolerated being connected with everything, now I have turned a cold shoulder to it and have irrevocably divorced myself from everything that I have loved."[30] That evening Dōst Muḥammad initiated him into the Naqshbandiyya.

After experiencing the travails of searching for a spiritual guide, the seeker must be formally accepted by the spiritual mentor and participate in an initiation ceremony *(bayʿa)*. This ritual officially links the disciple by an oath of allegiance to the shaykh and, by extension, to Muḥammad via the spiritual lineage of the Naqshbandiyya or any other chosen pedigree. After initiation the seeker, as a disciple of the shaykh, learns certain responsibilities and a code of behavior before proceeding on the sufi path.

Becoming a Disciple

In the Prophet's time *bayʿa* generally meant "recognizing authority and pledging obedience to that authority" whether in the context of becoming a Muslim, association with the Medinan community *(hijra)*, participation in battle *(jihād)*, or leadership succession *(khilāfa)*.[31] Before the advent of Islam, *bayʿa* was the traditional way of pledging allegiance to a tribal chief. The handclasp as an established way of pledging allegiance refers to the Companions performing *bayʿa* at Hudaybiya in 6/628: "Those who swear allegiance to you [Muḥammad] actually swear allegiance to God. God's hand is over their hands." [Q. 48:10] Companions had no need for *bayʿa* to begin spiritual traveling, says Shāh Walīullāh, since this was a natural outcome of Muḥammad's companionship.[32] Over time Muslims began to associate *bayʿa* with government leadership succession, especially when Muslim rulers continued the practice of *bayʿa* to affirm political allegiance. Eventually as the sultans abandoned the practice, sufis began giving robes (sing. *khirqa*) to their disciples as a token of

[30]*Mawāhib raḥmāniyya fī fawāʾid wa-fuyūḍāt ḥaḍarāt thalātha dāmāniyya: kamālāt-i ʿuthmāniyya* [hereafter cited as *Kamālāt-i ʿuthmāniyya*], pp. 37–38. The *qibla* points Muslims to the Kaʿba; the shaykh is a pointer to God.

[31]Walīullāh, *Al-qawl al-jamīl*, p. 16.

[32]Ibid., p. 17.

bay'a, reactivating an abandoned sunna practice.[33] At that point *bay'a* took on the added meaning of affiliation with a spiritual master, summarized by, "The sufi robe signifies being in the shadow of intimacy with God; wearing it is a sign of the shaykh's acceptance [which in turn] indicates God's acceptance."[34]

Among sufis the three steps in initiation are, first, repentence from sins *(tawba)*, an oath swearing on the Prophet and the collective presences of the shaykhs of a particular sufi lineage that one will conscientiously perform the ritual duties expected of a Muslim according to the five pillars of Islam and abstain from major sins.[35] The second is an affiliation of blessedness *(tabarruk)* with the goal of accumulating auspiciousness *(baraka)* transmitted through the chain leading back to Muḥammad.[36] Often this type of bond is created between a student and a hadith teacher.[37] Shāh

---

[33]Ibid. After the middle of the tenth century caliphs in Baghdad expected those to whom they delegated their authority to take an oath of fealty *(bay'a)* even though the caliphs often had no control over these princes *(umarā'*, sing. *amīr)*. After the Mongol conquest of Baghdad in 656/1258 even these formalities were abandoned. The sufi robe is mentioned as early as the ninth century by al-Ḥārith al-Muḥāsibī (d. 243/857). See Louis Massignon, *Essai sur les origines du lexique technique de la mystique musulmane*, p. 128, and *La Passion de Husayn Ibn Mansūr Hallāj*, 1:62, [English trans. 1:72]. Apparently Abū Bakr Shiblī (d. 334/946) pioneered the ceremony of passing on the robe that symbolized the transformation of the disciple into a shaykh. See Kamil Mustafa Al-Shaibi, *Sufism and Shi'ism*, p. 69. The Prophet's robe mentioned in the Shī'ī *ḥadīth-i kisā'* is not the robe of the sufis. See Seyyed Hossain Nasr, *Sufi Essays*, pp. 109–10. For further information on sufi robes, see Richard Gramlich, *Die schiitischen Derwischorden Persiens*, 3 volumes, 2:172–73 n. 924–26; Muḥsin Kiyānī, *Tarīkh-i khānaqāh dar Īrān*, pp. 447–558; 'Alī Ibn 'Uthmān al-Jullābī al-Hujwīrī, *Kashf al-Maḥjūb*, pp. 49–65 [English trans., pp. 45–57]; Bākharzī, *Awrād al-aḥbāb*, 2:23–42.

[34]Nūruddīn Ḥamza b. 'Alī b. 'Abdulmalik Ṭūsī Bayhaqī, *Jawāhir al-asrār*, cited in Aḥmad 'Alī Rajā'ī Bukhārā'ī, *Farhang-i ash'ār-i Ḥāfiẓ*, p. 107. For an extensive but uncritical survey of the sufi robe, see 'Ali Muḥammad Sajjādī, *Jāma-yi zuhd: khirqa wa-khirqapūshī.*

[35]Bahrā'ichī, *Ma'mūlāt i maẓhariyya*, p. 34. The five pillars of Islam are testifying that there is no god but God and that Muḥammad is His messenger; performing the five daily ritual prayers; fasting during the month of Ramaḍān; paying of alms tax *(zakāt)*; and performing the pilgrimage to Mecca once in one's lifetime if possible. Major sins are associating others with God, theft, adultery, unlawful killing, lying, slandering, cheating, and killing children.

[36]The more chains leading back to Muḥammad the better. Raḍīuddīn 'Alī Lālā Ghaznawī, a contemporary of Najmuddīn Kubrā (d. 617/1220), supposedly had acquired 124 sufi robes, 113 of which he still had in his possession at the time of his death. See Jāmī, *Nafaḥāt al-uns*, p. 436, cited in R. Gramlich, *Die schiitischen Derwischorden*, 2:173 n. 928.

[37]Another form of *bay'a* that has been described as an Indo-Muslim rite of passage between circumcision and marriage often accompanies religious instruction and would probably fall in the category of *tabarruk.* See Jafar Sharif, *Qanoon-e-Islam or the Customs of the Mussulmans of India*, pp. 281–84.

Walīullāh acquired five such affiliations from his hadith teacher, Abū Ṭāhir Muḥammad, just as Aḥmad Sirhindī became affiliated with the Kubrāwiyya through his hadith teacher, Yaʿqūb Kashmīrī (d. 1003/1595).[38] Some interpret this type of *bayʿa* as an affiliation of intercession *(bayʿat-i tawassul)* where the shaykh acts as the intermediary between the believer and God in this world and the next.[39] A Qur'ānic justification for such a concept is "O believers, fear God and seek the way of approach *(al-wasīla)* to Him." [Q. 5:35][40] Most multiple sufi affiliations are of this second type.[41]

The third type of affiliation includes the requirements of the first two, i.e., abandoning serious sins, avoiding minor sins, and performing the ritual requirements, and adds a fourth, the practice of spiritual exercises. The committed seeker "has the firm intention to perform completely almighty God's decrees with a sincere heart and to save [oneself] from [committing] what God prohibits, [thereby] creating a connection with the heart and God (J)."[42] This initiation involves an outward agreement to remain in companionship *(ṣuḥbat)* and obedience to the shaykh in order to proceed on the path *(kasb-i sulūk)* to God. Through the special connection *(rābiṭa)* with the spiritual mentor, whom Naqshbandīs consider the Prophet's representative, the aspirant develops both an inner and outer connection to Muḥammad.[43] Such an encompassing affiliation differentiates initiation from the mere ritual of declaring allegiance to a pir. It requires cultivating a very close relationship with a spiritual guide which then connects one into a series of like-minded mystics consciously linked to the Prophet. This third type of initiation commits a disciple to a relationship of unquestioning obedience to a single living spiritual guide. In

---

[38]For two of Sirhindī's *ḥadīth isnāds,* see Zawwār Ḥusayn, *Ḥaḍrat mujaddid alf-i thānī,* pp. 141–42.

[39]Jaipūrī, *Miʿyār al-sulūk,* p. 42.

[40]Nūr Aḥmad Maqbūl, *Khazīnat-i karam,* p. 606, and Ṣiddīq Aḥmad, *Dhikr-i maḥbūb,* p. 39. Another Qur'ānic justification for the shaykh is "Those they call upon [to remove afflictions] are themselves seeking the means *(al-wasīla)* to approach their Lord" (Q. 17:57). See ibid. where this verse was suggested as a textual defense for those doubting the need for a shaykh. Given the context of the preceding verse (Q. 17:56) chastising those calling on anyone else but God, the verse cited above gives more support to an argument against intermediaries between God and humankind.

[41]For one of the most detailed and revealing examples of multiple initiations see Aḥmad b. Muḥammad al-Qushshāshī's (d. 1071/1660–61) *Al-simṭ al-majīd.*

[42]Zawwār Ḥusayn, *'Umdat al-sulūk,* p. 46, which is taken from Shāh Walīullāh, *Al-qawl al-jamīl,* p. 28.

[43]Muḥammad Ḥusayn Assī, *Anwār-i Lā Thānī,* p. 36.

the words of Aḥmad Riḍā Khān Barēlwī (d. 1340/1921), the founder of an Indian *"ahl-i sunnat"* or "People of the Prophet's Way" movement (which outsiders call the Barelwi movement), "People seek *bai'a* as a matter of course. They do not know its [true] meaning. *Bai'a* is as Hazrat Yahya Muneri's disciple understood it to be: He was drowning in a river, when Hazrat Khizr (upon him be peace) appeared and asked him for his hand, so that he could pull him out. The disciple replied, I have already given my hand [in discipleship] to Hazrat Yahya Muneri. I can no longer give it to anyone else. Hazrat Khizr (upon him be peace) disappeared, and Hazrat Yahya Muneri appeared and pulled his disciple ashore to safety."[44]

Before initiation, Naqshbandīs assume that the aspirant is an adult of sound mind and already performs the ritual practices of Islam, particularly the communal daily prayers.[45] Often the shaykh tests the sincerity and correct religious dogma *('aqīda)* of the aspirant before initiation.[46] Other Naqshbandīs encourage the potential disciple to visit other sufis before his initiation so that when he returns to request initiation both the guide and the aspirant know he has made a correct choice by the process of *istikhāra*.[47]

Once the decision to become initiated has been formally made, the next procedures vary with each pir. Some begin the process by thanking the Prophet and spirits of the great sufis *(pīrān-i a'ẓām)* and then reciting Qur'ān 112 *(sūrat al-ikhlāṣ)* an odd number of times while expressing the desire for these spirits' mediation *(tawassul)*.[48] Others do two cycles (sing. *rak'a*) of a repentance prayer with the intention of being blessed on the sufi path, after which the opening chapter *(al-fātiḥa)* of the Qur'ān is recited and sufi shaykhs are summoned.[49] Then the aspirant sits crosslegged

---

[44]Aḥmad Riḍā Khān, *Malfūẓāt*, 2:41, cited in Usha Sanyal, "In the Path of the Prophet: Maulana Aḥmad Riza Khan Barelwi and the Ahl-e Sunnat wa Jama'at Movement in British India, c. 1870–1921," p. 101 [comments in brackets are Sanyal's]. Shara fuddīn Yaḥyā Manērī (d. 782/1381) was a Firdawsī shaykh of Bihar, India.

[45]Some pirs initiate children who have not reached puberty; see Zawwār Ḥusayn, *'Umdat al-sulūk*, p. 46. Naqshbandīs have also initiated invisible beings *(jinns)*. See Zawwār Ḥusayn, *Ḥayāt-i sa'diyya*, (Karachi: Aḥmad Brothers Printers, 1987), pp. 62–63.

[46]'Āshiq 'Alī Khān Nāṭiq Kalānūrī, *Lama'āt-i kamālāt-i qādiriyya ma' mu'āwin-i tabarrukāt-i khāliqiyya*, p. 59.

[47]Jaipūrī, *Mi'yār al-sulūk*, p. 166.

[48]Ibid.

[49]Bahrā'ichī, *Ma'mūlāt-i maẓhariyya*, p. 34. Mīrzā Maẓhar Jān-i jānān allowed each person to choose which *ṭarīqa* he or she would like to be initiated in, although he taught Mujaddidī spiritual practices to all his disciples. Mīrzā Maẓhar's spiritual grandson, Ghulām Murtaḍā (d. 1321/1903), initiated aspirants

facing Mecca in ritual purity clasping the pir's right hand in both of his hands and repents by repeating after the shaykh: "Praise be to God! We praise Him; we ask Him for guidance; we ask Him for forgiveness; we believe in Him; we put our trust in Him. We take our refuge in God from the sins of our souls and from our evil actions. Whoever God guides is not led astray and whoever God leads astray is not rightly guided. We testify that there is no god but God and that Muḥammad is His slave and messenger (S)."[50]

The aspirant, still clasping the shaykh's right hand with both of his hands, then repeats after the pir that he pledges allegiance to the Prophet by means of the presences of the shaykhs of the lineage on the condition that he dutifully performs the ritual requirements on Islam and abstains from major sins.[51] Reciting such a formula in the presence of a shaykh by itself constitutes a formal repentance corresponding to the first type of initiation described above.

Before initiation into the Naqshbandiyya-Mujaddidiyya some shaykhs recite statements of religious dogma for the aspirants to repeat, e.g., "I believe in God, His angels, His books, His messengers, the last day, that one's fate both good and bad is from God almighty, and resurrection after death. I believe in God as He is with His names and His attributes and I accept all of His ordinances [for humankind]."[52]

At this point, still clasping hands, the aspirant requests formal initiation into the Naqshbandiyya-Mujaddidiyya in the name of the initiating shaykh, Bahā'uddīn, Abū Bakr, or Muḥammad.[53]

---

into the Qādirī *ṭarīqa* yet they did Mujaddidī exercises and called upon the great Naqshbandī shaykhs in their *khatm-i khwājagān*. See Muḥammad Qamaruddīn, *Anwār-i murtaḍawī*, pp. 30, 45. Successors to both these Naqshbandī masters identified themselves as Naqshbandīs.

[50]Zawwār Ḥusayn, *'Umdat al-sulūk*, p. 277. Some shaykhs have the aspirants repeat parts of this three times. See Jaipūrī, *Mi'yār al-sulūk*, p. 166, and Bahrā'ichī, *Ma'mūlāt-i maẓhariyya*, p. 34.

[51]This is described as generic repentance *(ijmālī tawba)*. See ibid., p. 35.

[52]Zawwār Ḥusayn, *'Umdat al-sulūk*, p. 277.

[53]Jaipūrī, *Mi'yār al-sulūk*, p. 166. Shaykhs initiate disciples in various ways. Shēr Muḥammad, for example, gave Muḥammad 'Umar lessons in correct behavior *(ādāb)* and had him recite specific Qur'ānic verses before he imparted the heart *dhikr*. After Muḥammad 'Umar received the heart *dhikr*, Shēr Muḥammad gave him invocatory prayers and Qur'ānic verses to recite. Although Shēr Muḥammad usually did not initiate with a handclasp, he did so with Muḥammad 'Umar. See Bīrbalī, *Inqilāb al-ḥaqīqat*, pp. 17–18. If there are a lot of people to be initiated the pir can also spread out his sheet or turban and have each person grip a part of it instead of individually clasping each person's hand. See Maḥbūb 'Alī, *Khayr-i khayr, marghūb al-sulūk*, p. 104. Other variations include Ghulām Murtaḍā initiat-

Then the shaykh imparts the recollection of God *(talqīn-i dhikr)* into the disciple's heart by putting his forefinger on the disciple's chest and subsequently "writing" Allāh on it. For some this feels "like an arrow penetrating the inner recesses of the disciple's heart," sending pulsations through the chest.[54] Before imparting the recollection of God formula the pir instructs the disciple to sit with closed eyes and, eliminating all stray thoughts, to visualize divine light and energy coming from its origin by means of the pir's heart to the disciple's heart. Throughout the initiation the shaykh is energizing the disciple's heart by focusing his spiritual energy *(tawajjuh)* on it.[55] At the end of the session, the pir recites the opening chapter of the Qur'ān *(al-fātiḥa)*, supplicating God to bless the occasion. Depending on the available time, he instructs the disciple(s) in the basics of correct behavior *(ādāb)*, the necessity of spiritual companionship *(ṣuḥbat)*, and the necessity of performing recollection of the heart at all times whether awake or asleep.[56]

Initiation for Women

For women, initiation is not considered to be sunna, although there is Qur'ānic precedent (60:12):[57] "O Prophet, when believing women come to you, pledging allegiance to you that they will not associate anything with God, will not steal, will not commit adultery, will not kill their children, will not bring trouble that they have devised between their hands and feet, nor disobey you in what is right, then accept their allegiance and ask God to forgive them."[58]

---

ing his eldest son, Maulwī Ḥāfiẓ Ma'ṣūm, with a ceremonial turban at the grave of Aḥmad Sirhindī. See Muḥammad Qamaruddīn, *Anwār-i murtaḍawī*, p. 174.

[54]Muḥammad 'Ināyatullāh, *Maqamāt-i irshadiyya*, p. 361.

[55]Bahrā'ichī, *Ma'mūlāt-i maẓhariyya*, p. 35; Jaipūrī, *Mi'yār al-sulūk*, p. 166. It is said that the origin of the Naqshbandī initiation process is modeled after the first time Gabriel came and ordered Muḥammad to recite *(iqra')*. Gabriel hit Muḥammad's chest three times and, after the third time, Muḥammad began to recite. It is said that one day the Prophet wrapped himself in Abū Ḥurayra's sheet and hit his own chest three times. Returning the sheet Muḥammad instructed Abū Ḥurayra to wrap himself in this sheet and not to forget this day; see ibid., p. 167.

[56]For an example of a non-Naqshbandī *bay'a* ceremony, see Kīyānī, *Tārīkh-i khānaqāh*, p. 395, and Fritz Meier, *Vom Wesen der islamischen Mystik.*

[57]Kalānūrī, *Lama'āt-i kamālāt*, p. 61.

[58]Men were expected to fulfill the same conditions in addition to military responsibilities. In the *bay'at al-riḍwān* women could declare allegiance to Muḥammad made on condition that they abstain from lamenting the dead; see Shāh Walīullāh, *Al-qawl al-jamīl*, p. 16.

In nineteenth-century Muslim India these Qur'ānic concerns were translated into special conditions for female initiation. Women had to agree to give up practicing non-Muslim customs, e. g., stop praying to the Hindu goddess Sītalā, who was believed to cure smallpox, stop giving to divālī celebrations, stop sacrificing animals at shaykhs' graves, stop fasting on auspicious days determined by astrology, and stop resorting to magic. In addition, each woman had to pledge not to steal from her husband, to dance, or to sing (the last activity was supposed to lead to adultery).[59]

A major concern of the Naqshbandīs during the British colonial period was to keep men separate from women, i.e., to perpetuate and spread the practice of *parda*. Naqshbandī shaykhs were supposed to set a good example by not touching the hands of women aspirants and by keeping men and women disciples separated "so that *parda* continues to be established and becomes common with other religious figures."[60] Women are to be physically separated by at least a sheet; instead of a handclasp one grasps a turban cloth or other ritually clean piece of cloth. A women is never supposed to be alone with the shaykh and needs to be accompanied by a guardian *(maḥram)* from her family. To impart recollection of the heart the shaykh focuses his spiritual energy while the women disciple visualizes the name of God written on her heart.[61] Given the close supervision of Muslim women in Indian society and the need for a guardian from her family to be present at her initiation, one assumes that women usually become initiated by the same shaykh as other men in her family. Numerous family members having spiritual bonds to one pir also safeguard and consolidate a shaykh's influence in the local society.

With certain exceptions, the disciple is prohibited from breaking the tie with his spiritual mentor.[62] If seekers could change allegiance to their masters at will, shaykhs would lose the authority they need to guide others. All three types of affiliation with a

[59]Bahrā'ichī, *Ma'mūlāt-i maẓhariyya*, pp. 37–44. For a much fuller treatment of reformist concerns for women, see the nineteenth-century work by Ashraf 'Alī T'hanawī, *Bihisht-i zewar*, translated by Barbara Metcalf as *Perfecting Women: Maulana Ashraf Ali Thanawi's Bishisht-i zewar: A Partial Translation with Commentary.*

[60]Zawwār Ḥusayn, *'Umdat al-sulūk*, p. 278.

[61]Jaipūrī, *Mi'yār al-sulūk*, p. 167. Naqshbandīs have informed me that recollection of the heart can also be imparted by a rosary or piece of wood first dipped in water and placed by the woman where the shaykh would otherwise put his fingers.

[62]For rules outside a Naqshbandī milieu specifying allegiance to only one shaykh and conditions to transfer allegiance to another shaykh, see Gramlich, *Die schiitischen Derwischorden*, 2:238–41.

sufi master are broken if the disciple commits a major sin or ceases to perform regular worship, but the Prophetic precedent is for the shaykh not to accept a disciple's desire to break his or her initiation agreement, though if the disciple simply abandons the master the initiation is said to be canceled.[63] Disciples are admonished not to declare allegiance indiscriminately to various mentors since ungrateful spiritual dilettantes will receive no divine grace.[64]

There are numerous valid reasons why someone might wish to go to another spiritual guide. Even though the master may be perfect and perfection-bestowing, not every disciple will necessarily benefit from him. If the aspirant follows the guide properly and sincerely, it is incumbent *(wājib)* upon him or her to search for another shaykh if no results are achieved after a period of time.[65] If a seeker cannot see his or her shaykh any longer for whatever reason, or finishes the exercises of one sufi lineage, or achieves the same degree of spiritual development as the guide, then it is permissible to look for a new spiritual mentor, so long as one does not break ties with the first guide by keeping in mind his positive qualities.[66] Any shaykh can do something accidentally against the shariʿa, and in the case of such a lapse the disciple should first excuse the mentor on the basis of his or her own faulty understanding of the situation.[67] Often such behavior is simply the result of the pir's involuntary intoxicated ecstasy. A shaykh who continually acts contrary to the dictates of Islamic law and the practices of the Prophet, however, should be abandoned without a second thought.

Shaykhs' tombs, some of which become the center of extensive shrine activity, are generally recognized to be places where devotees can receive divine grace. Mujaddidīs assert that there is certainly divine grace radiating from the tombs of deceased pirs, but it is not sufficient to bring a disciple to perfection. For this type of transformation to occur, the connection depends on the person

[63]Zawwār Ḥusayn, *ʿUmdat al-sulūk*, pp. 46–47. Even if the pir is angry with the disciple, this is not cause for the master to terminate the relationship.

[64]Jaipūrī, *Miʿyār al-sulūk*, pp. 40–41.

[65]Ibid., p. 41.

[66]Ibid., pp. 40–42.

[67]Muḥammad ʿInāyatullāh, *Maqāmāt-i irshādiyya*, pp. 227–28. The precedent for this statement is the Qur'ānic story of Moses and Moses's companion, commonly thought to be Khiḍr (Q. 18:65–82). Khiḍr's outwardly inexplicable and unacceptable behavior confounded Moses yet had a deeper meaning. The assumption that a shaykh can perceive the inner reality of events allows him occasionally to appear to behave outwardly against the shariʿa.

giving divine energy *(fayḍ)* and the person receiving it both being in corporeal form. Only adepts who have gone beyond the circle of contingent existence *(dāʾira-yi imkān)* and who have a suitable connection can receive divine energy from the deceased shaykh.[68] Logically, if the *fayḍ* from a dead and live pir were equal, then all the residents of Medina from the time of the Prophet until now would have the same spiritual rank as the Companions and would not require companionship *(ṣuḥbat)* with intimates of God.[69] Given the Mujaddidīs' concentration of authority in the living pir, it is not surprising that visiting a shaykh's tomb would not substitute for companionship with a living pir. In addition, given the number of tomb shrines dotting the Panjabi countryside, the market for spiritual mentors would already be saturated if deceased shaykhs were as efficacious as live ones.

Becoming a Spiritual Guide

Once the elementary recollection exercise becomes firmly established, the newly initiated disciple's subtle centers are activated in sequence before he or she practices the recollection of negation and affirmation *(nafy wa-ithbāt)* and proceeds through the Mujaddidī contemplations *(murāqabāt)*. This constitutes the disciple's practical *(ʿamalī)* training. Ideally, the practice of spiritual exercises is complemented by spiritual *(ruḥānī)* and theoretical *(ʿilmī)* education, the combination of which is necessary for a connection with inner truth.[70] Spiritual education involves sitting in the presence of the shaykh's spiritual attention *(tawajjuh)*, while so-called theoretical training teaches disciples the practical application of outwardly following the practices of Muḥammad. Shēr Muḥammad is one shaykh who provided a well-rounded education for his disciples with regular gatherings where he discussed

---

[68]Zawwār Ḥusayn, *ʿUmdat al-sulūk*, p. 42.

[69]Pānīpatī, *Irshād al-ṭālibīn*, p. 25.

[70]Bīrbalī, *Inqilāb al-ḥaqīqat*, p. 26. Muḥammad ʿUmar (d. 1386–87/1967) complained that contemporary pirs usually did not teach refinement of character *(akhlāq)*, correct manners *(ʿādāt)*, different ways of recollecting God, or mystical exercises *(ashghāl)*. In his travels, Muḥammad ʿUmar went around asking disciples about their contemplation exercises and discovered that even the most advanced were only doing variations on heart recollection. Apparently the teaching of special sufi terminology, necessary for each sufi exercise, had been abandoned by Muḥammad ʿUmar's contemporaries. See ibid., pp. 69–70. Such a general report, perhaps to some extent a glorification of his spiritual mentor, Shēr Muḥammad, who did give his disciples a well-rounded spiritual education, might still reflect the prevailing sufi conditions of the time.

problems particular to sufism and read Sirhindī's *Maktūbāt*.[71] The acquisition of religious knowledge, the formulation of correct religious dogma, and the learning of other "exoteric" religious lessons is usually completed before initiation.[72] By the late nineteenth century this type of "outer" religious education tended to be the domain of specialists in madrasas specially appointed for the purpose.

There are no uniform criteria among the Naqshbandī shaykhs for deciding when a person is qualified to become a successor *(khalīfa)*.[73] When he is regarded as qualified the disciple usually receives a printed certificate authorizing him or her to teach Naqshbandī practices *(ijāzatnāma)*.[74] There are three types of authorization: conditional *(muqayyad)*, unrestricted *(muṭlaq)*, and a third which is given only to the one person chosen to be the master's principal successor (literally, one who sits on the prayer carpet), the *sajjādanishīn*.[75] Dōst Muḥammad (d. 1284/1868), for

---

[71]Ibid., p. 69. To illustrate points in sufi practice *(sulūk)* Muḥammad ʿUmar Bīrbalī says Shēr Muḥammad used *Tafsīr-i wāʿizī*, a popular Qur'ān commentary by Ḥusayn Wāʿiẓ-i Kāshifī, the father of the author of *Rashaḥāt-i ʿayn al-ḥayāt*, Fakhrruddīn ʿAlī; see ibid., p. 90. *Tafsīr-i Wāʿiẓī*, still in print with Shāh Walīullāh's interlinear translation in Persian, is usually not used by contemporary Naqshbandīs as a sufi exegesis in the Indo-Pakistani subcontinent. Instead, contemporary Naqshbandīs use Ismāʿīl Ḥaqqī's *Rūḥ al-bayān fī tafsīr al-qur'ān* and Shihābuddīn al-Alūsī's *Rūḥ al-maʿānī fī tafsīr al-qur'ān al-ʿaẓīm wa'l-sabʿ al-mathānī.*

[72]An excess of this outer knowledge often caused individuals to become arrogant to the point that religious knowledge became the "greater veil" *(ḥijāb al-akbar)*; see Bīrbalī, *Inqilāb al-ḥaqīqat*, p. 86 n. 1.

[73]Some specify that having continuous recollection of the heart is the absolute minimum qualification. Preferably the disciple will have traveled along the path sufficiently to have reached "lesser intimacy with God" *(wilāyat-i ṣughrā)* and have the ability to perform *sulṭān-i adhkār*. See Jaipūrī, *Miʿyār al-sulūk*, pp. 4, 168. Some specify a requirement of arriving at "greater intimacy with God" *(wilāyat-i kubrā)*; see Muḥammad ʿInāyatullāh, *Maqāmāt-i irshādiyya*, p. 287. Neither source identifies what kind of successor *(muqayyad* or *muṭlaq)* is intended.

[74]Some Naqshbandīs justified the issuing of printed certificates for spiritual successors as a development of the long-established practice of writing a will to clarify inheritance issues not covered by shariʿa. See Muḥammad Ismāʿīl, *Mawāhib raḥmāniyya fī fawā'id wa-fuyūḍāt ḥaḍarāt thalātha dāmāniyya: maqāmāt-i sirājiyya* [hereafter *Maqāmāt-i sirājiyya*], p. 187. By 1347/1928 Sirājuddīn was using printed forms for his successors. See Zawwār Ḥusayn, *Ḥayāt-i saʿdiyya*, pp. 29–30. The ambition to obtain a teaching certificate often overshadowed other motives for traversing the Path, causing some shaykhs, e.g., Irshād Ḥusayn, to write very few of these certificates. See Muḥammad ʿInāyatullāh, *Maqāmāt-i irshādiyya*, p. 379. For a collection of *ijāzatnāma*s given by Ghulām ʿAlī Shāh; see Imām ʿAlī Shāh, *Maktūbāt-i quṭb-i rabbānī*. Translations of some representative certificates are in appendix 4. For examples of non-Naqshbandī *ijāzatnāmas*, see Kīyānī, *Tārīkh-i khānaqāh dar Īrān*, pp. 365–68.

[75]In the cases of shrines, i.e., where religious specialists act in the capacity of

example, acquired the first two of these after fourteen months of practice from his shaykh Aḥmad Saʿīd (1277/1860); it gave him conditional permission to teach *(ijāzat-i muqayyad)*.[76] In addition, his spiritual mentor gave him a turban, a shirt, and a hat *(kulāh)*.[77] He was taken aback when hordes of people suddenly began expecting him to accept them as disciples, asked for cures, or demanded amulets. A few years later he returned to Delhi, where he reviewed with Aḥmad Saʿīd the fine points of sufi practice *(sulūk)* before being granted unrestricted authorization to teach *(ijāzat-i muṭlaq)*.[78]

The third category of successor, the *sajjādanishīn*, is naturally the rarest, since it is handed only to the one person who will sit on the spiritual mentor's prayer rug after he passes away. For shaykhs in the large sufi lodges, much more is at stake than merely inheriting a prayer rug, for with it one not only acquires an army of disciples, but often incurs the responsibility of administering a small empire of landholdings and villages. In theory, the *sajjādanishīn* should be the most spiritually qualified person from those who have obtained unrestricted permission to teach. In practice the shaykh's eldest son often became his father's successor, a type of succession that drastically altered Naqshbandī sources of authority.

Such a situation is elaborated in the recent succession history of the sufi lodge in Musa Zai near Dera Ismail Khan.[79] Muḥammad ʿUthmān (d. 1314/1896), Dōst Muḥammad's chosen successor, proved to be the first and last nonlineal successor at the Musa Zai sufi lodge complex. Sirājuddīn (d. 1333/1933), the eldest son of Muḥammad ʿUthmān, received unrestricted permission to teach and simultaneously was formally chosen as the future *sajjāda-*

caretakers rather than directing-shaykhs, lineage is a determining factor. In Indo-Pakistan usually a caretaker is either a person who is a lineal descendant of the deceased sufi, a *pīrzāda* (literally, son of the pir), or a lineal descendant of one of the successors of the deceased sufi, often called a *mutawallī*. For an example of complicated leadership claims and the financial intricacies of a popular contemporary Qādirī shrine near Islamabad, see Hafeez-Ur-Rehman Chaudhry, "Traditional and State Organizations of the Shrine of Bari Imam." See also Christian Troll, ed., *Muslim Shrines in India.*

[76]Conditional authorization means the successor is still under the direction of the shaykh and must follow his advice. Unrestricted permission allows the successor complete independence in training disciples, including whether or not to follow his shaykh's advice.

[77]Muḥammad Ismāʿīl, *Al-tajalliyāt-i dōstiyya*, pp. 32–35.

[78]Ibid.

[79]For a parallel example in the Chishtiyya, see Richard Eaton's "Court of Man, Court of God."

nishīn at the legally adult age of fourteen.[80] For this occasion all the religious notables and successors of Musa Zai were invited to witness his "turban-tying" ceremony. After the religious exercises following post-sunrise prayer were completed, everyone gathered at the grave of Dōst Muḥammad. Muḥammad ʿUthmān performed three sets of supplications to bring divinely emanating energy *(fayḍ)* down upon those assembled for the occasion of his son's succession. When the grand moment came for Sirājuddīn to have his turban put on, his father tied it halfway and then three of his religious teachers finished tying it.[81] His principal teachers and a classmate each then received turbans of honor. Sweets were distributed before Muḥammad ʿUthmān performed a final supplication.

After this, Sirājuddīn received a certificate of unrestricted authorization to teach, signed by fourteen religious notables. He also received a prayer rug. These were the tangible symbols of a *sajjādanishīn.* The signatures and the tacit approval of the assembled ulama were officially considered to validate Muḥammad ʿUthmān's decision.[82] From his deathbed Muḥammad ʿUthmān ordered all his disciples to renew their initiation *(tajdīd-i bayʿat)* with Sirājuddīn, as the Companions had done with the first three successors of Muḥammad.[83]

After Sirājuddīn's death, two religious notables decided upon Muḥammad Ibrāhīm, Sirājuddīn's son, as successor, as a result of a divination from al-Ḥakīm al-Nīsābūrī's *al-Mustadrak.*[84] Others apparently had misgivings about the outcome, for the hagiographer states, "Anyone who doubts his [Muḥammad Ibrāhīm's]

---

[80]Muḥammad Ismāʿīl, *Maqāmāt-i sirājiyya,* pp. 6–22. A boy of fourteen, according to Ḥanafī *fiqh,* is considered an adult and eligible to marry. Among Indian sufis, however, this would be a minimum age to accept someone as a disciple. Readers of *Maqāmāt-i sirājiyya* are reminded that a certain Saʿduddīn Taftāzānī (d. ca. 1289/1872) wrote a commentary on one of ʿIzzuddīn Ibrāhīm b. ʿAbduwahhāb Zanjānī's works entitled *Sharḥ Saʿduddīn al-Taftāzānī ʿalā taṣrīf al-ʿizzī* at the age of fourteen. See Muḥammad Ismāʿīl, *Maqāmāt-i sirājiyya,* p. 23.

[81]Ibid., pp. 9–10. This is a pre-Islamic Arabic custom, the best-known exemplar of which is ʿAbdullāh b. Ubayy, who was about to be crowned this way in Yathrib as Muḥammad arrived. R. B. Serjeant also notes the practice among Yemeni tribes in "The ʿAwdhillah Confederation with Some Reference to al-Hamdānī," p. 101. The Arab monarch, Imru' al-Qays, was also crowned in this fashion, described as *dhū aṣr at-tāj.* See Irfan Shahid, "Philological Observations on the Namāra Inscription."

[82]Muḥammad Ismāʿīl, *Maqāmāt-i sirājiyya,* p. 14. This choice was also said to be confirmed by visions *(murāqabāt-i ilhāmī).*

[83]Ibid., p. 21.

[84]Muḥammad b. ʿAbdullāh al-Ḥakīm al-Nīsābūrī, *Al-mustadrak ʿalā al-ṣaḥīḥayn fiʾl-ḥadīth.*

successorship should ask God for forgiveness and repent, as these suspicions are the delusions of the ego and the devil."[85]

Since Sirājuddīn had already let his son wear his turban and sit on his prayer carpet the week before his death, the precedent of Abū Bakr, who had led the prayer when Muḥammad had been ill, was cited to support the validity of Sirājuddīn's having chosen Muḥammad Ibrāhīm as his successor. To seal the argument, the hagiographer invoked community consensus, enumerating the number of people who renewed their initiation and began to visualize the new *sajjādanishīn* in their spiritual practices.[86] During Muḥammad Ibrāhīm's tenure, what used to be a subsidiary lodge of Musa Zai at Khundian Sharif became an independent institution with nonlineal succession.[87]

The sufi lodge was the territory between worldly and other-worldly concerns. The day-to-day maintenance and feeding of hundreds involved considerable resources, but the land and villages owned or administered by the sufi lodge, combined with pious donations, usually covered most of these needs. Short-term visitors of the sufi lodge, like children in a well-to-do family, would not be aware of the behind-the-scenes activity designed to make ends meet, at least until the pivotal dynamics of succession brought worldly issues to the foreground. Events occurring after the shaykh's death reflect the same kind of interpersonal dynamics that one finds in families. In such cases the intensity of intra-family quarreling corresponds to the wealth and power which is at stake, and very little is forgotten. Naqshbandī sources, both written and oral, retrospectively and briefly describe these transitional periods in a very conciliatory fashion. An exposé of the pettiness of some sufi families could all too easily contribute to undermining sufi authority in general, and during the troubled times of British colonial India the sufis had enough problems already. In this milieu we find a new type of Mujaddidī shaykh, a mediating-shaykh who encouraged a love of the sufi guide that dispensed with the need both for spiritual travel and for a shaykh's focused spiritual attention.

---

[85]Muḥammad Ismāʿīl, *Maqāmāt-i sirājiyya*, pp. 185–86 [additions mine].

[86]Ibid., pp. 187–88. This latter confirmation was called a "practical consensus" (*ʿamalī ijmāʿ*). Muḥammad Ibrāhīm is not mentioned in the hagiographical work of what used to be a subsidiary sufi lodge of Musa Zai at Khundian Sharif.

[87]Abū Saʿīd Aḥmad, a disciple of Sirājuddīn, was the first to preside at Khundian independently of the authorities at Musa Zai. In 1941 a Deobandi, Muḥammad ʿAbdullāh, was chosen over his pir's three sons. For Abū Saʿīd Aḥmad's last testament declaring Muḥammad ʿAbdullāh as his successor, see Maḥbūbilāhī, *Tuḥfa-yi saʿdiyya*, pp. 144–48. In 1954 Khān Muḥammad, became the nonlineal spiritual successor to his mentor.

CHAPTER 8

Mediational Sufism and Revivalist Currents in British Colonial India

A tourist brochure published in 1985 reads as follows:

Muslim shrines and tombs of Sufi Saints represent Muslim culture [and] traditions. . . . These Sufi Saints still rule over the hearts of Pakistanis and Muslims of other countries. With the passage of time the number of devotees has increased. The visit to shrines by millions of people every year is an abiding testimony of their absolute and undisputed sway over their followers and of their divine blessings emanating from their hallowed graves.[1]

Since the nineteenth century some Indian Muslims have become so distressed at the type of Islam described in this brochure that they have formed organizations to contest sufism and the mediatory role of the sufi shaykh. In colonial India the Naqshbandiyya were already responding with revivalist initiatives as institutional expressions of Naqshbandī authority shifted from directing-shaykhs to mediating-shaykhs.[2] The colonial revivalist milieu during one of the most religiously volatile times in the region had much to do with the development of mediational sufism. Mediational sufism is a perspective which posits shaykhs, both living and deceased, who mediate between individual Mus-

[1]Ubaidullah Baig and A. A. K. Brohi, *Journey into Light: An Instant Guide to Devotional Tours*, pp. 3–4.

[2]Based on research of colonial Panjab chapters 8–10 discuss post-1857 modern developments representative of institutionalized sufism throughout Northern India, including Sind and the United Provinces. For colonial Sind see Sara F.D. Ansari's, *Sufi Saints and State Power: The Pirs of Sind, 1843–1947;* and for the United Provinces see Farhan Nizami's, "Madrasahs, Scholars and Saints: Muslim Response to the British Presence in Delhi and the Upper Doab 1803–1857."

lims and God (via Muḥammad), the existence of a spiritual hierarchy which is a function of how one is connected to Muḥammad, and a variegated religious topography of tomb-shrines which are potent places to contact God.

Panjabi Islam was structured in a mediational pattern from the beginning. The spread of Islam throughout the western Panjab has been attributed to the efforts initiated by the grand sufi masters of the Chishtiyya and Suhrawardiyya, Bābā Farīd Ganj-i Shakar (d. 664/1265) of Pakpattan and Bahā'uddīn Zakariyā (d. 666/1267) of Multan, respectively.[3] Richard Eaton has argued that conversion resulted in nomadic Jat tribes becoming agriculturists while simultaneously adapting to the influences of Mughal government. This enabled the families and caretakers of the sufi tomb-shrines to control intractable Jat groups by the sixteenth century.[4] Smaller, local shrines associated with villages or subtribes augmented these major shrines creating, by the nineteenth century, a Panjabi countryside dotted with graves of holy people.[5]

In the mind of the typical rural Panjabi, sufi shaykhs, whether dead or alive, derive their palpable worldly authority from their closeness to an utterly transcendent and distant God. These connections to God enable sufis to intercede on behalf of the believer in the same way that political and social relationships and interactions in northern Indian society require the use of mediators between various levels of the sociopolitical hierarchy. Communication between the spiritual and mundane realms is conceived in an identical fashion. Sharafuddīn Manērī of Bihar (d. 782/1381) states that "the sheikhs are kings close to the King, and their requests are acceptable to Him. All those who come to the sheikhs and bind themselves to the sheikhs attain what they desire."[6]

[3]The British gazetteers and census takers recorded that Muslims attributed their conversions to these and other sufi notables. Thomas Arnold, in his *Preaching of Islam*, and Murray Titus, in *Indian Islam: A Religious History of Islam in India*, both relied upon these reports to support a counterargument refuting the conventional European attitude that conversions in India resulted from force.

[4]Richard M. Eaton, "Approaches to the Study of Conversion to Islam in India," pp. 106–23. Eaton actually charts an inverse relationship between Muslim political penetration, i.e., the sword, and conversion to Islam, citing the most dramatic conversion rates in regions on the fringes of Indo-Muslim rule, eastern Bengal and western Panjab. For conversion in Bengal, see Richard M. Eaton, *The Rise of Islam and the Bengal Frontier, 1204–1760*.

[5]Rural Muslims, Sikhs, and Hindus not only frequented sufi lodges and Muslim tombs *(mazārs)* but minor sufi shrines *(pīrkhānas)*, cremation sites of village ancestors *(jatherās)*, and graves of Sikh and Hindu holy men *(samādhis)*. See Harjot Oberoi, *The Construction of Religious Boundaries: Culture, Identity and Diversity in the Sikh Tradition*, p. 198.

[6]Sharafuddīn Manērī, *The Hundred Letters*, p. 28.

For many Indian Muslims, the activities associated with the sufi shrines were their only contact with Islam, and they saw no need to change their dress or lifestyle to differentiate themselves from Hindus. To counter this tendency Aḥmad Sirhindī had pioneered his Islamic revival movement and Shāh Walīullāh had continued it.[7] Both a master of the Islamic religious sciences and a sufi, Shāh Walīullāh emphasized the study of hadith, becoming a specialist in it *(muḥaddith)*. His sons, led by the hadith scholar Shāh ʿAbdulʿazīz (d. 1239/1824), continued his work, which was to influence most of the reform and revival groups during the British colonial period.[8] The most obvious legacy appears in the idiom of religious polemics. By 1900 no argument justifying revivalist sufism would be considered serious unless supported by numerous Qur'ānic and hadith citations, the more the better.[9] In addition, the majority of those who articulated these principles of revivalist Islam and mediational sufism were, unlike Shāh Walīullāh and his family, intentionally scattered in the towns over North India—for very good reasons.

For 150 years before the 1857 rebellion notables had been moving out from the cities to the towns (Urdu, sing. *qaṣba*) as the breakdown in central governmental authority allowed marauding bands of Afghans, Jats, and Marathas to loot the larger cities. The relative calm of the towns allowed for more continuous and

---

[7]This revitalization process continues the original Islamization impetus in that it seeks among other things to teach nominal Muslims appropriate Islamic orthopraxy and develop a more self-conscious Muslim identity. It tends to emphasize personal authority of Muḥammad and the Prophetic model rather than scriptural authority. In this regard Ahl-i Hadith would be more of a reform *(iṣlāḥ)* movement, attempting to re-form Indian Islam in a radical way (in the sense of a complete reconstruction) rather than in an incremental manner. Reformers tend to stress the scriptural basis of authority to justify their religious perspectives.

[8]Chishtīs in the Panjab played an important role in revivalist activity. Khwāja Sulaymān (d. 1267–68/1850) of Taunsa, who established his sufi lodge in a remote area of Dera Ghazi Khan near the Indus River, continued the work of revivalist Chishtī Shāh Kalīmullāh (d. 1142/1729). During British colonial rule the most prominent revival shaykh of this sufi lineage, Mihr ʿAlī Shāh (d. 1355–6/1937) of Golra, extended the Chishtī revivalist influence over many western Panjabi tribal leaders affiliated with the British administration. See David Gilmartin, *Empire and Islam: Punjab and the Making of Pakistan*, pp. 56–59.

[9]This has always been the case to some degree since the tenth century, but it was exaggerated in British India. In Jamāʿat ʿAlī Shāh's article, "Ḍarūrat-i murshid," there are 29 scriptural proofs given to justify the need for a spiritual guide. An argument frequently was clinched by having more citations than the opponent; see Barbara Metcalf, *Islamic Revival in British India: Deoband, 1860–1900*, p. 308. Often these Qur'ānic and hadith proofs were extremely strained, e.g., *Risāla-yi anwār al-ṣūfiyya* 7, no. 1, p. 16 [hereafter cited *Risāla* 7.1.16]. Pagination is very irregular in this journal.

dynamic cultural activities less influenced by political or economic catastrophe.[10] Towns scattered throughout northern India sustained intellectual life and served as refuges for religious notables, both ulama and sufis.[11]

Living in towns did not always guarantee security. To the east of Delhi, the nawwāb of Rampur provided a refuge for Aḥmad Sirhindī's descendants after the Sikhs had razed Sirhind in 1758.[12] One of Aḥmad Saʿīd's successors, Irshād Ḥusayn (d. 1311/1893–94), whose sons later gave the Friday sermons at the Bādshāhī Mosque in Lahore, had a lodge in Rampur. Faḍlurraḥmān Ganjmurādābādī (d. 1312–13/1895) and his successors provided spiritual guidance to many ulama at Nadwat al-Ulama in Lucknow.[13] In Kashmir, the descendants of Khāwand Maḥmūd's fourth son, Muʿīnuddīn Hādī (d. 1085/1674–75), still represent the Naqshbandiyya. Through this lineage, Ḥusayn Shāh (d. 1304/1886–87 Nepal) took the Naqshbandiyya to Nepal in the nineteenth century.[14] The Naqshbandiyya arrived in East Bengal via the efforts of Ṣūfī Nūr Muḥammad, whose grandfather shaykh was Shāh ʿAbdulʿazīz Dihlawī (d. 1239/1824), the son of Shāh Walīullāh. Ṣūfī Fatḥ ʿAlī (d. 1293/1876), Ghulām Salmānī (d. 1330/1912),

---

[10]The importance of these towns is reflected in the names of religious notables who come from towns all over northern India, e.g., Sirhind, Ganj Muradabad, Gangoh, Thanabhawan, Qusur, Bilgram, and Rae Bareilly.

[11]Farhan Nizami has provided a groundbreaking discussion of Muslim-dominated towns (sing. *(qaṣba)* and their importance in Indian culture. See Nizami, "Madrasahs, Scholars and Saints," pp. 37–42. In Delhi this trend was accentuated after the 1857 revolt when the British eliminated the last outward symbolic traces of the Mughal Empire. The effect on the Delhi ulama was devastating. David Gilmartin writes, "Though many *sajjādanishīns* kept their political influence in the localities even after the Mughal collapse, the decline of the Mughals seemed for the ulama at Delhi nothing less than a catastrophe. It signaled the disappearance of the cultural axis around which the entire Indian Islamic system had developed." See Gilmartin, *Empire and Islam*, p. 53. Many Delhi ulama and sufis dispersed to small towns throughout the Panjab. Ulama and sufis often were the same person. According to a two-volume biographical work of non-Barelwi ulama in nineteenth- and twentieth-century Panjab, Safīr Akhtar, *Tadhkira-yi ʿulamāʾ-i Panjāb*, out of 173 ulama with a specified sufi affiliation, 42 percent were Naqshbandīs, 35 percent Chishtīs, 20 percent Qādirīs, and 2 percent Suhrawardīs. Naqshbandī ulama were more prominent (61 percent) among Lahori Barelwi ulama.

[12]Personal communication, Professor Iqbāl Mujaddidī. After the first Sikh takeover of Sirhind in 1122/1710 the descendants of Aḥmad Sirhindī fled to Delhi, first taking refuge in the sufi lodges of Mīrzā Maẓhar Jān-i jānān and Shāh Walīullāh. See Ghulām ʿAlī Shāh, *Maqāmāt-i maẓharī*, pp. 49–50, 191 n. 104.

[13]Metcalf, *Islamic Revival*, p. 344. See Abū'l-Ḥasan ʿAlī Nadwī, *Tadhkira-yi Ḥaḍrat Maulānā Faḍl Raḥmān Ganj Murādābādī (r)*.

[14]Miyān Akhlāq Aḥmad, *Tadhkira-yi Haḍrat Īshān*, pp. 105–06.

and Sayyid ʿAbdulbārī (d. 1318/1901) continued the Naqshbandī lineage in Bengal.[15]

The Northwest Frontier Province of present-day Pakistan, which was included in the Panjab by the British until 1318–19/1901, might have been a bastion of the Naqshbandiyya-Mujaddidiyya if Jahāngīr had not forced Ādam Banūrī (d. 1053/1644), a very popular shaykh among the Pathans, to leave India in 1052/1642–43. ʿAbdurraḥmān Bahādur Kilmī (d. 1340/1921–22), Akbar Shāh Bukhārī (d. 1347/1928–29), and Ḥāfiẓ ʿAbdullāh (d. 1372–73/1952), the leading Naqshbandīs of British colonial Peshawar, received their spiritual guidance from Muḥammad ʿUthmān of Musa Zai or from Muḥammad Qāsim (d. 1380/1960) of Muhrah near Murray Hill Station.[16] In the British colonial period, two Naqshbandī lodges in the province continued to act as spiritual magnets attracting disciples from Pathan tribes. Amīr Kuṭla Mullā Ṣāḥib (d. 1295/1878) established one lodge, located at Kutla Manda Sharif in the Mardan district, while Muḥammad Ḥusayn (d. 1315/1897–98) founded the other lodge at Zakura Sharif near Dera Ismail Khan.[17] The Naqshbandī presence in the province at least from the middle of the nineteenth century has been overshadowed by the Qādiriyya, which still predominates there.

By the twentieth century, Naqshbandī centers were scattered throughout northern India.[18] In the Sind, Muḥammad Maʿṣūm's

[15]Hamid Algar, "Brief History of the Naqshbandī Order," p. 26.

[16]Muḥammad Qāsim is the spiritual descendant of Sirhindī's successor, Shāh Ḥusayn, thirteen generations removed. For other the prominent Mujaddidīs in the Panjab and their genealogy, see figure 3.

[17]His spiritual grandson, Muḥammad ʿAbdullaṭīf (d. 1398/1978), is known for his involvement in the Pakistan Movement. Both Sayyid Amīr and Muḥammad Ḥusayn share the same spiritual genealogy as fifth-generation lineal descendants of Aḥmad Sirhindī, Faḍl-i Aḥmad Faruqī Sirhindī, commonly called Haḍrat Jīyū (d. 1231/1815 in Peshawar) whose father died while fighting the Sikhs. See Niẓāmuddīn Balkhī Mazārī, *Ṭuḥfat al-murshid.*

[18]Swat was not a Naqshbandī center. The famous figure of Miyān ʿAbdulghafūr (d. 1292–93/1877), the Akhūnd of Swat, is variously described as a Qādirī or a Naqshbandī. Amīr Shāh Qādirī in his *Tadhkira-yi ʿulamāʾ wa-mashāʾikh-i Sarḥad,* p. 150, describes the Akhūnd as reaching perfection in the Qādiriyya and then being successively initiated into the Naqshbandī, Chishtī, and Suhrawardī *ṭarīqas.* Iʿjāzulḥaqq Quddūsī, in his *Tadhkira-yi ṣūfiyāʾ-i Sarḥad,* p. 551, asserts that the Akhūnd was a Naqshbandī. Hamid Algar, in his "Political Aspects of Naqshbandī History," p. 136, also asserts that Miyān ʿAbdulghafūr was a Naqshbandī. Textually the Akhūnd's primary Qādirī affiliation (since he had both Qādirī and Naqshbandī shaykhs) is confirmed by his most famous disciple, Qāḍī Maḥmūd, a Qādirī. In *Maqāmāt-i Maḥmūd,* Qāḍī Maḥmūd unambiguously describes the Qādirī spiritual training received under the tutelage of his preceptor. See Maʿshūq Yār Jang Bahādur, *Maqāmāt-i Maḥmūd.*

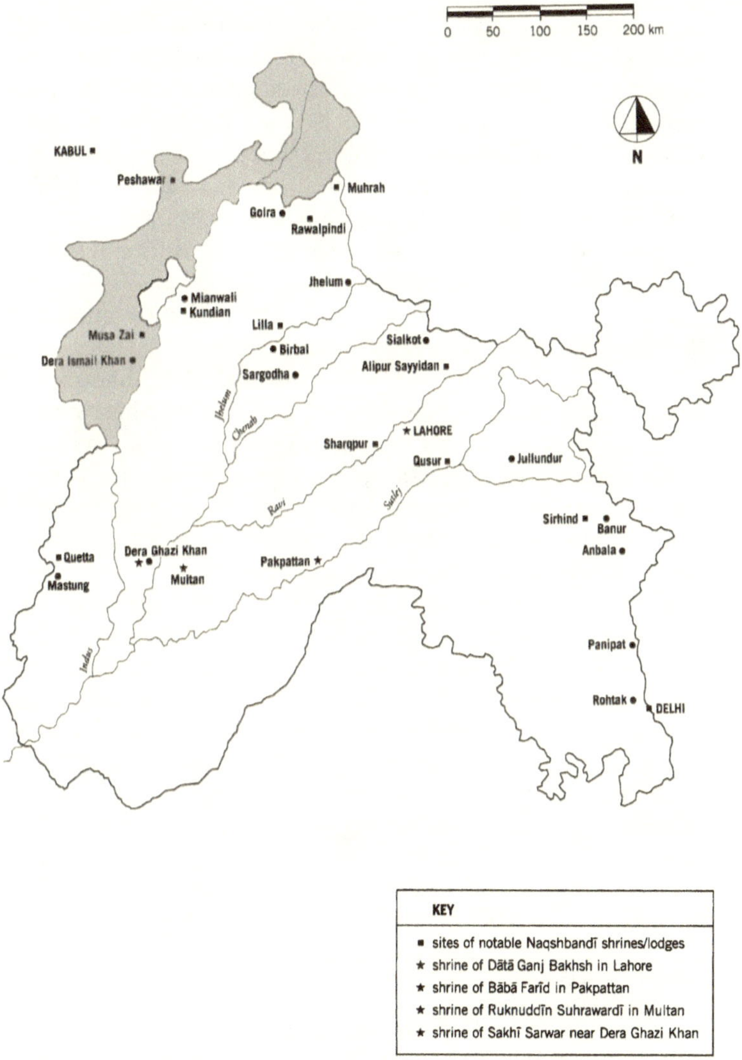

The Panjab before 1901, including the present-day Northwest Frontier Province (shaded)

great-grandson, ʿAbdurraḥmān Mujaddidī (d. 1315/1897), emigrated from Qandahar to Takhar, approximately thirty kilometers from Hyderabad, Sind. His principal successor, Muḥammad Ḥasan Khān (d. 1365/1946), moved the sufi lodge to Tando Sa'indad, where it was more convenient to the railroad.[19]

[19]Tando Sa'indad was a more accessible location two kilometers from the railroad station at Tando Muhammad Khan. See Muḥammad Iqbāl Ḥusayn Naʿīmī,

In Baluchistan Muḥammad Ṣiddīq Mastūngī (d. 1327/1909–10) established a sufi lodge and school in Mastung.[20] In the neighboring region of Qandahar, political turbulence forced Dōst Muḥammad Qandahārī in 1266/1850 to relocate his lodge near the village of Musa Zai, seventy kilometers from Dera Ismail Khan.[21] His shaykh, Aḥmad Saʿīd of Delhi, advised him to establish the new sufi lodge in a place where both Panjabi and Pashtu were spoken.[22] Although there were some initial difficulties with the neighboring Pashtu-speaking tribes, the remote sufi lodge attracted disciples from Afghanistan, the Peshawar area, and the Panjab.

Muḥammad ʿUthmān (d. 1314/1896), Dōst Muḥammad's successor, continued the Naqshbandī tradition at Musa Zai and in 1311/1893–94 had a new lodge built near Mianwali in the village of Khundian, Panjab, to take advantage of the relatively moderate climate there. Situated on the frontier between Pashto- and Panjabi-speaking groups, the new, more accessible location continued to fulfill the mandate of his grandfather pir. The train station at Khundian is about two kilometers from the sufi lodge. In comparison, the original sufi lodge at Musa Zai even today is a bumpy thirteen-hour bus ride from Peshawar. His son and successor, Sirājuddīn (d. 1333/1915), spent his summers at the Khundian lodge, and, through his teaching, the Naqshbandiyya spread to Hyderabad, Sind.[23] These two lodges, like those of the other prominent Naqshbandīs of this period, were located in villages. (One exception is ʿAbdulkarīm [d. 1355/1936], whose lodge was in Rawalpindi.)

In the environs of Lahore, Muḥyīddīn Quṣūrī (d. 1270/1854) carried on the teachings of Ghulām ʿAlī Shāh.[24] Ghulām Nabī

Tadhkira-yi awliyā-i Sindh, pp. 110–11, 190–92; and Ghulam Mustafa Khan, "The Naqshbandi Saints of Sind."

[20]Muḥammad Ṣiddīq was a fourth-generation spiritual descendant of Faqīrullāh Shikārpūrī (d. 1195/1781); see Muḥammad Ḥasan Jān, *Tadhkirat al-ṣulaḥā' fī bayān al-atiqiyā'*, p. 7, and Amīnullāh ʿAlawī, "Khwāja Ḥājjī Muḥammad Ṣiddīq Mastūngī," pp. 233–44.

[21]Muḥammad Ismāʿīl, *Mawāhib raḥmāniyya fī fawā'id wa-fuyūḍāt ḥaḍarāt thalātha dāmāniyya: al-tajalliyāt al-dōstiyya*, pp. 65–66.

[22]Maḥbūbilāhī, *Tuḥfa-yi saʿdiyya*, pp. 40–42.

[23]Zawwār Ḥusayn (d. 1400/1980) and his disciple, Dr. Ghulām Muṣṭafā Khān, two prolific Naqshbandī scholars from the Sind, are spiritual descendants of Sirājuddīn.

[24]Ghulām ʿAlī Shāh's sufi lodge was probably one of the most important Naqshbandī centers in the world during his lifetime. In addition to Khālid al-Baghdādī, who later spread the Naqshbandiyya throughout Arabia and Turkey, his other three major successors were Muḥyīddīn Quṣūrī (d. 1270/1854), Ghulām Nabīlillāhi (d. 1306/1888), and Dōst Muḥammad Qandahārī (d. 1284/1868).

Lillāhī (d. 1306/1888) set up his sufi lodge in the hinterlands of Jhelum. Other disciples of Muḥyīddīn Quṣūrī went on to establish their lodges in Dera Ismail Khan, Bhera, and Namak Miyānī.[25] Shēr Muḥammad Sharaqpūrī (d. 1347/1928), a revivalist pir of the Arain *birādarī*,[26] attracted large numbers of disciples to his lodge in Sharaqpur, located roughly forty kilometers from Lahore. His most renowned disciples were Muḥammad ʿUmar Bīrbalī (d. 1387/1967), the editor of Shēr Muḥammad's recorded discourses, *Inqilāb al-ḥaqīqat*, who later became the *sajjādanishīn* at his father's sufi lodge in the village of Bīrbal in the Sargodha district;[27] Muḥammad Ismāʿīl Kirmānwālī (d. 1385/1966 in Lahore), who received permission to teach disciples upon his first meeting with Shēr Muḥammad; and Sayyid Nūrulḥasan Bukhārī Kīliyānwālī (d. 1373/1953), an ex-Shīʿī of the Gujranwala district.[28] Innumerable other Naqshbandīs were scattered throughout the Panjab, many of whose spiritual pedigrees could be traced back to a handful of shaykhs in pre-1857 Delhi.

The British takeover of Delhi does not entirely explain why the northern Panjab became the major center of Naqshbandī activity in British India. In spite of the Mujadiddī version of the Naqshbandiyya rapidly adapting to the Indian environment after Sirhindī's death, it has never had mass appeal in the subcontinent. The atmosphere in a Naqshbandī lodge, reflected in the strict Islamic behavior of disciples, contrasts sharply with the festive atmosphere of rural Panjabi shrine practices that demanded little from the visitor except a material contribution for services rendered. Yet Naqshbandīs shared a similar mediational paradigm and would visit shrines themselves, e.g., those of Bahā'uddīn Naqshband, Muʿīnuddīn Chrishtī, or Aḥmad Sirhindī. One factor contributing to Naqshbandī success in the revivalist religious environment of rural colonial Panjab was the ability to bridge the gap between the urban ulama and the activities associated with

[25]Muḥammad Ibrāhīm Quṣūrī, *Khazīna-yi maʿrifat*, p. 61. These lodges were still functioning in 1977.

[26]Most Panjabis marry within their own *birādarī* or clan; the Arains were one of these *birādarīs*, whom the British classified as an "agricultural tribe." See Gilmartin, *Empire and Islam: Punjab and the Making of Pakistan*, pp. 89–95. For an analysis of kinship systems in the Panjab, see David Gilmartin, "*Biraderi* and Bureaucracy: The Politics of Muslim Kinship Solidarity in Twentieth Century Punjab."

[27]Tawakkulī, *Tadhkira-yi mashā'ikh-i naqshband*, p. 550. Muḥammad ʿUmar's father was Ghulām Murtaḍā Bīrbalī (d. 1321/1903), the spiritual grandson of Muḥyīddīn Quṣūrī.

[28]Muḥammad ʿUmar Bīrbalī, *Inqilāb al-ḥaqīqat*. For information concerning Muḥammad Ismāʿīl, see Nūr Aḥmad Maqbūl, *Khazīna-yi karam*, and for Nūrulḥasan, see Munīr Ḥusayn Shāh, *Inshirāḥ al-ṣadūr bi-tadhkirat al-nūr*.

Panjabi sufi shrines. Mediational sufis, Naqshbandī or otherwise, benefited to a large measure because of Aḥmad Riḍā Khān's reform and revivalist activity.

Ulama Support

No one bolstered the Indian mediational type of sufism with more scriptural citations than the erudite Aḥmad Riḍā Khān Barēlwī, a prolific writer who produced thousands of legal opinions. He wanted to give the predominantly rural practices of northern Indian sufi shrines legitimacy in reformist terms, that is, legitimizing its activities and worldview in terms of the Qur'ān and the hadith. His followers, the Barelwis, saw no contradiction between the reformist ideal of each Muslim behaving in conformity to the Prophetic model and adherence to the beliefs and practices of a predominantly rural, shrine-centered Islam.[29] This legitimacy enabled a mediational sufism to become increasingly popular in the cities. It is this unique blend of predominantly rural shrine activity and modern urban institutions that has produced the distinctive South Asian perspective on Islam and on sufi practice.

Aḥmad Riḍā formulated an original Sunnī prophetology to support and enhance his mediational version of Islam. His operating principle was to develop beliefs and customs that would considerably elevate the status of Muḥammad and the sufis. Instead of divine energy *(fayḍ)* from God, the Barelwis emphasize the "Muḥammadan light" *(nūr-i muḥammadī)* which existed from the beginning of creation.[30] They believe the Prophet to be present

[29]Aḥmad Riḍā's followers identified themselves as "Ahl-i Sunnat wa-Jamāʿat" (members of the rightly guided Sunnī mainstream), but they became known to outsiders as "Barelwis." Since many other communities also considered themselves "Ahl-i Sunnat wa-Jamāʿat," Barelwi is used here in a non-pejorative sense. For the movement in general, see Metcalf, *Islamic Revival*, pp. 296–314, and for a detailed treatment of Aḥmad Riḍā Khān and the non-sufi aspects of his movement, see Usha Sanyal, *Devotional Islam and Politics in British India: Ahmad Riza Khan Barelwi and His Movement, 1870–1920*.

[30]The idea of the Muḥammadan light was fully developed by the beginning of the tenth century; see Annemarie Schimmel, *Mystical Dimensions of Islam*, pp. 214–15. There are numerous apparent resemblances between Aḥmad Riḍā's emphasis on the centrality of Muḥammad and his lineal descendants *(ahl-i bayt)* and Twelver Shīʿī concepts. Aḥmad Riḍā arrived at his prophetology through devotion to Muḥammad and an ardent desire faithfully to imitate his Prophetic example. Barelwis justified their practices and self-identity, which revolved around the figure of Muḥammad, by citing Sunnī sources. To the extent that Barelwi and Shīʿī positions overlapped it should be understood to be development from two different traditions rather than "Shīʿī influence." See Sanyal, *Devotional Islam*, pp. 212–16.

and observing *(ḥāḍir wa-nāẓir)* at all times and places; and that he can be called upon whenever needed.[31] According to the Barelwis Muḥammad has a comprehensive knowledge of the unknown *(ʿilm-i ghayb)*.[32]

Given this theological background, Aḥmad Riḍā opposed the Deobandis and other Muslim groups because they did not accord Muḥammad his status as a holy superman.[33] For Aḥmad Riḍā, Medina, the city where the Prophet's tomb was located, was the holiest place in the world, even more sacred than Mecca, the location of the "House of God" (the Kaʿba). One of his verses says,

> O pilgrims! come to the tomb of the king of kings
> you have seen the Kaʿba, now see the Kaʿba of the Kaʿba.[34]

Anyone who decreased the glory of Muḥammad in any way was for Aḥmad Riḍā guilty of infidelity to Islam *(kufr)*. The Deobandis, and any other ulama and sufis who venerated the Prophet as a perfect but human model for human behavior, fell far short of what Aḥmad Riḍā considered proper love and adulation of the Prophet.

Focusing all his love on Muḥammad, Aḥmad Riḍā considered himself "Muḥammad's slave" *(ʿAbd al-Muṣṭafā)*.[35] He put Mu-

---

[31]The shorthand for this belief is the expression "O Messenger!" *(Yā rasūl)*. In contemporary Pakistan it is not unusual to see Barelwis identifying themselves by wearing green buttons with this written on them. Benazir Bhutto, not generally considered a Barelwi but a Shīʿī, had this written on many of her campaign posters in Lahore during the 1989 elections.

[32]This notion was denounced by Shāh Ismāʿīl Shahīd (d. 1831) as associating limited human knowledge with the knowledge that only God possesses *(ishrāk fi'l-ʿilm)*. See Shāh Ismāʿīl Shahīd, *Radd al-ishrāk*, pp. 20–22.

[33]Aḥmad Riḍā declared any person who did not share each detail of his prophetology to be an infidel in the same fashion that a person not adhering to each article of the Sunnī credal dogma *(ʿaqāʾid)* would be considered a non-Muslim. Aḥmad Riḍā defines numerous kinds of infidels in his *Ḥusām al-ḥaramayn*, including those following Mīrzā Ghulām Aḥmad, the leader of the Ahmadis who had declared himself a prophet, and Deobandi leaders, Muḥammad Qāsim Nānautawī, Rashīd Aḥmad Gangōhī, and Ashraf ʿAlī T'hānawī. Aḥmad Riḍā labeled the latter three "Wahhābīs." See Usha Sanyal, *Devotional Islam*, pp. 235–37. Deobandis were a group of nineteenth-century revivalist ulama who supported a sufism devoid of what they considered non-Islamic practices.

[34]Ibid., p. 157.

[35]Ibid., p. 156. This is how he often signed his name, yet another example of the blurring of distinctions between God and the Prophet. Some Muslims might consider this excessive devotion to the Prophet, since each believer is supposed to be a slave of God. Aḥmad Riḍā justified his pen name on the basis of Caliph ʿUmar's precedent.

Veneration and love of the Prophet, which had emerged very early in the Is-

ḥammad much "closer" to God, declaring that the Prophet was not "other than God." [36] According to his formulation, only Muḥammad reaches God without intermediaries, so that on the Day of Judgment all other prophets, ulama, and intimates of God will be imploring him to intercede for them.[37] Citing ʿAbdulḥaqq Muḥaddith Dihlawī (d. 1052/1642) and the Egyptian poet, al-Buṣīrī (d. ca. 695/1296), Aḥmad Riḍā declared: "Setting aside the claim that Christians make [about Jesus being divine], you can say whatever you wish in praise of the Prophet for there was no limit to the Prophet's qualities."[38] Thus the Prophet's knowledge also included the five things mentioned in the Qur'ān and hadith said to be known only to God.[39]

If there were not ample evidence to the contrary throughout Aḥmad Riḍā's work, a reader seeing these passages out of context might come to the conclusion that Aḥmad Riḍā was equating God and Muḥammad. It would be more accurate to say that for Aḥmad Riḍā, God and Muḥammad constituted a seamless reality. Aḥmad Riḍā said, "If his heart were to be broken into two pieces it would be found that on one part would be inscribed the first part of the *kalima*, 'There is no god but Allah,' and on the other would be written the second half, 'And Muḥammad is his messenger.' "[40] This same rapport between God and Muḥammad is expressed in Aḥmad Riḍā's poetry:

> The two worlds seek to please Allāh
> God seeks to please Muḥammad
> Muḥammad is the threshold to Allāh
> Allāh is the threshold to Muḥammad
> A vow was made for all time
> to unite Khuda's [God's] happiness with Muḥammad's.[41]

---

lamic tradition, were expressed through a poetic genre in India called *naʿt* during the Mughal period; *naʿt* is still recited today in the vernacular languages of South Asia. See Annemarie Schimmel's *And Muhammad Is His Messenger: The Veneration of the Prophet in Islamic Piety* for a full treatment of these developments throughout the Islamic world. Aḥmad Riḍā discussed the Prophet's attributes in his legal opinions *(fatāwā)* and in conversations *(malfūẓāt)*; he also composed an entire *dīwān* of his own *naʿt* poetry, *Ḥadā'iq-i Bakhshish.*

[36]Sanyal, *Devotional Islam*, p. 154.

[37]Ibid., p. 179.

[38]Aḥmad Riḍā, *Malfūẓāt*, 2:58–59, cited in ibid., p. 153.

[39]These were knowledge of the Day of Judgment, of when it would rain, of the sex of an unborn child, of what a person would earn the following day, and of where one would die. Aḥmad Riḍā's interpretation was that being known to God did not imply that *only* God knew and the Prophet did not. See ibid., p. 180.

[40]Aḥmad Riḍā, *Malfūẓāt*, 3:67, cited in ibid., p. 157.

[41]Aḥmad Riḍā, *Ḥadā'iq*, p. 47, cited in Usha Sanyal, "In the Path of the Prophet:

For the Barelwis exuberant praise of the Prophet is the touchstone of correct religious practice and belief, enabling them to legitimize both weak hadiths, if they elevate Muḥammad's stature, and innovations in practice, if they honor the Prophet.[42] They express their devotion in a typically Indian manner, paralleling the practices of Indian bhaktas by writing love poetry, adorning holy persons with flowers, and using rosewater and incense when in their holy presence—a far cry from the paradigmatic practices of Muḥammad, an Arabian prophet that Ahl-i Hadith members use as the exclusive criterion for appropriate Islamic orthopraxy. These kinds of Indian devotional practices did not usually trouble Deobandis, although such activities provoked serious clashes between Barelwis and the Ahl-i Hadith.

During the British colonial period, the Ahl-i Hadith vehemently denied the institutions of sufism and any notions that there could be intermediaries between God and the believer. Ahl-i Hadith challenged the customary Indian Islamic ethos and associated practices, making it one of the most radical groups of Indian ulama.[43] They categorically excluded all later developments in Islam,[44] thereby declaring both medieval schools of jurisprudence and sufism, institutions which had guided Muslims for a millennium, to be superfluous. Emphasizing a direct and literal interpretation of the Qur'ān and hadith, the Ahl-i Hadith believed that each Muslim could derive guidelines for ritual performance and for life situations from these original sources. Experiencing God, a sufi goal, was for them not a proper Muslim goal. Although never very popular, this group's relatively few adherents came from the elite who did not mind that Ahl-i Hadith ulama rejected both the traditional Indian Sunnī Ḥanafī ritual observances (by reciting "āmīn" out loud [*āmīn bi'l-jahr*] and raising their hands [*raf' al-yadayn*] in prayer) and the customary master-disciple relationships.[45]

Maulana Ahmad Riza Khan Barelwi and the Ahl-e Sunnat wa Jamaʿat Movement in British India, c.1870–1921," pp. 182–83 (brackets and diacritics mine).

[42]Ibid., pp. 348, 448. It is this mode of thinking that justified admirable innovations (sing. *bidaʿt al-ḥasana*) since it is not against general proof *(dalīl ʿāmm)* and leads one to the shariʿa and practice of the sunna. See Aḥmad Saʿīd, *Bi'l-fawā'id al-ḍābiṭa fī ithbāt al-rābiṭa*, pp. 16–31, where visualization of the shaykh is justified as an admirable innovation. General proof in this context most likely means community consensus.

[43]Metcalf, *Islamic Revival*, pp. 268–96.

[44]The Ahl-i Hadith are forced to include the first three centuries of Islam because of their reliance on the canonical tenth-century hadith collections.

[45]There is no reliable information on how many people claimed to be Ahl-i Hadith followers. According to Muḥammad Jaʿfar T'hānesarī's *Tawārīkh-i ʿajibān*,

In 1867 a group of ulama founded a Dār al-ʿUlūm at Deoband to propagate a shariʿa-minded revivalist/reformist Islam.[46] The Deobandi orientation emphasized adherence of individuals to Islamic behavioral norms just as Sirhindī and his spiritual successors had been urging for the past three centuries. In contrast to the popular mediational Islam centered on practices around sufi shrines and annual shrine celebrations, Deobandis conceived of religious leaders as teachers of Islamic religious duties and exemplars of the Prophetic sunna for the common people. Although the Deobandi leadership pattern challenged the basis of the predominantly rural sufi mediational style of religious authority, Deobandi teachers shared much in common with their nonreformist brethren. Deobandi ulama thought of themselves primarily as legal consultants *(muftīs)* while also acting as sufi shaykhs to their students.

Each religious scholar at Deoband functioned as a directing-shaykh, training and shaping morals and outward behavior of disciples in accordance with the shariʿa and the Prophetic ideal. One noteworthy Deobandi teacher, Chishtī Rashīd Aḥmad Gangōhī (d. 1322–23/1905), developed relationships with disciples that were oriented toward individual instruction and counseling, in contrast to the mediational style of rural shaykhs who met with large groups of disciples. The goal was not to intercede for the disciple or to transmit information from religious books, but to train and educate each disciple in such a way as to transform character and subdue the ego *(nafs)*.

Like other sufi shaykhs, Rashīd Aḥmad taught his disciples to love and emulate him, stressing the need for an affinity *(munāsabat)* in the heart between the spiritual mentor and disciple. He did not hesitate to visit the tombs of spiritual forebears, for example, that of Aḥmad Sirhindī or other renowned sufis. Rashīd Aḥmad Gangōhī's disciples compared their shaykh's speech to that of Muḥammad, while Muḥammad Qāsim Nānautawī's (d. 1294/1877) contemporaries continually compared him to the

---

there were only ten Wahhābīs in the Panjab in 1861; by 1879 a quarter (!) of the Muslims "were followers of Muḥammad Ismāʿīl," cited in Abū'l-Ḥasan Zayd Fārūqī, *Maulānā Ismāʿīl awr Taqwiyat al-Īmān*, p. 10. According to a 1979 report conducted by the Pakistani Ministry of Religious Affairs on religious schools in Pakistan, 354 were Deobandi, 267 Barelwi, 126 Ahl-i Hadith, and 41 Shīʿī. There were no figures on how many students were in each school, so the relationship between schools and popularity of a religious perspective is difficult to establish. See P. Lewis, *Pirs, Shrines and Pakistani Islam*, p. 83.

[46]Metcalf, *Islamic Revival*, pp. 157–83. Unless otherwise noted I am relying on Metcalf's treatment of Deobandis in this section.

Prophet. When Muḥammad Qāsim heard the Prophet's name he would tremble. Like other modern Indo-Muslim disciples, Nānautawī's disciples considered themselves his lovers. Indeed, those who knew the teachers and shaykhs of Deoband would say that to see their faces was to "be reminded of God."[47] Although the Deobandis and the Barelwis appeared to oppose each other, they had much in common.

The Deobandis specialized in formulating legal judgments *(fatāwā)* which propagated their reformist ideas and reinforced the status quo of following the legal school of Abū Ḥanīfa, the legitimacy of which was continually being contested by the Ahl-i Hadith. Through these legal decisions Deobandi ulama clarified in a practical fashion their credal critique of the Ahl-i Hadith and Shīʿīs and discouraged what they considered to be un-Islamic customs, e.g., elaborate death anniversary celebrations at the graves of sufis, monthly *gyārhwīñ* (literally, eleventh) celebrations on the eleventh day of each Islamic month commemorating ʿAbdulqādir al-Jīlānī (d. 561/1166), sufi music assemblies *(samāʿ)*, special pilgrimages to sufi shrines, and solicitations for the assistance of deceased sufis, who could hear supplications at any time or place. Since the Barelwis considered all of these practices compatible with the Prophetic sunna and the Deobandis did not, the two groups spent much of their time fighting each other.[48]

One source of friction between the Deobandis and the Barelwis was their conflicting idea of the spiritual mentor's role: the Deobandis were directing-shaykhs and the Barelwis were mediating-shaykhs. For Deobandis the shaykh was an educator and an exemplar of moral character and piety, while for the Barelwis the shaykh was an intercessor and patron. The implications for disciples were manifold. The Deobandis expected the disciple to make an effort to transform his or her character and insisted on individual accountability in religious matters. A Deobandi disciple yielded his or her ego in loving obedience to the shaykh in addition to practicing spiritual exercises under his guidance. In contrast, the Barelwis placed considerably less stress on the disciples' personal responsibility and regarded a disciple's spiritual growth as depending on the intercession of the shaykh, which in turn was tied to the intercession of Muḥammad. The Barelwis

---

[47]Ibid., p. 179.

[48]For a more comprehensive view of what Deobandi reformers considered to be un-Islamic, particularly among women, see Barbara Metcalf's translation of Maulānā Ashrafʿ Alī T'hānawī's *Bihishtī zēwar—Perfecting Women: Maulana Ashraf Ali Thanawi's Bihisht-i Zewar: A Partial Translation with Commentary.*

considered a direct approach to God to be a sign of arrogance, an insult to Muḥammad and his heirs, being a foolish rejection of the means God had provided to become close to Him.

Voluntary Associations in the Panjab

After 1880 the religious milieu of the Panjab was increasingly stirred up by various Hindu and Sikh reformist and revivalist movements as well as Muslim ones.[49] The alarming success of Christian missionary activity,[50] initiated by the American Presbyterians in November 1849 after the British conquest of the Panjab, was one reason for it. Christian missionary endeavors began to show results in the 1880s: the 3,912 Christian converts in 1881 had increased 410 percent by 1891 to total 19,750.[51] Although this represented a minuscule proportion (.08 percent) of the population, Muslim, Hindu, and Sikh groups perceived these conversions to be a harbinger of the fate that would befall them. Conversion had symbolic socioeconomic and political repercussions far beyond the numbers in the British decennial census. As each religious community was tallied according to geographical and social/caste affiliation, a community's triumph or decline was registered in the census figures.[52]

Lahore was the Panjabi center for Hindu and Muslim revivalist publications because of its role as the British administrative center. The city's population increase from 100,000 in 1860 to 430,000 in 1931 resulted from an influx from the countryside, as well as Panjabis seeking an English education to qualify for employment in the colonial administration.[53] This Indian-educated class, increasingly communicating in the language and cultural expressions of the British, adopted British organizational styles and modern forms of communication such as newspapers and journals. Among Indian groups, the Hindus pioneered these voluntary associations, which Urdu speakers called *anjumans*, in

[49]See Oberoi's *Construction of Religious Boundaries*.

[50]See Avril A. Powell, *Muslims and Missionaries in Pre-Mutiny India*.

[51]Kenneth W. Jones, *Arya Dharm: Hindu Consciousness in 19th-Century Punjab* p. 10.

[52]In 1923 the Anjuman-i Khuddām aṣ-Ṣūfiyya began recording their numerical successes with names (non-Muslim and Muslim) in their journal *Risāla-yi anwār al-ṣūfiyya;* see 19.10.20. This practice continued at least through 1925. See also Arjun Appadurai, "Number in Colonial Imagination."

[53]Gilmartin, *Empire and Islam*, pp. 76–77.

imitation of the British.[54] In 1884 Muslims formed their own voluntary association, the Anjuman-i Ḥimāyat-i Islām, to defend Muslim interests against Christian missionary and Hindu Arya Samaj attacks. It published pamphlets and journals to counter polemic tracts by other religious communities and established Islamic high schools and the Islamia College in Lahore to promote an Islamic education and to prepare students for jobs in the British civil-service system.[55]

The development of these voluntary associations in the 1880s coincided with the appearance of an English-speaking Indian middle class who were politically very powerful. These first English-speaking, college-educated Panjabis were neither rooted in the ideals and paradigms of the past nor totally at ease with the fast pace of change and innovation brought by the British. Membership in these voluntary organizations represented one manifestation of a cross-cultural phenomenon that allowed the elites of all religious communities to be swept along by British modernizing influences. By the turn of the century anglicized Panjabis had created a novel cross-cultural synthesis with corresponding organizations that would transform the Panjab and dramatically alter their perceptions and lifestyles.

Panjabis fashioned the voluntary organization, called variously *sabhā, samāj,* club, *anjuman,* or society, to conform to their new Indian middle-class life. With them British forms of organization hitherto alien to Panjabi culture, complete with annual meetings, officers, budgets, executive committees, reports, appeals, and fund raising, were adapted wholesale into Indian life. The organizations generated by these societies included schools, libraries, orphanages, and presses, all of which reached significant numbers of Panjabis for whom English was still a foreign language. Finally, voluntary organizations, in addition to providing a convenient way to meet other educated men, had the potential to act

[54]Dr. G. W. Leitner, soon after becoming the principal of the newly organized Government College, founded the Anjuman-i Panjāb in 1865. The British formed the Anjuman-i Islāmiyya in 1869 in Lahore to administer the Bādshāhī Mosque and encourage Muslim loyalty to British rule.

[55]Gilmartin, *Empire and Islam,* p. 77. The Arya Samaj opened its Dayanand Anglo-Vedic High School in 1886. See Kenneth Jones, *Arya Dharm,* pp. 67–93. Muslim anjumans proliferated in the first few decades of the twentieth century. Jamā'at 'Alī's Anjuman-i Khuddām, aṣ-Ṣūfiyya was one of the most prominent in the Panjab. Others include Anjuman-i Mustashār al-'Ulāma' (*Risāla* 4.1.9), Anjuman-i Khuddām-i Musulmān in Jhang (*Risāla* 4.6.40), Anjuman-i Ḥanafiyya (*Risāla* 10.3.25 and 21.3.1), and Anjuman-i Nāṣir at-Ta'līm headed by Jamā'at 'Alī (*Risāla* 10.4.12). For detailed coverage of early Muslim anjumans see Edward D. Churchill, "Muslim Societies of the Punjab, 1860–1890."

as a support group, an alternate tribal-kinship network *(birādarī)* parallel to family and other social networks.[56] There were other Indo-Muslims who absolutely would not compromise with non-Muslim British cultural differences; revivalist sufis often fit in this category and at times even deliberately highlighted these religio-cultural divergences.

Indo-Muslim Identity

For revivalist Naqshbandīs defending sufism was the equivalent to preserving Islamic identity in the face of this anglicizing trend brought about by British political dominance, Christian missionaries, Hindu revivalism, and the Ahmadis, a group led by the self-proclaimed prophet, Ghulām Aḥmad.[57] Some Indian Muslims formed voluntary associations; others concentrated on maintaining (and making others aware of) their Islamic identity through what they considered the total observance of the Prophetic sunna. Outward behavior reflected what Indian Muslims perceived as a deeper spiritual malaise which was either caused or accelerated by British colonial rule. For Naqshbandīs and other juristic sufis of the time, following the sunna was a religious obligation. Neglect of any aspect of this Prophetic imitation indicated a grievous lack of respect to the Prophet himself. Ultimately, to follow the sunna was to observe the correct etiquette toward God and achieve a very tangible connection with Him. A person fol-

---

[56]A note in the margin of an article *Risāla-yi anwār al-ṣūfiyya* had a thirty-year-old disciple of Jamā'at 'Alī advertising for a marriage partner; see *Risāla* 20.4.3. This was not only unusual for Muslim Panjabi society of the 1920s but it was atypical for the journal. Now, such advertisements appear regularly in Lahore newspapers.

[57]One article of credal dogma accepted for over a millennium by the Sunnī community declared Muḥammad to be the last prophet. The Muslim community defined a Muslim by his or her acceptance of all statements of the creed. Rejecting even one statement automatically made a person a non-Muslim. It was on these grounds that nineteenth-century Sunnī Indian ulama declared Ahmadis not to be Muslims, a decision confirmed in 1974 by the Pakistani Parliament. The practice of Western scholars is to recognize any group as Muslim that defines itself as Muslim. See Yohanan Friedmann's *Prophecy Continuous: Aspects of Ahmadi Religious Thought and Its Medieval Background*. In 1922 Jamā'at 'Alī issued an edict *(farmān)* declaring that each knowledgeable Muslim, especially if initiated into a sufi lineage, has a religious obligation *(farḍ)* vigorously to propagate Islam so that Muslims would not convert to Hinduism; see *Risāla*, 19.8.14. Nine years earlier Jamā'at 'Alī had spoken out against Ahmadis, accusing them of causing Muslims to become infidels and demanding that they use separate mosques. See *Risāla*, 10.5.7.

lowing the Prophetic sunna was sancified by the love of the Prophet.[58]

Shēr Muḥammad (d. 1347/1928), based in a small village forty kilometers outside Lahore, expected all those coming to his sufi lodge to comply with the sunna from "head to foot." Any Muslim coming into his presence and not looking like a Muslim in appearance, with the proper head covering for men—which included a cap with a turban wound around it—would be severely reprimanded.[59] If people came into his presence bareheaded he would put a rimless cap on their heads so they would minimally comply with the sunna. If they came wearing a hat he would ask them why they were not wearing a turban *(ʿimāma).*[60]

Shēr Muḥammad accused the British of corrupting Muslims and spoke out against English shoes, English haircuts, and English food.[61] Since such Christian customs were against the sunna, he accused Muslims adopting English clothes or hairstyles of looking like Christians.[62] The following anecdote reveals the kind of collisions encountered by well-educated English-speaking Indian Muslims when they visited Shēr Muḥammad:

When [Shēr Muḥammad] saw their clean-shaven faces and their close-cut English haircuts he would ask, "Do your fathers look like this—with no beard and hair? Do you consider your fathers' appearance to be bad looking? Our Sikh brothers do not act like this." [Shēr Muḥammad], ad-

[58]Bīrbalī, *Inqilāb al-ḥaqīqat,* pp. 30–33.

[59]Ibid., p. 27.

[60]Ibid., p. 28. According to the Ḥanafī school, which almost all South Asian Sunnīs follow, it is reprehensible *(makrūh)* for men to pray without some kind of head covering. As a result there are often baskets of thatched rimless caps at the door of mosques for use during prayer. It is also impolite in Indo-Pakistan for a man not to cover his hair when in the presence of a sufi shaykh. A handkerchief is the minimum acceptable covering and a cap with a turban is the most preferred. Wearing a turban as a mark of following the sunna has also been strongly advocated by the leaders of the modern Tablīghī Jamāʿat movement.

[61]Muḥammad ʿAlī, a successor of revivalist Chishtī Sulaymān Taunsawī, who had a sufi lodge in Khayrabad, expressed displeasure at any Muslim wearing European shoes since it was a part of Christian culture; see Nizami, "Madrasas, Scholars, and Saints," p. 98. The symbolically charged nature of dress also affected the British, who for a time did not allow non-Christian Indians to wear European shoes; see J. S. Jha, ed., *Imperial Honeymoon with Indian Aristocracy,* pp. 425–36. Shāh Walīullāh and later Shāh ʿAbdulʿazīz were two of the first to stress the importance of dress as a symbol of Islamic identity. See Nizami, "Madrasas, Scholars, and Saints," p. 179. At Kakori Sharif (near Lucknow) Shāh Ḥabīb Ḥaidar (d. 1935) disliked hearing English words in his sufi lodge. See Claudia Liebeskind, "Sufism, Sufi Leadership and 'Modernization' in South Asia since c. 1800," p. 329.

[62]Bīrbalī, *Inqilāb al-ḥaqīqat,* pp. 28–36.

> dressing the others in the group, asked how this act had been perpetrated on them [the English-educated Muslims] and what had happened to Muslims. . . . "Do not Sikhs find jobs? It is a sad thing that they shave and cut the hair of Muslim prisoners but leave the Sikhs alone. The English also have come to know that Muslims are fainthearted in their religion." Then [Shēr Muḥammad] would ask how many years they had studied English. They would answer fifteen or sixteen years. When he asked them what *bismillāh* meant they did not know. . . . "There is nothing they do not know in English, but they read the blessed Qur'ān without understanding [a word]. Everyone knows the English laws but no one is informed of God's laws. . . . Now you have become English. Now your attestation of faith is *There is no god but God and the English are the messengers of God.*"[63]

The story would end with English-educated Muslims repenting. If they came back again, they returned wearing a beard and conscientiously performing their ritual prayers. At that point Shēr Muḥammad would carefully observe their behavior and write prescriptions like those of a practitioner of Greek medicine *(ḥakīm)*. After this, Qur'ānic verses in harmony with each individual's character would be given for recitation after each prayer. When the person was ready, he or she would be initiated and learn the first Naqshbandī *dhikr*, the continual repetition of "Allāh."[64]

In this chaotic religious environment a valid Bakrī connection to Muḥammad no longer sufficed to legitimize Naqshbandī authority. For most Naqshbandīs the British were many levels removed from their day-to-day life.[65] A much more immediate

---

[63]Muḥammad Ibrāhīm Quṣūrī, *Khazīna-yi ma'rifat*, p. 122.

[64]Bīrbalī, *Inqilāb al-ḥaqīqat*, p. 42.

[65]Naqshbandīs and other Indian sufis still continued educational activities to defend a mediational Islam and to counter modern British educational models, which had inspired Sayyid Aḥmad Khān to have the Muhammadan Anglo-Indian College at Aligarh become the "Muslim Oxford University." Two Naqshbandī groups set up religious schools, the Dār al-'Ulūm Abīdiyya Naqshbandiyya near Dera Ghazi Khan in 1922 and the Madrasa-yi 'Arabiyya Sa'diyya at the Khundian sufi lodge near Mianwali in 1917. See Nadhr Aḥmad, *Jā'iza-yi madāris-i 'arabiyya maghribī pākistan*, pp. 27–29, 120–21, 351–52. Since independence five more Naqshbandī Arabic schools have been established: Madrasa-yi Naqshbandiyya (1951) in Qusur, Panjab; Jāmi'a-yi Naqshbandiyya Mujaddidiyya Fayḍ Lā Thānī (1966) in Raiwind, Panjab; Jāmi'a-yi Naqshbandiyya Riḍwiyya Fayḍ Muṣṭafā (1960) in Pakpattan, Sahiwal; Dār al-'Ulūm Naqshbandiyya Riḍwiyya (1952) in Sangla Hal, Shaykhpura; and Dār al-'Ulūm Mujaddidiyya (1970) in Tanda, Gujarat. All except the first declared a Ḥanafī-Barēlwī affiliation; see ibid., pp. 55, 63, 174, 209, 225–26. Following the Deobandi model, a network of Barelwi schools began in Lahore with Dār al-'Ulūm Nu'māniyya (named after Abū Ḥanīfa and founded in 1304–5/1887) and Dār al-'Ulūm Ḥizb al-Aḥnāf (founded in 1342–43/

threat was that of scripturalist-minded groups like the Ahl-i Hadith, who defined religious authority solely on the basis of the Qur'ān and authoritative hadith collections. Their alternative orthodoxy simply did not recognize the validity of traditional law schools and sufism. Indeed, this not only put Naqshbandī and other sufi authority in jeopardy, but caused them to react as if the quintessence of Islam itself was endangered.

The Naqshbandīs responded by declaring that allegiance to a sufi pir was incumbent upon each Muslim. In this fashion, late nineteenth- and twentieth-century Naqshbandī revivalist shaykhs justified themselves in Islamic legal terminology by declaring (1) inner knowledge *('ilm-i bāṭin)* to be a religious obligation *(farḍ)*, (2) the search for the Way to be legally incumbent *(wājib)*, and (3) the initiation ceremony *(bay'a)* by a spiritual guide to be an exemplary model (sunna) of the Prophet and his Companions.[66] Interpreting the sufi shaykh as the literal heir of the Prophet, Naqshbandīs never ceased to remind their disciples that they must obey the spiritual mentor in the same unquestioning fashion as the Companions were said to have complied with Muḥammad's decisions. That such exhortations were necessary indicated that many were questioning sufi authority. Undoubtedly many did visit sufi lodges but it is unlikely that this was a result of coercion. Instead, the need to make sufi initiation a religious obligation suggests that the sufis' charismatic authority had seriously eroded. Typically the decision to pursue the sufi path, as in other supererogatory Islamic practices, had been left up to each individual. However, for that small number with the spiritual capacity, sufi practice had been considered obligatory.[67] The mediatory

1924), both of which received direct financial support from revival pirs. For further information on Dīdar 'Alī Alwarī (d. 1353–54/1935), *khalīfa* and student of Naqshbandī Faḍlurraḥmān Ganjmurādābādī and the founder of the Dār al-'Ulūm of the Ḥizb al-Aḥnāf, see Sanyal, *Devotional Islam*, pp. 80–81. Naqshbandī Jamā'at 'Alī Shāh provided teachers (all of whom were his disciples) in addition to supporting these schools financially. See Iqbāl Aḥmad Fārūqī, *Tadhkira-yi ahl-i sunnat wa-jamā'at Lāhūr* (Lahore: Maktaba-yi Nabawiyya, 1987), p. 272, and Gilmartin, *Empire and Islam*, pp. 60–61. Of 23 prominent sufi-affiliated Barelwi ulama in British colonial Lahore, 14 were Naqshbandīs, 6 Chishtīs, and 3 Qādiris. See Fārūqī, *Tadhkira-yi ahl-i sunnat.*

[66]It is understood in a revivalist milieu that following the Prophetic model is a religious obligation. Hidāyat 'Alī Jaipūrī in his *Mi'yār al-sulūk*, p. 26, emphasizes this formulation, attributing it to Qāḍī Thanā'ullāh Pānīpatī.

[67]Within the Naqshbandiyya making sunna practices incumbent *(wājib)* was standard practice. One Naqshbandī shaykh, Shēr Muḥammad (d. 1347/1928), even declared *mustaḥabb* practices to be required. See Bīrbalī, *Inqilāb al-ḥaqīqat*, p. 39. This type of orthopraxical attitude is consistent with the Naqshbandiyya since they do not give permission *(rukhṣa)* to bend the dictates of Ḥanafī jurispru-

sufism of colonial India became a "movement," a reified entity rather than a spiritual lineage with which one connected in a circumscribed context. What had become obligatory for the few under the aegis of a directing-shaykh now became obligatory for all with the mediating-shaykh.

Twentieth-century arguments cited Shāh Walīullāh, who had declared *bay'a* to be sunna,[68] and Qāḍī Thanā'ullāh Pānīpatī (d. 1225/1810), who interpreted Qur'ān 3:102—"O those who believe! Piously perform your obligations to God in a reverent manner"—to mean that Muslims should avoid everything not pleasing to God. One's inner and outer character *(akhlāq)* and dogma *('aqā'id)* should perfectly reflect piety *(taqwā)*.[69] From this, Pānīpatī concludes that seeking the path *(ṭalab-i ṭarīqat)* in order to achieve inner perfection is religiously incumbent upon each Muslim because piety is inconceivable without intimacy with God *(wilāyat)*. He also uses Qur'ān 49:13, "The noblest of you in the sight of God is the one whose conduct reflects the most fear of God," to justify the assertion that cultivating piety is a religious obligation.[70] Perfect piety is not possible to attain without developing one's subtle entities *(laṭīfas)*, which in turn depends upon the acquisition of inner knowledge *('ilm-i bāṭin)*. Enhancing this latter quality, according to Pānīpatī, is a Muslim's religious obligation, since God ordered Muḥammad to say, "My Lord! Increase me in knowledge" (Q. 20:114).[71] Concluding the argument, Pānīpatī mentions that the search for the perfect and perfection-bestowing pir therefore becomes necessary, since few can arrive near God without the intermediary *(tawassul)* of a spiritual guide.[72]

---

dence. This latter point is one more aspect of Naqshbandī identity which Naqshbandīs use to justify their superiority over other sufi lineages.

[68]Shāh Walīullāh, *Al-qawl al-jamīl*, p. 18.

[69]Qāḍī Thanā'ullāh Pānīpatī, *Irshād al-ṭālibīn* p. 21. I have purposely translated this Qur'ānic verse in the way Pānīpatī has interpreted it while not ignoring its original meaning. The context for Q. 3:102 is the so-called "Constitution of Medina" and the verb *ittaqā*, often later associated with being pious or God-fearing, which in the original context had a meaning closer to "honorably discharging obligations" or "keeping oneself to a contract" in the new tribal alliance at Medina. See R. B. Serjeant, "The Constitution of Medina," p. 12, and "The *Sunnah Jāmi'ah*, Pacts with the Yathrib Jews, and the *Tahrīm* of Yathrib: Analysis and Translation of the Documents Comprised in the So-called 'Constitution of Medina,' " pp. 21–23, both in his *Studies in Arabian History and Civilization* chapters 5 and 6.

[70]Pānīpatī, *Irshād al-ṭālibīn*, p. 22.

[71]Ibid., pp. 22, 31.

[72]Ibid., p. 23. Zawwār Ḥusayn (d. 1400/1980), writing over one century later, repeats Pānīpatī's argument and then proceeds to justify the institution of initia-

The presuppositions of Pānīpatī's declaration of sufi orthodoxy involve the necessity of "connecting to God" via an inner transformation involving the mediation of a spiritual guide instead of relying solely on transmitted religious knowledge, a scriptural connection. In other words, connecting to Muḥammad via many sources of authority makes a person a better Muslim. The sufism that Pānīpatī describes is clearly not the mediational sufism declared obligatory a century later. Many Naqshbandīs of the Panjab, by the first decades of the twentieth century, had ceased to be directing-shaykhs and had already adopted the practice of choosing their lineal descendants as their principal spiritual heirs. Such practices often meant that the lineal successor did not possess the minimum qualifications expected of a spiritual guide, especially the ability to project spiritual power *(tawajjuh)*. If Muḥammad ʿUmar Bīrbalī's (d. 1387/1967) observations of twentieth-century sufis are correct, very few sufis achieved an ability to go beyond an elementary level of *dhikr*.[73] When hereditary succession becomes the norm, thereby curtailing spiritual practice even more, one can expect a corresponding modification in the role and authority of the Naqshbandī sufi shaykh. This is exactly what happened as mediating-shaykhs replaced directing-shaykhs.

---

tion *(bayʿa)* in the same fashion as Shāh Walīullāh before him; see *ʿUmdat al-sulūk*, pp. 30–37.

[73]Bīrbalī, *Inqilāb al-ḥaqīqat*, pp. 70, 73–74.

CHAPTER 9

Redefining the Shaykh's Role in the Naqshbandī Sufi Tradition

In the pir's majesty and his blessed face are all of God's inner and outer benefits.
Ḥāfiẓ Nūr 'Alī,
pensioner District Judge and disciple of Jamā'at 'Ali Shāh

Visualization of the pir has created the heart's mirror.
Visualization of the pir has rubbed out the blackness of the heart.
From this it is easy to see the face of the Messenger in the heart.
Visualization of the pir is meeting God Almighty. . . .
Munawwar Husayn, "Taṣawwur-i shaykh"

The mediating-shaykh reflects a new form of Naqshbandī personal authority, a mediational sufism radically departing from the symbols and practices of directing-shaykhs and indicating a paradigm shift which fundamentally alters what earlier Naqshbandīs conceived to be sufism.[1] The mediating-shaykh as the sole intermediary between the Prophet and believers dramatically contrasts with Naqshbandī directing-shaykhs who taught disciples how they themselves could arrive near God and manipulate supernatural power. Yet these kinds of mediatory roles were not

[1]This is not to say that there have not been any Naqshbandī mediating-shaykhs before the twentieth century. Sufis have typically functioned as implicit, if not explicit, mediators between heaven and earth but this has been in combination with their role as directing-shaykhs. One cannot comment on the vast majority of Naqshbandīs throughout history who, by an absence of written sources, have remained effectively anonymous. (Did they refrain from writing because they were mediating-shaykhs?) If I had not had access to twenty years of Jamā'at 'Alī's monthly magazine, the kind of information necessary to establish him as a mediating-shaykh would not have been available.

new to hereditary shrine-shaykhs and caretakers of sufi shrines in northern India.[2] Hereditary shrine-shaykhs specialized in "passing on messages to God" instead of guiding and educating their disciples in spiritual travel. Although sharing overlapping conceptual frameworks of mediation, the Naqshbandī mediating-shaykh used a different idiom than his hereditary shrine-shaykh counterpart.

Naqshbandī mediating-shaykhs reformulated spiritual practices to emphasize love; the goal itself became love. With love of the pir, everything else, including salvation, followed. Only love could traverse the ever-increasing hierarchical distance between a seeker and an ever-remote shaykh. Paradoxically, as Muḥammad and God appeared to be going further away from a believer on an outward trajectory, love drew them closer on a returning arc into the heart of the believer. This devotionalism, or *bhakti* (not a term used by Naqshbandīs), attracted many English-educated Muslims, who had been the group most influenced by the radically changed social conditions of colonial India. A new expression of Naqshbandī religiosity came into being, replete with a modern, English-inspired organizational style, a monthly magazine, and shaykhs who traveled thousands of kilometers a year on the new Indian railway.

Jamāʿat ʿAlī, who earns the distinction of being the most renowned Naqshbandī revivalist pir of the colonial period, was a paradigmatic mediating-shaykh. Like Chishtī Mihr ʿAlī Shāh, he had been educated among the leading reformist ulama, yet he strongly advocated the popular mediatory Islam of the rural Panjab that coincided more often than not with the Barelwi perspective.[3] He created an organization, the Anjuman-i Khuddām aṣ-

---

[2]The most popular shrine in nineteenth-century western Panjab was that of Sakhī Sarvar, not a sufi but presumably a Muslim (the shrine attendants are Muslim). See O. P. Ralhan and Suresh K. Sharma, ed., *Documents on Punjab: Folklore*, vol. 15, pp. 141–50, and Harjot Oberoi, *The Construction of Religious Boundaries: Culture, Identity and Diversity in the Sikh Tradition* (New York: Oxford University Press, 1994), pp. 147–60.

[3]Sayyid Karīm Shāh (d. 1319–20/1902), Jamāʿat ʿAlī Shāh's father, was a landowner in ʿAlipur. He had Ḥāfiẓ Shihābuddīn Kashmīrī come from nearby Qalʿah Subha Singh to teach Jamāʿat ʿAlī Shāh the Qur'ān. After studying with ʿAbdurrashīd ʿAlīpūrī, ʿAbdulwahhāb Amritsarī, and Ghulām Qādir Bhīrawī, Jamāʿat ʿAlī Shāh studied religious sciences with two well-known revivalist Naqshbandīs, Irshād Ḥusayn Rampūrī (d. 1311/1893–94) and Shāh Faḍlurraḥmān Ganj Murādābādī (d. 1312–13/1895). He also studied with Muḥammad ʿAbdullāh Tonkī (d. 1338–39/1920) and with the first rector of Nadwat al-Ulama, Muḥammad ʿAlī Mongīrī (d. 1346–47/1928). Jamāʿat ʿAlī Shāh received permission to transmit hadith from Muḥammad ʿAbdurrahmān Pānīpatī (d. 1313–14/1896) and, when he traveled to Mecca, Shāh ʿAbdulḥaqq Allāhābādī Makkī (d. 1333–34/1915) gave

Ṣūfiyya (hereafter Anjuman), to promote a mediatory brand of sufism and to meet the attacks of Deobandis, Ahmadis, Ahl-i Hadith, and Arya Samajis. His enterprise and its ramifications, which contributed to his designation as the leader of the Muslim community *(amīr-i millat)* in 1935, represent one kind of modern mediating-shaykh. Among Naqshbandīs, Jamāʿat ʿAlī Shāh best typified this mediational style in his ability to draw together under one banner three apparently disparate groups of Muslims: rural peasants, urban ulama, and English-educated elite.

Ittiḥād-i millat, a coalition of prominent urban leaders (with a certain degree of popular support) headed by Ẓafar ʿAlī Khān, poet and editor of the popular Lahore newspaper *Zamīndār*, designated Jamāʿat ʿAlī Shāh (d. 1370/1951) leader of the Indian Muslims *(amīr-i millat)* in 1935, an appointment that demonstrated Jamāʿat ʿAlī's mediatory talent among both the rural and urban elites and common people. The mediational sufism represented by Jamāʿat ʿAlī and supported by the erudite Aḥmad Riḍā Barēlwī knew no such rural/urban cleavage (nor does it today). With this kind of learned support from the ulama, his rural landowning ties, and the influential support of urban leaders, Jamāʿat ʿAlī departed radically from his Indian Naqshbandī predecessors. Yet he was not alone among his Muslim contemporaries when he established both a voluntary sufi association *(anjuman)* and a monthly published magazine to propagate his views.

Jamāʿat ʿAlī's Sufi Organization

Sources say that Jamāʿat ʿAlī was born in the village of ʿAlipur Sayyidan in the Sialkot district of the Panjab in 1841. His parents were lineal descendants of Sayyid Muḥammad Saʿīd Nawrūz Shāh Shirāzī, who came to India with the contingent of Persians who accompanied the Mughal ruler Humāyūn (d. 963/1556) on his campaign to reconquer India. Jamāʿat ʿAlī received an extensive religious education, achieving distinction as a memorizer of the Qur'ān *(ḥāfiẓ)* and a hadith specialist *(muḥaddith)*.

Coming from a family of Qādirī *sajjādanishīns*, Jamāʿat ʿAlī's first informal contact with the Naqshbandiyya was through his father, who had been initiated by Sayyid Ḥusayn Shāh, Jamāʿat ʿAlī Shāh's maternal grandfather. Bābā Faqīr Muḥammad Chūrāhī (d. 1315/1897), in nearby Chak Qurayshian (in Sialkot

him authorization to narrate additional hadiths. See Muḥammad Ṣādiq Quṣūrī, "Asātidha-yi amīr-i millat," and Arthur Buehler, "Jamāʿat ʿAlī Shāh."

Jamā'at 'Alī Shāh, circa 1935 (courtesy of the Naqshbandiyya Foundation)

district), formally initiated Jamāʿat ʿAlī into the Naqshbandiyya-Mujaddidiyya in 1891. Soon after, Jamāʿat ʿAlī received permission to initiate disciples into the Naqshbandiyya. He established his religious leadership in the sufi revival movement by propagating Islam *(tablīgh)* as he traveled on foot to many villages and towns throughout the Panjab. He not only encouraged regular performance of required religious duties according to Islamic law and supervised the construction of mosques but advocated a sufi-revival Islam, a mediational form of Islam based upon the leadership of sufi shaykhs who were also ulama.

In 1904, to institutionalize his sufi revival movement and to expand its activities beyond the Panjab, Jamāʿat ʿAlī founded the first successful sufi *anjuman* in the Panjab, and Anjuman-i Khuddām aṣ-Ṣūfiyya, (Voluntary Association for Sufi Servants). The genesis of the Anjuman begins with an English-educated district judge and landowner from Rohtak, Panjab, Anwar ʿAlī (1862–1920),[4] who was a sufi disciple and successor to his Naqshbandī-Mujaddidī shaykh, Maḥmūd Shāh Jālandarī.[5] He had achieved a modicum of fame as the author of books explaining Sufism and around the turn of the century founded the Muḥammadan Sufism Society, but it only attracted a few members. In 1904 the society was renamed the Voluntary Association for Sufi Servants with Jamāʿat ʿAlī at its head.

Anwar ʿAlī assumed responsibility for establishing the Anjuman's monthly magazine, *Risāla-yi anwār al-ṣūfiyya* (Magazine of Sufi Illuminations) and also served as Jamāʿat ʿAlī's right-hand man.[6] The fundamental purpose of the organization was to unify Indian sufis against scripturalist-minded groups (pejoratively labeled Wahhābīs) such as the Ahl-i Hadith. The goals of the Anju-

---

[4]For a short biography of Anwar ʿAlī, see *Risāla-yi anwār al-ṣūfiyya* 1, no. 2, p. 5, and 16, no. 9, pp. 20–31 [hereafter *Risāla* with volume, number, page; e.g., *Risāla* 1.2.5 and 16.9.20–31]. Pagination is very irregular in this magazine. I have found no mention of his pivotal contribution to Jamāʿat ʿAlī's efforts in the voluminous biography (752 pages) of Jamāʿat ʿAlī other than a casual mention along with other shaykhs and ulama. See Akhtar Ḥusayn, *Sīrat-i amīr-i millat* [hereafter cited as *Sīrat*], p. 353.

[5]The anglicized spelling is Jullundurī.

[6]*Risāla* 1.2.6. Anwar ʿAlī's central role in the Anjuman is indicated in the list of notables attending the first annual conference of the Anjuman on 20 March 1904; his name was listed after that of Jamāʿat ʿAlī and the son of the noted Naqshbandī shaykh Imām ʿAlī Shāh (d. 1282/1865), Mīr Luṭfullāh. Anwar ʿAlī gave the keynote speech at the 1904 annual conference which, reprinted in its entirety, comprised almost half of the first issue of the *Risāla*. At the tenth conference in 1913 Jamāʿat ʿAlī bestowed sufi robes on certain worthy successors from Mysore and Hyderabad in the Deccan, and Anwar ʿAlī gave them hats and turbans.

man, written in large script on the frontpiece of the first issue of the *Risāla,* were (1) to unify all the sufi lineages, e.g., Naqshbandiyya, Chishtiyya, Qādiriyya, and Suhrawardiyya; (2) to spread knowledge of Sufism; (3) to make books on Sufism available; and (4) to circulate the *Risāla,* in which sufi hagiography, exemplary character, and conduct were featured.[7] The Anjuman strived to unify what had always been disparate, segmented sufi lineages, creating a newly defined Suf-ism, an unprecedented "imaginary" institution engendered by a journal that would bolster and preserve mediational sufism as an institution.

The sufi activity of Jamāʿat ʿAlī and Anwar ʿAlī, although novel in Naqshbandī history, was right in step with the times. Jamāʿat ʿAlī, with his traditionally impeccable credentials of sufi shaykh and religious scholar, complemented Anwar ʿAlī's modern qualifications as an English-educated sufi who wrote about Sufism in both Urdu and English. Moreover, both these sufis availed themselves of modern technologies to propagate Sufism.

Aside from performing the pilgrimage to Mecca, directing-shaykhs rarely left their sufi lodges for any length of time. To assist their disciples along the spiritual path directing-shaykhs had always to be on call, regularly providing spiritual energy *(tawajjuh)* and spiritual companionship *(ṣuḥbat)* on a daily basis. Disciples knew that their directing-shaykh would be at his lodge so they could visit him whenever possible. Many senior disciples had spent years living at the sufi lodge in the company of their guides. Typically, but not always, a prominent sufi controlled an area around his lodge, commonly known as his spiritual territory *(wilāyat).* Normally his ability to exercise supernatural power only extended to the boundaries of this territory, and if a sufi did not observe the correct protocol when entering the spiritual domain of another sufi, it could have fatal consequences.[8]

These considerations did not apply to the peripatetic habits of Jamāʿat ʿAlī, whose authority could not easily be associated with any particular place or territory. The enterprise of propagating Sufism *qua* Sufism was in itself a modern phenomenon. Jamāʿat ʿAlī, rather than have seekers come to him, as directing-shaykhs had done for a millennium, took advantage of the mobility provided by the modern Indian railroad network and traveled the

[7]*Risāla* 1.1.n.p.

[8]See Khaliq Ahmad Nizami, *Some Aspects of Religion and Politics in India during the Thirteenth Century,* pp. 175–77; and Simon Digby, "Encounters with Jogis in Indian Sufi Hagiography." For types of difficulties over spiritual territory in Egypt, see Kathryn Virginia Johnson, "The Unerring Balance: A Study of the Theory of Sanctity *(Wilāyah)* of ʿAbd al-Wahhāb al-Shaʿrānī," pp. 126–34.

length and breadth of India. A very different dynamic ensued as disciples of traveling mediating-shaykhs like Jamāʿat ʿAlī had to wait in loving anticipation until the spiritual mentor decided to come to them. There were only two times a year when a disciple could be sure of finding Jamāʿat ʿAlī: at the annual meeting of the Anjuman, often held in May, and the anniversary of Jamāʿat ʿAlī's mother's death on the fourth of Shaʿbān, both held in Jamāʿat ʿAlī's village of Alipur.[9] With the kind of mediational sufism evolving in Jamāʿat ʿAlī's circle, the constant companionship with the shaykh was no longer necessary—indeed the longing created by the master's absence nurtured the love for the shaykh.[10]

Seldom otherwise could Jamāʿat ʿAlī be found at home in Alipur. In 1908, for example, he was on the road for at least eight months of the year, spending five months in Mysore, Bangalore, and Hyderabad, Deccan. For the long return train trip north, the nawwāb of Hyderabad rented a private car for him. As the train stopped along the way people came to see him and to give him fruit and flowers, a small-scale version of how Mahatma Gandhi was to be greeted when traveling later.[11] Six years later, after another long absence from the Panjab, eager followers in Sialkot decorated Jamāʿat ʿAlī and his son, Khādim Ḥusayn, with garlands. The press of people waiting to see them was so great that disciples had to cordon off a path so they could leave the station. It is said that when he returned to Alipur shortly after, a distance of fifty kilometers from the train station in Sialkot, people from Sialkot and Alipur lined up for two kilometers outside the village to receive the skaykh.[12] Jamāʿat ʿAlī's days of unobtrusively walking barefoot from village to village in the Panjab were over.

After 1880 there was a publishing boom of newspapers and magazines in the Panjab, as each religious group attempted to win converts and to defend its orthodoxy.[13] Indeed, the number

[9]The first three annual meetings of the Anjuman were held in the Bādshāhī Mosque in Lahore. See Akhtar Ḥusayn, *Sīrat,* p. 350. Akhtar Ḥusayn in *Sīrat* says incorrectly that the first annual meeting took place in 1901 instead of the 1904 indicated by the date of the first issue of *Risāla*. Jamāʿat ʿAlī attended the *ʿurs* of his own spiritual mentor, Bābā Faqīr Muḥammad Chūrāhī, whenever possible, but sometimes he was not able to visit due to his frequent travels.

[10]This change in the configuration of sources of personal authority contrasts with previous directing-shaykhs, e.g., ʿUbaydullāh Aḥrār, who altered their techniques due to extensive travel responsibilities but yet who managed to train a cadre of successors who themselves were potent directing-shaykhs.

[11]*Risāla* 4.4.3.

[12]*Risāla* 10.3.25–30.

[13]In the period 1880–1906 publishers printed 82 percent of all the Panjabi publications in Urdu. See N. Gerald Barrier and Paul Wallace, *The Punjab Press, 1880–*

and circulation of these publications served as a barometer of the political and religious ferment of the times.[14] The *Risāla-yi anwār al-ṣūfiyya,* the first issue of which was personally paid for by Jamāʿat ʿAlī, was the first sufi magazine in the Panjab. Unlike most other religious magazines written and published by Muslims, it assiduously avoided acting as a forum for religious debate.[15] Although there were occasional references to Ahmadīs and "Wahhabis," most of the *Risāla*'s articles interpreted diverse facets of mediational sufism, explaining how one arrived near God by loving Muḥammad and one's spiritual mentor.

In 1923 the *Risāla* added a regular section on the "calamity of apostasy" *(fitna-yi irtidād)* and on the monthly progress of the Anjuman in propagating Islam. Along with other Muslim groups, the Anjuman geared up to defend themselves and fight against the activities of the Arya Samajis, whose goal was to "reconvert" the Muslims whose ancestors had been Hindus.[16] By

---

1905, p. 159. An overwhelming majority (197) of these newspapers were published in Lahore, with Delhi taking second place with 60; see ibid., p. 160. Of these, 63 percent had a circulation of less than 500 per issue, 22 percent had a circulation of 500–999; see ibid., p. 163. After the turn of the century the number of newspapers increased dramatically: 55 in 1895–99 to 144 in 1900–04; see ibid., p. 165. From 1880–1905 419 newspaper/magazines were published in the Panjab, and from 1905–37 over 900; see ibid, p. 4. See also Edward D. Churchill, "Printed Literature of the Punjabi Muslims, 1860–1900." In regard to Arabic printing, Muhsin Mahdi states, "The state and the mystical fraternities seem to have been the initial sponsors of the printed book in secular and religious fields respectively." See "From the Manuscript Age to the Age of Printed Books," pp. 6–7.

[14]Not all these publications could be categorized as wholly religious. Political discussions had to be circumspect; a journal openly criticizing the British would be forced to close down and the editors penalized under the Vernacular Press Act of 1867. During the period 1880–1905 there were sixteen Muslim religious magazines published in the Panjab. The British descriptions indicate that all sixteen had an explicit polemical religious agenda. Four were pro-Ahmadi, one pro-Ahl-i Hadith, two anti-Ahmadi, five anti-Christian and Hindu, two against non-Sunnīs, and one journal against Sayyid Aḥmad Khān. See Barrier and Wallace, *Punjab Press,* pp. 9–155. For more details on the Vernacular Press Act, see Merrill Tilghman Boyce, *British Policy and the Evolution of the Vernacular Press in India, 1835–1878.*

[15]Letters to the editor were answered individually but not in the magazine itself. In the twenty years of *Risāla* in my possession (1904–25) there was only one exception to this rule, when the editor addressed the issue of whether a person could ask help to someone other than God; see *Risāla* 4.7.8–11. Other sufi magazines circulating in the Panjab that are mentioned in *Risāla* are *Al-ʿirfān* [13.4.1], *Al-faqīh* [14.9.21], *Al-jihād* [20.9.1]. Short-lived local magazines associated with the Anjuman and *Risāla* are *Muballigh* in Qusur, *Lamaʿāt aṣ-ṣūfiyya* in Sialkot, and *Al-jamāʿat.* See Akhtar Ḥusayn, *Sīrat,* p. 360.

[16]Christians also were formidable rivals in proselytization, although no mention was made of Christians as opponents. If Christians converted to Islam, however,

1925 Jamāʿat ʿAlī had led thirty-one delegations all over the Panjab to counter the Arya Samaj movement. In 1923 the *Risāla* began featuring monthly articles describing the Anjuman's efforts in building schools, mosques, and hospitals—a shift in emphasis that was already foreshadowed in 1915 with an article "The Ṭarīqa Should Help People."[17] Jamāʿat ʿAlī regarded these efforts to improve people's lives as part of the propagation of Islam.[18]

One of the most intriguing aspects of sufi authority was the relationship between Jamāʿat ʿAlī, the magazine, and his followers. Economically, the *Risāla,* as one of many other publications attempting to influence Indian Muslims, needed paying subscribers to survive.[19] Just as increased numbers of Muslims in the Panjab census reports indicated Muslim success, increased subscribers to the *Risāla* favorably reflected the Anjuman's achievements. The Anjuman expected that readers would be influenced by the *Risāla* and would spread the message. Jamāʿat ʿAlī sent a free copy of the *Risāla* to all the hereditary shaykhs, whose anticipated praise for the magazine was expected to increase readership or listenership.[20]

In 1911 Jamāʿat ʿAlī declared that each of his literate disciples must read the *Risāla,* making it religiously incumbent *(farḍ)* upon disciples to propagate the reading of the magazine.[21] Four months later the manager of *Risāla* urged each reader to enroll three new subscribers, commenting that "service to the knowledge of Sufism should be each Muslim's religious obligation *(farḍ)*."[22] The editor would congratulate readers who succeeded in finding three or more new subscribers and list their names in the next issue. If circulation had not increased appreciably from

---

this was duly noted. The *Risāla*'s editor highly praised Maulwī Muḥammad ʿAẓīm, Jamāʿat ʿAlī's disciple, who converted an English chief engineer named C. F. Linton.

[17]*Risāla* 12.9.15–16.

[18]*Risāla* 20.3.21–28.

[19]*Risāla* had an almost continuous publication (except possibly a break in 1959–61) to 1987—the longest circulation of any sufi magazine in the Panjab. The Naqshbandiyya Foundation in the United States is in the process of reviving this magazine, entitled *Sufi Illuminations,* with the first issue appearing in 1997.

[20]Written in Urdu, the *Risāla*'s actual circulation could have been many times the number of paying subscribers. The British thought that the vernacular press had a more extensive impact on illiterates because noneducated people supposedly had a less critical attitude toward written ideas than those communicated orally. See Prem Raman Uprety, *Religion and Politics in Punjab in the 1920's*, p. 95.

[21]*Risāla* 8.1.2.

[22]*Risāla* 8.5.16. Although the manager signed this and other announcements, any mention of religious duty was understood to originate with Jamāʿat ʿAlī.

the previous month, the subscribers were collectively chastised.[23] Acknowledging that there were many other magazines competing with the *Risāla,* the manager would then again exhort both Jamāʿat ʿAlī's disciples and Muslims not formally affiliated with him to propagate the magazine. Disciples must recite it to others so that these Muslims too could benefit from divine grace *(fayḍ).*[24]

In 1922 Jamāʿat ʿAlī issued an edict *(farmān)* declaring that each person able to read Urdu must read the *Risāla* and the magazine *Al-faqīh* (from Amritsar) in addition to communicating the information to others.[25] As a final step Jamāʿat ʿAlī declared the following year that his literate disciples must all purchase the *Risāla* and read it, otherwise they would have no further connection with him.[26] According to the mediational sufism of Jamāʿat ʿAlī, if this warning were not heeded, one would effectively be barred from any hope of intercession in this world or on Judgment Day. Such edicts indicate a tension between the new style of a modern mediating-shaykh and the expectations and authoritarian style of the directing-shaykh.

The Mediational Sufism of Jamāʿat ʿAlī

Incorporating an English organizational style and modern means of communication into Jamāʿat ʿAlī's sufi network not only altered the practice of Panjabi sufis but also coincided with dramatic symbolic and conceptual changes for the participants. Seekers going to a directing-shaykh encountered an entirely different experience than they would have going to a mediating-shaykh. Both types of shaykhs had arrangements to assist people having worldly problems or those seeking amulets. Likewise, in nineteenth-century Panjab, both revivalist mediating-shaykhs and directing-shaykhs emphasized adherence to the Prophetic model while justifying their practices in the reformist terms of Qur'ān and hadith. Unlike directing-shaykhs, however, there is no evidence that mediating-shaykhs concerned themselves with the individual spiritual development of their disciples in the context of a rigorous spiritual discipline. In the Naqshbandī case,

[23] *Risāla* 20.1.cover page.

[24] *Risāla* 11.9.n.p. The same announcement was signed by Jamāʿat ʿAlī instead of the manager the following year; see *Risāla* 12.11.n.p. By 1916 similar announcements were posted upon the first pages with an explanation that the magazine was losing money; see *Risāla* 13.1.2.

[25] *Risāla* 19.2.last page.

[26] *Risāla* 20.4.1.

Jamāʿat ʿAlī did not instruct seekers in Mujaddidī spiritual exercises or exhibit the use of supernatural power associated with such training.[27]

Such a spiritual education had no place in mediational sufism. The theoretical framework of mediation conceptually eliminated the possibility that a believer could travel close to God through his or her own efforts, much less manipulate supernatural power. The mediational construct placed Muḥammad beyond anyone except pirs. The only way to God was through the mediation of a shaykh connected with Muḥammad, who in turn would intercede with God on behalf of the believer.

For Naqshbandīs and many other sufis prior to the twentieth century, the shaykh often functioned as a bridge *(barzakh)* between God and the believer, between the "higher" and the "lower" worlds. Regarded as the heir of the Prophet who had followed in the (inner and outer) footsteps of Muḥammad, the Naqshbandī shaykh had a function similar to that of the Prophet. However, once Muḥammad became elevated and, for all practical purposes, as distant as God, the spiritual mentor in mediational sufism became the intermediary between humans and Muḥammad. Instead of one intermediary between God and the believer now there were two: (1) the pir, the minor intermediary *(barzakh-i ṣughrā)*, and (2) Muḥammad, the major intermediary *(barzakh-i kubrā)*.[28] The shaykh, no longer conceived as a bridge guiding others to God via Muḥammad, now himself served as the necessary means *(wasīla)* to bridge the distance between the believer and Muḥammad.

Yet paradoxically, God and Muḥammad drew closer to the seeker, who had relinquished any expectation of reaching God through his or her own efforts. Love of the pir, upon whom salvation and communication with God depended, brought the seeker into a more intimate relationship with God. The mediating-shaykh's remoteness from the seeker disappeared if the seeker cultivated love for the shaykh. A hierarchical distance that could not be traversed with rigorous meditation practices or in any other manner was instantly bridged through love of the pir.

---

[27]Nor did Aḥmad Riḍā concern himself with teaching his disciples meditation or contemplation exercises for their spiritual development. Instead he concentrated on intercession, divination, and amulets in his capacity as a patron and Qādirī shaykh. See Barbara Metcalf, *Islamic Revival in British India: Deoband, 1860–1900*, p. 307.

[28]*Risāla* 16.2.13.; Aḥmad Riḍā Khān Barēlwī, *Naqā' al-salāfa fī aḥkām al-bayʿa wa'l-khilāfa*, p. 12; and Jamāʿat ʿAlī Shāh, "Ḍarūrat-i murshid," p. 17. The vocabulary here with *barzakhs* is the same used by directing-shaykhs, but the meaning is radically different.

Using Pānīpatī's formulation—love for the pir, love for Muḥammad, and love for God—Jamāʿat ʿAlī inextricably connected sufi practice with love:[29] love of God comes from the love of the Prophet, and the love of the Prophet comes from the love of the pir.[30] Instead of a means to facilitate spiritual practices and focus divine grace in the company of a directing-shaykh, love of the mediating-shaykh allows one to achieve annihilation of the ego in God *(fanāʾ fīʾllāh)*, since the pir has already achieved it.[31] Loving all the heirs of the Prophet is an utmost religious obligation *(farḍ-i aʿlā)*, but one must love the pir before all else in the world.[32] It is also religiously incumbent *(sharʿ kā farḍ)* on the disciple to love the pir's children.[33] Jamāʿat ʿAlī reinterpreted and explained all Naqshbandī exercises in terms of love.

The *Risāla* would have its readers believe that the Mujaddidī techniques of *dhikr, tawajjuh, rābiṭa*, and *taṣawwur-i shaykh* had been redefined by love of the shaykh and Muḥammad. For example, "By repeating 'Allāh' *(dhikr)* one is immersed in the love of the Prophet."[34] Spiritual attention *(tawajjuh)* is equated with true love *(sachchī maḥabbat)*.[35] Instead of love of the shaykh developing spontaneously, for Jamāʿat ʿAlī any connection *(rābiṭa)* with the shaykh requires love of the shaykh first.[36] The shaykh-disciple *rābiṭa* itself is equated with the love of Muḥammad and of God. Visualization of the shaykh *(taṣawwur-i shaykh)* is also equated with the disciple's complete love for the pir.[37] What used to be de-

---

[29]Aḥmad Sirhindī, perhaps to distinguish Indian Naqshbandīs from Hindu and Sikh bhaktas, did not overly stress love in his collected letters. In one of the instances love is mentioned, he states, "Progressing *(sulūk)* in this exalted lineage [the Naqshbandiyya] is linked with a connection of love *(rābiṭa-yi maḥabbat)* with the shaykh." See *Maktūbāt-i imām-i rabbānī*, 3 volumes, vol. 1, letter 260, pp. 92–93. By the beginning of the nineteenth century, Mujaddidīs, identifying the shaykh as an intimate of God and as an heir of the Prophet, began to declare love of the Prophet, love of intimates of God *(awliyāʾ)*, and love of God to be religious obligations. See Qāḍī Thanāʾullāh Pānīpatī, *Irshād al-ṭālibīn*, p. 26. Yet this love was to develop spontaneously and be a means of creating an affinity *(munāsabat)* with the directing-shaykh. Love was intended to be one of many means for the aspirant to draw nearer to God, not an end in itself.

[30]*Risāla* 8.1.18.

[31]Ibid. and *Risāla* 8.2.6.

[32]*Risāla* 10.8.9–10.

[33]*Risāla* 10.8.12. There are parallels with this doctrine and that of Shīʿīs who revere the Prophet's family *(ahl-i bayt)*. Loving the shaykh's children is an important principle in mediational sufism, since the next *sajjādanishīn* will be one of the shaykh's children, and not necessarily the most spiritually qualified.

[34]*Risāla* 19.2.16.

[35]*Risāla* 20.12.27.

[36]*Risāla* 5.9.8

[37]*Risāla* 18.2.22.

scribed as divine energy emanating from God *(fayḍ)* has been transformed into the effulgence of Muḥammadan electricity *(Muḥammadī bijlī kā fayḍ)*: "The effulgence of Muhammadan electricity keeps on arriving inside the true disciple's inner self *(bāṭin)* from the beloved pir's *(piyārē pīr)* inner self. . . . and [the true disciple] traverses and completes all the stages of the Path by [means of] true love's electricity *(sachchī maḥabbat kī bijlī)* . . . and because of true love, perfected pirs cause a connection *(nisbat)* to be made in the hearts of their sincere disciples."[38] Without love for the pir the seeker cannot receive divine energy or profit from companionship with the spiritual mentor; any benefit from the spiritual mentor is a direct function of how much one loves the pir.[39] Indeed, love of the pir is reason enough to enter heaven.[40]

This redefinition process was especially noticeable in the abstraction of spiritual methods used in Jamāʿat ʿAlī's mediational sufism. Companionship *(ṣuḥbat)* with the intimates of God *(awliyāʾ)* now gave the seeker eternal life instead of merely being a means toward that end.[41] Instead of teaching disciples the Naqshbandī-Mujaddidī practices that usually took years of disciplined effort, the son of Jamāʿat ʿAlī's shaykh at Churah Sharif, Muḥammad ʿĀdil Shāh, declared that the easiest way to train the *nafs* was to recite litanies *(awrād)* of the chain of shaykhs, the blessed genealogical tree *(shajara sharīfa)*, leading from him back to Muḥammad.[42] Jamāʿat ʿAlī did not instruct and supervise his disciples in the diligent performance of sufi practices such as silent recollection of God *(nafy wa-ithbāt)* and the contemplations *(murāqabāt)*.[43] Exercises contained in pocket-sized devotional

---

[38]Ibid.; in *Risāla* 1.1.7 it is implied that the spiritual guide gets his light from Muḥammad.

[39]*Risāla* 14.7/8.16 and 16.12.39.

[40]*Risāla* 18.2.18.

[41]*Risāla* 16.1.11.

[42]*Risāla* 1.9.33.

[43]It is not certain which exercises, if any, Jamāʿat ʿAlī taught his disciples. He declared, "People from all social classes are in my circle. I only give people exercises in remembering God *(dhikr)*, nothing else"; see *Risāla* 19.8.14. Whatever exercises he may have taught, he did not follow the same principles as his predecessors, who only permitted intermediate and advanced disciples to perform *tahajjud* prayers (supererogatory prayers performed at night). Allegedly Jamāʿat ʿAlī influenced Jinnah to perform these *tahajjud* prayers. See Muḥammad Ṣādiq Quṣūrī and Muḥammad ʿAbdulqayyūm Khān, *Amīr-i millat (r) awr al indiyā sunnī kānfarans*, p. 71. In mediational sufism these prayers became an elixir for salvation. One source indicated that doing these prayers enabled one to arrive at Muḥammad; see *Risāla* 20.6.7. It is almost certain that Jamāʿat ʿAlī's disciples did not practice the Mujaddidī contemplations *(murāqabāt)*. One author defines contemplation as shutting down the senses, which differs radically from what the

pamphlets stressed repetition of the genealogical chains of shaykhs leading back to Muḥammad, short praises of the Prophet *(durūd)*, devotional poems praising the shaykh, and supplications to the Naqshbandī shaykhs *(khatm-i khwājagān)*.[44]

The style and conceptual construct of mediating-shaykhs, although largely departing from Naqshbandī directing-shaykhs, appropriated and adapted many symbols and practices from rural sufi shrine practices where a mediational Islam had long been the custom. Although the paradigms underlying the activities at sufi shrines had not appeared to change significantly, the Anjuman initiated new rituals, including annual conferences heavily laced with speeches about loving the shaykh and the Prophet. This redefinition introduced incongruities in this "Anglo-Indian" sufi assembly and its associated practices.

The Anjuman's annual meeting was a hybrid mix of the death anniversary (*ʿurs*, literally, marriage) celebration at a holy person's shrine and English organizational patterns, a combination accurately representing Jamāʿat ʿAlī's mediational sufism. In 1911 Miles Irving counted forty thousand devotees squeezing through the "door of Paradise" at Bābā Farīd's mausoleum in an evening. These faithful believed that whoever passed through it would go to heaven.[45] Other anniversary activities included a ceremonial parade of relics, placing of flowers and a new grave cover on the tomb, singing sufi poetry *(qawwālī)*, and reciting of poems praising the Prophet.[46] Since many believed that the decreased sufi is more readily available to forward requests to God (or grant requests) during the two or three days of the anniversary ceremonies, there was always a throng around the tomb during the *ʿurs* celebration.

Mujaddidī term means; see *Risāla* 12.7.8. One of Jamāʿat ʿAlī's successors discusses *dhikr* in a letter dated 21 February 1902 as a means to create love *(ʿishq)*; *murāqaba* is referred to as a "sitting posture." See Muḥammad Ḥusayn Quṣūrī, *Maktūbāt-i sharīf*, pp. 4–10. Written articles detailing the Mujaddidī contemplations, however, would not be sufficient evidence that they were actually practiced. See appendix 1 in this study.

[44]See Munawwar Ḥusayn, *Shajaratun tayyibatun*, and ʿAlī Aḥmad, *Shajaratun ṭayyibatun*. Although these devotional pamphlets were printed after Jamāʿat ʿAlī's death and originate from two different lineages of Jamāʿat ʿAlī's successors, the formats of both are nearly identical and resemble similar booklets advertised in *Risāla* 4.5.44 and 4.6.39.

[45]Miles Irving, "The Shrine of Bābā Farīd at Pākpattan," p. 55. He ironically remarks, "One may imagine that they have little time to linger in the shrine." The same tradition exists at Muʿīnuddīn Chishtī's (d. 633/1236) *ʿurs*. See Liyaqat Hussain Moini, "Rituals and Customary Practices at the Dargah of Ajmer," p. 72.

[46]Tahir Mahmood, "The Dargah of Sayyid Salar Masʿud Ghazi in Bahraich: Legend, Tradition and Reality," p. 34.

Anglicized sufis took the concept of conducting an annual Anjuman meeting from the British model. Anwar ʿAlī usually presided over this yearly conference, and either he or the editor of the *Risāla* gave the keynote address. The editor and various English-educated Muslims delivered more than two-thirds of the lectures during the 1911 two-day conference.[47] Other than his blessed presence at the conference, Jamāʿat ʿAlī's only role in the "British" program written in Urdu was to give the Friday sermon.[48]

Advertised months in advance by the *Risāla*, the annual meeting represented an oral version of a double-issue journal, that is, eight lectures per day, punctuated by prayer, Qur'ān recitation, poetry praising the Prophet *(naʿt)*, and meals. Apparently the idea of an annual conference of sufi lectures appeared foreign to many members of the Anjuman, because its administrative head, Muḥammad Karam Ilāhī, B.A., LL.B., felt it necessary to write a lengthy five-part article to justify and explain it.[49]

Anniversary celebrations with a sufi as their *axis mundi* would have been the closest analog that an Indian Muslim would have had to make sense of the Anjuman's annual sufi gathering. This not-so-remote resemblance might not have been enough to bridge the gap between the familiar and the new, the Indian and the English. The focus around which everything revolved was a dais where all the distinguished *sajjādanishīns* and ulama sat and from where Qur'ān recitation, *naʿt*, and speeches were delivered.[50] The cultural ambiguity of such a platform and gathering makes one wonder whether it was a scaled-down version of Lord Lytton's ten-foot-high dais surrounded by eighty-four thousand Indians and Europeans at his 1877 extravaganza, the Imperial Assemblage, or a scaled-up version of a Mughal court *(darbār)* where the royal personage sat on cushions surrounded by an assembly of a few hundred people.[51]

---

[47]This is based on the only complete program published during a twenty-year period. See *Risāla* 7.7.39.

[48]Ibid.

[49]To justify the need for the annual conference Muḥammad Karam Ilāhī wrote a five-part article entitled "The Necessity of the Annual Conference and the Blessed 'Urs," *Risāla* 7.8,7.10,8.2,8.3,8.4. Despite the title, the article attempted to justify the annual conference, not making any parallels with the shrine *ʿurs*.

[50]*Risāla* 14.7/8.4, and Akhtar Ḥusayn, *Sīrat*, p. 351.

[51]For an insightful analysis of how the British appropriated Indian symbols, especially how the Mughal court was used as a model for the Imperial Assemblage of 1877, see Bernard S. Cohn, "Representing Authority in Victorian India." My sources do not specify the height of the platform at the annual meeting or whether the dignitaries sat on chairs or on carpets.

The central issue, however, is that a reconceptualization had taken place. What had been an anniversary ritual of mediation between heaven and earth around a common symbolic spiritual center now became a ritual *darshān* enacting the ever-increasing hierarchical distance between the shaykh and the disciple,[52] much in the same way as the colonial political structure had become distant from the people it ruled. Speakers offered lectures on the love of the shaykh or love and praise of Muḥammad to ease any tensions of the potentially uneasy cultural-symbolic gray area of the Anjuman's annual conference.[53]

Anglicized Indians attempted to graft the ritual idiom of anniversary celebrations onto the agenda of mediational sufism in these meetings. According to the *Risāla,* the annual meeting was designed "to provide companionship with the pure-hearted, to increase the love of God, and to develop love in the heart for the Prophet and sufis."[54] There was no "door of Paradise," much less a sufi's mausoleum, but those participating in the annual meeting not only had their sins forgiven but were "to be accepted by God and be blessed on the Day of Judgment."[55] Attendance at the annual conference *(jalsa)* was considered service to God. Those who went to the annual meeting did so "out of their love of God's protégés."[56] In Jamāʿat ʿAlī's mediational sufism, where love of sufis was also the key to heaven, the result was clear: "Those who go to the conference will be in the rows with sufis on the Day of Judgment."[57] Comparable to anniversary celebrations, the conference gave participants frequent opportunities for listening to poetry praising the Prophet.[58] A devotee who could not linger at the shrine during an *ʿurs* could at least touch the shrine or its

[52]*Darshān* is not a Naqshbandī term, nor a term frequently used by Indian sufis because of its Hindu connotations. It is a South Asian act of worship where one is blessed with seeing and being seen by a holy person, holy image, or holy place. See Diana Eck, *Darśan: Seeing the Divine Image in India.* I found *darshān* used once in the *Risāla* as a title of a short poem honoring Jamāʿat ʿAlī entitled "Darshan of [my] own shaykh" *(Darshān-i shaykh khud);* see *Risāla* 11.4.last page.

[53]In the fourteen years from 1911 to 1925 the reports on the annual meetings listed most of the lecture topics. The subjects addressed three general areas: (1) the shaykh, particularly love of the shaykh; (2) praise and love of the Prophet; and (3) aspects of Sufism. Roughly half of all the lectures emphasized love of the shaykh or of the Prophet.

[54]*Risāla* 7.8.28 and 7.10.22.

[55]*Risāla* 7.10.20 and 8.2.20.

[56]*Risāla* 8.3.7.

[57]*Risāla* 8.3.6–7.

[58]A sample program for the two-day 1911 conference indicates that the program of lectures was punctuated eleven times by the recitation of *naʿt*. See *Risāla* 7.7.39.

threshold. In a throng of seven to fourteen thousand people a participant at an Anjuman conference could not expect to have personal contact with Jamāʿat ʿAlī.[59] Their seeing and being seen by him, a *darshān* of sorts, was their way of interacting with the mediating-shaykh.

What has been driving the changes making mediating-shaykhs the norm in northern India and many other parts of the world?[60] Such a mode of spiritual guidance appealed to the rural masses, but Jamāʿat ʿAlī's mediational sufism also attracted significant numbers of urban anglicized Muslims. In the *Risāla* the Anjuman is frequently lauded for bringing Muslims of all social backgrounds together, especially during these annual meetings.[61] The

---

[59]In the years 1912–15 roughly seven thousand participated. In 1916 and 1917 this number almost doubled after Jamāʿat ʿAlī convinced the British to extend the railroad line and build a station at Alipur. His many disciples in Sialkot still had to find other means of transport to travel the fifty kilometers separating the two towns. These numbers might be relatively accurate because an estimate could be made from the quantity of food consumed, and Jamāʿat ʿAlī supplied all the food for the participants during the two days. After 1919 the *Risāla* no longer mentioned the number of participants.

[60]This development of mediating-masters superseding directing-masters is not without precedent in South Asia. Mediational sufism in the Naqshbandiyya closely parallels that of the southern (Teṅkalai) school of Śrī Vaiṣṇavas founded by Piḷḷai Lokācārya (b. 1264 C.E.) By the fourteenth century C.E., veneration of Śrī Vaiṣṇava teachers *(ācāryas)* gave them near-total temporal power over their devotees. With its emphasis on *prapatti* (surrender to divine grace), the Teṅkalai school diverged from the teachings of the prominent Śrī Vaiṣṇavan, Rāmānuja (d. 1137 C.E.), in the same fashion as the religious enterprise of mediating-shaykhs deviated radically from their predecessors. Emphasizing an arduous meditational practice tempered with love, Rāmānuja's bhakti-yoga resembles the Naqshbandī directing-shaykh's discipline of contemplative exercises and love of the shaykh. *Ācāryas* and mediating-shaykhs, by consolidating religious authority in themselves as they became the sole means to salvation, render individual striving redundant, even counterproductive. See Vasudha Narayanan, *The Way and the Goal: Expressions of Devotion in the Early Śrī Vaisnava Tradition,* and Arjun Appadurai, *Worship and Conflict under Colonial Rule: A South Indian Case.* I am indebted to Professor Steven Hopkins for bringing these parallels to my attention. See also Holmes Welch's *The Practice of Chinese Buddhism, 1900–1950,* in which he compares the differences between Pure Land and Cha'n Buddhism in the premodern period of China, which structurally exhibit the same kind of polarities between the sufism of mediating-shaykhs and directing-shaykhs. The changes in Chinese Buddhism match closely those in Indian sufism during the same period as many of the same dynamics, e.g., colonialism and access to publications, set irreversible social changes into motion.

[61]After Jamāʿat ʿAlī's disciples had directed their love toward hierarchical superiors, they needed to be reminded to share this feeling among themselves. Jamāʿat ʿAlī's spiritual mentor, Faqīr Muḥammad, who emphasized the need for fellow disciples to love each other and to overlook each other's shortcomings, advised, "If the disciple wants to be loved by God, Muḥammad, and the pir then . . . it is

emphasis on love in the Anjuman undoubtedly enhanced the feeling of equality among the disciples, in addition to serving as a medium for feeling close to a hierarchically and physically distant mentor and even more distant Prophet and God. For the English-educated Muslims, already culturally marginalized to the extent that they were cut off from the Persian sources of their cultural heritage, sufi expressions of Islam became accessible through love.

Many anglicized Hindus and Muslims exposed to modern Western relativizing and rationalizing theoretical frameworks might have had difficulties blindly participating in the types of religiosity that their parents had accepted without question. In the Islamic case one might expect that most of them would not accept even the first condition inherent in the sufi lodge *communitas*, i.e., that the spiritual master (though unlikely to know either English or modern science) is functionally infallible and one must become "like a corpse in his hands."[62] This kind of unquestioning submission to a directing-shaykh would be extremely difficult to understand for a person who has been taught that only the ignorant and superstitious have such childish attitudes. Loving the shaykh bypasses these cognitive problems while also appealing to those still living in an "enchanted universe" of the typical villager who had not yet been influenced by modern education. Nonetheless, those without English education became exposed to a new conceptual universe that eventually led to social changes and modifications of worldviews. The modern Islamic ideas of thinkers like Muḥammad Iqbāl had a tremendous symbolic impact, especially when circulated widely through modern publications to eager audiences.

The British colonial presence communicated an unspoken su-

---

an utmost necessity to love [one's] fellow disciples"; see *Risāla* 10.9.3. Later, Jamā'at 'Alī wrote his essay, "Companions of the Path or Fellow Disciples" *(Yārān-i ṭarīqat yā pīr bhā'ī)*, stressing the need for fellow disciples to get along with each other. See Jamā'at 'Alī Shāh, *Irshādāt*, pp. 63–111. To what extent disputes between disciples created schisms or caused followers to leave the Anjuman cannot be ascertained from available Anjuman sources. Friction between the two cultures, one with rural roots and customary practices, and the other, urban and English-educated, would be likely. A treatise emphasizing love between fellow disciples does not get written without a need.

[62]The point here is that the revivalist directing-shaykh would seriously challenge English-educated people (see Shēr Muḥammad's remarks in this chapter). Each person would have to decide which was more important: pleasing the British or pleasing the shaykh. In contemporary Pakistan English-educated individuals have no problem deferring to their mediating-shaykhs; often these shaykhs themselves have Western educations; see P. Lewis, *Pirs, Shrines, and Pakistani Islam*, p. 1.

periority of worldview. How could a directing-shaykh's exercise of supernatural power compete successfully with the British raj? No one asked sufis to marshall their spiritual power in the 1857 rebellion against the British. A set of presuppositions (an entire worldview?) was in the process of being transformed as more and more Indian Muslims (following British attitudes) contemptuously looked down on those who accepted the authority of sufis.[63] If generic sufi practices were perceived as superstitious, then *tawajjuh, ṣuḥbat,* and *fayḍ* had no meaning at all, and there was no reason to undergo the discipline necessary for spiritual practice under a directing-shaykh. A science of universal, unchanging laws denied the supernatural suspension of those laws and thereby undercut the fundamental credibility of most sufi activity. The abandoning of spiritual exercises among the Panjabi Naqshbandīs followed the demise of the conceptual existence of supernatural power, which in turn had been relegated to superstition by the material success of rationalized technological power.

Printing undermined the local sources of authority for Islamic religious knowledge, i.e., the person-to-person transmission and interpretation of oral texts. In Francis Robinson's words, "Printing, by multiplying texts willy nilly, struck right at the heart of [personal] Islamic authority."[64] A pan-Islamic world permeated the imaginations of South Asian Muslims as they came increasingly into contact with the larger Islamic world through improved transportation and publication. This stimulated a "universalization process" whereby Indian Muslims took on an increasingly pan-Islamic identity.

The synergistic combination of these and other developments directly challenged the exercise of local personal authority in Islam. Before the "print revolution," a person did not read a religious book without the guidance of the sole interpreter, the teacher. Person-to-person learning was an inherently conservative process where interpretive possibilities were limited. In the

---

[63]In 1946 on the eve of the Muslim League victory in Panjab, the district organizer for the Unionist Party lamented "that 80% population of this district is 'Pirridden.' They are blind followers of Pirs. . . . No amount of individual propaganda can convert the blind adherents of the Pirs." Quoted in the Unionist Party Papers File D-44, cited in David Gilmartin, "Religious Leadership and the Pakistan Movement," p. 513. For British antecedents, of which there are many, see Major Aubrey O'Brien, "The Mohammedan Saints of the Western Punjab."

[64]Francis Robinson, "Technology and Religious Change: Islam and the Impact of Print," p. 234. Much of my discussion of the "print revolution" in this and the next paragraph comes from this article.

sufi environment especially, "a person who is said to have really studied the subject is called *ustād dīdah,* literally one who has "seen" a master, that is, one who has benefited from the oral teachings and also the presence *(ḥuḍūr)* of the master who embodies those teachings and who renews and revives them through the very act of living their truths."[65] After printed books became available a person could interpret the same texts in a radically different way—a process which could only undermine the traditional authority of ulama and sufis. Print brought on a "scriptural revolution," simultaneously undermining personal authority while strengthening a scripturalist-minded interpretation of Islam. It is no coincidence that two books denouncing mediational practices in Islam, *Taqwiyat al-islām* and *Ṣirāṭ al-mustaqīm,* were among the earliest books that Muslims published in India.[66]

Print materials nurtured a pan-Islamic layer in Indian Muslim identity by creating links to the larger community of Muslims, both in and outside India. Such a situation relativized the personal authority of sufi masters, who represented the local, segmented kinship systems of rural India. Not only did print allow new innovative combinations of ideas, but it created novel types of larger collective units where members would never have contact with each other, for example, the recipients of Jamāʿat ʿAlī's monthly magazine or Ahl-i Hadith groups who united in their opposition to mediational sufism. These new forms of pan-Islamic identity effectively competed with local loyalties. Muḥammad Iqbāl continually stressed the larger Muslim community through the symbols of the Qur'ān and the Kaʿba ("The body of our Faith's Community throbs vital to the Word of the Koran" and "In circumambulation of its shrine [the Kaʿba] our pure Community draws common breath").[67] Iqbāl's poetry, printed

---

[65]Seyyed Hossein Nasr, "Oral Transmission and the Book in Islamic Education," p. 63.

[66]See Muḥammad Ismāʿīl, *Taqwiyat al-īmān* (Calcutta: Maṭbaʿ-i Aḥmadī, 1826) and Sayyid Aḥmad and ʿAbdulḥayy, *Ṣirāṭ-i mustaqīm,* (Calcutta: Maṭbaʿ-i Shaykh Hidāyatullāh, 1822).

[67]Muḥammad Iqbāl, *Rumūz-i Bēkhūdī,* pp. 42, 51. Peter Brown notices that the societal role of the Christian holy man diminished in the sixth century and attributes this phenomenon to a "new sense of majesty of the community," manifested in a revival of towns in the Eastern Empire and the development of an ecclesiastical hierarchy in western towns. See his "The Rise and Function of the Holy Man in Late Antiquity," p. 100. In a similar fashion the marginalizing of sufis in British India and later could be a function of increasing numbers of Indian Muslims becoming connected to a larger pan-Islamic community, one majestically extolled by Iqbāl.

and orally transmitted to a larger illiterate audience, captured the imaginations of Indian Muslims who heretofore had conceived of Islam on very local and personal terms (if they even identified themselves as Muslims at all). The inherent disruption of a colonial power which forcibly linked Indians to a distant Britain was compounded by inevitable contacts with Muslims outside India and the proliferation of printed materials. Once such social forces were unleashed, local personal sufi authority lost its monopoly and had to compete on increasingly unfavorable terms with other perspectives and worldviews.

Often people most affected by urbanization and modern structures took Iqbāl's advice and held firm to the "protection" of the Qur'ān.[68] Others, including urban Muslims, were drawn to a mediating-shaykh like Jamāʿat ʿAlī, whose "universal" path of love combined some practices of hereditary shrine pirs with a shariʿa-minded Islam of revivalist shaykhs. The appeal of a mediational mode of Islam tied to the charismatic authority of a sufi shaykh exhibiting Prophetic qualities cut across urban-rural and literate-illiterate boundaries. At once local in his legitimization of shrine activities and international in terms of Naqshbandī membership and familiarity with the Qur'ān and hadith, Jamāʿat ʿAlī and his Anjuman, by cutting through traditional social polarities (e.g., urban/rural), attracted Muslims of all types from all over India.

Mediational Sufism and Politics

For the rural Panjabis mediational sufism was the spiritual analog of the worldly economic, social, and political reality they experienced. The vast majority of visitors to sufi masters were not interested in the exacting demands of a directing-shaykh. One's choice of shaykh was primarily geographically and socially determined. A villager would share a spiritual mediator with many other members of his or her clan and select a local intermediary who could produce results. Choice of a pir was not simply a spiritual decision, since he and his network of contacts might also be needed for mundane matters as well. A British colonial officer in the western Panjab commented, "Saints are windows through which the light of heaven shines, and, even if windows are sometimes dirty, ordinary mortals must be content with such light as they may get through them."[69] Divine intercession and worldly

---

[68]Iqbāl, *Rumuz-i Bēkhūdī*, p. 42.

[69]See O'Brien, *Mohammadan Saints*, p. 517.

intervention with higher economic and political powers both demanded a mediator.

Long before the British arrived in the Panjab, spiritual influence had joined with political power. The Mughals had also given lands and privileges to leaders of shrine families *(sajjādanishīns).* Irfan Habib notes that the Mughals legitimized themselves by employing urban ulama and rural shrine families as mediators with the populace.[70] Although the British seriously attempted to divest their colonial regime of any official connections to religious institutions, they could not help but exploit the local influence of the powerful landowning families,[71] many of whom were associated with sufi shrines and had been mediating between the central government and the local people for centuries,[72] and as landed gentry had also collected taxes. The British ended up imitating the Mughal practice of supporting religious dignitaries and shrines.[73]

The hereditary shaykhs on their side would have preferred not to have binding relationships with the colonial power, because it brought loss of face or prestige *(ʿizzat)* in the eyes of their Muslim peers, but they found themselves involuntarily drawn into supporting the British colonial administrative system. The colonial district officer was the patriarchal king (*mā-bāp,* literally, mother-father) of the district who controlled affairs by distributing prestige. The landed gentry relied on the British to confirm their status and allow them to assert their power.[74] For a pir, prestige

[70]Irfan Habib, *The Agrarian System of Mughal India,* p. 309, cited in David Gilmartin, *Empire and Islam: Punjab and the Making of Pakistan,* p. 45. Gilmartin comprehensively outlines the structure of rural Panjabi Islam, pp. 40–46.

[71]By the twentieth century the shrine family of Babā Farīd in Pakpattan owned one tenth of all the land in the district, 43,000 acres, some of which was donated by Ranjīt Singh's Sikh government. In Multan 5,000 acres belonged to the shrine of Bahā'uddīn Zakariyā. See Ian Talbot, *Punjab and the Raj, 1849–1947,* p. 24.

[72]Dick Eaton explains that the qualifications for *sajjādanishīns* shifted from spiritual merit to political loyalty to a central government in his *Sufis of Bijapur (1300–1700): Social Roles of Sufis in Medieval India,* pp. 241–42.

[73]The former Sikh government of the Panjab also conformed to this practice. See B. N. Goswamy and J. S. Grewal, *The Mughal and Sikh Rulers and the Vaishnavas of Pindori.* For examples of British colonial policy using sufis' local political authority, see Gilmartin, *Empire and Islam,* pp. 46–52. The British supported sufis solely for political purposes and did not share the paradigm of divine intervention.

[74]Kenneth W. Jones, *Arya Dharm: Hindu Consciousness in 19th-Century Punjab,* pp. 6–7, and Sara F. D. Ansari, *Sufi Saints and State Power: The Pirs of Sind, 1843–1947,* pp. 45–52. Ansari's sociopolitical description and analysis of the relationship between rural Sindi pirs and the British provides parallels of how the British ruled in the Panjab in almost identical circumstances. Moroccan sufis in nineteenth-century northern Africa also made necessary compromises with colonial authorities to preserve their status. See Julia Clancy-Smith in *Rebel and Saint: Mus-*

was not a mere luxury but the means through which he could muster support from smaller landowners and attract disciples.

Using an elaborate system of bestowing prestige, the British kept the rural landowners at least passively supporting the colonial system. The greatest honor in the British colonial system for a shaykh was to be exempt from personal appearance in civil courts. Not every shaykh was in this exclusive circle, so for those who were, it was best not to have this precious prize revoked.[75] Pirs did not upset the colonial status quo and the British did not disturb the equilibrium of the rural landowner.[76]

Formally, the emergence of an intermediary rule elite in the British administration of the Panjab resulted from the passage of the Alienation of Land Act in 1900.[77] In an attempt to establish rural stability by preventing large-scale appropriation of peasant land by moneylenders, the British restricted landowning to British-defined categories of "agricultural" and "tribal" groups. Muslims, particularly sayyids and custodians of shrines *(mujāwirs)*, benefited from this legislation and, with other landowners, became drawn into the orbit of British colonial authority. The British became the formal patrons of the landowning *(zamīndār)* class, protecting and legitimizing the Panjabi system of hierarchy and mediation. In 1914 this relationship between the British and hereditary pirs became even more explicit when the British

---

lim Notables, Populist Protest, Colonial Encounters (Algeria and Tunisia, 1800–1904), p. 259.

[75]Ansari, *Sufi Saints*, pp. 50–51. Ansari notes that threatening to withdraw this exemption was the most powerful lever the British had to control powerful Sindi landowners. It worked successfully in Awadh also. See Claudia Liebeskind, "Sufism, Sufi Leadership and 'Modernization,' in South Asia since c. 1800," pp. 180–81. Gilmartin, who has studied the political relationships between the British and revival shaykhs, does not give any examples of exemption from court appearances being used to manipulate rural pirs in the Panjab. I cite exemption from court appearance merely as an example of how the British controlled landowners. Surely there were many other devices which would not necessarily have been recorded in the political files.

[76]The neutrality of rural landowning shaykhs with respect to the British does not appear to have diminished their authority in the eyes of their followers. It was always a point of argument, however, for detractors. Although there is no evidence, Aḥmad Riḍā, the founder of the Barelwi perspective, has been (and is still being) accused of having been a "British agent" in the pay of the colonial government. See Sanyal, "Ahmad Rida Khan Barelwī," pp. 7–8. Jamā'at 'Alī was criticized for his connection with the British government. Ansari examines Pīr Pāgārō and his dramatic balancing act between the British authorities and his supporters; see *Sufi Saints*, pp. 57–76.

[77]This legislation was particular to the Panjab. I am relying on David Gilmartin's discussion of this legislation in his *Empire and Islam*, pp. 26–38.

awarded "landed gentry" grants to influential Panjabi Muslims. Through this move, many members of sufi families became rural administrators, honorary magistrates, and district board members.[78] Jamāʿat ʿAlī came from such a family of Qādirī hereditary shaykhs in the Sialkot district, whose influence was defined by the British colonial system. He was therefore inextricably associated with the rural Panjabi social structure, and his rural landowning connections had contributed to his rise to prominence as a sufi revival shaykh. Eventually, however, they would prove to be a liability.

Jamāʿat ʿAlī presided over the first All-India Sunnī Conference in 1925 and gave the keynote address.[79] Ten years later, having been declared the "leader of the Muslim community" *(amīr-i millat)* in August 1935 at a special conference of the United Muslim Community *(Ittiḥād-i millat)*, he again gave the keynote address at the All-India Sunni Conference. It began by stressing the need for love of the Prophet and for the propagation of Islam, for the unity of sufis and ulama, for keeping up the agitation to reclaim the Shahīdganj Mosque, which had been appropriated by the Sikhs when they controlled Lahore from 1799 to 1849, and for preserving Muslim shariʿa laws and Muslim graves.[80] With numerous followers all over India, both rural and urban, his credentials as a religious scholar and his status as a sayyid, Jamāʿat ʿAlī embodied a variety of sources for spiritual authority, which allowed him to transcend many of the problems that restricted the activities of his predecessors.[81]

---

[78]Ibid., p. 50. The British often became much more involved with the religious affairs of shrines than they desired. See ibid., pp. 46–50.

[79]This conference was held roughly every ten years and was actually a name for an organized body of Barelwi ulama founded by Naʿīmuddīn Murādābādī to counter the Jamʿiat al-Ulama-yi Hind and the Khilafat Committee. See Usha Sanyal, "In the Path of the Prophet: Maulana Ahmad Riza Khan Barelwi and the Ahl-e Sunnat wa Jamaʿat Movement in British India, c. 1870–1921," pp. 409–18.

[80]Muḥammad Ṣādiq Quṣūrī, *Amīr-i millat*, pp. 49–52.

[81]On the other hand Jamāʿat ʿAlī was very old at the time (over one hundred years old, if his birthdate is correct) and "easily accessible to influence, and prone to listen to the last person who talks to him." See Home Political File, F. H. Puckle, 6 September 1935, cited in David Gilmartin, "The Shahidganj Mosque Incident: A Prelude to Pakistan," p. 160. This type of critique is mirrored in Fazl-i Husain's comment (letter dated 26 September 1935) that Mir Maqbool ("a thoroughly unprincipled liar and government informer," according to Fazl-i Husain) interviewed Jamāʿat ʿAlī in order to write a memorandum to be sent to the British. See Fazl-i Husain, *Diary and Notes of Mian Fazl-i Husain*, pp. 178–79. Yet Jamāʿat ʿAlī has "all cliques and adventurers . . . at work to get him do all sorts of works . . . he is said to have played into the hands of all by turns, and got out of their hands afterwards" (letter 7 November 1935); see ibid., pp. 191–92.

For the Muslim community, the test for Jamāʿat ʿAlī was whether or not he could coerce the British into returning the site of the Shahīdganj Mosque, which had been demolished by the Sikhs in July 1935. Although he had the support of government officials and many followers, only the British had the power to force the Sikhs to return the mosque. The strategy was for Jamāʿat ʿAlī to put pressure on the British through the Muslim community, especially the thousands of his disciples who were serving in the British army.

Within a few months the Shahīdganj movement collapsed. Politically, the principal reason arose out of the differences between British and Islamic law. According to Fazl-i Husain, a prominent Panjabi Unionist Party politician,[82] the failure was the fault of the Muslims who had let the *waqf* lapse after the British took over the Panjab. British law placed time limits on these charitable endowments, although Islamic law did not.[83] An experienced politician, Fazl-i Husain remarked that because the *waqf* had been allowed to lapse there was no way that the site would be restored to Muslims unless "there was a revolution and some new Muslim government was established."[84]

As a rural pir and landowner, Jamāʿat ʿAlī had limited ability to confront the British to the degree needed for effective political action without jeopardizing his family's position. Nor could he free himself from the influence of wealthy disciples and advisers in rural Panjab who provided his political leverage.[85] As Maulānā Ḥabīburraḥmān of the opposing urban Panjabi Aḥrār Party put it, "How can a man who calls the government *mai-bap* (mother and father) be entrusted with leading the Muslims?"[86] The limitations of Jamāʿat ʿAlī's political authority were clearly demonstrated, although the sufi networks remained the most effective means of marshalling rural political support on the provincial level.

---

[82]Fazl-i Husain was president of the fifth Panjab Provincial Conference in 1917, founder and important politician in the National Unionist Party (1923–37), Panjab minister of education (1921–25), Panjab revenue minister (1926–27, 1929–30), and member of the Governor General's Executive Council (1930–35). See Muhammad Azim Husain, *Fazl-i Husain: A Political Biography.*

[83]Fazl-i Husain, *Letters of Mian Fazl-i Husain,* p. 569.

[84]Ibid., p. 584.

[85]Gilmartin, "The Shahidganj Incident," p. 161. Gilmartin also notes the limitations of his leadership over those who did not subscribe to the Barelwi mediational paradigm of Islam; one Delhi Muslim stated, "In the opinion of Pir Jamaat ʿAli Shah I am a 'great infidel.' " Jamāʿat ʿAlī declared those who opposed his initiative to be outside the Muslim community. See ibid., pp. 161–62 and Gilmartin, *Empire and Islam,* pp. 103–7.

[86]Gilmartin, *Empire and Islam,* p. 104.

The Shahīdganj affair also had ramifications much more profound than merely demonstrating the limited provincial political clout of Jamā'at 'Alī. The mosque represented more than a century of non-Muslim rule in Lahore.[87] When the Sikhs under Ranjīt Singh had conquered Kashmir and Panjab in the nineteenth century they had deliberately desecrated the most treasured Lahori mosques, the Bādshāhī Mosque (built by Aurangzīb in 1044/1634) and the Wazīr Khān Mosque (completed 1084/1673), by killing swine in them and converting their courtyards into stables, because the mosque had become a symbol of Indo-Muslim identity.[88] At the same time Ranjīt Singh contributed to sufi shrines in Lahore, presumably because their doors were open to all, including Sikhs and Hindus. It was one thing to retain a sacred space like a sufi shrine where religious identity was permeable and quite another to have a mosque whose rigid boundaries excluded non-Muslims.

In the twentieth century, the popular press spread the more rigid "Islam of the mosque," including many of Muḥammad Iqbāl's pan-Islamic notions of a non-mediational Islam, rather than the local Islam of the sufi lodge.[89] This universal Islam stressed a "special inheritance—symbolized by the Prophet, the Qur'ān, and the mosque—that every Muslim could claim as a birthright."[90] Ẓafar 'Alī Khān, poet and editor of the popular Lahore newspaper *Zamīndār*, championed pan-Islam, stressing the symbolic caliph in Istanbul and defending the Prophet and the mosque as he transformed Urdu poetry into a popular political

---

[87]The mosque site was the place where many Sikhs had been executed by the Mughal governor (hence the name Shahīdganj or "place of martyrs"). When the Sikhs occupied the city in 1762 the mosque was closed to Muslim prayer until its destruction in 1935. See Gilmartin, "The Shahidganj Mosque Incident," p. 148.

[88]Charles Masson (James Lewis), *Narrative of Various Journeys in Balochistan, Afghanistan, and the Panjab, Including a Residence in Those Countries from 1826–1838*, 3 vols. (London: R. Bentley, 1842), 1:409–10. Professor Iqbāl Mujadddī informed me of this crucial aspect of Panjabi history that, to the best of my knowledge, is totally ignored in the sources discussing Sikh history.

[89]The popular press was anything but monolithic, although newspapers like the *Zamīndār* (with a circulation over 15,000 in 1915) numerically dwarfed all other Urdu publications (it is unlikely that the circulation of Jamā'at 'Alī's *Risāla* was more than 500 per month). In the Panjab, Fazl-i Husain, using subsidies from the Āghā Khān, established both English and vernacular papers to act as Unionist Party papers in addition to publication of leaflets and regular local news summaries sent to England. On 24 June 1936 before the crucial 1937 elections, the Āghā Khān sent 10,000 rupees from his Derby winnings for this purpose with another 10,000 rupees sent two months later. See Fazl-i Husain, *Letters*, pp. 596–98.

[90]Gilmartin, "The Shahidganj Mosque Incident," p. 153.

idiom.[91] This newly conceived notion of the Muslim community formulated and propagated by urban Muslims, combined with Iqbāl's forceful poetry, did much to create a distinctly new identity for many Indian Muslims that contrasted with both the local identity of the sufi shaykh and sufi shrine and the identity of revivalist sufis and ulama who stressed conformity with the Prophetic model. It was the same Ẓafar ʿAlī Khān who led the urban Ittiḥād-i Millat that declared Jamāʿat ʿAlī to be the leader of the Muslim community.

Although Jamāʿat ʿAlī's mediational sufism transcended conventional polarities it did not bridge the gap between what might be called "mosque Muslims" and "lodge Muslims." To some extent, the ulama had already paved the way for the mosque = Muslim identity. During the Shahīdganj affair Lahore's ulama confirmed their authority by instigating protests.[92] In the cities the mosque as the symbol of government power "conquered" the sufi shrine.[93] Mosques, as symbols of Muslim government, therefore had literally to be conquered by non-Muslim invaders, such as the Sikhs in eighteenth-century Lahore and the British in Delhi after the 1857 rebellion.

Rural Muslims did not always share the monumental excitement generated over the Shahīdganj Mosque. Abū'l-Saʿīd Aḥmad Khān (d. 1941), a rural Naqshbandī shaykh at Khundian, remarked that "if the Shahīdganj Mosque has passed from Muslim hands, one should not lament [it since] additional mosques will be constructed through the grace of God Almighty."[94] His notion of Muslim identity, shared by earlier generations of Naqshbandīs, remained one centered on doctrine and inner transformation. For both directing-shaykhs and many revivalist pirs, buildings had nothing to do with the important task of faithfully duplicating and embodying the Prophetic model. One should concentrate on recapturing the experience of the Companions rather than on re-

[91]Ibid., p. 155.

[92]The Minister of Education, Firuz Noon, tried to get a legal decision from the ulama of Lahore to prevent the sacrifice of lives but only three out of thirteen ulama came. Although they agreed to his proposal they were afraid of losing their popularity with the masses; see Fazl-i Husain, *Letters*, p. 416.

[93]Prominent examples include the Wazīr Khān Mosque overshadowing Iṣḥāq Kāzarūnī's (d. 1037/1627–28) tiny tomb; the Fatehpūr Sīkrī Mosque dominating Salīm Chishtī's (d. 978–9/1571) shrine; and more recently, the newly constructed mosque dwarfing Dātā Ganjbakhsh's tomb in Lahore.

[94]Maḥbūbilāhī, *Tuḥfa-yi saʿdiyya*, p. 118. He adds that the real problem is dealing with the Ahmadis. Aḥmad Khān states, "Constructing mosques is quite virtuous but refining one's character and purifying one's ego are worthwhile inner constructions." See ibid., p. 164.

covering a dilapidated, abandoned mosque. Of course it was easier to maintain this position in a remote area where the sacred space and time of the sufi lodge remained undisturbed by Sikhs and British alike. But the result was that revivalist pirs both before and after Jamāʿat ʿAlī remained restricted in their activities almost exclusively to local contexts. In the ensuing years of independent Pakistan, rural sufi shaykhs have occasionally influenced provincial politics but have hardly made any impact on national politics, just as in colonial India.

After the Shahīdganj affair, the reigning landowner/sufi-pir Unionist Party overwhelmingly won the 1937 Panjab provincial elections; the Muslim League captured only two of the eighty-six legislative seats allotted to Muslims.[95] Less than ten years later, on the eve of independence, the Muslim League captured seventy-five of eighty-six seats in the 1946 Panjab provincial elections. In that election Jamāʿat ʿAlī abandoned the provincial Unionist Party to support Muhammad Ali Jinnah and the Muslim League, who represented all-India politics. At the 1946 All-India Sunnī Conference Jamāʿat ʿAlī, by then physically weak, was given a place of honor and is reported to have said, "Jinnah is an intimate of God *(walī Allāh)*,"[96] although many believed that he was not a practicing Muslim.[97]

Ian Talbot attributes Jamāʿat ʿAlī's abrupt shift in Panjab politics to a sequence of events involving the Muslim League's ability both to gain the support of the landowners and pirs and to address the wartime grievances of the peasants. After the Simla conference in July 1945, where Jinnah declared that all nominees of the interim Pakistan government must be Muslim League members, it was clear that future political patronage would be with the Muslim League, not with a Unionist Party loyal to the British government.[98]

From a religious perspective, the Muslim League program appealed to revivalist pirs, since a government based on the shariʿa

[95]Before this crucial election (19 June 1936) Fazl-i Husain was sent a list of fifteen pirs who would be called upon to assist the Unionist Party; Jamāʿat ʿAlī and Mihr ʿAlī Shāh of Golra Sharif were among these fifteen. See Fazl-i Husain, *Letters*, p. 593.

[96]Quṣūrī, *Amīr-i millat*, p. 71.

[97]Many considered Jinnah to have forsaken Islam when he married a Parsi in a civil ceremony in 1918. Others, because of his lack of beard and love for English ways, did not consider his leadership to be particularly religious, except when it suited his political purposes. Jinnah's being an Ismāʿīlī could only add to the problems.

[98]Ian A. Talbot, "The Growth of the Muslim League in the Punjab, 1937–46."

would lend support to their individual religious activities.[99] In effect, the Muslim League promised to expand the scope of their religious activities from the rural periphery to the center of provincial and national concerns. Thus, Muḥammad Ḥusayn Shāh, the son of Jamāʿat ʿAlī, was reported to have toured the Jhelum district where he issued a *fatwā* declaring the Muslim League to be the only Islamic community and all others to be infidels.[100] Prior to the 1946 elections Muslim League propagandists went disguised as sufi pirs in the Northwest Frontier Province, as did many Panjabi landlords, who dressed in immaculately white clothing with turbans and long beards in the manner of sufi pirs when they campaigned for the Muslim League.[101] Another *fatwa* from Faḍl Aḥmad Shāh, the *sajjādanishīn* of Shāh Nūr Jamāl Chishtī's shrine in Jalalpur (Jhelum) states: "An announcement from the Dargarh [*sic*, shrine] of Hazrat Shah Jamal. I command all those people who are in my Silsilah to do everything possible to help the Muslim League and give their votes to it. All those people who do not act according to this message should consider themselves no longer members of my Silsilah."[102] By this decree the Muslim League effectively gained the political endorsement of the rural pirs.[103] Sufi shaykhs mobilized the moving ideas of Iqbāl to convince Muslims to vote for Pakistan: "If you are in love with Islam you should do things in the way Iqbal asked you to do it."[104] It did them no good, however: these same sufis later remained on the periphery of Pakistani affairs. A government-

[99]David Gilmartin, "Religious Leadership and the Pakistan Movement in the Punjab." For a more detailed discussion of the Muslim League in the Panjab and the 1946 elections, see Gilmartin, *Empire and Islam,* pp. 189–224. Before the 1946 elections Qamaruddīn, Mihr ʿAlī Shāh's pir, urged other sufis to support the Muslim League, ". . . it is Islamic to ask for votes and 'religious' to give them. The Muslim League is purely a religious movement in which all the rich, poor, sufis, and scholars are participating." See Talbot, *Punjab and the Raj,* pp. 212–13. For other strategies manipulating religion for electoral ends, see David Gilmartin, " 'Divine Displeasure' and Muslim Elections: The Shaping of Community in Twentieth-Century Punjab."

[100]Letter, Bashir Husain, Jhelum District Organizer, to Mian Sultan Ali Ranjha, Zamindara League (Unionist Party) Secretary, 13 December 1945. Unionist Party Papers, file D-44, cited in Gilmartin, "Religious Leadership," p. 226.

[101]Talbot, *Punjab and the Raj,* p. 211.

[102]*Nawā-i waqt* (Lahore), 19 January 1946, in Talbot, "The Growth of the Muslim League," p. 252 [comments in brackets mine].

[103]For a brief synopsis of parallel processes in the Sind, see Sara Ansari, "Political Legacies of Pre-1947 Sind."

[104]This is from a speech supporting the Muslim League and the glory of Muslim government by Imdād ʿAlī Shāh Gīlānī, *sajjādanishīn* at the shrine of Shāh Muqīm Mujrāwī, on 1 January 1946. See Ian Talbot, *Punjab and the Raj, 1849–1947,* p. 212.

supported, amorphous, urban, impersonal, universal Islamic symbol of the mosque and Qur'ān (and to some extent the ulama) keeps the mediational, personal, and local Islamic symbols of the sufi shrine on the periphery.[105]

The shift from directing-shaykhs to mediating-shaykhs who were then banished to the periphery meant also a shift from personal to impersonal authority. The mosque, in contrast to either the ultrapersonal *axis mundi* of the directing-shaykh in his sufi lodge or the living,[106] disembodied pir in his sufi shrine, is intentionally impersonal. It facilitates prayer to an utterly transcendent God as it spatially represents a universal Islamic symbol. Sufi lodges and shrines reflect the diverse localities and customs of the persons living there. The mosque (architectural diversity aside) is universally the same: one wall indicates the direction of Muslim prayer. The sufi lodge or shrine has many layers in a hierarchical space reflecting different levels of involvement ranging from non-Muslim visitors to authorized successors of the master who reside with their families at the lodge. These distinctions between personal and impersonal Islamic space extend back to medieval Islam or even earlier.

In British colonial India mechanisms came into play which overwhelmingly favored an impersonal, homogenizing, and rationalizing matrix of Islamic symbols. The enchanted universe of local Islams, offering intense personal contact with a charismatic personality, had little impact on the imaginations of those beyond its short radius.[107] The abstract Islamic symbols of the anglicized educated elite, who had the political power both before and after Independence, was configured to transcend all differences, whether ethnic, genealogical, or linguistic. Bolstered by increased international communications and Western ideas, the symbols of an urban, universal matrix of Islamic symbols challenged the localized, personal Islam of the shaykh to produce a more rational, disenchanted religious universe.[108] As the government of Paki-

[105]For an analysis of how this is occurring, see Katherine Ewing, "The Politics of Sufism: Redefining the Saints of Pakistan."

[106]Supplicating visitors who go to a shrine say they are going to visit the *living person* buried there, not the building.

[107]There were extensive networks throughout the history of Islam which connected places as far as Java, Central Asia, and Arabia together—but all of these were personal contacts.

[108]There are many parallel processes driving the development of both the normative Sikh community and the Muslim community in colonial Panjab. See Oberoi, *The Construction of Religious Boundaries*. The kinds of diversity that were attenuated in the Sikh community still thrive in the Indo-Muslim community (at the price of sectarian strife).

stan took over the administration of larger sufi shrines, impersonal bureaucratic social services, medical assistance, and government education replaced the personal charismatic authority of the sufi and his contact with the sacred/supernatural.[109]

Jamāʿat ʿAlī himself bridged the gap between the two modes of Islam by focusing on a universal love that spanned a variety of views in colonial India. Barelwi ideas bolstered this devotional Islam through methods of praising and glorifying the Prophet, a universal symbol of the Muslim community. Freely using publication and other forms of modern communication, mediating-shaykhs encouraged a universal love of the Prophet and therefore the sufi master. Although a personal mode of Islam in some respects, it eliminated the sufi lodge/shrine center. Social interaction in Jamāʿat ʿAlī's circle, whether through his magazine, his sporadic visits, or the annual meetings of the organization, exhibited a fundamental asymmetry. His disciples had almost no way of responding personally and directly. The sheer number of disciples made this mediational mode of Islam impersonal.

Centers based on religion, language, and locale were often in conflict. Prominent lawyer-politicians were accused of locating their cultural homeland in England—Fazl-i Husain wrote his diary in English and Jinnah could communicate effectively only in English.[110] Arabia was the cultural homeland for thinkers like Iqbāl and others whose notion of Islam centered on the Qurʾān and the Kaʿba. Those associated with a sufi shaykh or a local shrine had their own centers. Most Indian Muslims "constructed" a bricolage of multiple centers.

The Western-educated politicians had both the resources and the power to manipulate the dissemination of cultural symbols to propagate their impersonal (and often Arabia-centered) version of Islam to the masses. The relation between the sacred and profane had been drastically altered. In this radical disjuncture a subtle, impersonal secularization had been set in motion, the ef-

[109]See Ewing, "Politics of Sufism." As of 1991 there were 255 sufi shrines administered by the Endowments Department of the Panjab: 84 Qādirī, 36 Chishtī, 7 Suhrawardī, 5 Naqshbandī, and 123 unaffiliated, according to the internal records of this ministry. See Endowments Department, *Fihrist-i aʿrās-i mazārāt,* unpublished list, 9 pp. There are many more sufi shrines that are not under government control.

[110]This is an interpretive statement that would reflect the perspective of a revivalist shaykh like Shēr Muḥammad and other like-minded Indo-Muslims and not necessarily the individuals themselves. I am not equating the use of English language, the administrative imposed language of the British, with a necessary cultural identification.

The tomb building in Alipur Sharif where Jamāʿat ʿAlī is buried

Jamāʿat ʿAlī's grave

fects of which combined to limit or even eliminate the scope of the supernatural. To say that a revolutionary alteration and transformation of consciousness has affected much of the Indian Muslim community over the last one hundred years would be to understate the situation.

The *communitas* of the sufi lodge with its fervently personal and transformative environment intended to re-create and experience Prophetic realities had shifted by the 1930s to a Prophet designed to further the nation state. In 1935 ʿAṭāʾullāh Shāh Bukhārī said, "A man may be a sinner, a liar, a thief and a *dacoit* [highway brigand], but if he is prepared to lay down his life when the question of defending the honour of the Prophet comes up, then he is truly pious. . . . I would fain allow myself to be thrown before fierce lions as a punishment for my love of the Prophet."[111] This clearly represents a notion of the Prophet designed to fit in with the nation-state. The establishment of Pakistan presented many Indian Muslims with a powerful vision: independence from a colonially calculated minority status to fulfill their destiny as an independent majority in the Land of the Pure (a literal meaning of "Pakistan"). They too could follow in the footsteps of Muḥammad by replicating his *hijra* from Mecca to Medina. How many of the hundreds of thousands of Muslims who lost their lives in the 1947 Partition did so with Islamic visions crafted by orators and politicians?

Jamāʿat ʿAlī passed away in 1951. His son and *sajjādanishīn*, Muḥammad Ḥusayn Shāh (d. 1972), succeeded him; today Jamāʿat ʿAlī has many successors and disciples throughout Pakistan (the larger centers are in Qusur, Sialkot, Lahore, and Multan) and even in England and the United States.[112] The annual festival honoring Jamāʿat ʿAlī's death date is held on the second month of the *sambat* calendar, Bīsakh 28–29, roughly corresponding to May 11–12. Although a definitive study remains to be done of contemporary Naqshbandī practices in the Panjab, mediating-shaykhs are now the norm in the Naqshbandī lodges.

---

[111]Gilmartin, "The Shahidganj Mosque Incident," pp. 155–56.

[112]The Naqshbandiyya Foundation for Islamic Education, Post Box 3526, Peoria, IL 61612-3526, founded by a disciple in Jamāʿat ʿAlī's lineage, Ahmad Mirza M. D., promotes a better understanding of Indo-Muslim sufi practice and knowledge in the United States.

CHAPTER 10

The Role of the Naqshbandī Sufi in Pakistan

You can deny God but you cannot deny the Prophet.

Muḥammad Iqbāl, *Jāvīdnāma*

The development of the sufi shaykh begins with the eastern Mediterranean holy person of late antiquity via Muslim ascetics to the teaching-shaykhs and then to directing-shaykhs as Muslims became the majority community. Their emphasis on hadith study and the assiduous replication of the Prophet's behavior preserved the outward aspects of Muḥammad's charismatic behavior; their specialized spiritual practices replicated inner Prophet realities. When the most spiritually qualified became the chief successor and followed faithfully in his predecessor's footsteps, personal Prophetic authority was rejuvenated and transmitted to the next generation. Sufis occupied a pivotal mediational role in society

Directing-shaykhs in particular derived power and authority from their positions as mediators. In the first transformation of sufi authority from teaching-shaykhs to directing-shaykhs in the tenth century, sufis often situated themselves on the boundary between pre-Muslim and Muslim, bridging the old pre-Islamic society and new emerging Islamic society by adapting prior agencies of authority to the Islamic mythic worldview and substituting a spiritual lineage to the most perfect human, Muḥammad, for tribal or aristocratic lineage.

When a sharīʿa-minded or juristic sufism developed sufis "occupied" the boundary between transmitted religious knowledge (here credal dogma [*ʿaqāid*], hadith, and jurisprudence [*fiqh*]) and sufism. Although this overlap of jurist and sufi knowledge has not been unusual for directing-shaykhs, the further development of a consciously formulated juristic sufism, e.g., the Mujaddidiyya beginning in seventeenth-century India, occurred after sufi activity that both integrated and accepted pre-Islamic elements. This ability to spread juristic sufism enabled the Mujaddidiyya to become an international lineage that adeptly mediated both juristic knowledge and sufi practice.[1] The "ulama connection" led to political liaisons which then involved yet another set of potential intersecting boundaries. The "mother of coups" would be to have the ruler himself become the sincere disciple of a directing-shaykh, a goal occasionally achieved in fifteenth-century Central Asia but never realized by Indian Mujaddidīs.

In the wake of the first transformation of sufi authority there was a centrifugal movement by sufis both within emerging Islamic societies and geographically beyond them, to combine old and new elements, to re-present prior sociocultural forms in new combinations. Sufis, strategically located at the margins, had considerable success in this endeavor as they mediated between the old and new. In their authoritative liminal positions as holy persons, whether consciously or by trial and error, they progressively Islamicized old behavioral patterns by incorporating them into Islamic models, gradually transforming society in the process. Liminality and mediation went hand in hand with strategic positioning on constantly shifting multiple margins which made sufis indispensable to the functioning of decentralized Islamic agrarian/herding societies.

The second transformation of sufi authority occurred when Naqshbandī directing-shaykhs became mediating-shaykhs, a shift that for the Indian Naqshbandiyya coincided with the British colonial impulse. This second transformation was the inverse of the first. When Muslims started becoming the majority community in the tenth century, it was the silent but resounding triumph of Islamic conquest, the victory of a sociocultural religious construct that united many diverse tribal lineages and ethnic groups under one relatively unified banner. The formal termina-

[1]In India the Mujaddidiyya contrasted with the Chishtiyya. Chishtī pirs skillfully mediated local Indian culture and Islamic practice to a much greater extent that the Mujaddidiyya. There were Chishtī sufis who strove to make the Chishtī lineage more shariʿa-minded, but generally Chishtī popularity among common people, Muslim and non-Muslim, demonstrates the ability of their pirs to operate on the boundary between Muslim and non-Muslim—at least relative to the Naqshbandīs. Not surprisingly, the Chishtiyya are the most popular sufi lineage on the subcontinent.

tion of Mughal rule in 1857 combined with Muslim minority status had the opposite effect. By the turn of the century, it was increasingly difficult for Muslims not to see the Islamic worldview as just one of many, and on the world stage a not very powerful one. The new world order was not Islamic.

The institutional expression of the directing-shaykh depended on an unquestioned single worldview. By transcending relatively bounded religious constructs, effectively the modern-scientific worldview undermined both psychologically and socially the institution of the directing-shaykh. For urban sufis the demise of the Islamic government meant the effective end of patronage and with it the severe reduction in the scale of institutional activities. In addition there was no larger political system that legitimized Islam, symbolically or literally. The absolute nature of the Islamic sociocultural construct had disappeared when the British ruled over Muslims. In addition, religious arguments for patronage and support had in one stroke been annuled by the British separation (on paper at least) of religion and politics.

The personal authority of the directing-shaykh utilized the universal symbol of Muḥammad in the context of an apparently unchanging Islamic worldview. The sudden onslaught of other alternative Muslim conceptions of religion, e.g., Ahmadis and Ahl-i Hadith, raised doubts in the minds of many Muslims, as more and more English-educated Indian Muslims applied Western rationalism to the mythological constructs of Indian Islam. The directing-shaykh was most vulnerable to this criticism, since bracketed rational inquiry was the very foundation of the master-disciple relationship.

The crowning blow was the British destruction of the educational system. Before 1857 and long before the formation of the Islamic seminaries of Deoband, Nadwat al-Ulama, and Aligarh, the upper class was educated privately before going on to higher education. Everyone else learned through the voluntary efforts of sufis or ulama,[2] which gave them well-deserved prestige in addition to providing a cadre of disciples who would continue their religious education through the spiritual practices they taught.

This two-tiered educational system became much more decentralized as religious notables fled Delhi after 1857 and networks of religious leaders developed between northern Indian towns. The British, by destroying the schools in Delhi, did much to

[2]Farhan Nizami, "Madrasahs, Scholars and Saints: Muslim Response to the British Presence in Delhi and the Upper Doab 1803–1857," p. 14.

spread the voluntary nature of Islamic education. One of the most famous Muslim schools in Delhi, the Madrasa-yi Raḥīmiyya founded by Shāh Walī Allāh's father, Shāh ʿAbdurraḥīm (d. 1130/1718), continued until 1857 when the British auctioned it off to a Hindu raja.[3] Delhi College, which had opened in 1825 as a Muslim college and shortly thereafter received a large endowment from Nawwāb Iʿtimāduddawla, had by 1870 forty-nine Hindu students for each Muslim student.[4] By 1882, when a gifted Hungarian linguist and educator working for the British, G. W. Leitner, made his survey of indigenous education in the Panjab, British land reforms had almost obliterated all trace of indigenous education in both the cities and villages.[5] Some ulama could at least find jobs in the British courts and a small number of landowning hereditary sufis could continue their activities under British rule, but the institutional infrastructure for directing-shaykhs, both political and educational, had by the 1920s eroded considerably.

Throughout Islamic history conceptions of Muslim community reflect sociopolitical structures. In modern times the pan-Indian Muslim community created through loving the pir as the way to salvation and connected together by the monthly *Risāla* mirrors the creation of nation as community where democratic "love for all" focuses upon the imagined community (connected together by Urdu newspapers) of an emerging nation-state. A parallel relationship between notions of sufi community and social institutions occur with directing-shaykhs in the decentralized *ʿayān-amīr* system. Many sufi behavioral codes come from court practices, as do the terms used to designate their sufi dwellings, e.g., a king's court *(dargāh)* and prince's audience chamber *(darbār)*, along with appelations of King *(shāh)*. Directing-shaykhs command in their lodges in much the same way as rulers in their palaces. Likewise when sufis are in tribal environments, the heroic model of the tribal chieftain is stressed, particularly in "spiritual competi-

[3]Ibid., pp. 18–19.

[4]G. W. Leitner, *History of Indigenous Education in the Panjab Since Annexation and in 1882*, p. 47. Leitner documents how the British destroyed a vibrant educational system in the Panjab.

[5]Each village, whether Muslim, Sikh or Hindu, invariably had at least one teacher whose subsistence was provided for by a small plot of land. The British appropriated these lands, saying that the government would provide teachers. In Leitner's paraphrased words, "The government educational system . . . [had] little real hold on the people, who in sullen silence felt themselves to be disregarded, and their ancient civilisation despised." Ibid., p. v.

tions."[6] Personal authority (not institutional or bureaucratic) represent the norm for rulers and sufis in both social contexts.

Jamāʿat ʿAlī, like his directing-shaykh predecessors, adroitly placed himself in a mediating position between sociopolitical factions. There are few frontiers where he was not found. In the first decade of the twentieth century, he sought to bring together all sufi lineages and English-educated Muslims. In the 1920s he worked toward the active proselytization of Islam to counter Hindu and Christian attempts to convert Muslims. In the following decade we find him bridging rural-urban political differences, the Shahīdganj incident being the best-known example. His use of modern transportation and publications enabled him to convey his sufi message in a rapidly changing environment with constantly shifting boundaries.

The authority Jamāʿat ʿAlī derived from this position was in principle the same as his directing-shaykh counterpart, except that one can no longer locate any *communitas* arising from this modern threshold (note Turner's observation, "It is in liminality that communitas emerges").[7] There is no longer the necessarily authoritarian normative *communitas* of the sufi lodge to simulate the ideal community of the Prophet and his Companions. It has been replaced by an imaginary macrocommunity created through the dissemination of a monthly sufi magazine which reflects the emerging modern nation-state as imagined community.[8] United in its love of the shaykh and the Prophet, Jamāʿat ʿAlī's community was an expression of the emerging Muslim nation, the spiritual antistructure that existed independently of the actual structure of political power, a convenient configuration since the British (theoretical) conception of politics kept religion and politics in separate domains.[9]

The Indian Muslim community during the colonial period was itself on a threshold between relatively stable Muslim institutions with Muslim rulers of the past and an unknown, uncertain fu-

[6]Clifford Geertz, *Islam Observed: Religious Development in Morocco and Indonesia*, and Stephen L. Pastner, "Sardar, Hakom, Pir: Leadership Patterns among the Pakistani Baluch," pp. 164–79.

[7]Victor Turner, *Dramas, Fields, and Metaphors: Symbolic Action in Human Society*, p. 232.

[8]See Benedict Anderson, *Imagined Communities: Reflections on the Origin and Spread of Nationalism.*

[9]The sufi lodge of the directing-shaykh also paralleled this relationship; the hierarchical directing-shaykh structure parallels the person-centered authoritarian decentralized political structure.

ture.[10] The Muslim community found itself in an uncomfortable, disunited, conflicting "liminal situation." Significant numbers of Muslims yearned for a united, harmonious Muslim community that transcended all religious, lineage, economic, tribal, and social differences just as the idealized community of the Prophet had. Such a desire was eminently modern, born out of modern impulses that transcended local concerns while connecting these diverse locales and pepole within a maze of conflicting viewpoints. There was an urge to find suitably universal Islamic symbols to bring the community back together from the powerful modern centrifugal forces which highlighted difference and juxtaposed them in all too often uncomfortable proximity.

It was this modern universalizing impulse that rallied the Barelwis in love around the universal, personal, omnipresent Prophet in the same way that the Ahl-i Hadith based their perspective on the universal, impersonal, scriptural sources of Islam. Jamāʿat ʿAlī's notion of an ideal community mirrored the Prophet-centered Barelwi conceptions with the sufi pir, as heir of the Prophet, at the center. Sufi lineage was to be transcended as the bond of love drew all Muslims under the comprehensive association of "Voluntary Sufi Servants" just as the Prophet was conceived to have gathered all types of people as Companions. In this enterprise Jamāʿat ʿAlī and other Barelwi ulama loosely drew together diverse Muslims from all over India under one banner of love.

This necessarily unfulfilled love, a yearning for a transformative *communitas*, fueled the movement for Pakistan as a Muslim nation, a concretely defined imaginary community that provided a modern symbol for Muslim unity. The universalizing notion of the modern nation-state, Pakistan, managed to transcend the conflicting universal symbols of personal authority (sufi pir) and scriptural authority (Qur'ān and hadith). In this imaginary *communitas* of homogeneous, equal voters, the primary rite of passage was the 1946 Indian provincial elections, which enabled the temporarily united Muslim *communitas* to enter en masse into collective modern political adulthood: the Muslim nation of Pakistan.[11] Muhammad ʿAli Jinnah, in his role as sole spokesman for

[10]Note Turner's observation: "Major liminal situations are occasions on which a society *takes cognizance of itself.*" Turner, *Dramas, Fields, and Metaphors,* pp. 239–40 [italics Turner's].

[11]I have been stimulated in this discussion by David Gilmartin's insightful unpublished paper, "The Rhetoric of Muslim Elections: Community and Pakistan in 1946."

the Indo-Muslim community,[12] led the movement which brought Muslims from conflict and a minority status to the fulfillment of a politically united (majority) Muslim nation. As the directing-shaykh led the community-building rituals of an individually transformative *communitas* of the sufi lodge, so Jinnah directed the political process for the modern imaginary *communitas* that radically transformed the Indo-Pakistani Muslim community. In this context Jamāʿat ʿAlī's declaration that Jinnah was a "friend of God" *(walī Allāh)* begins to take on a counterintuitive plausibility.

These momentous changes utterly change the nature of Naqshbandī sufi lodges. Personal transformation in the *communitas* of a sufi lodge is no longer the norm. In the modern state of Pakistan an increasingly modern sociopolitical system of bureaucratic authority predominates over personal authority. The relatively impersonal nature of the mediating-shaykh's master-disciple relationships parallels the more modern, rationalized political forms of authority. Sufi institutions continue to remain in flux.

Post-Independence patterns include the Pakistani government attempting to control the institutional expression of sufism directly, redefining it in the process.[13] The government strategy has been to put forth a new ideology of sufi shaykhs and shrines that undermine their traditional authority as caretakers and brokers of supernatural power. By taking over shrines, creating highly visible improvements to the buildings, and making social centers out of them that include schools, libraries, and hospitals, the government has endeavored to preempt the hereditary's pir's prerogative as caretaker. Sufi shrines have become community centers rather than sacred places of divine potency with a hereditary mediating-shaykh dispensing God's grace. Often the government builds hospitals within a shrine-complex where allopathic medicine is administered in place of potent handmade amulets with Qur'ānic passages prepared by those residing at the sufi shrine.

This policy, which was begun by Pakistani president Ayub Khan, was extended by Zulfiqar Bhutto, who emphasized governmental participation in the shrine rituals themselves. At death-anniversary ceremonies his officials performed the principal rituals of washing the grave and laying on a new cloth *chaddar* to cover it, tasks usually delegated to the chief religious specialist at the shrine, the *sajjādanishīn*. Al-Hujwīrī (d. 463–64/1070), com-

[12]Ayesha Jalal has articulated this role in her *The Sole Spokesman: Jinnah, the Muslim League and the Demand for Pakistan.*

[13]See Katherine Ewing, "The Politics of Sufism: Redefining the Saints of Pakistan."

A poster dated 21 May 1991 advertising the arrival at the Lahore airport of an Afghan sufi shaykh, Sayfurraḥmān. Locations (mosques) and times (usually in the afternoon) of *dhikr* sessions during his four-day stay are described in the four boxes at the bottom.

monly known as Dātā Ganjbakhsh, was presented as a sufi who "preached egalitarianism and visualized a classless society based on the concept of *musawat-i Muhammadī* (Muhammadan equality).[14] Ayub Khan and Bhutto, as secularists, linked themselves with sufi shrines to identify themselves with religious authority and thereby legitimize their political power. While promoting shrines and sufi doctrines associated with these shrines for the glory of Pakistan and Islam, they were attempting to co-opt the personal authority of the pirs.[15] The colonial impact upon Indo-Muslims, combined with increasing Pakistani governmental regulation of institutional sufism,[16] leads one to the conclusion that contemporary sufi lodges would not be the first place one would expect to find directing-shaykhs.[17]

Whether a person is a directing-shaykh or a mediating-shaykh is not of concern to the vast majority of South Asian Muslims. The paths to God have metaphorically meant anything from "relaying a message" via a mediating-shaykh to being in the presence of a shaykh, either deceased or living, to spiritually traveling into God's presence. The mystical quest actually to have direct knowledge of God or to encounter God in this world attracts few individuals. Most people are content to be with God after their death; how or when they get there is unimportant. Reading scripture, following the spiritual giants of Islam, loving one's shaykh, arduous mystical practice, or fulfilling the ritual requirements of Islam—all these paths eventually lead to God.

In his *Jāvīdnāma* Muḥammad Iqbāl asserted that one can deny God but one cannot deny Muḥammad. One way of interpreting this saying is that by rejecting Muḥammad one also rejects God. A sufi carries this one step further by stating that a denial of the shaykh, as heir of the Prophet, is a denial of both Muḥammad and God. As Naqshbandīs have integrated a seamless scriptural truth with the continuous living authority of the shaykh, Muḥammad, and God, they have infused day-to-day ritual observance

---

[14]*The Pakistan Times*, 23 September 1980, cited by P. Lewis, *Pirs, Shrines, and Pakistani Islam*, p. 54.

[15]Perhaps living sufis and caretakers have a lower profile at certain shrines, but the devotional behavior at the large shrines continues unabated. For example in the early 1980s the annual income of the Dātā Ganj Bakhsh (The Treasure-bestowing Master) shrine was estimated at 12.3 million rupees, or close to a million dollars; see *Pakistan Times* 2 December 1982, cited in ibid.

[16]Such a process is paralleled in Egypt by the Supreme Council of Sufi Lineages; see Valerie Hoffman, *Sufism, Mystics, and Saints in Modern Egypt*, pp. 9–11, 14–15.

[17]Interview, Hakīm Muḥammad Mūsā, Lahore, 14 March 1990, when he also assured me that none would be found in Panjabi sufi lodges, which I later confirmed.

with the living spark of the Prophet. Resourcefully re-creating the paradigmatic community of the Prophet and Companions throughout the Islamic world has enabled the Naqshbandiyya to maintain exceptional threads of continuity from early Islam, through Aḥmad Sirhindī to Jamāʿat ʿAlī.

APPENDIX 1

Written Sources for Spiritual Exercises

The Naqshbandiyya emphasize the lineage that differentiates them from other sufis and their adherence to the practices of the Prophet and performance of ritual duties according to a strict interpretation of Ḥanafī jurisprudence. Naqshbandī identity, whether described by Naqshbandīs or by Western scholars, almost always includes ʿAbdulkhāliq Ghujduwānī's formulation of eight guiding principles related to Naqshbandī spiritual practice, i.e., awareness of breath *(hūsh dar dam)*, being conscious of following in the steps of the Prophet *(naẓar bar qadam)*, traveling on the internal mystical path *(safar dar waṭan)*, solitude in society *(khalwat dar anjuman)*, constant repetition of God's name *(yād kard)*, returning to the world after performing *dhikr (bāzgasht)*, guarding one's spiritual progress *(nigāhdāsht)*, and concentration on God *(yāddāsht)*.[1] Bahā'uddīn Naqshband's three additional principles are also mentioned: awareness of time *(wuqūf-i zamānī)*, counting of *dhikr* repetitions *(wuqūf-i ʿadadī)*, and a heart constantly attentive to God *(wuqūf-i qalbī)*.[2]

Few written records survive from the early Naqshbandiyya explaining how these eleven principles were actually applied.[3] Most likely detailed information on spiritual practices was not dissem-

[1]The first four of these principles are from Ghujduwānī's spiritual mentor, Abū Yaʿqūb Yūsuf Hamadānī (d. 534/1140). See ʿAbdulkhāliq Ghujduwānī, *Risāla-yi Ṣāḥibiyya*, p. 91.

[2]For a scholarly discussion of these principles, see Faqīrullāh Shikārpūrī, *Futūḥāt al-ghaybiyya*, unpublished manuscript, Khundian Sharīf, n.d., pp. 164–68, and Warren Fusfeld, "The Shaping of Sufi Leadership in Delhi: The Naqshbandiyya-Mujaddidiyya, 1750–1920," pp. 85–90.

[3]ʿAbdurraḥmān Jāmī, *Sarrishta-yi ṭarīqa-yi khwājagān*, discusses *dhikr*, *rābiṭa*, *waqūf zamānī*, and *murāqaba* in very general terms.

inated in written form but passed from master to disciple as part of an initiatory tradition. The Mujaddidīs of the British Indian period were unusual in this respect since they did write and even publish so many aspects of this initiatory tradition.

Before the nineteenth century, Indian Mujaddidī shaykhs, following Sirhindī's example, wrote letters elaborating details of Naqshbandī cosmology and spiritual practice to their disciples. The first work devoted to a description of the Mujaddidī path was written by one of Aḥmad Sirhindī's disciples, Mīr Nuʿmān, who produced a manual explaining the Naqshbandī-Mujaddidī path.[4] If the spiritual practices outlined in later nineteenth-century documents are representative of earlier practices, then Mīr Nuʿmān's description of the Mujaddidī path and subsequent eighteenth-century written discussions of Mujaddidī spiritual practices can be considered sketches of what disciples actually did in their mystical exercises.[5] The initiatory tradition, including exercises, supplications, and prayers the shaykh instructed the disciple to perform, was still being transmitted orally.

By the nineteenth century, particularly among Ghulām ʿAlī Shāh's lineage, an entirely new genre of sufi literature emerged, that of *maʿmūlāt* works. The name of the genre is related to the words *ʿamalīyāt* and *iʿmāl* both having a meaning of "causing to act" or "making something work," which technically cover a variety of "spiritual prescriptions" often containing Qur'ānic verses used by Muslims to solve worldly problems such as averting evil and curing diseases.[6]

Shāh Walīullāh's (d. 1176/1762) *Al-qawl al-jamīl* and *Intibāh fi*

[4]Mīr Nuʿmān, *Risāla-yi sulūk*. In this short manual (32 pages) the established positions of the *laṭīfas* in the human body, the color of light associated with the each *laṭīfa*, the origins *(uṣūl)* of each *laṭīfa*, and the stages of *murāqabāt* are explained. It is a manual defining a new Mujaddidī system without including any details of *dhikr*, *nafy wa-ithbāt*, or any other instructions for the disciple.

[5]ʿAbdulaḥad Waḥdat Sirhindī's *Sabīl ar-rushād* does not appreciably add to Mīr Nuʿmān's treatise. Shāh Walīullāh's *Intibāh fī salāsil awliyā' Allāh* and *Al-qawl al-jamīl* are more explicit about *nafy wa-ithbāt*, but do not discuss spiritual practices in significantly greater detail than the preceding works. In some aspects Walīullāh has abridged his discussion, e.g., the issue of contemplations of prophetic and divine realities is avoided. See *Intibāh fī salāsil awliyā' Allāh*, p. 77.

[6]Such formulae would often be written on paper enclosed by leather to be used as amulets *(taʿāwīdh*, sing. *taʿwīdh)* or were in the form of numerical charts *(nuqūsh*, sing. *naqsh)*. In the subcontinent sufis have been religious specialists knowledgeable in this system of curing disease and solving problems using such methods. A medical anthropological study of Indo-Pakistani sufis, their various systems of healing, and what diseases they treat would be a valuable scholarly contribution. For the pir as a curer and exorcist, see Katherine Ewing, "Sufi as Saint, Curer, and Exorcist in Modern Pakistan."

salāsil awliyā' Allāh are precursors to the genre. Both are intended for a general educated audience and have neither technical or detailed discussions of sufi practices.[7] *Al-qawl al-jamīl* generally discusses the sufi exercises *(ashghāl)* of the Chishtiyya, Qādiriyya, and Naqshbandiyya, with one section supplying practical formulae for things like repelling rabid dogs, protecting children, and keeping bothersome disembodied spirits from one's house. *Intibāh fī salāsil awliyā' Allāh* discusses other aspects of sufism; it also contains a letter by ʿAbdulaḥad (d. 1126/1715) and the genealogical links to Muḥammad authorizing him to recite popular devotional prayers, e.g., Abū'l-Ḥasan ʿAlī ash-Shādhilī's (d. 656/1258) *Ḥizb al-baḥr*, or to transmit the contents of popular compendiums of devotional prayers, e.g., *Dalā'il al-khayrāt* by al-Jazūlī (d. 869/1465). Both treatises emphasize the need to be affiliated with a sufi shaykh. It would be unlikely that persons recited these formulae themselves. They either had a sufi perform the recitation for them or, in the case of devotional prayers, received permission *(ijāza)* from a shaykh to recite specific devotional prayers. Such nontechnical works by Shāh Walīullāh encouraged educated Muslims in a practical unapologetic fashion to become affiliated with a sufi master.

Maʿmūlat-i maẓhariyya, as its title suggests, initiated the *maʿmūlāt* genre of Naqshbandī sufi literature explicating both reformist notions of sufi practice and traditional Naqshbandī practices.[8] Written by a disciple of Mīrzā Maẓhar Jān-i jānān (assassinated

---

[7]These two books are the basis for Mīr Valīuddīn's posthumously published *Madārij al-sulūk*, translated as *Contemplative Disciplines in Sufism*. The latter book contains numerous errors and makes only oblique references to the large chunks taken *en toto* from Shāh Walīullāh's works.

[8]The *maʿmūlāt* genre is a Naqshbandī phenomenon although it may have been more of a widespread phenomenon among revivalist sufi lineages than my research indicates. Shāh Muḥammad Ashraf ʿAlī T'hānawī's massive 1270-page *Tarbiyat al-sālik* shares many characteristics with Naqshbandī materials. Professor Iqbāl Mujaddiī, one of the foremost scholars of the Indian Naqshbandiyya, describes the contents of Naʿīmullāh Bahrā'ichī's *Maʿmūlāt-i maẓhariyya*, in terms of sufi practices *(maʿmūlāt)*, ritual and supererogatory prayers *(ʿibādat)*, and practical formulae *(waḍā'if)*. The latter indicate how to cure inner and outer disease and how to attract benefits and repel harmful influences. See his informative introduction to Ghulām ʿAlī Shāh's *Maqāmāt-i maẓharī*, p. 180. Among non-Naqshbandī Indian sufis *waḍā'if* can also be a term for sufi practices and *maʿmūlāt* can be a term for pious formulae. *Maʿmūl* also has the meaning of "established customary practice," explaining such titles as *Maʿmūlāt-i khayr*, which have pious formulae and supplications to be used daily. Pakistani booksellers specializing in religious books, when asked for books on *maʿmūlāt*, will most likely associate this genre with practical devotional prayers, e.g., *Al-ḥisn al-ḥasīn* or *Dalā'il al-khayrāt*.

1195/1781), Naʿīmullāh Bahrā'ichī (d. 1218/1803–4), the book was given a seal of approval by one of Mīrzā Maẓhar's senior disciples, Qāḍī Thānā'ullāh Pānīpatī (d. 1225/1810).[9] Although similar in content to its predecessors written by Shāh Walīullāh, *Maʿmūlāt-i maẓhariyya* is much more a consciously Naqshbandī treatise, emphasizing a sober shariʿa-minded sufism. It is unique in its extensive hagiographic treatment of Mīrzā Maẓhar and the inclusion of several of his letters to prominent disciples.[10]

The next manual discussing Mujaddidī practice is Abū Saʿīd Dihlawī's (d. 1250/1835) concise *Hidāyat al-ṭālibīn,* which is said to be used today at Khundian Sharif.[11] Aḥmad Saʿīd's (d. 1277/1860) *Arba ʿanhār* followed. It briefly discusses Mujaddidī, Qādirī, Chishtī, and Naqshbandī sufi practices; the latter three he includes in his Mujaddidī spiritual heritage.[12]

A popular successor to *Maʿmūlāt-i maẓharī* appeared in 1911. Muḥammad ʿInāyatullāh named his book *Maqāmāt-i irshādiyya* after his shaykh, Muḥammad Irshād Ḥusayn.[13] Unlike either of its predecessors, it begins by emphasizing the superiority of the Naqshbandiyya and the necessity of a shaykh. The first half is devoted to a description of the Naqshbandī ontology and stages along the Naqshbandī path; the second explains many sufi tech-

---

[9]It was written in 1205/1790–91 and first lithographed seventy years later. See *Maʿmūlāt-i maẓhariyya.* The second edition was printed in Lahore by Maṭbaʿ-i Muḥammadī in 1284/1867–68; the first edition is a better copy.

[10]Naʿīmullāh was the first to write about Mīrzā Maẓhar Jān-i jānān and the first to publish his letters. For a survey of both Naʿīmullāh's publications and Mīrzā Maẓhar's letters, see the detailed introduction to the Urdu translation of Ghulām ʿAlī Shāh's *Maqāmāt-i maẓharī* by Iqbāl Mujaddidī, pp. 1–223.

[11]It is strictly a manual giving background information for Naqshbandī disciples, although the oral tradition of the intentions (see appendix 3) is not included. The *mashārib-i khamsa,* the contemplations putting each *laṭīfa* to its origin, are also not mentioned, even though his shaykh, Ghulām ʿAlī Shāh, mentions it in *Makātīb-i sharīfa,* pp. 104–05. The best edition of *Hidāyat al-ṭālibīn* is edited by Nūr Aḥmad (the editor of Sirhindī's *Maktūbāt*) with his accompanying Urdu translation.

[12]Aḥmad Saʿīd had intended to discuss Suhrawardī sufi exercises in this book but, informed that Bahā'uddīn was displeased with him, named the fourth river "Naqshbandī" instead (the book title *Arbaʿ anhār* means four rivers). For the last section he lists the eleven principles of the Naqshbandiyya. See Muḥammad Maẓhar Mujaddidī, *Manāqib-i aḥmadiyya wa-maqāmāt-i saʿīdiyya,* p. 168, cited in Fusfeld, "The Shaping of Sufi Leadership," pp. 205–06.

[13]First published in 1329/1911 in Persian, it was reprinted in 1342–43/1923 and went out of print six years later. In 1360/1941 Muḥammad Allāh Khān's Urdu translation was published and has been reprinted at least twice since: Muḥammad ʿInāyatullāh Khān, *Maqāmāt-i irshādiyya,* Urdu trans. Muḥammad Allāh Khān, *Maʿārif-i ʿināyatiyya.*

nical terms used by Naqshbandī-Mujaddidī pirs.[14] A short hagiography of Irshād Ḥusayn completes the 81-page Persian treatise.

In 1927 another book, *Miʿyār al-sulūk,* more along the lines of *Maʿmūlāt-i maẓharī,* was written by Hidāyat ʿAlī Jaipūrī, a disciple of ʿAlī Shēr Shān. He defends and bolsters the institution of revivalist Naqshbandī sufism by establishing correct credal dogma and emphasizing the obligatory nature *(farḍ)* of acquiring inner knowledge *(bāṭinī ʿilm)* with a shaykh's guidance. After discussing the Naqshbandī path, such diverse material as supererogatory prayers, supplications, hagiographical presentations of the Prophet, and selected Indian Naqshbandī shaykhs are covered. The last few pages are devoted to "necessary amulets" and include numerical charts *(nuqūsh)* to protect against such ailments as black magic, fever, and weak eyesight.

Zawwār Ḥusayn developed the genre to its fullest in his *ʿUmdat al-sulūk.* Written for a general audience, the first part explains each aspect of Naqshbandī sufism which, in reformist terms, is copiously supported by appropriate Qurʾānic and hadith references.[15] Sections outline conditions for disciples and the responsibilities of a shaykh, followed by prescriptions to cure various illnesses and pious supplications. The second part is for a more specialized audience, sufis on the path. Discussing the Naqshbandī path and technical terminology, it also includes a section on supererogatory prayers and ends in an extensive hagiographical section with thirty-six half-page hagiographies of each sufi master in the author's spiritual lineage from Muḥammad to his shaykh, Muḥammad Saʿīd Qurayshī (d. 1363/1944). Typical of the genre, the book ends with 119 different formulae *(taʿwīdhāt wa-iʿmaliyāt)* to solve various problems.

The most modern production of the *maʿmūlāt* genre, *Manāhij al-sayr* by Abu'l-Ḥasan Fārūqī Dihlawī, is a synthesis of the preceding, mostly out-of print works. Discussing sufi terminology and the specifics of the Naqshbandī path in an academic fashion, it does not overtly encourage the reader to find a sufi master. Only at the end of the work is initiation mentioned, and almost all the dozen pious formulae are directly related to sufi needs, e.g., how to be aware of one's *laṭīfas* or how to benefit from a sufi grave.

Until Shāh Walīullāh's time separate treatises explaining spiri-

---

[14]An educated Muslim reading this book would be able to make the transition to Sirhindī's *Maktūbāt* with relative ease.

[15]For example, there are 52 Qurʾānic proofs and 41 hadith citations to support the practice of *dhikr*.

tual practices defined Mujaddidī identity much in the same way as the eleven principles established by Bahā'uddīn still define the Naqshbandī path. These short works discussing the Mujaddidī path, however, were the exception. What transpired between the Naqshbandī shaykh and disciple, outside of written letters, was part of an oral initiatory tradition. Shāh Walīullāh's writing about various practices of the major Indian sufi lineages was an attempt to harmonize these different lineages while buttressing the authority of the sufi shaykh. This is not typical of the Naqshbandiyya, who have perceived their practices as superior to other sufi lineages and their path as "closer" to God than others. Subsequent writing of *maʿmūlāt* works by Ghulām ʿAlī Shāh's disciples included certain elements of Shāh Walīullāh's work, e.g., practical formulae and the necessity of a shaykh, but emphasized shariʿa-minded aspects of the Naqshbandiyya instead of an inclusive pan-Indian sufism.[16]

By the twentieth century, the *maʿmūlāt* genre reflected the concerns of revivalist sufism, defining a normative Islam with sufism at center stage and the shaykh as the primary religious authority. If the distribution of sufi books at that time followed the contemporary pattern, they were read inside the Naqshbandī community and passed around to those interested in sufism.[17] In addition to providing valuable background information to disciples who could no longer spend twenty to thirty years at the foot of their master, *maʿmūlāt* works furnished supporting arguments for beliefs likely to be attacked by scripturalist-minded "Wahhābī" groups.

The only two Naqshbandī-Mujaddidī *maʿmūlāt* books in print today are the Urdu translation of *Manāhij al-sayr* by Abu'l-Ḥasan Fārūqī Dihlawī and *ʿUmdat al-sulūk. Manāhij al-sayr* presumably is of more academic interest than practical use since there has been little if any recent interest in pursuing the Mujaddidī path at Chatli Qabr.[18] In retrospect the Naqshbandī *maʿmūlāt* genre has

[16]Fusfeld suggests a divergence of thought and emphasis between the school of Shāh Walīullāh's son, Shāh ʿAbdulʿazīz, and Ghulām ʿAlī Shāh, citing a description given in Christian W. Troll's *Sayyid Aḥmad Khan: A Reinterpretation of Muslim Theology*, pp. 30–36. There might have been significant differences between these two schools, but no conclusions can be made on the basis of Troll's very vague allusions; see Fusfeld, "The Shaping of Sufi Leadership," p. 240.

[17]Another impetus for Mujaddidī publications, including the genre of *maʿmūlāt*, was the ownership of lithograph presses by Naqshbandīs. One example is the Maṭbaʿ-i Ṣiddīqī in Bareilly acquired in 1862 by a Mujaddidī, Muḥammad Iḥsān. His stepson, ʿAbdulaḥad, acquired the prestigious Maṭbaʿ-i Mujtabā'ī in 1886. See Barbara Metcalf, *Islamic Revival in British India: Deoband, 1860–1900*, pp. 243–44.

[18]Personal communication from the late Abū'l-Ḥasan Fārūqī, January, 1991. The

been a relatively short-term phenomenon in the Panjab. Its use in Mujaddidī circles diminished rapidly after Partition in 1947, when the sufi revival movement lost its momentum and fewer aspirants traveled along the Mujaddidī path.[19]

---

same situation apparently exists at other Naqshbandī *khānaqāhs* in the Panjab. I was unable to find out to what extent *'Umdat al-sulūk* was being used in contemporary Sind.

[19]One cannot surmise from textual information alone that a Naqshbandī shaykh is a directing-shaykh, that is, training disciples to proceed along the Mujaddidī path according to the principles outlined in chapter 5. One example is a hagiographical work on the Naqshbandī lineage of Muḥammad 'Abdullāh Jān, a contemporary Naqshbandī pir. It includes an entire chapter on the Mujaddidī path and methods although these do not reflect the contemporary practices of this pir. Instead the inclusion of such information demonstrates the use of spiritual methods and ideas to affirm Mujaddidī identity. See Khālid Amīn Makhfī al-Khayrī, *Silsila-yi khayriyya ma' tadhkira-yi naqshbandiyya,* pp. 85–111. I suspect that the increasing number of published manuals detailing Mujaddidī practices relates to the decreasing number of Mujaddidī directing-shaykhs.

APPENDIX 2

Mujaddidī Contemplations

The performance of contemplation *(murāqaba),* according to Shāh Walīullāh, is the "particular excellence of the Naqshbandiyya."[1] As the disciple progresses through the contemplations *(murāqabāt)* he or she is able to travel in the Essence *(dhāt).*[2] Naqshbandī define *murāqaba* as "waiting for the *laṭīfas* to attract divine energy." In the words of Bāqībillāh's son, Khwāja Khurd, "*Murāqaba* is leaving behind one's power and strength; it is turning from all states and attributes waiting in expectation of the encounter [while] longing for its beauty and being immersed in its desire and love."[3]

The Naqshbandī cosmology represented by intersecting circles is a "geographical" map of the worlds between the Essence and the physical world; the Naqshbandī path to God described by the series of intentions in the various contemplations is a more detailed road map of the same spiritual continuum.[4] The spiritual

[1]Here he means the Naqshbandiyya-Mujaddidiyya; see J. M. S. Baljon, *Religion and Thought of Shāh Walī Allāh Dihlawī, 1703–1762,* p. 85.

[2]Contemplation is being used here in a technical sense. Mystical practice often involves three processes: concentration, meditation, and contemplation. The first stage, concentrating the mind, is the act of sharpening a pencil; the second, meditation, is like learning to form letters; and the third, contemplation, is writing words and sentences. For the Naqshbandīs these stages correspond to *dhikr-i qalbī, nafy wa-ithbāt,* and *murāqaba.* The principal difference between meditation and contemplation is the clear sense of dynamic motion in the latter. There are twenty-six different contemplations in the Naqshbandī system; collectively they will be referred to as the *murāqabāt.* For a philosophical analysis of meditation and contemplation, see Peter Moore, "Mystical Experience, Mystical Doctrine, Mystical Technique."

[3]Fārūqī, *Manāhij al-sayr,* p. 81. Fārūqī relates an apocryphal story transmitted from Saʿduddīn Kāshgharī (d. 860/1455–56) describing how Junayd was taught how to perform *murāqabāt* by a cat: one should wait with completely undivided attention like a cat ready to pounce on a mouse.

[4]See figures 5 and 7.

terrain, the series of manifestations between the Essence and the corporeal world including the path to negotiate this terrain, all of it "uphill,"[5] is described in detail throughout the twenty-six stages of the *murāqabāt.* A comparison of figures 5 and 7 shows the difference in scale between the four emanations from the essence and the twenty-one circles representing twenty-six individual meditations in the *murāqabāt,* the third stage for travelers on the Naqshbandī-Mujaddidī path. Before embarking on this journey through the *murāqabāt,* the recollection of the heart which "created a vehicle" and the *nafy wa-ithbāt* of "warming up the engine" have already been performed under the close supervision of the shaykh.

When the disciple is ready to begin, the first contemplation focuses on exclusive unity *(aḥadiyat)* before proceeding to the five contemplations of the prophetic wellsprings *(murāqabāt-i mashārib).*[6] This is the last "tour" through the attributes of God before proceeding to the Essence.[7] These five Prophetic contemplations emulate the model of the Prophet-Companion spiritual companionship *(ṣuḥbat)* as the disciple visualizes him- or herself in front of the Prophet, receiving divine energy via the "connecting chain" of Naqshbandī shaykhs.[8] As each of the five subtle centers receives divine grace from its origin *(aṣl)* above the Throne,[9] the goal is for each *laṭīfa* to go to its origin to realize its annihilation

[5]Moving from the physical world towards the Essence is described as an ascent *(ʿurūj),* a word having the same root as the Prophet's midnight journey into the heavens *(al-miʿrāj).*

[6]This is also called the contemplation of the five subtle centers *(murāqabāt-i laṭāʾif-i khamsa).* See Fārūqī, *Madārij al-khayr,* pp. 88–89. Each meditation attempts to guide *fayḍ* from the Essence to a specific *laṭīfa* by means of the Prophet via the great Naqshbandī shaykhs *(pīrān-i kibār).* For the differences coined by Ṣadruddīn Qūnawī (d. 673/1274), Ibn al-ʿArabī's chief disciple, between "exclusive unity" *(aḥadiyyat)* in the sense of the complete negation of corporeal manifestation and "inclusive unity" *(wāḥidiyyat)* in the sense of negation from outward existence but not from knowledge, see William Chittick, "The Five Divine Presences: From al-Qūnawī to al-Qayṣarī."

[7]Naqshbandīs emphasize that their goal is to travel in the essence *(dhāt)* not the attributes *(ṣifāt).* This means they are traveling in the first manifestation of creation instead of lower manifestations, not the undifferentiated Essence *(lā taʿayyun).*

[8]Evidently some Naqshbandīs concentrated on the individual prophets in these contemplations, since Ghulām ʿAlī Shāh said that it was unacceptable for anyone to concentrate on other prophets "although faith and certainty can be obtained from them." He recommends focusing on Muḥammad and God using the Naqshbandī shaykhs as mirrors. See Ghulām ʿAlī Shāh, *Makātīb-i sharīfa,* letter 81, p. 105.

[9]See figure 6 for correspondences between the *laṭīfas* and the location of their origins.

(fanā᾿). Extremely few travelers can annihilate these five *laṭīfas* in rapid succession, most associating themselves with a certain *laṭīfa* (also described as being under the foot of a certain prophet) until that is annihilated and then progressing on to efface the next *laṭīfa*. The minimum requirement for progress on the path is to return the heart *laṭīfa* to its origin. Then the disciple can move out of the circle of contingent existence *(dā᾿ira-yi imkān)* and proceed to the next realm of names and attributes.

Adam governs the first contemplation of the five prophetic ways; the active attributes *(ṣifāt-i fiʿliyya)* are most concentrated in him, since he knew the names of everything in creation. Naqshbandīs describe spiritual travelers who are at the "station of the heart" in the presence of *dhikr* while observing God's creation to be "under the foot" of Adam.[10] In contrast, the "station of the spirit" involves looking at God and negating God's creation by returning the *rūḥ* to its origin in the eight immutable divine attributes. This is the second prophetic contemplation associated with Abraham and Noah who manifest the special rank of having denied corporeal realities, e.g., fire did not harm Abraham, and the Flood did not drown Noah. Travel in the mystery *(sirr)* begins after the spirit *laṭīfa* as the *sirr*'s origin in the divine qualities *(shu᾿ūn-i dhātiyya)* begin at the end of the eight immutable divine attributes.[11] This is the domain of Moses who was the first to speak to God (hence he is often called *kalīmullāh*).

The next subtle center's origin is located in the attributes of negation (*ṣifāt-i salbiyya* or *ṣifāt-i tanzīhiyya*), the origin of the arcanum *laṭīfa*, which are like a "mirror image" of the previous divine qualities. Jesus, associated with the arcanum *laṭīfa*, established the meaning of negation *(nafy)* by utterly transcending the laws associated with the circle of contingent existence, e.g., being born without a father, reviving the dead, and transcending death. The last of the prophetic contemplations includes all the divine qualities in its origin just as Muḥammad, the prophet associated with the super-arcanum *laṭīfa*, is the source of the prophethood and the divine intimacy *(wilāya)* of the other prophets.

As Jesus established negation through his being, Muḥammad established the principle of affirmation *(ithbāt)* through his prophethood. The quality of comprehensive synthesis *(sha᾿n-i*

---

[10]Zawwār Ḥusayn, *ʿUmdat al-sulūk*, pp. 208–09.

[11]From the perspective of *waḥdat al-wujūd*, i.e., the formulation of Ibn al-ʿArabī's school, there are four divine qualities: light *(nūr)*, knowledge *(ʿilm)*, witnessing *(shuhūd)*, and existence *(wujūd)*. See Dhawqī, *Sirr-i dilbarān*, p. 344. Naqshbandīs do not restrict the *shu ᾿ūn* to these four qualities.

jāmiʿ) is the transition between the Essence and the divine qualities, associated with the Muḥammadan reality and the source of divinely emanating grace for all the rest of creation. Muḥammad is the greater bridge *(barzakh al-kubrā)* to God. Naqshbandīs therefore believe no spiritual path can arrive at God unless it includes the Muḥammadan reality and is blessed with divine grace from the quality of comprehensive synthesis. When the disciple has annihilated at least the heart *laṭīfa* he or she has exited the reflections *(zilāl)* and can proceed in the contemplations to the lesser intimacy with God *(wilāyat-i ṣughrā).*

Bahā'uddīn's elaboration of the Naqshbandī path went as far as the contemplation of "being together with God" *(maʿiyyat).*[12] By this point the traveler is out of the boundaries of the circle of contingent existence *(dā'ira-yi imkān)* and is now "traveling to God" *(sayr ila'llāh).* Although most other sufi shaykhs give disciples permission to teach at this point, Mujaddidīs do not necessarily let their students teach at this level if they are still subject to uncontrollable *jadhba* or fits of ecstasy.

From here the traveler enters the stage of greater intimacy with God *(wilāyat-i kubrā).* The adept travels in the *nafs* during this stage of spiritual development since it is only this subtle center that spans the spiritual heights and the world of creation.[13] This is the realm of the intimacy of prophets *(wilāyat-i anbiyā')* who return from spiritual heights to convey their message to humanity. It is also the station *(maqām)* of "the expanded breast" *(sharḥ-i ṣadr),*[14] pointing to the perfection of the *akhfā* subtle center which expands to fill the entire chest, forming a single unit of light *(hay'at-i waḥdānī,* literally, the unitary form).[15]

[12]Zawwār Ḥusayn, *'Umdat al-sulūk,* pp. 289–90. It is uncertain whether the preceding prophetic contemplations, at least in the form used by the Mujaddidiyya, were a part of Bahā'uddīn Naqshband's spiritual practices. Naqshbandıs have informed me that the eighteen further stages of spiritual journeying elaborated by Sirhindī (from the contemplation of *aqrabiyat* to the contemplation of *lā taʿayyun)* used to be reached by Uwaysī instruction before Sirhindī's elaboration of them. It was only after Sirhindī that these additional stages could be reached by exercises taught by a living shaykh. For a history of *maʿiyyat* and its meaning for Rūmī's father Bahā-i Walad, see Fritz Meier, *Bahā-i Walad: Grundzüge seines Lebens und seiner Mystik,* pp. 160–89.

[13]Note the emphasis on the *fayḍ* going to the *nafs* in these next five contemplations. Beyond that point the *hay'at-i waḥdānī* is formed as the subtle "vehicle" to go to the highest realms.

[14]Mentioned in the Qur'ān (6:125, 20:25, 39:22, 94:1).

[15]Muḥammad 'Ināyatullāh, *Maqāmāt-i irshādiyya,* pp. 251–52, and Zawwār Ḥusayn, *'Umdat al-sulūk,* pp. 291–92. I have not found any Naqshbandīs mentioning this light in the chest in connection with the cleansing of the Prophet's heart by angels.

At the stage of greater intimacy the ten *laṭīfas*, including the subdued, tranquil ego *(al-nafs al-muṭma'inna)*, have become purified in the station of contentment *(riḍā)*.[16] The larger circle of "greater intimacy" is represented by three smaller circles and a bow. Cosmologically, nearness *(aqrabiyat)*, the first of the smaller circles, is a transition *(barzakh)* including the names and attributes in its lower half and the divine qualities *(shu'ūn-i dhātiyya)* in its upper half, while the two higher circles of love *(maḥabba)* correspond with the attributes of negation *(ṣifāt-i salbiyya)* and the quality of comprehensive synthesis *(sha'n-i jāmiʿ)*, respectively.[17] The bow *(qaws)* is associated with the highest of God's qualities, knowledge *(sha'n-i ʿilm)*. The distinction of the "greater intimacy" is its cycling and unifying the higher and lower. The last contemplation of the Outward *(ism-i ẓāhir)* involves a return (*nuzūl*, literally, descent) to those things of the created world which had been negated and now can be affirmed to be included when traveling towards God. It is only from this greater intimacy that, in imitation of the prophets and Companions, one can return to the created world from the lofty heights of spiritual travel.

The Mujaddidīs specify one more degree of closeness to God, the "highest intimacy" *(wilāyat-i ʿulyā)*, that of the highest angels *(al-malā' al-aʿlā)*, involving the three elements of water, air, and fire. Upward/inward from the contemplation of the Inward *(ism-i bāṭin)* all traveling is in *dhāt*, i.e., the first manifestation of the Essence.[18] Above this are the three circles of perfections *(kamālāt)*, a domain to which angels cannot go because perfection is a function of integrating the highest, the most subtle body of light, with the lowest, the coarsest body of earth. This human potential to manifest the highest and the lowest aspects of creation makes humans superior to angels; it is for this reason that God ordered the angels to prostrate themselves in front of Adam (Q. 2:34). Beginning with the second contemplation of perfections, the perfections of Messengership *(kamālāt-i risālat)*, the consolidation of *laṭīfas (hay'at-i waḥdānī)* has become perfected as a vehicle.[19] It is this contemplation that is associated with the station of "the dis-

[16]Fārūqī, *Madārij al-khayr*, p. 72.

[17]Zawwār Ḥusayn, *ʿUmdat al-sulūk*, pp. 290–92.

[18]Muḥammad ʿInāyatullāh, *Maqāmāt-i irshādiyya*, pp. 252–53. Indian Abū Saʿīd (d. 1250/1835) received permission to teach at this stage in his contemplation exercises. See Abū Saʿīd, *Hidāyat al-ṭālibīn*, p. 76.

[19]All messengers of God (*rusul*, sing. *rasūl*) are prophets *(anbiyā')* but only relatively few prophets qualify as messengers of God. The distinction is that the messengers of God bring scriptures to humankind such as the Torah, Psalms, Bible, and Qur'ān.

tance of two bow lengths" *(qāba qawsayn)*, alluding to Muḥammad's exalted station (Q. 53:9).[20]

By the time of Ghulām ʿAlī Shāh (d. 1240/1824), discrepancies occur in the Mujaddidī path. According to nineteenth- and twentieth-century manuals of Naqshbandīs spiritual practice, the sufi, after traversing the contemplations of the perfections, should proceed to the divine realities *(ḥaqāʾiq-i ilāhiyya)* before embarking on the path of prophetic realities *(ḥaqāʾiq-i nabawiyya)*.[21] This was not always the case. Aḥmad Sirhindī had originally declared the reality of the Qurʾān *(ḥaqīqat-i qurʾan)* and the reality of the Kaʿba *(ḥaqīqat-i kaʿba-yi rabbānī)* to be above the reality of Muḥammad *(ḥaqīqat-i Muḥammadī)*.[22] This caused a fury of opposition, particularly among certain sufis and ulama of the Hijaz who objected to the Kaʿba having a more exalted spiritual "rank" than the Prophet.[23] Sirhindī argued in response that the reality of the Prophet is superior to any other creature. The real Kaʿba is worthy of prostration since it is not created and is covered with the veil of nonexistence. It is this Kaʿba in the essence of God that Sirhindī was referring to as the reality of the Kaʿba, not the appearance of the Kaʿba *(ṣūrat-i kaʿba)*, which is only a stone.[24]

The earliest sources detailing the Mujaddidī spiritual path follow Sirhindī's hierarchy, placing divine realities closer to God than prophetic realities.[25] By the latter part of the nineteenth cen-

---

[20]Ibid., p. 88. The association of the Prophet's night journey through the heavens and the *qāba qawsayn* occurs as early as Anas b. Mālik (d. ca. 92/710). See Louis Massignon, *La Passion de Husayn Ibn Mansūr Hallāj*, 4 volumes, 3:312, n. 3 (trans. 3:295, n. 114). There are very few references even alluding to progress on the Naqshbandī path and Muḥammad's heavenly journey in Naqshbandī literature—perhaps this is a conscious attempt to indicate the exalted nature of Muḥammad's experience which no other prophet had.

[21]There is a shortcut bypassing these two sets of realities, the path of *qayyūms*, which is reserved for very special travelers.

[22]Aḥmad Sirhindī, *Mabdaʾ wa-maʿād*, p. 78.

[23]The principal contenders in this controversy were Ādam Banūrī, one of Sirhindī's major successors, and Aḥmad Qushshāshī (d. 1071/1600). ʿAbdullāh Khwīshagī Quṣūrī has documented the correspondence in his *Maʿārij al-wilāyat*, pp. 606–46. The background of this controversy is fully discussed by Iqbāl Mujaddidī in *Aḥwāl wa-āthār-i ʿAbdullāh Khwīshagī Quṣūrī*, pp. 150–53.

[24]Aḥmad Sirhindī, *Maktūbāt-i imām-i rabbānī*, 3 volumes, vol. 3, letter 124, p. 147, and Muḥammad ʿInāyatullāh, *Maqāmāt-i irshādiyya*, pp. 261–63.

[25]The earliest source on the Mujaddidī path other than Sirhindī's *Maktūbāt* is by Mīr Nuʿmān, one of Sirhindī's successors. See his *Risāla-yi sulūk*, pp. 14–23. The contemplations of the perfections of prophetic realities precede the higher divine realities. Writing almost a century later, ʿAbdulaḥad Waḥdat Sirhindī (d. 1126/1715), in his *Sabīl al-rashād*, acknoweldges the divine realities to be closer to God than the prophetic realities.

tury, the consensus of the Naqshbandī community had placed the prophetic realities closer to God than the divine realities. The rationale for this development may have been to neutralize unnecessary discord with the larger Muslim community whose emotional attachment to Muḥammad was greater than any understanding of philosophical fine points. Like many believers, they could not imagine any entity closer to God than Muḥammad. This would be a logical move in the interest of shariʿa-mindedness and affirmation of the Sunnī creed especially (in retrospect) when viewed against the vehement Naqshbandī opposition to the Aḥmadīs. In the popular imagination at least, the Naqshbandīs would have had difficulty being leaders of revivalist sufism in British India if they needed continually to defend the ontological superiority of the Kaʿba over Muḥammad. There were more important issues at stake. In any case, few reached these heights of spiritual traveling and those who did were wise enough not to stir up unnecessary controversy over the mystical experience of an elite.

Ghulām ʿAlī Shāh of Delhi was the first to redefine Sirhindī's spiritual path.[26] He asserted that "together the reality of Muḥammad *(ḥaqīqat-i Muḥammadī)* and the reality of Aḥmad *(ḥaqīqat-i Aḥmadī)* are the closest [realities] to the Essence *(ḥaḍrat-i dhāt)*. . . . According to Ḥaḍrat Mujaddid (r) the first manifestation [from the Essence] is love and [contained in] the center of that manifestation of love is the reality of Aḥmad, an aspect of being a beloved of God *(maḥbūbiyat)*, [which] is the spiritual *(rūḥī)* manifestation of that Presence (S) [Muḥammad] and [in an outer circle from the Aḥmadī reality is] the reality of Muḥammad [being] mixed with belovedness *(maḥbūbiyat)* and being a lover *(muḥibbiyat)* which is the physical manifestation of that Presence (S) [Muḥammad]."[27]

---

[26]His contemporaries Qāḍā Thanāʾullāh Pānīpatī (d. 1225/1810) and Naʿīmullāh Bahrāʾichī (d. 1218/1803) both avoided the issue by not discussing the *murāqabāt* beyond the contemplations of perfections. See Pānīpatī, *Irshād al-ṭālibīn,* p. 67, and Naʿīmullāh Bahrāʾichī, *Maʿmūlāt-i maẓhariyya,* p. 72. By the early part of the twentieth century apparently other Indian Mujaddidī lineages also redefined the Mujaddidī path in the same fashion as Ghulām ʿAlī. See Jaipūrī, *Miʿyār al-sulūk,* pp. 153–61.

[27]Ghulām ʿAlī, *Makātīb-i sharīfa,* p. 148. Sirhindī developed an original interpretation of the Prophet Muḥammad, postulating two individuations: the bodily-human, representing Muḥammad as a messenger, and the spiritual-angelic, reflecting Muḥammad as a prophet. According to Sirhindī's inspiration, the former became transformed into the latter over a period of one thousand years after the Prophet's death. As a result the Muslim ulama were awarded the same rank as the prophets of Israel and the renewer *(mujaddid)* was supposed to fulfill the comparable task of a steadfast prophet; see Yohanan Friedmann, *Shaykh Aḥmad Sirhindī: An Outline of His Thought and a Study of His Image in the Eyes of Posterity,*

Among sufis this type of reinterpretation is seen as a mystical *ijtihād,* legitimate independent judgment based on spiritual experience.[28] All the manuals explaining the spiritual methods of the Mujaddidīs written in nineteenth- and twentieth-century India follow this new pattern. It is part of a larger pattern that exalted the status of Muḥammad and resulted in an increased status of the sufi shaykh. Although there appear to be few sources of the period documenting the controversies, they apparently involved opposition to Aḥmad Sirhindī.[29] To avoid unnecessary controversy and act in accordance with the community, a consensus of Mujaddidī shaykhs recognized the superiority of Muḥammad over other realities, both prophetic and divine.

pp. 15–17. The relationship between Sirhindī's prophetology and his elaboration of the spiritual path has yet to be investigated.

[28]Ghulām ʿAlī (d. 1240/1824) explains in one letter that the contemplations of divine realities are higher than the contemplations of prophetic realities in agreement with Sirhindī. See Ghulām ʿAlī, *Makātīb-i sharīfa,* p. 176. In another letter he reverses the two sets of contemplations according to subsequent usage among Mujaddidīs. See ibid., pp. 207–08. This situation illustrates one difficulty using sufi letters as sources, since each recipient of each letter had a different level of understanding and the shaykh addresses each person accordingly. Even if every letter were addressed to the same person, letters written over a period of time reflect the disciple's development and the shaykh's changing understanding of reality.

[29]Ibid., letters 1, 6, 67, 86, 88, 96.

APPENDIX 3

The Intentions Guiding the Disciple through the Mujaddidī Contemplations

One aspect of Mujaddidī practice that remained in oral tradition until quite recently was the series of mentally spoken intentions while traveling through the contemplations. To what extent the first six of these intentions changed after the advent of the expanded Mujaddidī system is not indicated in any of the sources. We only know that living shaykhs using Bahā'uddīn's methods trained disciples to go as far as the *maʿiyyat* contemplation. In Pakistan the usual time to perform these exercises is after the afternoon *(ʿaṣr)* prayer when the shaykh and his disciples gather in a circle silently to perform the Mujaddidī contemplations. Individual performance of the contemplations is recommended before or right after the morning prayer. From the Indian Mujaddidī *maʿmūlāt* works the original intentions in Persian with occasional Qur'ānic verses are only found in *ʿUmdat al-sulūk,* which I have supplemented by a more complete set of intentions from *Maʿmūlāt-i sayfī.*[1]

The Intentions

1. The Intention of the Contemplation of Exclusive Unity *(aḥadiyyat)*
   Divine grace comes from the eternal Essence that comprehen-

[1]This latter work is a Mujaddidī manual with an added set of intentions *(wuqūf-i murāqabāt),* formulated by an Afghan Mujaddidī, Shāh Rasūl aṭ-Ṭālqānī (d.1382/ 1962–3), which precede the ones given in *ʿUmdat al-sulūk.* See Abū'l-Asfār ʿAlī Muḥammad al-Balkhī, *Maʿmūlāt-i sayfī,* pp. 22–31. The intentions in *ʿUmdat al-sulūk* are found on pp. 285–301.

sively encompasses the [divine] attributes and [divine] perfections, is free from all imperfections and defects, and is incomparable [to anything created]. [This divine grace comes] to my heart *laṭīfa* by means of the great [Naqshbandī] pirs (r) *(pīrān-i kibār)*.

2. The Intention of the Contemplation of the Origin of the Heart
   O God, my heart faces the Prophet's (S) heart. The divine energy emanating from the active attributes which you have sent from the Prophet's (S) heart to Adam's (R) heart, convey it also to my heart by means of the great [Naqshbandī] pirs (r).
3. The Intention of the Contemplation of the Origin of the Spirit *(rūḥ)*
   O God, my spirit faces the Prophet's (S) spirit. The divine energy emanating from the eight immutable divine attributes which you have sent from the Prophet's (S) spirit to the spirits of Abraham and Noah, convey it also to my heart by means of the great [Naqshbandī] pirs (r).
4. The Intention of the Contemplation of the Origin of the Mystery
   O God, my mystery faces the Prophet's (S) mystery. The divine energy emanating from the divine qualities which you have sent from the Prophet's (S) mystery to Moses's mystery, convey it also to my mystery by means of the great [Naqshbandī] pirs (r).
5. The Intention of the Contemplation of the Origin of the Arcanum
   O God, my arcanum faces the Prophet's (S) arcanum. The divine energy emanating from the attributes of negation which you have sent from the Prophet's arcanum to Jesus's arcanum, convey it also to my arcanum by means of the great [Naqshbandī] pirs (r).
6. The Intention of the Contemplation of the Origin of the Super-Arcanum
   O God, my super-arcanum faces the Prophet's (S) super-arcanum. The divine energy emanating from the quality of comprehensive synthesis which you have sent to the Prophet's (S) super-arcanum, convey it also to my super-arcanum by means of the great [Naqshbandī] pirs (r).
7. The Intention of the Contemplation of Being Together With God *(maʿiyyat)*
   Divine energy comes from the eternal Essence that is with me and with all creation just as each atom of creation is with the Divine as understood in the blessed verse, "He is with you wherever you are" (Q. 57:4). [This divine energy comes] to my heart by means of the great [Naqshbandī] pirs (r).[2]
8. The Intention of the Contemplation of Close Proximity *(aqrabiyyat)*
   Divine energy comes from the eternal Essence which is the origin of the [divine] names and attributes and which is nearer to me than myself, even nearer to me than my jugular vein, an ineffable

[2]In *Maʿmūlāt-i sayfī* this reads the five *laṭīfas* of the world of divine command. For a complete overview of the different opinions concerning which *laṭīfa* should be associated with this contemplation, see *Manāhij al-sayr*, pp. 89–95.

(bilā kayf) nearness as understood in the blessed verse, "We are nearer to him than his jugular vein" (Q. 50:16). [This divine energy comes] to my soul *nafs laṭīfa* and the five *laṭīfas* of the world of divine command by means of the great [Naqshbandī] pirs (r).

9. The Intention of the First Contemplation of Love *(maḥabbat)*
   Divine energy comes from the eternal Essence, which is the origin's origin of the [divine] names and attributes, who loves me and I love Him as understood in the blessed verse, "He loves them and they love Him" (Q. 5.54). [This divine energy comes] to my soul *laṭīfa* by means of the great [Naqshbandī] pirs (r).
10. The Intention of the Second Contemplation of Love *(maḥabbat)*
    Divine energy comes from the eternal Essence, which is the origin's origin's origin of the [divine] names and attributes, who loves me and I love Him as understood in the blessed verse, "He loves them and they love Him" (Q. 5:54). [This divine energy comes] to my soul *laṭīfa* by means of the great [Naqshbandī] pirs (r).
11. The Intention of the Contemplation of the Arc's Circle
    Divine energy comes from the eternal Essence, which is the origin's origin's origin's origin of the [divine] names and attributes and the Arc's Circle, who loves me and I love Him as understood in the blessed verse, "He loves them and they love Him" (Q. 5:54). [This divine energy comes] to my soul *laṭīfa* by means of the great [Naqshbandī] pirs (r).
12. The Intention of the Contemplation of the Outward *(ism-i ẓāhir)*
    Divine energy comes from the eternal Essense who is called the outward name as understood in the blessed verse, "He is the first and the last and the outward and the inward and is the Knower of all things (Q. 57:3). [This divine energy comes] to my soul *laṭīfa* by means of the great [Naqshbandī] pirs (r).
13. The Intention of the Contemplation of the Inward *(ism-i bāṭin)*
    Divine energy comes from the eternal Essence who is called the inward name, is the origin of "highest proximity" [sometimes called] the proximity of the highest angels *(malā' al-a'lā)* as understood in the blessed verse, "He is the first and the last and the outward and the inward and is the Knower of all things" (Q. 57:3). [This divine energy comes] to three of my elements, water, air, and fire by means of the great [Naqshbandī] pirs (r).
14. The Intention of the Contemplation of the Perfections of Prophethood
    Divine energy comes from the eternal Essence, which is the origin of the perfections of prophethood, to my element earth by means of the great [Naqshbandī] pirs (r).
15. The Intention of the Contemplation of the Perfections of Messengership
    Divine energy comes from the eternal Essence, which is the origin of the perfections of messengership, to my consolidated *laṭīfas (hay'at-i waḥdānī)* by means of the great [Naqshbandī] pirs (r).

16. The Intention of the Contemplation of the Perfections of the Great Prophets *(anbiyā'-i ūlū al-ʿaẓm)*[3]
    Divine energy comes from the eternal Essence, which is the origin of the perfections of the great prophets to my consolidated *laṭīfas* by means of the great [Naqshbandī] pirs (r).
17. The Intention of the Contemplation of the Reality of the Divine Kaʿba
    Divine energy comes from the eternal Essence, to which all of creation prostrates and which is the origin of the reality of the divine Kaʿba. [This divine energy comes] to my consolidated *laṭīfas* by means of the great [Naqshbandī] pirs (r).
18. The Intention of the Contemplation of the Reality of the Glorious Qurʿan
    Divine energy comes from the [infinite] vastness of the eternal Divine Presence, which is the origin of the reality of the glorious Qur'an, to my consolidated *laṭīfas* by means of the great [Naqshbandī] pirs (r).
19. The Intention of the Contemplation of the Reality of Prayer *(ṣalāt)*
    Divine energy comes from the perfect [infinite] vastness of the eternal Divine Presence, which is the origin of the reality of prayer, to my consolidated *laṭīfas* by means of the great [Naqshbandī] pirs (r).
20. The Intention of the Contemplation of Pure Worshippedness *(maʿbūdiyyat-i ṣirfa)*
    Divine energy comes from the eternal Divine Presence, which is the origin of pure worshippedness, to my consolidated *laṭīfas* by means of the great [Naqshbandī] pirs (r).
21. The Intention of the Contemplation of the Reality of Abraham (R)
    Divine energy comes from the eternal Divine Presence who is the lover of His own attributes and who is the origin of the reality of Abraham (R). [This divine energy comes] to my consolidated *laṭīfas* by means of the great [Naqshbandī] pirs (r).
22. The Intention of the Contemplation of the Reality of Moses (R)
    Divine energy comes from the eternal Divine Presence who is the lover of His own essence and who is the origin of the reality of Moses (R). [This divine energy comes] to my consolidated *laṭīfas* by means of the great [Naqshbandī] pirs (r).
23. The Intention of the Contemplation of the Reality of Muḥammad (S)
    Divine energy comes from the eternal Divine Presence who is the lover and beloved of His own essence and who is the origin of the reality of Muḥammad (S). [This divine energy comes] to my consolidated *laṭīfas* by means of the great [Naqshbandī] pirs (r).
24. The Intention of the Contemplation of the Reality of Aḥmad (R)
    Divine energy comes from the eternal Divine Presence who is the beloved of His own essence and who is the origin of the reality of

[3]They are usually considered to be Adam, Abraham, Moses, Jesus, and Muḥammad.

Aḥmad (R). [This divine energy comes] to my consolidated *laṭīfas* by means of the great [Naqshbandī] pirs (r).

25. The Intention of the Contemplation of Pure Love
    Divine energy comes from the eternal Divine Presence, who is the source of pure love, to my consolidated *laṭīfas* by means of the great [Naqshbandī] pirs (R).
26. The Intention of the Contemplation of the Undifferentiated
    Divine energy comes from the absolute eternal Essence that is existent [along] with created existence and is free from all [created] manifestations. [This divine energy comes] to my consolidated *laṭīfas* by means of the great [Naqshbandī] pirs (r).

APPENDIX 4

Examples of Teaching Certificates

To give the reader an idea of the development of the certificate *(ijāzatnāma)* entitling Indian Mujaddidī shaykhs to teach, three samples from Aḥmad Saʿīd's (d. 1277/1860) lineage and two from Imām ʿAlī Shāh's (d. 1282/1865) lineage are reproduced below. The first two, translated from Persian and Arabic, illustrate how Aḥmad Shāh gave his successor, Dōst Muḥammad, first conditional *(muqayyad)* and then unconditional *(muṭlaq)* permission to teach.[1] The lengthy third certificate, originally written in Arabic, is the one Dōst Muḥammad gave to his successor, Muḥammad ʿUthmān (d. 1314/1896).[2] Following these is the certificate Ṣādiq ʿAlī Shāh (1317–8/1900) received from Imām ʿAlī Shāh and the certificate Ṣādiq ʿAlī Shāh gave to another pir's son, Farīd-uddīn, in 1865.[3]

The Certificate of Conditional Permission Given to Dōst Muḥammad

In the name of God, the Compassionate and Merciful after praise [to the Prophet this] poor one, Aḥmad Saʿīd Mujaddidī, [who is a Mujaddidī] both by spiritual pedigree *(nisbatan)* and by spiritual method *(ṭarīqan)*. God has clearly desired that [the one possessing] integrity and perfection of rank, Pilgrim of the two sacred places [Mecca and Medina] Mullā Ḥājjī Ḥaḍrat Dōst Muḥammad (may God love and be satisfied with him) come to this nobody

[1]Muḥammad Ismāʿīl, *Mawāhib raḥmāniyya fī fawāʾid wa-fuyūḍāt ḥaḍarāt thalātha dāmāniyya: al-tajalliyāt al-dōstiyya*, pp. 35–40.

[2]Muḥammad Ismāʿīl, *Mawāhib raḥmāniyya fī fawāʾid wa-fuyūḍāt ḥaḍarāt thalātha dāmāniyya: kamālāt-i ʿuthmāniyya*, pp. 49–55.

[3]Imām ʿAlī Shāh, *Maktūbāt-i Quṭb-i Rabbānī*, pp. 107–13.

[Aḥmad Saʿīd] for inner growth. For more than a year he has stayed near [this] poor one [Aḥmad Saʿīd] and during this time has quickly activated his ten subtle entities *(laṭīfas)*. May God be blessed that he has experienced the auspiciousness of the great pirs in each station, discovering the effects and lights found in each subtle entity and witnessing the signs of annihilation *(fanāʾ)* and remaining *(baqāʾ)* in himself. Therefore I gave permission to teach the way of the Naqshbandiyya-Mujaddidiyya, Qādiriyya, Chishtiyya, and Suhrawardiyya. May God Almighty favor him for life. It is necessary for him to adhere to the honored Path. The conditions of this permission are: to be established in the shariʿa, to follow the sunna, to avoid innovation, to continually recollect God, and to work with God Almighty (may He be praised) [to remove] people's obstacles and despair. Hope is from God Almighty as are patience and trust in God, contentment, satisfaction, and peace. End.

The Certificate of Unrestricted Permission Given to Dōst Muḥammad

In the name of God, Compassionate and Merciful, may the God of the two worlds be blessed. [May there be] blessings on the seal of the prophets and all his companions. The poor one, Aḥmad Saʿīd al-Mujaddidī, may God forgive him for everything, asks that God (may He be blessed) safeguard [this] Pilgrim who is righteous, honest, [and] honored with sincere integrity of the two sacred places [Mecca and Medina] and who comprehends the two worlds. Make [this Pilgrim], Maulānā Dōst Muḥammad, a beloved soul, a leader and guide among his people. When he entered the Path and began practicing the recollections *(adhkār)* of God and the contemplations, I supervised him in all the stations of the [following] paths: Naqshbandī-Mujaddidī, Qādirī, Chishtī, Suhrawardī, Kubrawī, and others. The confluence of oceans became the source of lights. He has unconditional permission to guide students while being inspired in the presence of God and being present in the hearts of the Elect. [In addition he has permission] to initiate seekers of the aforementioned paths according to Prophetic practice. He is my successor. His hand is my hand. How excellent is he who follows him. God (J) said that "Those who pledge allegiance to you [Muḥammad] pledge allegiance to God; the hand of God is over their hand" [Q. 48:10]. May God bless the best of his creation, our lord Muḥammad, and all his companions. End.

The Certificate of Unrestricted Permission Given to Muḥammad ʿUthmān

Blessings be to God and the Prophet. It is not hidden from the Elect of humankind nor the commoners that my righteous brother, repository of inner and outer perfections, the Maulwī Muḥammad ʿUthmān Ṣāhib (may God grant him peace) entered the exalted path of the Naqshbandiyya Mujaddidiyya Maʿṣūm-iyya Maẓhariyya from this poor nothing, Dōst Muḥammad, commonly named "Ḥājjī" (may God forgive him for everything). I supervised him in the heart *laṭīfa* and the progression of *laṭīfas* in the world of archetypes, whereupon lights and secrets were revealed to him. He experienced strong attractions *(jadhabāt)* [by God], manifest lights, total presence of God, and the pleasure of being overwhelmed [in the unity of God] which is the beginning of annihilation in God, the prerequisite of remaining in God.

Then I supervised him in the *nafs* and *qālab laṭīfa* where he experienced annihilation and vanishing [of self] of *fanāʾ* and descended from the source of effects. Then I supervised him in the contemplation of *aḥadiyya,* the circles of three intimacies *(wilāyat-i ṣughrā, kubrā, ʿulyā),* and he achieved the necessary presences of the intimates of God *(awliyāʾ),* the prophets, and the great angels. After this I supervised him in the three perfections and the seven realities, pure love, non-differentiation, and the cutting sword [see above, figure 7]. He achieved these stations by the favor of God. Whoever the great shaykhs (r) favor has good fortune and [experiences] many [mystical] states which are suitable for each station in their completeness of detail. Then I took him through all the stages of the path again until I helped him complete the path one more time. May God reward him.

Therefore he was my constant companion for seventeen years. [going] wherever I went, serving me in every way. May God Almighty bestow His treasures upon him. He became distinguished among both my companions and my loved ones. I gave him unrestricted permission *(ijāzat muṭlaq)* [to teach] the methods of the Naqshbandiyya Mujaddidiyya Maʿṣūmiyya Maẓhariyya and the Qādiriyya, Chishtiyya, Suhrawardiyya, Kubrawiyya, Shaṭṭāriyya, Madāriyya, Qalandariyya, and other sufi lineages.

So he became one of the Mujaddidī successors (r) based upon the authority of my guidance. After I go to God, the Guide, I will have transferred all my belongings to him. All the seekers, travelers, and others who have entered my group are among the companions who must follow his orders and not go against him after I pass away. His hand is like my hand and his acceptance is like my acceptance. How excellent is he who follows him and is patient with his orders. May God Almighty (may He be praised) make him one of the pious believers and make his soul *(nafs)* pure like [that of] Muḥammad (S).

Thus it is incumbent upon him [Muḥammad ʿUthmān] to follow the honored path and teach it to my students seeking God Almighty the Most Holy. May he find lights from among them through the pure attention he gives them. I urge him to maintain continuous recollection and thought of God, contemplation, solitude, [removing] people's despair and [giving] them hope in God. [He should in addition have] patience, contentment, satisfaction and trust in God, being satisfied in His judgment and being inclined toward God Almighty by means of the blessed shaykhs (r) to solve problems and difficulties. The condition of this permission is to act with integrity according to the Prophetic shariʿa and the Prophetic (S) sunna and to love the blessed shaykhs (r).

May God make him a [true] worshiper, ascetic, a grateful person, lover, putting His trust in God. May He bless him through his life and guide his acts so that he is protected and victorious in whatever he does. Amen. O Lord of the two worlds, honoring the lord of the messengers (S) [Muḥammad], sublime above the best of His creation, our lord Muḥammad, may he and all his companions have your mercy, O most Merciful One. May you put him in my care like my shaykh, my leader, exemplar, and protector from error safeguarded me, the person who memorized the blessed Qur'an, Shāh Aḥmad Saʿīd Ṣāḥib (through whom God blessed me with his most holy secret). [May God] put his [Aḥmad Saʿīd's] noble shaykh, the hundred and thirteenth renewer *(mujaddid)*, the representative of the best human (S) [Muḥammad], [with] the ten who go directly to paradise (R). Shāh ʿAbdullāh, known as Ghulām ʿAlī Shah [d. 1240/1824] (may God sanctify his honorable secret) is in the front of the foremost, without any defect. And with that, God benefits and gives to whom He wishes. God is the Master of Sublime Grace. The twenty-sixth of Ramaḍān, 1284 [1868]. End.

The Certificate of Permission Given to Sādiq ʿAlī Shāh

[Praise to God, Muḥammad, and his companions] To the masters of the shaykhs and the presences of the ulama (may their affairs be firmly and resplendently grounded in God) that in every place may God (be He praised) cause my guided son Ṣādiq ʿAlī to reach his goal. He came to me, to the most remote degree of men, to perform the practices *(sulūk)* of those on the path to God and to perform the exercises in the origins of states.

He encountered the connection of attraction [by God] and annihilation of self, so that he became blessed with [both] attraction and *sulūk.* With the help of divine attractions [by God] he traversed extensive stations of contingency, experiencing travel in the necessary stages from struggle to witnessing the divine essence and from [ordinary] travel to [flying] like a bird. With my help he was conveyed to behold the lights of the realities [and through this] changed by the qualities of God on the path of divinity and the extremity of materiality, being the object through which [God] manifests, [realizing] the gnosis of God's oneness intellectually and experientially. Connected with the realities of annihilation and remaining, he went to God *(sayr ila'llāh),* traveling in God *(sayr fi'llāh),* returning [to the world of creation] for God and by means of God *(sayr ʿan Allāh billāh)* before returning [to live as an apparently ordinary person] in the created world *(sayr fi'l-ashyā').*

When his attraction [by God] in *sulūk* became advanced, he was trained as "those desired by God" *(murādān)* and the attraction of [divine] favor was endless. In focusing spiritual attention *(taṣarruf)* he reached such a level to be qualified to train and perfect seekers. The son (may he be honored) has permission to invite seekers of God and those traveling on the way of God to God (J). Seekers informed of his companionship, service, and agreeable advice consider him to be "red sulfur" *(kibrīt aḥmar)* [a very rare and valuable person]. God knows [who will] bring forth my redemption from the perils and fruits of nearness at the end of time. It is bequeathed for [you to] educate, counsel, and give condolence to seekers, worthy ones, and [those with] the fear of God Almighty in Muḥammad's midnight journey through the seven heavens *(al-isrā'),* and to observe the correct conduct of the Path. You are my hope from the favor of god (may His gifts be continuous) who will, in the station of guidance, take care of the person [needing assistance] until the next world. He [God] caused a world to become filled with divine energy. In veneration of the Prophet and God the most glorious [Blessings on the Prophet, his family, and companions].

The Certificate of Permission Given to a Pir's Son, Farīduddīn

[Praise to God, Muḥammad, and his companions] In view of the proper way regarding those with understanding, may [I] clarify the fruit of one who is close to God, the praised excellences of my son, Farīduddīn, who God singled out when He created the world. He earned the hereditary connection *(nisbat)* of those who have arrived [at God's presence], the proof of the perfection-bestowing ones, the presence of his great father, who is the soul *(rūḥ)* of God spiritually and more arrived [in God's presence] than us with respect to auspiciousness and revelations. By means of this poor one he entered the exalted Naqshbandiyya-Mujaddidiyya path (may God Almighty sanctify its secrets) and benefited greatly. He learned the methods of continual recollection, performing the required contemplations by the criterion [established in] the blessed verse, "We guide those who strive in Us to Our paths" [Q. 29:69]. God Almighty only honors.

By the grace of the doorkeeper he has acquired gifts in his heart, [including] attraction [by God], divine secrets, and ecstasy, [all of] which have changed his life. During the time of being attracted and being overwhelmed [by God] he witnessed the stages of *sulūk* in light. He passed the paths of the heart and ladder of the soul *(rūḥ)*, arriving at the world of unveiling *(kashf)* and certainty. After traveling and flying through that to the angelic station and [then] the sphere of divine power in an eternally manifesting manner described in terms of God's attributes, he was honored by annihilation and remaining [in God]. Then he proceeded to God *(sayr ila'llāh)*, traveling in God *(sayr fi'llāh)*. When he went on the path of choice and clearly saw the ways of guidance and stations, he benefited from each experience.

He has permission to teach students and receive those repenting sins. Those prepared on the Way are aware that he is qualified in the perfections described [here]. [Besides] being very talented in companionship *(ṣuḥbat)*, he is a great elixir. People coming for repentance and initiation put a finger on his hand and are immediately attracted [by God]. Inside they experience endless lights [brought about by his] spiritual power. Heedless ones will have awareness and continual presence [with God]. You are my hope from the favor of God (may His name be honored). He gives His divine energy to the worthy among the commoners and the Elect. By the truth of the poles *(al-aqṭāb)* and supports *(al-awtād)* [of religion] . . . 1282 [1865–6].

BIBLIOGRAPHY

Islamic names without *nisbas* are alphabetized by first name.

Sources in Arabic, Persian, and Urdu

Abarquhī, Shamsuddīn Ibrāhīm. *Majmaʿ al-baḥrayn.* Ed. Najīb Māyil Harawī, Intishārāt-i Mawlā, 1985.

ʿAbdulḥayy, Ibn Fakhruddīn al-Ḥasanī. *Nuzhat al-khawāṭir wa-bahjat al-masāmiʿ wa'l-nawāẓir.* 3d ed. 9 vols. Hyderabad, Deccan: Osmania Oriental Publications Bureau, 1989.

ʿAbdullāh Jān. *Mu'nis al-mukhliṣīn.* Karachi: ʿAbbāsī Letter Art Press, 1947.

ʿAbdullāh Shāh. *Sulūk-i mujaddidiyya.* Ed. by ʿAbdurra'ūf Musāfir. Hyderabad, Deccan: Maṭbaʿ-i Dā'īra Machine Press, 1958.

Aḥmad Saʿīd, *Arbaʿ anhar.* Delhi: Maṭbaʿ-i Mujtabā'ī, 1893.

———. *Bi'l-fawā'id al-ḍābiṭa fī ithbāt al-rābiṭa.* N.p.: Maṭbaʿ-i Ḥusnā, 1875.

Aḥrārī, Abū'l-ʿUlā'ī. *Isrār-i Abū'l-ʿUlā.* Agra: Shamsī Machine Press, n.d.

Akhtar Ḥusayn. *Sīrat-i amīr-i millat.* 2d ed. Karachi: A. Ayndālīs Printers, 1982.

ʿAlawī, Amīnullāh. "Khwāja Ḥājjī Muḥammad Ṣiddīq Mastūngī." *Nūr al-Islām, Awliyā'-i Naqshband Nambar* 24/2 (March–April 1979): 233–44.

ʿAlī Aḥmad. *Shajaratun ṭayyibatun.* N.p., n.d.

Alūsī, Shihābuddīn al-. *Rūḥ al-maʿānī fī tafsīr al-qur'ān al-ʿaẓīm wa'l-sabʿ al-mathānī.* Beirut: Dār Iḥyā' al-Turāth al-ʿArabī, 1970.

Assī, Muḥammad Ḥusayn. *Anwār-i Lā Thānī.* 3d ed. Multan: Ruḥānī Art Press, 1985.

ʿAṭā' Ḥusayn. "Daqīqat as-sālikīn." Unpublished manuscript. Khānaqāh-i Munīʿmiyya, Gaya, Patna, India, n.d.

———. *Kayfiyat al-ʿārifīn.* Gaya, 1932.

ʿAṭṭār, Farīduddīn. *Dīwān-i qaṣā'id wa-ghazaliyāt.* Ed. Saʿīd Nafīsī. Teheran: Kitābkhāna-yi Ṣanā'ī, 1960.

ʿAynul-quḍāt. *Tamhīdāt.* Ed. ʿAfīf ʿUsayrān. Teheran: Intishārāt-i Dānishgāh-i Tihrān, 1962.

ʿAẓma, Nadhīr al-. *Al-miʿrāj wa'l-ramz al-ṣūfī.* Beirut: Dār al-Bāḥith, 1982.

Bahrā'ichī, Naʿīmullāh. *Maʿmūlāt-i maẓhariyya.* Kanpur: Maṭbaʿ-i Niẓāmi, 1858.

Bākharzī, Abū'l-Mufākhir Yaḥyā. *Awrād al-aḥbāb wa-fuṣuṣ al-ādāb.* 2 vols. Ed. Īrāj Afshār. Teheran: Intishārāt-i Farhang-i Īrān-zamīn, 1980.

Balkhī, Abū'l-Asfār ʿAlī Muḥammad al-. *Maʿmūlāt-i sayfī*. 4th ed. N.p., 1989.

Bāqībillāh. *Kulliyāt-i Bāqībillāh*. Ed. Abū'l-Ḥasan Fārūqī and Burhān Aḥmad Fārūqī. Lahore: Dīn-i Muḥammadī Press, n.d.

Barēlwī, Aḥmad Riḍā Khān. *Al-yāqūtat al-wāsiṭa fī qalb ʿaqd al-rābiṭa* [1891]. Lahore: Maḥmūd Riyāḍ Printers, 1987.

———. *Ḥadā'iq-i bakhshish*. Karachi: Medina Publishing Company, 1976.

———. *Naqā' al-salāf fī aḥkām al-bayʿa wa'l-khilāfa*. N.p., n.d.

Bīrbalī, Muḥammad ʿUmar. *Inqilāb al-ḥaqīqat*. 2d ed. Lahore: Āftāb-i ʿĀlam Press, n.d.

Bukhārā'ī, Aḥmad ʿAlī Rajā'ī. *Farhang-i ashʿār-i Ḥāfiẓ*. Teheran: Intishārāt-i ʿIlmī, 1980.

Bukhārī, Khurshīd Ḥasan. "Mughal siyāsat par awliyā'-i naqshband kā athar," *Nūr al-islām, awliyā'-i naqshband nambar* 24/1 (March–April 1979): 135–61.

Charkhī, Yaʿqūb. *Risāla-yi unsiyya*. Edited and Urdu translation by Muḥammad Nadhir Rānjhā. Lahore: Zāhid Bashīr Printers, 1983.

Dhawqī, Muḥammad. *Sirr-i dilbarān*. 4th ed. Karachi: Mashhūr Offset Press, 1985.

Dihlawi, ʿAbdulḥaqq. *Akhbār al-akhyār*. Gumbat: Fārūqī Academy, n.d.

———. *Takmīl al-īmān*. Madras: Hāshimī Press, 1872.

Dihlawī, Abū Saʿīd. *Hidāyat al-tālibīn*. Urdu translation by Ghulām Muṣṭafā Khān. *Jawāhir-i maẓhariyya wa-maẓāhir-i zawwāriyya*. Karachi, 1954.

Fārūqī, Abū'l-Ḥasan Zayd. *Manāhij al-sayr*. Urdu translation by Muḥammad Naʿīmullāh Khiyālī. *Madārij al-khayr*. Delhi: Shāh Abū'l-Khayr Academy, 1983.

Fārūqī, Iqbāl Aḥmad. *Tadhkira-yi ahl-i sunnat wa-jamāʿat Lāhūr*. Lahore: Maktaba-yi Nabawiyya, 1987.

Furūzānfar, Badīʿuzzamān. *Aḥādīth-i mathnawī*. 3d ed. Teheran: Intishārāt-i Amīr Kabīr, 1983.

Ghazzālī, Abū Ḥāmid al-. *Iḥyā' ʿulūm al-dīn*. 5 vols. Cairo: Al-dār al-Miṣriyya al-Libnāniyya, n.d.

Ghujduwānī, ʿAbdulkhāliq. "Risāla-yi ṣāḥibiyya." Ed. S. Nafīsī. *Farhang-i Īrānzamīn* 1 (1954): 70–101.

Ghulām ʿAlī Shāh. *Makātīb-i sharīfa* [1916]. Istanbul: Ihlās Vakfı, 1989.

———. *Maqāmāt-i maẓharī*. Edited and Urdu translation by Muḥammad Iqbāl Mujaddidī. Lahore: Urdu Science Board, 1983.

Gunābādī, Muḥammad. *Walāyat nāma*. 2d ed. Teheran: Dānishgāh-i Īrān, 1965.

Ḥakīm al-Nīsābūrī, Muḥammad b. ʿAbdullāh al-. *Al-mustadrak ʿalā al-ṣaḥīḥayn fiʾl-ḥadīth*. Hyderabad, Deccan: Maṭbaʿat Majlis Dāʾirat al-Maʿārif al-Niẓāmiyya, 1915.

Hamadānī, Muḥammad Ṣādiq Dihlawī Kashmīrī. *Kalimāt al-ṣādiqīn*. Ed. Muḥammad Salīm Akhtar. Lahore: Īmān Printers, 1988.

Ḥaqqī, Ismāʿīl. *Rūḥ al-bayān fī tafsīr al-qurʾān*. 6 vols. Cairo: Al-maṭbaʿat al-Amīra, 1870.

Ḥasanī, Aḥmad b. ʿAjība al-. *Īqāẓ al-himam fī sharḥ al-ḥikam*. Cairo: Maṭbaʿat Muṣṭafā al-Bābī al-Ḥalabī, 1961.

Hujwīrī, ʿAlī Ibn ʿUthmān al-Jullābī al-. *Kashf al-maḥjūb*. Ed. Valentine Zhukovski. Leningrad: Dār al-ʿUlūm Ittiḥād Jamāhīr Shūrawī Sūsiyālīstī, 1926.

Humāʾī, Jalāluddīn. *Taṣawwuf dar islām*. Teheran: Sāzmān-i Wīrā, 1983.

Ibn al-ʿArabī, Muḥyīddin. *Al-futūḥāt al-makkiyya*. 14 vols. Ed. ʿUthmān Yaḥyā. Cairo: Al-hayʾat al-Miṣriyya al-ʿĀmma lil-Kitāb, 1987.

Ibn Khaldūn, ʿAbdurraḥmān Muḥammad. *Shifāʾ al-sāʾil li-tahdhīb al-masāʾil*. Ed. Muḥammad Ibn Tāwīt aṭ-Ṭanjī. Istanbul: Osman Yalçin Matbaası, 1958.

Imām ʿAlī Shāh. *Maktūbāt-i quṭb-i rabbānī*. Lahore: Lahore Cooperative Printing Press, 1940.

Jaipūrī, Muḥammad Hidāyat ʿAlī. *Miʿyār al-sulūk wa-dāfiʿ al-awhām waʾl-shukūk*. Kanpur: Maṭbaʿ-i Intiẓāmī, 1927.

Jamāʿat ʿAlī Shāh. "Ḍarūrat-i murshid." In *Irshādāt-i amīr-i millat*. Ed. Muḥammad Ṣādiq Quṣūrī. N.p., 1983, pp. 16–61.

———. "Yārān-i ṭarīqat yā pīr bhāʾī." In *Irshādāt-i amīr-i millat*. Ed. Muḥammad Ṣādiq Quṣūrī, N.p., 1983, pp. 63–111.

Jāmī, ʿAbdurraḥmān. *Nafaḥāt al-uns min ḥaḍarāt al-quds*. Ed. M. Tawḥīdīpūr. Teheran: Kitābfurūshī Maḥmūdī, 1959.

———. *Sarrishta-yi ṭarīqa-yi khwājagān*. Ed. ʿAbdulḥayy Ḥabībī. Kabul: Riyāsat-i Tanwīr-i Afkār dar Wazārat-i Maṭbūʿāt, 1964.

Jīlī, ʿAbdulkarīm al-. *Kitāb al-insān al-kāmil*. Ed. Marijan Molé. Paris: Adrien-Maisonneuve, 1962.

Kākūrī, Muḥammad Taqī Anwar ʿAlawī. *Ḥaḍrat Sulṭān al-awliyāʾ Khwāja ʿUbaydullāh Aḥrār Naqshbandī*. Faydabad, India: Nishāṭ Offset Press, 1986.

Kalābādhī, Abū Bakr Muḥammad al-. *Kitāb al-taʿarruf li-madhhab ahl al-taṣawwuf*. Cairo: Maktabat al-Khanjī, 1934.

Kalānūrī, ʿĀshiq ʿAlī Khān Nāṭiq. *Lamaʿāt-i kamālāt-i qādiriyya maʿ*

muʿāwin-i tabarrukāt-i khāliqiyya [1934]. Lahore: Khurram Printing, 1987.

Kāshānī, ʿIzzuddīn Maḥmūd. *Miṣbāḥ al-hidāya*, 2d ed. Ed. Jalāluddīn Humāʾī. Teheran: Kitābkhāna-yi Ṣanāʾī, 1946.

Kāshifī, Fakhruddīn ʿAlī Ṣafī. *Rashaḥāt-i ʿayn al-ḥayāt*. 2 vols. Ed. ʿAlī Aṣghar Muʿīnīyān. Teheran: Bunyad-i Nēkūkārī-yi Nūrānī, 1977.

Khayrī, Khālid Amīn Makhfī al-. *Silsila-yi khayriyya maʿ tadhkira-yi naqshbandiyya*. Lahore: Shirkat Pazang Press, 1981.

Kishmī Badakhshānī, Muḥammad Hāshim. *Nasamāt al-quds*. Urdu translation by Maḥbūb Ḥasan Wāsiṭī. Sialkot: Maktaba-yi Nuʿmāniyya, 1990.

———. *Zubdat al-maqāmāt*. Lucknow: Nawal Kishōr, 1890. Rpt. Istanbul: Işik Kitabevi, 1977.

Kiyānī, Muḥsin. *Tārīkh-i khānaqāh dar Īrān*. Teheran: Kitābkhāna-yi Ṭahūrī, 1990.

Kubrā, Najmuddīn. *Die Fawāʾiḥ al-ǧamāl wa-fawātiḥ al-ǧalāl des Naǧm ud-dīn al-Kubrā*. Introduction to Arabic edition by Fritz Meier. Wiesbaden: Franz Steiner, 1957.

Kulaynī, Muḥammad Ibn Yaʿqūb al-. *Al-uṣūl al-kāfī fī ʿilm al-dīn*. Lucknow, 1885.

Lāhūrī, Ghulām Sarvar. *Khazīnat al-aṣfiyāʾ*. 2 vols. Lucknow: Nawal Kishōr Press, 1864.

Maḥbūb ʿAlī. *Khayr-i khayr, marghūb al-sulūk*. Amritsar: Electric Press, 1917.

Maḥbūb-i ʿĀlam. *Dhikr-i kathīr: maḥbūb al-sulūk* [1918]. 3d ed. Lahore: Millī Printers, n.d.

Maḥbūbilāhī, *Tuḥfa-yi saʿdiyya*. Lahore: Al-ḥamra Art Printers, 1979.

Makkī, Abū Ṭālib al-. *Qūt al-qulūb fī muʿāmalāt al-māḥbūb wa-waṣf ṭarīq al-murīd ilā maqām al-tawḥīd*. 2 vols. Cairo: Muṣṭafā al-Bābī al-Ḥalabī, 1961.

Mānḍawī Ghawthī, Muḥammad. *Gulzār-i abrār*. Urdu translation by Faḍl Aḥmad Jēwarī. *Adhkār-i abrār, Urdū tarjuma-yi gulzār-i abrār* [1808]. Lahore: Islamic Book Foundation, 1975.

Manūfī, Maḥmūd Abū Fayḍ al-. *Jamharat al-awliyāʾ*. 2 vols. Cairo: Muʾassasat al-Ḥalabī, 1967.

Maʿshūq Yār Bahādur. *Maqāmāt-i Maḥmūd*. N.p., n.d.

Mazārī, Niẓāmuddīn Balkhī. *Ṭuḥfat al-murshid*. Lahore: Maṭbaʿ-i Fayḍ-i ʿĀmm, 1912.

Mīr Khurd. *Siyar al-awliyāʾ fī maḥabbat al-ḥaqq jalla wa-ʿalāʾ* [1885]. 2d ed. Lahore: Chāpkhāna-yi Maʿārif, 1978.

Mīr Nuʿmān. *Risāla-yi sulūk*. Karachi: Barqī Press, 1965.

Miyān Akhlāq Aḥmad. *Tadhkira-yi Haḍrat Īshān*. Lahore: Imtiyāz-i Fayāḍ Printing Press, 1985.

Muḥammad Amīn. *Ithbāt-i taṣawwur-i shaykh*. 3d ed. Lahore: Dīn-i Muḥammadī Press, n.d.

Muḥammad Faḍlullāh. *ʿUmdat al-maqāmāt*. Jalalabad, n.d.

Muḥammad Ḥasan. *Ḥālāt-i mashā'ikh-i Naqshbandiyya-Mujaddidiyya*. Lahore: National Printing Press, n.d.

Muḥammad Ḥasan Jān. *Al-uṣūl al-arbaʿ fī tardīd al-wahhābiyya* [1927]. Istanbul: Hakîkat Kitabevi, 1989.

———. *Tadhkirat al-ṣulaḥā' fī bayān al-atiqiyā'*. Kanpur: Al-maṭābiʿ-i Tupkāpūr, 1929.

Muḥammad Ibn Munawwar. *Asrār al-tawḥīd fī maqāmāt Shaykh Abī Saʿīd*. Ed. Muḥammad Riḍā Shāfīʿī Kadkanī. 2 vols. Teheran: Intishārāt-i Agāh, 1987.

Muḥammad ʿInāyatullāh. *Maqāmāt-i irshādiyya* [1911]. Urdu translation by Muḥammad Allāh Khān. *Maʿārif-i ʿināyatiyya*. Lahore: Muḥammadī Press, 1959.

Muḥammad Ismāʿīl. *Mawāhib raḥmāniyya fī fawā'id wa-fuyūḍāṭ ḥaḍarāt thalātha dāmāniyya: kamālāt-i ʿuthmāniyya*. Lahore: Urdu Art Printers, 1986.

———. *Mawāhib raḥmāniyya fī fawā'id wa-fuyūḍāt ḥaḍarāt thalātha dāmāniyya: al-tajalliyāt al-dōstiyya*. Lahore: Caravan Press, 1985.

———. *Mawāhib raḥmāniyya fī fawā'id wa-fuyūḍāt ḥaḍarāt thalātha dāmāniyya: maqāmāt-i sirājiyya*. Lahore: M. S. Printers, 1989.

Muḥammad Masʿūd Aḥmad. *Sīrat-i mujaddid-i alf-i thānī*. Karachi: Medina Publishing Company, 1974.

Muḥammad Maʿṣūm. *Ḥasanāt al-ḥaramayn*. Ed. by Muḥammad ʿUbaydullāh. Urdu translation by Muḥammad Iqbāl Mujaddidī. Lahore: Ḥimāyat-i Islam Press, 1981.

———. *Maktūbāt-i maʿṣūmiyya*. 3 vols. Ed. by Ghulām Muṣṭafā Khān. Karachi: Walend Military Press, n.d.

Muḥammad Maṭlūb ar-Rasūl. *Anwār-i Haḍrat Lillāhī*. 2d ed. Rawalpindi: S. T. Printers, 1986.

Muḥammad Qamaruddīn. *Anwār-i murtaḍawī*. Sargodha: Qāḍī Muḥammad Riḍā Nallī, 1909.

Muḥāsibī, al-Ḥārith al-. *Kitāb al-riʿāya li-ḥuqūq Allāh*. Ed. Margaret Smith. London, 1940.

Mujaddidī, Muḥammad Iqbāl. *Aḥwāl wa-āthār-i ʿAbdullāh Khūshagī Quṣūrī*. Lahore: Ashraf Press, 1972.

Munawwar Ḥusayn. "Taṣawwur-i shaykh." In *Shajaratun ṭayyibatun*. Lahore, n.d., p. 31.

Munāwī, ʿAbdurra'ūf al-. *Al-kawākib al-durriyya fī tarājim al-sadāt al-ṣūfiyya*. Cairo: Maṭbaʿat Wūrshāt Tajlīd al-Anwār, n.d.

Munīr Ḥusayn. *Inshirāḥ al-ṣadūr bi-tadhkirat al-nūr*. Gujarat: Small State Industries, 1983.

Muslim. *Ṣaḥīḥ Muslim*. 5 vols. Ed. Muḥammad Fu'ād ʿAbdulbāqī. Beirut: Dār Iḥyā' al-Turāth al-ʿArabī, 1956.

Muʿtamadī, Mahīndokht. *Maulānā Khālid Naqshband*. Teheran: Pazhang Publishing, 1990.

Nadwī, Abū'l-Ḥasan ʿAlī. *Tadhkira-yi Ḥaḍrat Maulānā Faḍl Raḥmān Ganj Murādābādī (r)*. Lucknow: Tanwīr-i Barqī Press, 1958.

Naʿīmī, Muḥammad Iqbāl Ḥusayn. *Tadhkira-yi awliyā'-i Sindh*. Karachi: Shāriq Publishers, 1987.

Nāmaqī, Abū Aḥmad Jām. *Rawḍat al-mudhnibīn wa-jannat al-mushtāqīn*. Ed. ʿAlī Fāḍl. Teheran: Intishārāt-i Bunyād-i Farhang-i Īrān, 1977.

Naqshband, Ḥujjatullāh. *Wasīlat al-qabūl ilā Allāh wa'l-rasūl*. Hyderabad, Sind: Saʿīd Art Press, 1963.

Naushāhī, Aḥmad Sharāfat. *Sharīf al-tawārīkh*. 3 vols. in 14 parts. Lahore: Bakhtiyār Printers, 1979.

Nīsābūrī, Ḥasan b. Muḥammad al-. *Kitāb ʿuqalā' al-majānīn*. Ed. ʿUmar al-Asʿad. Damascus: Dār al-Nafās, 1987.

Nūr Aḥmad Maqbūl. *Khazīna-yi karam*. Karachi: Kirmānwālā Publishers, 1978.

Pānīpatī, Qāḍī Thanā'ullāh. *Irshād al-ṭālibīn*. Lahore: Fērūz Printing Works, n.d.

Panjab Endowments Department. *Fihrist-i aʿrās-i mazārāt*. Unpublished list.

Pārsā, Muḥammad. *Qudsiyya: Kalimāt-i Bahā'uddīn Naqshband*. Ed. Aḥmad Ṭāhirī ʿIrāqī. Teheran: Kitābkhāna-yi Ṭahūrī, 1975.

———. *Risāla-yi qudsiyya*. Ed. Malik Muḥammad Iqbāl. Lahore: Jadīd Press, 1975.

———. *Tuḥfa al-sālikīn: taḥqīqāt Khwāja Muḥammad Pārsā*. Ed. Ḥakīm Miṣbāḥuddīn. Delhi, n.d.

Pūrjawādī, Naṣrullāh, *Sulṭān-i ṭarīqat: sawānih zindagī wa-sharh-i athār-i Khwāja Aḥmad Ghazzālī*. Teheran: Intishārāt-i Agāh, 1979.

Qādirī, Amīr Shāh. *Tadhikira-yi ʿulamā' wa-mashā'ikh-i Sarḥad*. 2 vols. Peshawar, n.d.

Qānūngū'ī, Qā'imuddīn. *Dhikr-i mubārak: mashā'ikh-i sādāt-i Makān Sharīf*. Lahore: Muʿaẓẓam Printers, n.d.

Quddūsī, Iʿjāzulḥaqq. *Tadhkira-yi ṣūfiyā'-i Sarḥad*. Lahore: Markazī Urdu Board, 1966.

Qushshāshī, Aḥmad b. Muḥammad al-. *Al-simṭ al-majīd fī shā'n al-bayʿat wa'l-dhikr wa-talqīnihi wa-salāsil ahl al-tawḥīd*. Hyderabad, Deccan: Maṭbaʿat Majlis Dā'irat al-Maʿārif al-Niẓāmiyya, 1909.

Qushayrī, Abū'l-Qāsim ʿAbdulkarīm al-. *Al-risāla al-qushayriyya fī ʿilm al-taṣawwuf.* 2 vols. Ed. ʿAbdulḥalīm Muḥmūd and Maḥmūd b. ash-Sharīf. Cairo: Maṭbaʿt al-Ḥassān, 1974.

———. *Laṭāʾif al-ishārāt.* 3 vols. Ed. Ibrāhīm al-Basyūnī. Cairo: Markaz Taḥqīq al-Turāth, 1981.

Quṣūrī, Ghulām Muḥyīddīn. *Malfūẓāt-i sharīf.* Ed. Muḥammad Iqbāl Mujaddidī. Urdu translation by Iqbāl Aḥmad Fārūqi. Lahore: Al-maʿārif Press, 1978.

Quṣūrī, Muḥammad Ḥusayn. *Maktūbāt-i sharīf.* Delhi, n.d.

Quṣūrī, Muḥammad Ibrāhīm. *Khazīna-yi maʿrifat.* Lahore: Naqūsh Press, n.d.

Quṣūrī, Muḥammad Ṣādiq. "Asātidha-yi amīr-i millat." Unpublished manuscript, 1988.

———. *Tadhkira-yi Nashbandiyya-Khayriyya.* Lahore: Ḥāmid Jamīl Printers, 1988.

Quṣūrī, Muḥammad Ṣādiq, and Muḥammad ʿAbdulqayyūm Khān. *Amīr-i millat (r) awr al indiyā sunnī kānfarans.* Lahore: Abū al-Maʿālī Printing Press, 1991.

Raḥmān ʿAlī. *Tadhkira-yi ʿulamāʾ-i Hind.* Lucknow: Nawal Kishōr Press, 1894.

Rūmī, Maulānā Jalāluddīn. *Kitāb-i fīhi mā fīhi.* Ed. Badīʿuzzamān Furūzānfar. Teheran: Chāpkhāna-yi Majlis, 1951.

———. *Mathnawī-yi maʿnawī.* 10th ed. 6 vols. Ed. Reynold Nicholson. Teheran: Intishārāt-i Amīr Kabīr, 1988.

Safīr Akhtar, *Tadhkira-yi ʿulamā-i Panjāb.* 2 vols. Lahore: Zāʾid Bashīr Printers, 1980.

Sajjādī, ʿAli Muḥammad. *Hāma-yi zuhd: khirqa wa-khirqapūshī.* Teheran: Intishārāt-i ʿIlmī wa-Farhangī, 1991.

Samarqandī, Dawlatshāh. *Tadhkirat al-shuʿarāʾ.* Teheran: Intishārāt-i Padīda-yi Khawār, 1987.

Sarrāj, Abū Naṣr as-. *Kitāb al-lumaʿ fīʾl-taṣawwuf.* Ed. Reynold A. Nicholson. London, 1914.

Sayfuddīn. *Maktūbāt-i sayfiyya.* Comp. Muḥammad Aʿẓam. Ed. Ghulām Muṣṭafā Khān. Hyderabad, Sind: Saʿid Art Press, n.d.

Sharaf, Muḥammad ʿAbdulḥakīm. *Tadhkira-yi akābir-i ahl-i sunnat (Pākistān).* 3d ed. Lahore: Rūmī Printers, 1989.

Shārib, Ẓuhūr al-Ḥasan. *Tārīkh-i ṣūfiyāʾ-i Gujarāt.* Ahmadabad: Jamīl Academy, 1981.

Shikārpūrī, Faqīrullāh. "Futūḥāt al-ghaybiyya." Unpublished manuscript. Khundian Sharīf, n.d.

———. *Quṭb al-irshād.* Quetta: Maktaba-yi Islāmiyya, 1978.

———. *Maktūbāt-i Faqīrullāh.* Ed. Maulwī Karam Bakhsh. Lahore: Islāmiyya Steam Press, n.d.

Ṣiddīq Aḥmad, *Dhikr-i maḥbūb*. 3d ed. Gujranwala: Bazm-i Tawakkuliyya, 1977.

Simnānī, ʿAlāʾuddawla. "Khitām al-misk." In *Opera Minora*. Ed. Wheeler Thackson. Cambridge: Harvard University Office of the University Publisher, 1988.

Sīnā, Abū ʿAlī. *Miʿrājnāma*. 2d ed. Ed. Najīb Māyil Harawī. Teheran: Intishārāt-i Āstān-i Quds-i Riḍawī, 1987.

Sirhindī, ʿAbdulaḥad Waḥdat. *Gulshan-i waḥdat*. Ed. ʿAbdullāh Jān Fārūqī. Karachi: Educational Press, 1966.

———. *Sabīl al-rashād*. Urdu translation by Ghulām Muṣṭafā Khān. N.p., 1979.

Sirhindī, Aḥmad. *Mabdaʾ wa-maʿād*. Karachi: Aḥmad Brothers, 1984.

———. *Maktūbāt-i imām-i rabbānī*. 3 vols. Ed. Nūr Aḥmad. Karachi: Educational Press, 1972.

———. *Mukāshafa-yi ʿayniyya*. Urdu translation by Ghulām Muṣṭafā Khān. Karachi: Educational Press, 1965.

Sirhindī, Kamāluddīn Muḥammad Iḥsān. *Rawḍat al-qayyūmiyya*. 4 vols. Urdu translation by Iqbāl Aḥmad Fārūqī. Lahore: Maktaba-yi Nabawiyya, 1989.

Suhrawardī, Shihābuddīn ʿUmar as-. *Kitāb ʿawārif al-maʿārif*. Beirut: Dār al-Kutub al-ʿArabī, 1966.

Sulamī, Abū ʿAbdurraḥmān Muḥammad as-. *Adāb al-ṣuḥba wa-ḥusn al-muʿāshara*. Edited by M. J. Kister. Yafa: Maṭbaʿat al-Ḥukūma, 1954.

———. *Jawāmiʿ ādāb al-murīdīn*. Ed. Etan Kohlberg. Jerusalem: Jerusalem Academic Press, 1976.

———. *Kitāb ṭabaqāt al-ṣūfiyya*. Ed. Johannes Pedersen. Leiden: E. J. Brill, 1960.

———. *Manāhij al-ʿārifīn*. Ed. E. Kohlberg. From "A Treatise on Ṣūfism by Abū ʿAbd Al-Rahmām [sic] al-Sulami." In *Jerusalem Studies in Arabic and Islam* 1 (1979): 25.

Tawakkulī, Muḥammad Nūr Bakhsh. *Tadhkira-yi mashāʾikh-i naqshband*. With an afterword by Muḥammad Ṣādiq Quṣūrī. Gujarat: Faḍl-i Nūr Academy, n.d.

T'hānawī, Ashraf ʿAlī. *Tarbiyat al-sālik* [1911]. 2d ed. 3 vols. Karachi: Moss Printers, 1982.

Walīullāh, Shāh. *Al-qawl al-jamīl*. Urdu translation by Khurram ʿAlī. 2d ed. *Shifāʾ alʿalīl*. Karachi: Educational Press, 1974.

———. *Alṭāf al-quds*. Gujranwala, 1964.

———. *Anfās alʿārifīn*. Multan: Islāmī Kutubkhāna, n.d.

———. *Intibāh fī salāsil awliyāʾ Allāh*. Lyallpur: Panjab Electric Press, n.d.

———. *Shāh Walīullāh Dihlawī kē siyāsī maktūbāt.* Ed. K. A. Nizāmī. Dehli: Nadwat al-Muṣannifīn, 1969.

Yārkandī, Mīr Khāluddīn Kātib b. Maulānā Qāḍī Shāh Kūchak al-. *Hidāyat nāma.* British Museum mss. Oriental 8162.

Zarrīnkūb, ʿAbdulḥusayn. "Justujū dar taṣawwuf-i Īrān (3)." In *Majallah-i Dānishkadah-i Adabiyāt-i ʿUlūm-i Insānī* 21/2 (1974): 1–28.

Zawwār Ḥusayn. *Ḥaḍrat mujaddid-i alf-i thānī.* Karachi: Idāra-yi Mujaddidiyya, 1983.

———. *Ḥayāt-i saʿīdiyya.* Karachi: Aḥmad Brothers Printers, 1987.

———. *ʿUmdat al-sulūk.* 5th ed. Karachi: Aḥmad Brothers Printers, 1984.

Sources in European Languages

Addas, Claude. *Ibn ʿArabī ou la quête du soufre rouge.* Paris: Éditions Gallimard, 1989. Translated by Peter Kingsley, *Quest for the Red Sulphur: The Life of Ibn ʿArabi.* Cambridge: Islamic Texts Society, 1993.

Algar, Hamid. "Bahā Al-Dīn Naqshband." In *Encyclopaedia Iranica,* 1983.

———. "A Brief History of the Naqshbandī Order." In *Naqshbandis: Historical Development and Present Situation of a Muslim Mystical Order.* Ed. Marc Gaborieau, Alexandre Popovic, and Thierry Zarcone. Istanbul: Éditions Isis, 1990, pp. 1–44.

———. "Elements de provenance Malāmatī dans la tradition primitive Naqshbandī." Unpublished paper given at Colloque sur les Mélamlis et les Bayramis, Istanbul, 4–6 June 1987.

———. "Political Aspects of Naqshbandī History." In *Naqshbandis: Historical Development and Present Situation of a Muslim Mystical Order.* Ed. Marc Gaborieau, Alexandre Popovic, and Thierry Zarcone. Istanbul: Éditions Isis, 1990, pp. 123–52.

———. "Silent and Vocal Dhikr in the Naqshbandī Order." In *Akten des VII. Kongresses für Arabistik und Islamwissenschaft.* Göttingen: Vandenhoeck and Ruprecht, 1976, pp. 39–46.

Allāh Yār Khān. *Dalāʾil al-sulūk.* Trans. Abu Talha. *An Objective Appraisal of the Sublime Sufi Path.* 2d ed. Lahore: M. F. Printers, 1987.

ʿAllāmī, Abū'l-Faḍl. *Akbar nāma.* Trans. H. Beveridge. *Akbarnāmah: History of the Reign of Akbar Including an Account of His Predecessors* [1868–1894]. 3 vols. Delhi: Ess Ess Publications, 1977.

Amir-Moezzi, Mohammad Ali. *Le Guide Divine dans le Shiʿisme Originel.* Lagrasse: Éditions Verdier, 1993. Trans. David

Streight. *The Divine Guide in Early Shiʿism: The Sources of Esotericism in Islam.* Albany: State University of New York Press, 1994.

Anderson, Benedict. *Imagined Communities: Reflections on the Origin and Spread of Nationalism.* 2d ed. New York: Verso, 1991.

Andrae, Tor. *Die Person Muhammads in Lehre und Glaube seiner Gemeinde.* Stockholm: P.A. Vorstedt Og Söner, 1918.

Ansari, Abdul Haqq. *Sufism and Shariʿah: A Study of Shaykh Aḥmad Sirhindi's Effort to Reform Sufism.* Leicester: Islamic Foundation, 1986.

Ansari, Sara F.D. "Political Legacies of Pre-1947 Sind." In *The Political Inheritance of Pakistan.* Ed. D. A. Low. New York: St. Martin's Press, 1991, pp. 173–93.

———. *Sufi Saints and State Power: The Pirs of Sind, 1843–1947.* Cambridge: Cambridge University Press, 1992.

Appadurai, Arjun. "Number in Colonial Imagination." In *Orientalism and the Postcolonial Predicament: Perspectives on South Asia.* Ed. Carol A. Breckenridge and Peter van der Veer. Philadelphia: University of Pennsylvania Press, 1993, pp. 314–39.

———. *Worship and Conflict under Colonial Rule: A South Indian Case.* Cambridge: Cambridge University Press, 1981.

Arnold, Thomas. *Preaching of Islam: A History of the Propagation of the Muslim Faith.* London: Constable Press, 1913.

Awliyāʾ, Niẓāmuddīn. *Fawāʾid al-fuʾād.* Comp. Amīr Ḥasan Sijizī. Trans. Bruce B. Lawrence. *Nizam Ad-Din Awliya: Morals for the Heart.* New York: Paulist Press, 1992.

Awn, Peter. *Satan's Tragedy and Redemption: Iblis in Sufi Psychology.* Leiden: E. J. Brill, 1983.

Bābur. *Bābur Nāma.* Trans. Annette S. Beveridge. *The Memoirs of Babur* [1921]. 2 vols. Delhi: Low Cost Publications, 1989.

———. *The Baburnama: Memoirs of Babur, Prince and Emperor.* Trans. Wheeler Thackson Jr. Washington, D.C.: Smithsonian Institution, 1995.

Badāʾūnī, ʿAbdulqādir. *Muntakhab at-tawārīkh* [1884–1925]. Ed. W. Nassau Lees, Kabīruddīn Maulwī, and Maulwī Aḥmad ʿAlī. English translation by G. Ranking (vol. 1), W. H. Lowe (vol. 2), and T. W. Haig (vol. 3). 3 vols. Delhi: Idarah-i Adabiyat-i Delli, 1973.

Baig, Ubaidullah, and Brohi, A. A. K. *Journey into Light: An Instant Guide to Devotional Tours.* Islamabad: Pakistan Tourism Development Corporation, 1985.

Baljon, J. M. S. *Religion and Thought of Shāh Walī Allāh Dihlawī, 1703–1762.* Leiden: E. J. Brill, 1986.

Barrier, N. Gerald, and Paul Wallace. *The Punjab Press, 1880–1905.* East Lansing, Mich.: Asian Studies Center, 1970.

Bartol'd, V. V. "O Pogrebenii Timura." Translated by J. M. Rogers. "V. V. Bartol'd's Article *O Pogrebenii Timura* ("The Burial of Tīmūr")." In *Iran* 12 (1974): 65–87.

Berkey, Jonathan. *The Transmission of Knowledge in Medieval Cairo: A Social History of Islamic Education.* Princeton: Princeton University Press, 1992.

Bharati, Agehananda. "The Hindu Renaissance and Its Apologetic Patterns." *Journal of Asian Studies* 29/2 (February 1970): 267–88.

Bosworth, C. E. "Karrāmiyya." In *Encyclopaedia of Islam,* 2d ed., 1978.

Böwering, Gerhard. *The Mystical Vision of Existence in Classical Islam: The Qur'ānic Hermeneutics of the Sūfī Sahl At-Tustarī (d. 283/896).* New York: Walter De Gruyter, 1980.

Boyce, Merrill Tilghman. *British Policy and the Evolution of the Vernacular Press in India, 1835–1878.* Delhi: Chanakya Publications, 1988.

Brenner, Louis. *West African Sufi: The Religious Heritage and Spiritual Search of Cerno Bokar Saalif Taal.* London: C. Hurst and Company, 1984.

Brown, Peter. "The Rise and Function of the Holy Man in Late Antiquity." *Journal of Roman Studies* 61 (1971): 80–101.

———. "The Saint as Exemplar in Late Antiquity." *Representations* 1/2 (Spring 1983): 1–23.

Buehler, Arthur F. "Charismatic Versus Scriptural Authority: Naqshbandī Response to Deniers of Mediational Sufism in British India." In Frederik de Jong and Bernd Radtke, eds., *Islamic Mysticism Contested: Thirteen Centuries of Debate and Conflict.* Leiden: E. J. Brill, 1998.

———. "Jamā'at 'Alī Shāh." In *Dictionnaire biographique des savants et grandes figures du monde musulman périphériqe du XIXe siècle à nos jours.* Ed. Marc Gaborieau, Nicole Grancin, Pierre Labrousse, and Alexandre Popovic. Paris: CNRS, forthcoming.

———. "The Naqshbandiyya in Tīmūrid India: The Central Asian Legacy." *Journal of Islamic Studies* 7/2 (1996): 208–28.

Bulliet, Richard W. *The Patricians of Nishapur: A Study in Medieval Islamic Social History.* Cambridge: Harvard University Press, 1972.

Cahen, C. "Buwayhids or Būyids." In *Encyclopaedia of Islam,* 2d ed., 1979.

Calder, Norman. "Ikhtilâf and Ijmâ' in Shâfi'î's Risâla." *Studia Islamica* 58 (1983): 55–81.

———. "The Significance of the Term *Imām* in Early Islamic Jurisprudence." In *Zeitschrift für Geschichte der Arabisch-Islamischen Wissenschaften.* Ed. Fuat Sezgin. 1 (1984): 253–64.

Census of India. *Beliefs and Practices Associated with Muslim Pirs in Two Cities of India (Delhi and Lucknow).* Monogram Series. Vol. 1, 1961.

Chabbi, Jacqueline. "La fonction du ribat a Bagdad du Ve siècle au début du VIIe siècle." *Revue des études islamiques* 42 (1974): 101–21.

———. "Remarques sur le développement historique des mouvements ascétiques et mystiques au Khurasan." *Studia Islamica* 46 (1977): 5–72.

Chamberlain, Michael. *Knowledge and Social Practice in Medieval Damascus, 1190–1350.* Cambridge: Cambridge University Press, 1994.

Chaudhry, Hafeez-Ur-Rehman. "Traditional and State Organizations of the Shrine of Bari Imam." *Al-mushīr* 36/3 (1994): 85–104.

Chelhod, Joseph. "La baraka chez les Arabes ou l'influence bienfaisante du sacré." *Revue de l'histoire des religions* 74 (1955): 68–88.

Chittick, William C. *Faith and Practice of Islam: Three Thirteenth-Century Sufi Texts.* Albany: State University of New York Press, 1992.

———. "The Five Divine Presences: From al-Qūnawī to al-Qayṣarī." *Muslim World* 72/2 (April 1982): 107–28.

Chodkiewicz, Michel. *Un océan sans rivage: Ibn Arabî, le livre et la loi.* Paris: Éditions Seuil, 1992. Trans. David Streight. *An Ocean Without a Shore: Ibn ʿArabî, The Book, and the Law.* Albany: State University of New York Press, 1993.

———. "Quelques aspects des techniques spirituelles dans la *ṭarīqa* Naqshbandiyya." In *Naqshbandis: Historical Developments and Present Situation of a Muslim Mystical Order.* Ed. Marc Gaborieau, Alexandre Popovic, and Thierry Zarcone. Istanbul: Éditions Isis, 1990, pp. 69–82.

———. *Le sceau des saints: Prophétie et sainteté dans la doctrine d'Ibn Arabî.* Paris: Gallimard, 1986. Trans. Liadain Sherrard. *Seal of the Saints: Prophethood and Sainthood in the Doctrine of Ibn ʿArabī.* Cambridge: The Islamic Texts Society, 1993.

Churchill, Edward D. "Muslim Societies of the Punjab, 1860–1890." *The Panjab Past and Present* 7 (April 1974): 69–90.

———. "Printed Literature of the Punjabi Muslims, 1860–1900." In *Sources on Punjab History.* Ed. W. Eric Gustafson and Kenneth W. Jones. Delhi: Manohar, 1975, pp. 253–336.

Clancy-Smith, Julia. *Rebel and Saint: Muslim Notables, Populist Protest, Colonial Encounters (Algeria and Tunisia, 1800–1904).* Berkeley: University of California Press, 1994.

Cohn, Bernard S. "Representing Authority in Victorian India." In *The Invention of Tradition*. Ed. Eric Hobsbawn and Terence Ranger. Cambridge: Cambridge University Press, 1983, pp. 165–209.

Cole, Juan. *Roots of North Indian Shīʿism in Iran and Iraq: Religion and State in Awadh, 1722–1859*. Delhi: Oxford University Press, 1989.

Corbin, Henry. *L'homme de lumière dans le Soufism iranien*. Trans. Nancy Pearson. *The Man of Light in Iranian Sufism*. Boulder: Shambhala Press, 1978.

———. *En Islam iranien*. 4 vols. Paris: Éditions Gallimard, 1971.

Cornell, Vincent. "The Logic of Analogy and the Role of the Sufi Shaykh in Post-Marinid Morocco." *International Journal of Middle East Studies* 15 (1983): 67–93.

———. "Mirrors of Prophethood: The Evolving Image of the Spiritual Master in the Western Maghrib from the Origins of Sufism to the End of the Sixteenth Century." Ph.D. Dissertation, University of California Los Angeles, 1989.

Crone, Patricia, and Hinds, Martin. *God's Caliph: Religious Authority in the First Centuries of Islam*. Cambridge: Cambridge University Press, 1986.

Culianu, Ioan. *Out of This World: Other Worldly Journeys from Gilgamesh to Albert Einstein*. Boston: Shambhala, 1991.

———. *Psychanodia I: A Survey of the Evidence Concerning the Ascension of the Soul and Its Relevance*. Leiden: E. J. Brill, 1983.

Currie, P. M. *The Shrine and Cult of Muʿīn al-Din Chishtī of Ajmer*. Delhi: Oxford University Press, 1989.

Dabashi, Hamid. *Authority in Islam*. New Brunswick: Transaction Publishers, 1993.

Dale, Stephen. "The Legacy of the Timurids." In *The Legacy of the Timurids*. Ed. David Morgan and Francis Robinson. Delhi: Oxford University Press for the Royal Asiatic Society, forthcoming.

Damrel, David. "Forgotten Grace: Khwāja Khāwand Mahmūd Naqshbandī in Central Asia and Mughal India." Ph.D. Dissertation, Duke University, 1991.

———. "'The Naqshbandî Reaction' Reconsidered." Unpublished paper delivered at Duke University, 22 April 1995.

Davies, Paul. *Superforce: The Search for the Grand Unified Theory of Nature*. New York: Simon and Schuster, 1984.

De Boer, Tj. "Faiḍ." In *Supplement* to the *Encyclopedia of Islam*. 1st ed.

Deweese, Devin. *An "Uvaysi" Sufi in Timurid Mawarannahr: Notes of Hagiography and Taxonomy of Sanctity in the Religious History *of Central Asia.* Bloomington: Research Institute for Inner Asian Studies, 1993.

Digby, Simon. " 'Abd al-Quddus Gangohi (1456–1537 A.D.): The Personality and Attitudes of a Medieval Indian Sufi." In *Medieval India: A Miscellany 3.* New York: Asian Publishing House, 1975, pp. 1–66.

———. "Encounters with Jogis in Indian Sufi Hagiography." Unpublished paper. University of London, 1979.

———. "The Naqshbandīs in the Deccan in the Late Seventeenth and Early Eighteenth Century A.D.: Bābā Palangposh, Bābā Musāfir, and Their Adherents." In *Naqshbandis: Historical Development and Present Situation of a Muslim Mystical Order.* Ed. Marc Gaborieau, Alexandre Popovic, and Thierry Zarcone. Istanbul: Éditions Isis, 1990, pp. 167–208.

———. "The Sufi Shaikh as a Source of Authority in Mediaeval India." In *Islam et Société en Asie du Sud.* Ed. Marc Gaborieau. Paris: L'École des Hautes Études en Sciences Sociales, 1986, pp. 57–77.

Durkee, ʿAbdullāh Nūr ad-Din. *Orisons.* Vol. 1. Alexandria: Dār al-Kutub, 1991.

Eaton, Richard M. "Approaches to the Study of Conversion to Islam in India." In *Approaches to Islam in Religious Studies.* Ed. Richard C. Martin. Tucson: University of Arizona Press, 1985, pp. 106–23.

———. "Court of Man, Court of God." *Contributions to Asian Studies* 17 (1982): 44–61.

———. *The Rise of Islam and the Bengal Frontier, 1204–1760.* Berkeley: University of California Press, 1993.

———. *Sufis of Bijapur (1300–1700): Social Roles of Sufis in Medieval India.* Princeton: Princeton University Press, 1978.

Eck, Diana. *Darśan: Seeing the Divine Image in India.* 2d ed. Chambersburg, Penn.: Anima Books, 1985.

Eliade, Mircea. *Yoga: Immortality and Freedom.* 2d ed. Trans. Willard R. Trask. Princeton: Princeton University Press, 1969.

Elias, Jamal. *The Throne Carrier of God: The Life and Thought of ʿAlāʾ ad-dawla as-Simnānī.* Albany: State University of New York Press, 1995.

Ernst, Carl. *Eternal Garden: Mysticism, History, and Politics at a South Asian Sufi Center.* Albany: State University of New York Press, 1992.

———. "Mystical Language and the Teaching Context in the Early Lexicons of Sufism." In *Mysticism and Language.* Ed. Steven T. Katz. Oxford: Oxford University Press, 1992, pp. 181–201.

Ess, Josef van. *Theologie und Gesellschaft im 2. und 3. Jahrhundert Hidschra: Eine Geschichte des religiösen Denken im frühen Islam.* 5 vols. New York: Walter de Gruyter, 1991– .

Ewing, Katherine. "The Dream of Spiritual Initiation and the Organization of Self Representations Among Pakistani Sufis." *American Ethnologist* 17 (February 1990): 56–75.

———. "The Politics of Sufism: Redefining the Saints of Pakistan." *Journal of Asian Studies* 42/2 (February 1983): 251–68.

———. "Sufi as Saint, Curer, and Exorcist in Modern Pakistan." In *South Asian Systems of Healing.* Ed. E. Valentine Daniel and Judy F. Pugh. Contributions to Asian Studies Series. Vol. 18. Leiden: E. J. Brill, 1984, pp. 106–114.

Farah, Caeser E. "Rules Governing the Shaykh-Murshid's Conduct." Introduction by Annemarie Schimmel. *Numen* 21 (August 1974): 81–96.

Fazl-i Husain. *Diary and Notes of Mian Fazl-i Husain.* Ed. Waheed Ahmad. Lahore: Research Society of Pakistan, 1977.

———. *Letters of Mian Fazl-i Husain.* Ed. Waheed Ahmad. Lahore: Research Society of Pakistan, 1976.

Fleischer, Heinrich. "Über die farbigen Lichterscheinungen der Sufi's." In *Zeitschrift der Deutschen Morgenländischen Gesellschaft* 5 (1862): 235–41.

Fletcher, Joseph. "Aḥmad Kāsānī." In *Encyclopedia Iranica,* 1983.

Friedmann, Yohanan. *Prophecy Continuous: Aspects of Ahmadi Religious Thought and Its Medieval Background.* Berkeley: University of California Press, 1989.

———. *Shaykh Aḥmad Sirhindī: An Outline of His Thought and a Study of His Image in the Eyes of Posterity.* Montreal: McGill-Queen's University Press, 1971.

Fusfeld, Warren. "The Shaping of Sufi Leadership in Delhi: The Naqshbandiyya-Mujaddidiyya, 1750–1920." Ph.D. Dissertation, University of Pennsylvania, 1981.

Geertz, Clifford. *Islam Observed: Religious Development in Morocco and Indonesia.* New Haven: Yale University Press, 1968.

———. *Local Knowledge: Further Essays in Interpretive Anthropology.* New York: Basic Books, 1989.

Ghazzālī, Abū Ḥāmid al-. *The Remembrance of Death and the Afterlife.* Trans. T. J. Winter. Cambridge: The Islamic Texts Society, 1989.

Gibb, H. A. R. *Mohammedanism: An Historical Survey.* 2d ed. London: Oxford University Press, 1982.

Gilmartin, David. "*Biraderi* and Bureaucracy: The Politics of Muslim Kinship Solidarity in Twentieth Century Punjab." *International Journal of Punjab Studies* 1/1 (1994): 1–29.

———. " 'Divine Displeasure' and Muslim Elections: The Shaping of Community in Twentieth-Century Punjab." In *The Political Inheritance of Pakistan*. Ed. D. A. Low. New York: St. Martin's Press, 1991, pp. 106–29.

———. *Empire and Islam: Punjab and the Making of Pakistan*. Delhi: Oxford University Press, 1989.

———. "Religious Leadership and the Pakistan Movement in the Punjab." In *Modern Asian Studies* 13/3 (1979): 485–517.

———. "The Rhetoric of Muslim Elections: Community and Pakistan in 1946." Unpublished paper given at University of North Carolina at Chapel Hill, 25 May 1996.

———. "The Shahidganj Mosque Incident: A Prelude to Pakistan." In *Islam, Politics, and Social Movements*. Ed. Edmund Burke and Ira M. Lapidus. Berkeley: University of California Press, 1988, pp. 146–168.

Goldziher, Ignaz. "The Veneration of Saints in Islam." In *Muhammadanische Studien* [1889]. Trans. C. R. Barber and S. M. Stern. *Muslim Studies*. 2 vols. Ed. S. M. Stern. Albany: State University of New York Press, 1971, pp. 275–341.

Goswamy, B. N., and J. S. Grewal. *The Mughal and Sikh Rulers and the Vaishnavas of Pindori*. Simla: Indian Institute of Advanced Study, 1969.

Graham, William A. *Beyond the Written Word: Oral Aspects of Scripture in the History of Religion*. New York: Cambridge University Press, 1987.

———. *Divine Word and Prophetic Word in Early Islam: A Reconsideration of the Sources, with Special Reference to the Divine Saying or Ḥadîth Qudsî*. Paris: Mouton, 1977.

———. "Traditionalism in Islam: An Essay in Interpretation." *Journal of Interdisciplinary History* 23 (Winter 1993): 495–522.

Gramlich, Richard. *Die schiitischen Derwischorden Persiens*. 3 vols. Wiesbaden: Franz Steiner, 1965.

Gronke, Monika. *Derwische im Vorhof der Macht: Social- und Wirtschaftsgeschichte Nordwestirans im 13. und 14. Jahrhundert*. Stuttgart: Franz Steiner, 1993.

Gross, Jo-Ann, "Khoja Aḥrār: A Study of the Perceptions of Religious Power and Prestige in the Late Timurid Period." Ph.D. Dissertation, New York University, 1982.

Haar, J. G. T. ter. *Follower and Heir of the Prophet: Shaykh Aḥmad Sirhindī (1564–1624) as Mystic*. Leiden: Het Oosters Instituut, 1992.

———. "The Spiritual Guide in the Naqshbandī Order." In *The Legacy of Mediaeval Persian Sufism*. Ed. Leonard Lewisohn. London: Khaniqahi Nimatullahi Publications, 1992, pp. 311–21.

Habermas, Jürgen. *Communication and the Evolution of Society.* Trans. Thomas McCarthy. Boston: Beacon Press, 1979.

Habib, Irfan M. *The Agrarian System of Mughal India.* Bombay: Asia Publishing House, 1963.

———. "The Political Role of Shaikh Ahmad Sirhindi and Shah Waliullah." *Enquiry* 5 (1961): 36–55.

Hallstrom, Elizabeth Lassell. "My Mother, My God: Ānandamayī Mā (1896–1982)." Ph.D. Dissertation, Harvard University, 1995.

Hasrat, Bikrama Jit. *Dārā Shikūh: Life and Works* [1979]. 2d ed. Delhi: Munshiram Manoharlal, 1982.

Heinze, Ruth-Inge. *Proceedings of the International Conference on the Study of Shamanism.* Berkeley: Independent Scholars of Asia, 1985.

Hermansen, Marcia. *The Conclusive Argument from God: Shah Waliullah of Delhi's Hujjat Allah al-Baligha.* Leiden: E. J. Brill, 1996.

———. "Shāh Walī Allāh's Theory of the Subtle Centers (laṭā'if): A Sufi Model of Personhood and Self-Transformation." *Journal of Near Eastern Studies* 47/1 (1988): pp. 1–25.

Hodgson, Marshall G. S. *The Venture of Islam: Conscience and History in a World Civilization.* 3 vols. Chicago: University of Chicago, 1974.

Hoffman, Valerie J. *Sufism, Mystics, and Saints in Modern Egypt.* Columbia: University of South Carolina Press, 1995.

Husaini, A. S. "Uways Al-Qaranī and the Uwaysī Sufis." *Moslem World* 57 (April 1967): 103–13.

Hujwīrī, ʿAlī Ibn ʿUthmān al-Jullābī al-. *Kashf al-maḥjūb.* Ed. Valentine Zhukovski. Leningrad: Dār al-ʿUlūm Ittiḥād Jamāhīr Shūrawī Sūsiyālīstī, 1926. Trans. Reynold A. Nicholson, *The Kashf Al-Maḥjūb: The Oldest Persian Treatise on Sufism.* London: Luzac, 1911.

Iqbāl, Muḥammad. *Jāvīdnāma.* Lahore: Iqbal Academy, 1982. Trans. Arthur Arberry. London: Allen and Unwin, 1966.

ʿIrāqī, Fakhruddīn. *Divine Flashes.* Trans. William C. Chittick. New York: Paulist Press, 1982.

Irving, Miles. "The Shrine of Bābā Farīd at Pākpattan." In *Notes on Punjab and Mughal India: Selections from the Journal of the Punjab Historical Society.* Ed. Zulfiqar Ahmed. Lahore: Sang-e Meel Publications, 1988.

Isfarāyanī, Nuruddīn ʿAbdurraḥmān. *Kashf al-asrār.* Trans. Hermann Landolt. *Le révélateur des mystères.* Lagrasse, Aude: Verdier, 1986.

Jackson, Paul *The Way of a Sufi: Sharafuddin Maneri.* Delhi: Idarah-i Adabiyat-i Delli, 1987.

Jalal, Ayesha. *The Sole Spokesman: Jinnah, the Muslim League and the*

Demand for Pakistan. Cambridge: Cambridge University Press, 1985.

Jha, J. S., ed. *Imperial Honeymoon with Indian Aristocracy.* Historical Research Series no. 18. Patna: K. P. Jayaswal Research Institute, 1980.

Johnson, Kathryn Virginia. "The Unerring Balance: A Study of the Theory of Sanctity *(Wilāyah)* of ʿAbd al-Wahhāb al-Shaʿrānī." Ph.D. Dissertation, Harvard University, 1985.

Jones, Kenneth W. *Arya Dharm: Hindu Consciousness in 19th-Century Punjab.* Berkeley: University of California Press, 1976.

Katz, Steven T. "Language, Epistemology, and Mysticism." In *Mysticism and Philosophical Analysis.* Ed. Steven T. Katz. New York: Oxford University Press, 1978, pp. 22–74.

———. "Models, Modeling, and Mystical Training." *Religion* 12 (1982): 247–75.

Khalidi, Tarif. *Arabic Historical Thought in the Classical Period.* Cambridge: Cambridge University Press, 1994.

Khan, Ghulam Mustafa. " The Naqshbandī Saints of Sind." *Journal of the Research Society of Pakistan* 13/2 (1976): 19–47.

Klaniczay, Gábor. *The Uses of Supernatural Power: The Transformation of Popular Religion in Medieval and Early-Modern Europe.* Trans. Susan Singerman. Ed. Karen Margolis. Princeton: Princeton University Press, 1990.

Knysh, Alexander. "*Irfan* Revisited: Khomeini and the Legacy of Islamic Mystical Philosophy." *Middle East Journal* 46/4 (Autumn 1992): 632–53.

Kuhn, Thomas S. *The Structure of Scientific Revolutions.* 2d ed. Chicago: University of Chicago Press, 1970.

Lambton, Ann K. "Quis Custodiet Custodes: Some Reflections on the Persian Theory of Government." *Studia Islamica* 5 (1956): 125–48.

Lawrence, Bruce B. "The Chishtiyya of Sultanate India: A Case Study of Biographical Complexities in South Asian Islam." In *Charisma and Sacred Biography.* Ed. Michael A. Williams. Chico, Cal.: Scholars Press, 1982, pp. 47–67.

Le Gall, Dina. "The Ottoman Naqshbandiyya in the Pre-Mujaddidī Phase: A Study in Islamic Religious Culture and Its Transmission." Ph.D. Dissertation, Princeton University, 1992.

Leitner G. W. *History of Indigenous Education in the Panjab since Annexation and in 1882* [1882]. Delhi: Nirmal Publishers, 1986.

Lenski, Gerhard, Jean Lenski, Patrick Nolan. *Human Societies: An Introduction to Macrosciology.* 6th ed. New York: McGraw Hill, 1991.

Lewis, P. *Pirs, Shrines and Pakistani Islam.* Rawalpindi: Christian Study Centre, 1985.

Liebeskind, Claudia. "Sufism, Sufi Leadership and 'Modernization' in South Asia since c. 1800." Ph.D. Dissertation, Royal Holloway, University of London, 1995.

Lindholm, Charles. *Charisma.* Oxford: Basil Blackwell, 1990.

Madelung, Wilferd. "New Documents Concerning Al-Ma'mūn, Al-Faḍl Ibn Sahl, and ʿAlī Al-Riḍā." In *Studia Arabica and Islamica: Festschrift for Iḥsān ʿAbbās.* Ed. Wadād al Qāḍī. Beirut: Imprimerie Catholique, 1981.

———. "Sufism and the Khurramiyya." In *Religious Trends in Early Islamic Iran.* Albany: State University of New York Press, 1988, pp. 39–53.

Maharshi, Sri Ramana. *Talks with Sri Ramana Maharshi.* 7th ed. Tiruvannamalai: T. N. Venkataraman, 1984.

Mahdi, Muhsin. "The Book and the Master as Poles of Cultural Change in Islam." In *Islam and Cultural Change in the Middle Ages: Fourth Giorgio Levi Della Vida Biennial Conference.* Ed. Speros Vryonis Jr. Wiesbaden: Otto Harrassowitz, 1975, pp. 3–14.

———. "From the Manuscript Age to the Age of Printed Books." In *The Book in the Islamic World.* Ed. George N. Atiyeh. Albany: State University of New York Press, 1995, pp. 1–15.

Mahmood, Tahir. "The Dargah of Sayyid Salar Masʿud Ghazi in Bahraich: Legend, Tradition and Reality." In *Muslim Shrines in India.* Ed. Christian Troll. Delhi: Oxford University Press, 1989, pp. 24–43.

Makdisi, George. *The Rise of Colleges: Institutions of Learning in Islam and the West.* Edinburgh: Edinburgh University Press, 1981.

Malamud, Margaret. "Gender and Spiritual Self-Fashioning: The Master-Disciple Relationship in Classical Sufism." *Journal of the American Academy of Religion* 64/1 (Spring 1996): 89–117.

———. "Sufi Organization and Structures of Authority in Medieval Nishapur." In *International Journal of Middle East Studies* 26 (1994): 427–442.

Manērī, Sharafuddīn. *Maktūbāt-i ṣadī.* Trans. Paul Jackson. *Sharafuddin Maneri: The Hundred Letters.* New York: Paulist Press, 1980.

Margoliouth, David S. "The Relics of the Prophet Muhammed." *The Moslem World* 27 (1937): 20–27.

Marmor, Judd. "The Psychotherapeutic Process: Common Denominators in Diverse Approaches." In *The Evolution of Psycho-*

therapy. Ed. Jeffrey K. Zeig. New York: Brunner/Mazel, 1987, pp. 266–74.

Massignon, Louis. *Essai sur les origines du lexique technique de la mystique musulmane*. 2d ed. Paris: Vrin, 1968. Trans. Benjamin Clark. *Essay on the Origins of the Technical Language of Islamic Mysticism*. Notre Dame: University of Notre Dame Press, 1998.

———. *La Passion de Husayn Ibn Mansūr Hallāj*. 4 vols. Paris: Gallimard, 1975. Trans. Herbert Mason. *The Passion of Al-Hallaj: Mystic and Martyr of Islam*. 4 vols. Princeton: Princeton University Press, 1982.

Masson, Charles (James Lewis). *Narrative of Various Journeys in Balochistan, Afghanistan, and the Panjab, Including a Residence in Those Countries from 1826–1838*. 3 vols. London: R. Bentley, 1842.

Mayer, Adrian C. "Pir and Murshid: An Aspect of Religion Leadership in West Pakistan." *Middle Eastern Studies* 3 (January 1967): 160–69.

Meier, Fritz. *Zwei Abhandlungen über die Naqšbandiyya*. Istanbul: Franz Steiner, 1994.

———. "Nachtrag des Verfassers." In *Bausteine I: Ausgewählte Aufsätze zur Islamwissenschaft von Fritz Meier*. Ed. Erika Glassen and Gudrun Schubert. Istanbul: Franz Steiner Verlag, 1992, p. 130.

———. *Bahā-i Walad: Grundzüge seines Lebens und seiner Mystik*. Leiden: E. J. Brill, 1989.

———. *Abū Saʿīd-i Abū l-Ḫayr (357–440/967–1049): Wirklichkeit und Legende*. Leiden: E. J. Brill, 1976.

———. "Ḫurāsān und das Ende der klassischen Ṣūfik." In *La Persia nel medioevo*. Rome: Accademia Nazionale dei Lincei, 1971, pp. 545–72.

———. "Qushayrī's Tartīb as-sulūk." *Oriens* 16 (1963): 1–39.

———. "Ein Knigge für Sufis." *Rivista degli Studi Orientali* 32 (1957): pp. 485–524.

———. *Vom Wesen der islamischen Mystik*. Basel: B. Schwabe, 1943.

Messick, Brinkley. *The Calligraphic State: Textual Domination and History in a Muslim Society*. Berkeley: University of California Press, 1993.

Metcalf, Barbara. *Islamic Revival in British India: Deoband, 1860–1900*. Princeton: Princeton University Press, 1982.

———. "Living Hadīth in the Tablīghī Jamaʿāt (sic)." *Journal of Asian Studies* (1993): 584–608.

———. *Perfecting Women: Maulana Ashraf Ali Thanawi's Bihisht-i Zewar: A Partial Translation with Commentary*. Berkeley: University of California Press, 1990.

Michon, J. L. "L'autobiographie *(Fahrasa)* du soufi marocain Aḥmad Ibn Ajība (1747–1809) [3me partie]." *Arabica* 16 (June 1969): 113–54.

Mīrzā Muḥammad Haydar. *A History of the Mughals in Central Asia Being the Tarikh-i Rashidi of Mirza Muḥammad Haidar, Dughlát.* 2d ed. Ed. N. Elias. Trans. E. Denison Ross. London: Curzon Press, 1972.

Moini, Liyaqat Hussain. "Rituals and Customary Practices at the Dargah of Ajmer." In *Muslim Shrines.* Ed. Christian Troll. Delhi: Oxford University Press, 1989, pp. 60–76.

Moore, Peter. "Mystical Experience, Mystical Doctrine, Mystical Technique." In *Mysticism and Philosophical Analysis.* Ed. Steven Katz. New York: Oxford University Press, 1978, pp. 101–32.

Morony, Michael G. *Iraq after the Muslim Conquest.* Princeton: Princeton University Press, 1984.

Mottahedeh, Roy P. *Loyalty and Leadership in an Early Islamic Society.* Princeton: Princeton University Press, 1980.

Muhammad Azim Husain. *Fazl-i Husain: A Political Biography.* London: Longmans, 1946.

Muḥammad b. Munawwar. *Asrār al-tawḥīd fī maqāmāt Shaykh Abī Saʿīd.* Ed. Muḥammad Riḍā Shāfīʿī Kadkanī. 2 vols. Teheran: Intishārāt-i Agāh, 1987. Trans. John O'Kane. *The Secrets of God's Mystical Oneness.* Costa Mesa, Cal.: Mazda Publishers, 1992.

Mujeeb, M. *The Indian Muslims.* London: George Allen and Unwin, 1967.

Muqaddasi, al-. *Aḥsan al-taqāsīm fī maʿrifat al-aqālīm.* Trans. Basil Anthony Collins. *The Best Divisions for Knowledge of the Regions.* Reading: Garnet Publishing, 1994.

Narayanan, Vasudha. *The Way and the Goal: Expressions of Devotion in the Early Śrī Vaisnava Tradition.* Cambridge: Center for the Study of World Religions, 1987.

Nasr, Hossein Seyyed. "Oral Transmission and the Book in Islamic Education." In *The Book in the Islamic World.* Ed. George N. Atiyeh. Albany: State University of New York Press, 1995, pp. 57–70.

———. *Sufi Essays.* 2d ed. Albany: State University of New York Press, 1991.

Nizami, Farhan. "Madrasahs, Scholars and Saints: Muslim Response to the British Presence in Delhi and the Upper Doab 1803–1857." Ph.D. Dissertation, Oxford University, 1983.

Nizami, Khaliq Ahmad. "Naqshbandi Influence on Mughal Rulers and Politics." *Islamic Culture* 39 (January 1965): 41–52.

Nywia, Paul. *Exégèse coranique et langage mystique: Nouvel essai sur le lexique technique des mystiques musalmanes.* Beirut: Imprimerie Catholique, 1970.

Nyberg, H. S. *Kleinere Schriften des Ibn al-ʿArabī.* Leiden: E. J. Brill, 1919.

Oberoi, Harjot. *The Construction of Religious Boundaries: Culture, Identity and Diversity in the Sikh Tradition.* New York: Oxford University Press, 1994.

O'Brien, Major Aubrey. "The Mohammedan Saints of the Western Punjab." *Journal of the Royal Anthropological Institute* 41 (1911): 509–20.

Pastner, Stephen L. "Sardar, Hakom, Pir: Leadership Patterns among the Pakistani Baluch." In *Shariat and Ambiguity in South Asian Islam.* Ed. Katherine P. Ewing. Berkeley: University of California Press, 1988, pp. 164–79.

Paul, Jürgen. *Die politische und sociale Bedeutung der Naqšbandiyya in Mittelasien in 15. Jahrhundert.* New York: W. De Gruyter, 1991.

———. "Scheiche und Herrscher im Khanat Čaġatay." *Der Islam* 67/2 (1990): 278–321.

Piamenta, M. *Islam in Everyday Speech.* Leiden: E. J. Brill, 1979.

Potter, Lawrence. "The Kart Dynasty of Herat: Religion and Politics in Medieval Iran." Ph.D. Dissertation, Columbia University, 1992.

Powell, Avril A. *Muslims and Missionaries in Pre-Mutiny India.* London: Curzon Press, 1993.

Proclus. *The Elements of Theology: A Revised Text.* 2d ed. Trans. E. R. Dodds. Oxford: Clarendon Press, 1963.

Proudfoot, Wayne. *Religious Experience.* Berkeley: University of California Press, 1985.

Qureshi, Regula A. *Sufi Music of India and Pakistan: Sound, Context, and Meaning in Qawwali.* Cambridgeshire: Cambridge University Press, 1986.

Rahman, Fazlur. *Islam.* 2d ed. Chicago: University of Chicago Press, 1979.

Ralhan, O. P. and Sharma, Suresh K., eds. *Documents on Punjab: Folklore.* Vol. 15. New Delhi: Anmol Publications, 1994.

Rāzī, Najmuddīn. *Mirṣād al-ʿibād min al-mabdāʾ ilaʾl-maʿād.* Ed. Muḥammad Amīn Riyāḥī. Teheran: Intishārāt-i ʿIlmī wa-Farhangī, 1986. Trans. Hamid Algar. *The Path of God's Bondsmen from Origin to Return.* Delmar: Caravan Books, 1982.

Reinert, Benedikt. *Die Lehre vom Tawakkul in der klassischen Sufik.* Berlin: Walter De Gruyter, 1968.

Reinhart, Kevin. *Before Revelation: The Boundaries of Muslim Moral Thought.* Albany: State University of New York Press, 1995.

Rizvi, Athar Abbas. *A History of Sufism in India.* 2 vols. New Delhi: Munshiram Manoharlal, 1983.

———. *Muslim Revival Movements in the 16th and 17th Centuries.* Agra: Agra University Press, 1965.

Robinson, Francis. "Technology and Religious Change: Islam and the Impact of Print." *Modern Asian Studies* 27/1 (1993): 229–51.

Rosenthal, Franz. *Knowledge Triumphant: The Concept of Knowledge in Medieval Islam.* Leiden: E. J. Brill, 1970.

Rothberg, Donald. "Contemporary Epistemology and the Study of Mysticism." In *The Problem of Pure Consciousness: Mysticism and Philosophy.* Ed. Robert K. C. Forman. New York: Oxford University Press, 1990, pp. 163–210.

Rousselle, Erwin. "Spiritual Guidance in Contemporary Taoism." In *Spiritual Disciplines.* Trans. Ralph Manheim. New York: Pantheon Books, 1960.

Rubin, U. "Pre-existence and Light: Aspects of the concept of Nūr Muḥammad." *Israel Oriental Studies* 5 (1975): 63–119.

Rūmī, Jalāluddīn Maulānā. *Kitāb-i fīhi mā fīhi.* Ed. Badīʿuzzamān Furūzānfar. Teheran: Chāpkhāna-yi Majlis, 1951. Trans. Wheeler Thackson, *Signs of the Unseen: The Discourses of Jelaluddin Rumi.* Putney, Ver.: Threshold Books, 1994. Trans. Arthur Arberry. *Discourses of Rumi* [1961]. London: J. Murray, 1993.

———. *Mathnawī-yi maʿnawī.* 6 vols. 10th ed. Ed. Reynold Nicholson. Teheran: Intishārāt-i Amīr Kabīr, 1988. English translation by Reynold Nicholson. *Mathnawī-yi maʿnawī.* 8 vols. Cambridge: Cambridge University Press, 1925–1940.

Rundī, Ibn Abbād. *Maktūbāt.* Trans. John Renard. *Ibn ʿAbbād of Ronda: Letters on the Sufi Path.* New York: Paulist Press, 1986.

Samuel, George, "Tibet as a Stateless Society and Some Islamic Parallels." *Journal of Asian Studies* 41/2 (February 1982): pp. 215–229.

Sanyal, Usha. "Ahmad Rida Khan Barelwī." In *Dictionnaire biographique des savants et grandes figures du monde musulman périphérique du XIXe siècle a nos jours,* ed. Marc Gaborieu, Nicole Grancin, Pierre Labrousse, and Alexandre Popovic. Paris: CNRS, 1992, pp. 7–8.

———. *Devotional Islam and Politics in British India: Ahmad Riza Khan Barelwi and His Movement, 1870–1920.* Delhi: Oxford University Press, 1996.

———. "In the Path of the Prophet: Maulana Ahmad Riza Khan Barelwi and the Ahl-e Sunnat wa Jamaʿat Movement in British India, c. 1870–1921." Ph.D. Dissertation, Columbia University, 1990.

Schimmel, Annemarie. *And Muhammad Is His Messenger: The Veneration of the Prophet in Islamic Piety.* Chapel Hill: University of North Carolina Press, 1985.

———. *Deciphering the Signs of God: A Phenomenological Approach to Islam.* Albany: State University of New York Press, 1994.

———. *Islamic Names.* Edinburgh: Edinburgh University Press, 1989.

———. *Mystical Dimensions of Islam.* Chapel Hill: University of North Carolina Press, 1975.

———. *Pain and Grace: A Study of Two Mystical Writers of Eighteenth-Century Muslim India.* Leiden: E. J. Brill, 1976.

Scholem, Gershom G. *On the Kabbalah and Its Symbolism.* Trans. Ralph Manheim. New York: Schocken Books, 1965.

Serjeant, R. B. "The ʿAwdhillah Confederation with some Reference to al-Hamdānī." In *Customary Law and Shariʿah Law in Arabic Society.* Hampshire: Variorum, 1991, chapter 4.

———. "The Constitution of Medina." In *Studies in Arabian History and Civilization.* Ed. R. B. Serjeant. London: Variorum Reprints, 1981, chapter 5.

———. "The *Sunnah Jāmiʿah,* Pacts with the Yathrib Jews, and the Tahrīm of Yathrib: Analysis and Translation of the Documents Comprised in the So-called 'Constitution of Medina.' In *Studies in Arabian History and Civilization.* London: Variorum Reprints, 1981, chapter 6.

Shahid, Irfan. "Philological Observations on the Namāra Inscription." *Journal of Semitic Studies* 24/34. In *Byzantium and the Semitic Orient before the Rise of Islam.* London: Variorum Reprints, 1988, chapter 5.

Shaibi, Kamil Mustafa al-. *Sufism and Shiʿism.* Surrey: LAAM Ltd., 1991.

Sharif, Jafar. *Qanoon-e-Islam or the Customs of the Mussulmans of India.* Trans. G. A. Herklots. 2d ed. Madras: J. Higginbotham, 1963.

Shils, Edward. *Center and Periphery: Essays in Macrosociology.* Chicago: University of Chicago Press, 1975.

Smith, Huston. "Is There a Perennial Philosophy?" *Journal of the American Academy of Religion* 55/3 (1987): 553–66.

Smith, Wilfred Cantwell. "The Crystallization of Religious Communities in Mughal India." In *Understanding Islam: Selected Studies.* Ed. Wilfred Cantwell Smith. The Hague: Mouton, 1981, pp. 177–96.

Tabrīzī. *Mishkāt al-maṣābīḥ.* 4 vols. Trans. J. Robson. Lahore: Shaykh Muhammad Ashraf, 1965.

Talbot, Ian. "The Growth of the Muslim League in the Punjab, 1937–46." In *India's Partition: Process, Strategy, and Mobilization.* Ed. Munshirul Hasan. Delhi: Oxford University Press, 1993, pp. 230–53.

———. *Punjab and the Raj, 1849–1947.* Delhi: Manohar, 1988.

Titus, Murray. *Indian Islam: A Religious History of Islam in India.* London: Oxford University Press, 1930.

Trimingham, Spencer. *The Sufi Orders in Islam*. Oxford: Clarendon Press, 1971.

Troll, Christian W. *Sayyid Ahmad Khan: A Reinterpretation of Muslim Theology*. New Delhi: Vikas Publishing House, 1978.

———. "Two Conceptions of Daʿwá in India: Jamāʿat-i Islamī and Tablīghī Jamāʿat." *Archives de sciences sociales des religions* 87 (1994): 115–33.

———, ed. *Muslim Shrines in India: Their Character, History and Significance*. Delhi: Oxford University Press, 1989.

Turk, G. M. S. "Attitudes of 'Mureeds' Towards 'Pirs' in Two Selected Samples." M.A. Thesis, Punjab University, 1959.

Turner, Victor. *Dramas, Fields, and Metaphors: Symbolic Action in Human Society*. Ithaca: Cornell University Press, 1974.

———. *The Ritual Process: Structure and Anti-Structure*. 2d ed. Ithaca: Cornell University Press, 1977.

———. *From Ritual to Theatre*. New York: Performing Arts Journal Publications, 1982.

Uprety, Prem Raman. *Religion and Politics in Punjab in the 1920's*. New Delhi: Sterling Publishers, 1980.

Valiuddin, Mir. *Contemplative Disciplines in Sufism*. Ed. Gulshan Khakee. London: East-West Publications, 1980.

———. *Madārij al-sulūk*. Karachi: Medina Publishing Company, n.d.

Vett, Carl. *Dervish Diary*. Trans. Elbridge W. Hathaway. Los Angeles: Knud K. Mogensen, 1953.

Watt, W. Montgomery, "Ahl al-ṣuffa." In the *Encyclopaedia of Islam*, 2d ed., 1979.

Weber, Max. *Economy and Society: An Outline of Interpretive Sociology*. 2 vols. Ed. Guenther Roth and Claus Wittich. Berkeley: University of California Press, 1978.

Welch, Holmes. *The Practice of Chinese Buddhism, 1900–1950*. Cambridge: Harvard University Press, 1967.

Wensinck, A. J. *Concordance et indices de la tradition musulmane*. 8 vols. Leiden: E. J. Brill, 1936–1971.

———. *The Muslim Creed: Its Genesis and Historical Development*. Cambridge: Cambridge University Press, 1932.

Wilson, Peter Lamborn. *Scandal: Essays in Islamic Heresy*. New York: Automedia, 1988.

Zaehner, R. C. *Hindu and Muslim Mysticism*. London: Athlone Press, 1960.

Zwettler, M. "The Poet and the Prophet: Towards Understanding the Evolution of a Narrative." *Jerusalem Studies in Arabic and Islam* 5 (1984): 313–87.

INDEX

Islamic names are ordered alphabetically by first name.
Items in footnotes are indicated solely by page number.
Abbreviations: Ar.: Arabic
Per.: Persian
Skt.: Sanskrit
Turk.: Turkish

abdāl ("substitutes," members of the spiritual hierarchy), xxiv, 94, 118
ʿAbdulaḥad Waḥdat Sirhindī (d. 1126/1715), 246
ʿAbulghafūr, Akhund of Swat (d. 1292–96/1877), 172
ʿAbdulḥaqq Muḥaddith Dihlawī (d. 1052/1642), 74, 137, 178
ʿAbdulkhāliq Ghujduvānī (d. 575/1179): against sufi lodges, 44; and the "way of the masters," 58; part of the Ṭayfūriyya, 59; as Uwaysī pir, 89, 93; taught by Khiḍr, 94; reaches the *maqām-i shahādat*, 98; learns *dhikr-i khafī* from Khiḍr, 128; learns *nafy wa-ithbāt* from Khiḍr, 128; and eight guiding principles, 234
ʿAbdulqādir al-Jīlānī (d. 561/1166), 2, 70, 127, 132
ʿAbdulquddūs Gangōhī (d. 944/1537), 41, 112
ʿAbdurraḥmān Jāmī (d. 898/1492), 40, 73; and *rābiṭa*, 131–32; and *tawajjuh*, 133; and visualizing the shaykh, 135
Abraham, 109, 115, 243, 250; Reality of Abraham, 252
Abū ʿAbdullāh Muḥammad al-Jazūlī. *See* Jazūlī
Abū ʿAbdurraḥmān as-Sulamī (d. 412/1021), 34, 106
Abū ʿAlī al-Fārmadī (d. 477/1084), 86
Abū ʿAlī Muḥammad ath-Thaqafī. *See* Muḥammad ath-Thaqafī
Abū Bakr aṣ-Ṣiddīq: follows the model of the Prophet, 25; silent *dikhr* associated with, 52; distinctive lineage of Naqshbandiyya includes, 56; the Ṣiddīqiyya named after, 59; Aḥmad Sirhindī claims a higher rank than, 68; and Bakrī *silsila*, 88; distinctive features of Naqshbandiyya inherited from, 90; and Sunnī dogma, 90; exemplifies Prophetic sobriety, 92; *maqām-i ṣiddīqiyat* named after the station of, 98; and love for the Prophet, 140; formal initiation in the name of, 159; successorship according to the precedent of, 167
Abū Ḥafṣ as-Suhrawardī (d. 632/1234), 122, 132
Abū Ḥāmid al-Ghazzālī (d. 505/1111), 36, 106, 143
Abū Ḥanīfa, 3, 119, 181, 186
Abū'l-Ḥasan ʿAlī ash-Shādhilī (d. 656/1258), 85, 236
Abū'l-Ḥasan al-Kharaqānī (d. 425/1033), 41, 86, 94
Abū'l-Ḥasan Fārūqī, 238, 239
Abū'l-Ḥusayn an-Nūrī (d. ca. 295/908), 5, 6, 92
Abū'l-Qāsim al-Gurgānī (d. 469/1077), 89
Abū'l-Qāsim al-Qushayrī (d. 465/1072), 2, 3, 6, 33, 35, 36

Abū'l-ʿUlā Akbarābādī (d. 1061/1651), 73, 109
Abū Sahl Muḥammad aṣ-Ṣuʿlūkī. *See* Muḥammad aṣ-Ṣuʿlūkī
Abū Saʿīd (d. 1250/1835), 91, 153, 237
Abū Saʿīd Aḥmad (at Khundian), 167
Abū Saʿīd al-Kharrāz (d. 286/899), 98, 100
Abū Saʿīd-i Abū'l-Khayr (d. 440/1049), 34, 41; experiences of, 6, 29; and sufi lodge, 46, 51, 53
Abū Yazīd al-Bisṭāmī (d. 261/874), 38, 39, 45, 59, 147; experiences of, 6; had 113 teachers, 32; followed Jaʿfrī school of law, 33; in Naqshbandī genealogy, 85–86
adab (correct behavior, etiquette): follows the sunna, 19, 34, 36; emphasized by directing-shaykh, 34; everything depends on, 148; rules of, 149; and Persian court model, 150; toward God, 184; in presence of sufi shaykh, 185. *See also* protocol
Adam, 38; and *laṭīfas*, 108; and the *qālab laṭīfa*, 109; and the heart *laṭīfa*, 115, 120; God's creation to be "under the foot" of, 243; governs the first contemplation, 243; angels prostrating to, 245; the heart of, 250; as a Great Prophet, 252;
Ādam Banūrī (d. 1053/1644), 71, 73, 109, 172, 246
admirable innovations (sing. *bidaʿt al-ḥasana*), 179
Afghanistan, 64, 75
Āghā Khān, 23, 36, 215
Agra, 63, 64, 65, 73
agrarian economy: with a weak decentralized government, 14, 30; directing-shaykhs integral to, 31, 35, 48, 225: sufi lodge prospered in, 46;
aḥadiyyat (exclusive unity, the first intention in Mujaddidī contemplations), 242, 249
ahl al-ṣuffa ("people of the bench"), 48, 51
Ahl-i Hadith: as a reform group, 170; named Ahl-i Sunnat wa-Jamāʿat, 176; denial of sufism and Indian customs, 179; and Deobandis, 181; as alternative orthodoxy, 187, 226; and opposition to sufi groups, 192, 194, 209; and religious magazines, 197; centers on university scriptural sources, 229
Aḥmad b. Muḥammad Qushshāshī (d. 1071/1660), 59, 246
Ahmadis, 78, 177, 184, 192, 197, 216, 226
Aḥmad Khwājagī b. Jalāluddīn Kāsānī (d. 949/1542–43), 60, 62, 63
Aḥmad Riḍā Khān Barelwī (d. 1340/1921), 137, 158, 176–78, 192, 200, 212
Aḥmad Saʿīd (d. 1277/1860), 135; Delhi sufi lodge of, 74; as shaykh, 152, 165, 174; successors of, 171; and *Arbaʿ anhār*, 237; teaching certificates from his lineage, 254–55, 257
Aḥmad Sirhindī (d. 1034/1625), 66–74, 109, 233; founder-figure of the Mujaddidiyya, xv, 58, 59; his descendants' ties with Afghan notables, 64; introduced to Bāqībillāh, 65; and early Mujaddidī history, 68–71; and letters to rulers, 69; and later revival activity in India, 71–74; contributes to a new conception of Indian Muslim community, 78; redefining Naqshbandī principles, 90–93; as Uwaysī, 95; extended the Naqshbandī spiritual path, 99–100; emphasis

on credal dogma, 101; and emphasis on *waḥdat al-shuhūd*, 114, 123; defines *fayḍ*, 118; affiliated with the Kubrāwiyya, 157; his *ḥadīth isnāds*, 157; initiating disciples at his grave, 160; as revivalist, 170; descendants of, 171, 172; tomb of, 175, 180; writing about spiritual practice, 235; declared reality of the Kaʿba to be above the reality of Muḥammad, 246; prophetology of, 247; opposition to, 248. See *Maktūbāt* for collected letters of

Aḥmad Yasawī (d. 562/1166–67), 58, 60

Aḥrār. *See* ʿUbaydullāh Aḥrār

Aḥrār Party, 214

Akbar (Mughal emperor), 63, 64, 66, 68, 78, 172

Akbar Shāh Bukhārī (d. 1347/1928–29), 172

akhfā (super-arcanum *laṭīfa*, one of the subtle centers): location of, 105–6, 109, 111, 129; and Simnānī, 108; associated with Muḥammad, 114, 120; order of activation, 129; and the unitary form, 244; and the intentions, 250

ʿālam al-amr (world of divine command), 105, 115

ʿālam al-khalq (world of creation), 105

ʿālam-i ajsām (world of corporeal bodies), 115

ʿālam-i malakūt (world of divine sovereignty), 108, 115

ʿālam-i mithāl (world of image-exemplars), 115

ʿAlā'uddawla Simnānī (d. 736/1336): and Kubrawī *nafy wa-ithbāt*, 94; his sevenfold mystical system, 108; originating *waḥdat al-shuhūd*, 109, 114; the idea often *laṭifas* and a subtle, acquired body, 112; and the invisible teacher, 113; and essential attributes, 115; and *rabiṭa*, 132–33;

ʿAlāuddīn ʿAṭṭār (d. 803/1400), 135

Al-Azhar, 28, 72

ʿAlī al-Riḍā (d. 203/818): the eighth imam, 90

ʿAlī b. Abī Tālib (d. 41/661): and vocal *dhikr*, 52; in Naqshbandī genealogy, 86; sufi lineages raised to, 88; one of the three Shīʿī imams found in all sufi lineages, 90; lineage of disregarded by Sirhindī, 92

Alienation of Land Act, 212

Aligarh, 27, 186, 226

Alipur, 191, 192, 196, 206

All India Sunnī Conference, 213, 217

amīr millat (leader of the Muslim community), 192, 213

Amīr Kuṭla Mullā Ṣāḥib (d. 1295/1878), 172

Amīr Kulāl (the potter) as-Sūkhārī (772/1370), 89, 93, 94, 127

Amkanagī. *See* Muḥammad Amkanagī

amulets, 230, 238; supplied by sufis, xviii, 10, 37, 165, 199, 200, 235; Anglicized Indians during colonial period, 13, 183, 194, 204–7, 219

Anjuman-i Islāmiyya, 183

Anjuman-i Khuddām aṣ-Ṣūfiyya, 183; and propagating Islam, 182, 197; created in 1904 by Jamāʿat ʿAlī, 191, 194; annual meeting, 194, 196, 203–6; *Risāla-yi anwār alṣūfiyya* as monthly magazine of, 194; strove to unify sufi lineages, 195; members both rural and urban, 207, 210

Anjuman-i Panjāb, 183

Annihilation. See *fanā'*

annual conference/meeting sponsored by Jamā'at 'Alī. *See* Anjuman-i Khuddām aṣ-Ṣūfiyya
anti-structure, xvi, 8, 30, 35, 53–54, 228
Anwar 'Alī (1862–1920), 194, 195, 204
'aqīda/'aqā' id. *See* credal dogma
'aql-i kull (universal reason), 40
Arains, 175
arcanum (subtle center). See *khafī*
'arsh. *See* throne
Arya Samaj, 183, 197–98
ascension. See *mi'rāj*
ascent (*'urūj*), 116, 242
ascetics, 1, 24, 224
asceticism, 51, 121
ashrāf (sing. *sharīf* descendants of the Prophet), 20
Ashraf 'Alī T'hānawī, 177
asmā' wa'l-ṣifāt, al- (the names and attributes [of God]), 106, 115
aspirant. *See* disciple
'Aṭā' Ḥusayn (d. 1311/1893–4), 73–74
'Aṭṭār. *See* Farīduddīn
attributes of negation. See *ṣifāt-i salbiyya*
Aurangzīb (Mughal Emperor r. 1068/1658–1118–1707), 56, 68, 69, 70, 71, 78
Awḥaduddīn Kirmānī (d. 635/1238), 37
axis mundi, 219: sufi master as *axis mundi*, 204
a'yān-amīr system, 30, 46

Bābā Faqīr Muḥammad Chūrāhī (1315/1897), 192
Bābā Farīd Ganj-i Shakar (d. 664/1265), 169, 203, 211
Bābā Muḥammad Sammāsī (d. 755/1354), 89
Bābā Palangposh (d. 1110–11/1699), 62
Bābur, Ẓahīruddīn Muḥammad (d. 937/1530), 56, 61–64
Bādshāhī Mosque, 171, 183, 196, 215
Baghdad, 7, 33, 70, 90, 156
Bahā dur Shāh (the last Mughal ruler), 74
Bahā'uddīn Naqshband (d. 791/1389): conference on, ix; tomb of, ix, 58, 175; as founder-figure, xv, 55; as the first historical link in Naqshbandī genealogy, 88; many Uwaysī guides of, 89, 93–95; and broad conception of Naqshbandī spiritual pedigree, 92; reached the station of the credal formula (*maqām-i shahādat*), 98; unable to receive the *dhikr* from his living pir, 127; visualizing shaykh of, 135; initiation in the name of, 159; additional three guiding principles, 234; elaboration of the Naqshbandī path, 244, 249
Bahā'uddīn Zakariyā (d. 666/1267), 169, 211
Bakrī (having Abū Bakr aṣ-Ṣaddīq in the genealogical chain): *silsila*, 88; emphasis, 90; origins, 92; connection, 186
Balkh, 64
Baluchistan, 174
baqā' (literally, "remaining," the next station of one who has been annihilated in God): remaining in God, 100; remaining in the Messenger, 100; remaining in the sufi shaykh, 100; first *baqā'*, 123;
Bāqībillāh (d. 1012/1603): institutional affiliations when in Kabul, 62; most significant Naqshbandī in sixteenth-century India, 65; supported by one of Akbar's viziers, 66; non-Mujaddidī sub-lineage not continued, 74; discusses the seven subtle centers, 109; taught the way of bonding, 139; expediting others' arrival near God, 143; 'Umar Bīrbalī visiting his tomb, 154

baraka (Per. *barakat*, auspiciousness, "blessing,"), 56, 83, 117, 156. See also *fayḍ*
Barelwi ulama and school of ulama, 176–79; sufi affiliation of in Pakistan, 79; survey of Barelwi ulama, 79; founder, Aḥmad Riḍā Khān, 158; Barelwi ulama of Lahore, 171; both reformist and shrine-centered, 176; and Deobandis, 181; as mediating-shaykhs, 181; schools, 186; and mediatory Islam, 191, 214; sponsored the All-India Sunnī conference, 213; bolstered devotional Islam, 220; and universal symbol of the Prophet, 229
barzakh ("intermediary," "interface," "bridge"), 11, 114, 200, 245; *barzakh al-kubrā* (the major intermediary), 200, 244; *barzakh-i ṣughrā* (the minor intermediary), 200
*bay*ʿ*a*. *See* initiation
Bengal, 169, 171, 172
bhaktas, 179, 201
birādarī (Urdu, clan), 175, 184
Bīrbalī. *See* Muḥammad ʿUmar
British/British India: no written evidence for Naqshbandī *shaykhas* in, xxiv; religious figures/institutions have no legitimacy, 13; changed notions of sunna, 149; takeover of Delhi, 175; decennial census of, 182; forms of organization adopted in Panjab, 183; accused of corrupting Muslims, 185; communicated an unspoken superiority of worldview, 208; colonial policy, 211; forced to support religious dignitaries and shrines, 211; and Panjabi landowning class, 212; system of bestowing prestige, 212; and Shahīdganj affair, 216; destruction of the educational system, 226–27;
Budd'han Shāh (d. 1272/1855–6), 154
Bukhara, xv, 55, 60
Buyids/Buwayhids, 4, 24, 26, 30

Central Asia: contemporary importance of Naqshbandiyya in, ix; Mujaddidī success in, xvi; Naqshbandī directing-shaykhs in, 48; sufi lodges spread to, 48, 75; Naqshbandiyya gave assistance to landlords, 59; collapse of the nomadic hegemony in, 60; sufi economic interests in, 60; lasting impression on Indian Islam, 66; Uwaysī tradition in, 88; Kubrawiyya in, 108–9; in pan-Islamic networks, 219;
chakra (Skt. wheel), 110
charisma: Weber's theory of, 14; Prophetic charisma, 15, 20, 28; transformation into lineage charisma, 22; and Clifford Geertz, 25
charismatic community, 53, 96
Chatli Qabr, 74, 239
Chishtī(s): hereditary shaykhs at Chisht, 20; Akbar's affiliation, 66; holy men, 66; and Abū'-l-ʿUlā's Naqshbandī sub-lineage, 73; revivalists, 170
Chishtī-Ṣābirī: influences on Aḥmad Sirhindī, 68; use of *dhikr-i sulṭānī*, 112
Chishtiyya, 169, 195, 236, 255, 256
Christians: Christian-Muslim frontier, 3; give divine ontological status to Jesus, 178; missionary activity, 182–83, 197, 228; customs, 185; holy man, 209;
communitas: of Prophet and Companions, 48; Turner's notion of, 49; normative, 50; in sufi lodge, 50, 53, 146, 147, 207,

communitas (continued)
223; in Islamic society, 54; replaced by an imaginary macro-community, 228–30; yearning for, 229
community: ideal community of the Prophet, xvi; imaginary community, 229. *See also* charismatic community
Companions: paradigmatic community of the Prophet, xv, xvi; paradigmatic relationship with Muḥammad, 17; as part of the ideal Muslim community, 39, 44; *communitas* and, 48; and Sunnī dogma, 49; sufi lodge replicating community of Prophet and, 52–54, 228, 233; the *isnād* mechanism linking to, 83–84; Naqshbandīs duplicating the path of, 102, 116–17, 125, 187; did not experience intoxication, 123; nearness to God, 123; not infallible, 142; and precedents for initiation, 155; spiritual rank and, 163; and precedents for renewing allegiance, 166; recapturing the experience of, 216, 245; contemplations emulate, 242
companionship (*ṣuḥbat*): with Muḥammad, 16, 85; condition for master-disciple relationship, 33; involvement of the heart in, 84; precondition for religious wisdom, 85; Uways al-Qaranī's lack of with the Prophet, 93; with God, 132; and *rābiṭa*, 132, 136–37; pir purifies disciple's nature by 152; seekers investigate the effects of, 153; initiation as an agreement to remain in, 157; necessity of, 160; visiting a tomb does not substitute for, 163; and directing-shaykh, 195; with mediating-shaykh, 196, 202, 205; and love, 202
comprehensive synthesis (*sha'n-i jāmi'*), 114, 245
connection to God, the Prophet, or shaykh. See *nisba*
consolidation of religious authority, 97
contemplation(s) (*murāqabāt*), 104, 125, 130; Sirhindī formulated 25 of the 26, 99; Aḥrār and teaching of, 140; visualizing shaykh and, 146; and disciple's training, 163; discontinued in the twentieth century, 163; not taught by Jamā'at 'Alī, 202; Mujaddidī contemplations and their intentions, 241–53;
cosmology, xvi, 119, 120, 235, 241
credal dogma (*'aqīda/'aqā'id*): and Muḥammad, 10; Sunnī creed/dogma, 10, 49, 68, 184, 247; defining Indian Muslim community, 58; sufi seekers and, 75; as prerequisite to mystical practices, 79; written in numbered lists, 79; and the path of the Companions, 116; and cosmology, 117, 119; and the blocking of divine grace, 119; correct credal dogma before initiation, 158, 159, 164; importance of each article of, 177; and Ahmadis, 184; sufi overlap with, 224; and revivalist sufism, 238
crystallization of religious communities, 78

Dahbid, 60, 135
dā'ira-yi imkān (sphere of contingent existence), 104, 115, 163, 243, 244
Dalā'il al-khayrāt, 236
Damascus, 2, 45, 56
Dār al-'Ulūm Nu'māniyya, 186
Dārā Shikūh (d. 1069–70/1659), 69, 70

darbār (sufi shrine, original meaning: prince's audience chamber), 149, 204, 227
dargāh (sufi shrine, original meaning: king's court), 149, 227
darshān, 205, 206
Dātā Ganjbakhsh (The Treasure-bestowing Master), ʿAli b. ʿUthmān al-Jullābī al-Hujwīrī (d. 463–4/1070), 232; his tomb, 216
Delhi: Bāqībillāh migrates to, 62, 66; British capture in 1803, 74; great mosque of, 74; Naqshbandī activity in, 74; ulama, 171; Panjabi Naqshbandīs traced to, 175; newspapers published in, 197; notables fled after 1857, 226; schools destroyed in, 226–27
Deobandi(s): opposed by Barelwis, 177, 181; like directing-shaykhs with their students, 180; school of ulama, 180–81
dhāt. *See* Essence
dhikr (recollection of God): silent, ix, 56, 94, 127, 128, 202; changed meaning used by Tablīghīs, 22; ulama appropriation of, 35; a part of ritual in sufi lodge, 52; Aḥarī, 73; and Uways, 89; vocal, 89, 127; of the heart, 94, 127–29, 159, 241; beginning exercises of, 104, 186; when the entire body recollects God (*dhikr-i sulṭanī. sulṭān-i, adhkār*), 112–13, 129, 164; in a Shīʿī environment, 125; to cultivate subtle centers, 126; of "Allāh," 127; heart as starting point, 128; imparting, 128, 160; as one way to God, 131; and *rābiṭa*, 131–32; few go beyond, 189; redefined by Jamāʿat ʿAlī, 201, 202; hadith support for, 238
directing-shakyh (*shaykh al-tarbiyya*): as specific configuration of personal authority, xv, 12, 23; supplanted by mediating-shaykh, xviii; verifying activities of xix, xx; early history of, 1; annihilating ego in, 2; and mediation, 11; transformation from teaching-shaykh to directing-shaykh, 12–13, 29–30; role in herding/agrarian societies, 29–31; defined by ar-Rundī, 31–32; shift to directing-shaykh in Nishapur, 31–32; emphasis on correct behavior, 34; reaching superhuman status, 36; defining characteristic, 37; and the sufi lodge, 46–52; necessity of, 138–41; nineteenth-century training repertoire of, 145–46
disciple(s) (*murīd*): types of roles with the shaykh, 32; and unquestioning obedience, 33; number in shaykh's circle, 36; and re-creating the ideal Muslim community, 39, 54; should focus on one's living spiritual master, 93–94; modeling actions on the Prophet's behavior, 96; learning about spiritual centers, 105, 112; goal to receive divine grace, 120; exceptional, 122; abandoning the shaykh, 144, 162; following grand shaykh's, 153; being accepted for initiation, 154; becoming 155–63; pass through the contemplations, 241–45
divine energy/power or divine effulgence/grace (*fayḍ*): evidence of spiritual energy transference, xviii, xix; transmitted through the shaykh, 12; Mīrzā Maẓhar's experience of, 16–17; lineage as a conduit for, 20, 23, 84; channeling on the ruler's behalf, 69; need for proper connection to the Prophet, 83, 85; and an Uwaysī connection, 88; condition for knowledge to be considered as an inheritance of the Prophet, 95; God's friends mediate divine

divine energy (continued)
power to help people, 99; conceptual origins of, 107; mediated through the subtle centers, 114; via Muḥammad, 115, 118, 120; compared to electricity, 117; general and special, 118, 127; and credal dogma, 119; as inner light, 119; personal account of experiencing, 122, 152; receiving from the Essence, 128; ways of transmitting and effects on people, 133; and visualization of the shaykh, 136; and heart-to-heart communication, 138; becoming cut off from, 143; during initiation, 160–61, 166; tomb-shrines as places to receive, 162; Barelwis emphasized the "Muḥammadan light" instead of, 176; and spiritual territory, 195; from reading a sufi magazine, 199; and love of the pir, 202; reinterpreted as effulgence of Muhammadan electricity, 202; perceived as superstitious, 208; and the contemplations, 242. *See also* supernatural power, 117–20

Dōst Muḥammad Qandahārī (d. 1284/1867), xxii, 152, 154, 155, 164–66, 174; teaching certificate given to him, 254–55; teaching certificate given by him, 256–57

educational system, British destruction of, 226–27

ego: expected to annihilate/submit in the directing-shaykh, 2, 40, 133, 145; pir as touchstone for, 16; correct behavior as a means to subdue, 34; and becoming a *muslim*, 38, 41; egoism, 40; and escaping from, 40; and its annihilation in God, 43; controlling and transforming, 104; gives feeling of knowing better than the master, 139; control of as goal of sufi etiquette, 148; and Deobandi training 180, 181; love of the mediating-shaykh as a means to annihilate, 201; purifying, 216. See also *nafs*

Egypt, 4, 27, 46, 195

eleven principles of the Naqshbandiyya, 100, 237

enchanted universe, 53, 207

end of the Naqshbandi path being included in the beginning, 100, 121; begins where other paths end, x

endowments. *See* religious endowments

Endowments Department of the Panjab, 220

English shoes, 74, 185

Ernst, Carl, xxv, xxvi, 69, 103

Essence (*dhāt*): ten *laṭīfas* emanating from, 112; primary manifestation of, 114; grace is distributed to creation via the primary manifestation of, 115; sufi realizes the reality of, 117; emanation of special to Muḥammad, 118; remembering the name of, 127; contemplating, 132; grand shaykhs permanently in, 153; goal to travel in rather than the attributes, 242

"exclusive unity." See *aḥadiyyat*

exemplar (of the Prophet), xvi, 17, 18, 25, 39, 138, 143, 181; as a source of authority, 11; directing-shaykh as living, 22

Faḍl-i Aḥmad Fārūqī Sirhindī. *See* Ḥaḍrat Jīyū

Faḍlurraḥmān Ganjmurādābādī (d. 1312–13/1895), 171, 187, 191

fanā' (annihilation of the mystic's I-ness), 2, 100, 121, 129, 242–43

fanā' fi'llāh (*fanā'* in God), 2, 43, 100, 131, 137, 201

fanā' fi'l-rasūl (*fanā'* in Muḥammad), 100
fanā' fi'l-shaykh (*fanā'* in the shaykh), 2, 100, 131, 133, 137
Faqīrullāh Shikārpūrī (d. 1195/1781), 78, 111, 113, 120, 174
farḍ (religious obligation), 141, 151, 184, 187, 198, 201
fatwā (a religious legal opinion, pl. *fatāwā*), 21, 31, 178, 181, 218
fayḍ (effulgence). *See* divine energy/power
Fazl-i Husain, 213, 214, 215, 217, 220
friend of God. See *walī*
fu'ād (the inner heart), 5

Gabriel, 4, 5, 11, 160
Ganjmurādābādī. *See* Faḍlurraḥmān Ganjmurādābādī
Ghazzālī, Abū Ḥāmid al-. *See* Abū Ḥāmid al-Ghazzālī
Ghujduvānī. *See* ʿAbdulkhāliq Ghujduvānī
Ghulām Aḥmad, 177, 184. *See also* Ahmadis
Ghulām ʿAlī Shāh (d. 1240/1824), 153, 257; grave of, 74; effect on others, 152; sufi lodge of, 174; lineage of and sufi literature, 235, 239; and Shāh ʿAbdulʿazīz, 239; and concentrating on prophets, 242; and redefining the Mujaddidī mystical path, 246–48
Ghulām Murtaḍā (d. 1321/1903), 151, 158
Ghulām Nabīlillāhī (d. 1306/1888), 142
Gilmartin, David, xxv, 171, 212, 229
gnosis (Ar. *maʿrifa*, Per. *maʿrifat*), 6, 7, 118
Golden Chain (spiritual lineage which includes the Shīʿī imams), 90, 92
guide. See *murshid*
Gujarat, 56, 186
hadith: and religious knowledge, 3; Gabriel's, 4; sufi attitude toward, 6; example of a sufi lesson of, 16–17; teaching of is experienced as being in the presence of the Prophet, 16–17, 85; and transmission of, 21, 24; *isnād* of, 28, 83, 84; spiritual genealogy differs from a proper *isnād* of, 85; and support for the practice of *dhikr*, 126, 238; study of for sufi shaykhs, 152, 224; and revival activity, 170, 176; Shāh Walīullāh and emphasis on study of, 170; and Ahl-i Hadith, 179, 187; use of to praise the Prophet, 179; and Jamāʿat ʿAlī's teachers of 191–92
ḥadīth qudsī (Divine saying from God), 42, 43
ḥaḍrat-i dhāt (Divine Presence of the Essence), 247
Ḥaḍrat Jīyū (d. 1231/1815 Peshawar), 172
hagiography, xx, 195
ḥajar-i baht (so-called "philosopher's stone"), 108
Ḥakīm at-Tirmidhī, al- (d. 290/910), 5, 6, 45, 89
Ḥallāj, Ḥusayn b. Manṣūr al- (martyred 309/922), 36, 106, 121
Ḥanafī, 179, 185, 186: strife in Nishapur, 46; omitted from Dārā Shikūh's name, 70; credal dogma, 90; *fiqh*, 100; legal age according to, 166; Naqshbandīs not bending rules of, 187
Ḥanafī-Karrāmī alliance in Nishapur, 46
ḥaqīqa (Reality), 117, 120; *ḥaqīqa* as center of the circle with shariʿa as the circumference, 10
ḥaqīqat-i Aḥmadī (reality of Aḥmad), 247
ḥaqīqat-i ʿibādat (reality of worship), 9
ḥaqīqat-i kaʿba-yi rabbānī (reality of the Kaʿba), 246, 252

ḥaqīqat-i Muḥammadī (Muḥammadan Reality), 115, 245, 246, 252
ḥaqīqat-i qur'ān (reality of the Qur'ān), 246, 252
Ḥārith al-Muḥāsibī, al- (d. 243/857), 32, 52
hay'at-i waḥdānī (consolidation of all the *laṭīfa*s, literally, the "unitary form"), 112, 244, 245, 251–53
heart (*qalb*): as the locus of God's immanence, 84; as interface, 126. See also *qalb*
heir of the Prophet: sufi shaykh as, xvi, xix, 11, 15, 33, 36, 201; directing-shaykh as, 12, 48, 139; intimacy with God as a precondition for being, 14; jurist, sufi, and Shī'ī imam considered as, 14; functions like a prophet, 16; religious scholar as, 17, 36; supernatural power associated with, 18; living embodiment of the exemplary model of Muḥammad, 19; brings about personal transformation in others, 23; always exists, 41; Naqshbandī shaykh as, 98, 200
hereditary shaykh. *See* shrine shaykh
himma (Per. *himmat*). *See* divine energy/power; supernatural power; *tawajjuh*
Hindu(s): frequented sufi shrines, 169; and Christian converts, 182; publications of, 182; as revivalists, 182, 184; voluntary organizations of, 182–83; and reconverting Muslims, 197, 228; sufi shrines open to, 216; indigenous education of, 227
Ḥizb al-baḥr, 85, 236
Hodgson, Marshall, 3, 23, 31
Hudaybiya, 52
Ḥujjatullāh Naqshband (d. 1114/1702), 69
Hujwīrī al-. *See* Dātā Ganjbakhsh
Humāyūn (d. 963/1556), 56, 71, 192
Ḥusayn b. Manṣūr al-Ḥallāj. *See* Ḥallāj
Hyderabad, Deccan: Abū'l-'Ulā's sub-lineage in, 73; Jamā'at 'Alī's travels to, 196
Hyderabad, Sind: Naqshbandī spread to, 174

Iblisian Tawḥīd, 39, 40
Ibn 'Abbād ar-Rundī (d. 790/1388), 31, 34
Ibn al-'Arabī (d. 638/1240): mentions women in the spiritual hierarchy, xxiv; and travels of to deepen spiritual experiences, 32; and Ṣadruddīn Qūnawī, 37; and the arcanum *laṭīfa*, 108; and Naqshbandī cosmological terminology, 113; interpreters of 114
Ibn Taymiyya, 24
Ibrāhīm al-Kūrānī (d. 1101–2/1690), 73
identity: collective, 30; sufi, 44; redefining Naqshbandī, 58; and sobriety over intoxication, 65; Indian Muslim, 68, 209, 216; Indian Sunnī, 70; Islamic, 79, 184, 185; Mujaddidī constructs of, 90; Sunnī, 90; self, 101; Muslim, 170, 216; Barelwi, 176; Naqshbandī, 188; pan-Islamic, 208, 209; religious, 215; local, 216
iḥsān (perfection of the practice of islām), 4, 5, 7, 38
ijāza (permission to teach). *See* teaching permission
ijāzatnāma (written certificate to teach): and ambition to receive printed certificates, 164; examples of, 254–59
ijmā' (consensus), 83, 149, 167
ijtihād (literally, "striving," an independent legal judgment), 35, 110, 248; sufi *ijtihād*, 129

ʿ*ilm* (knowledge, typically religious knowledge): jurists' limited scope of, 6; as religious, 18; for legal opinions, 21; oral nature of, 27; of the heart and oral, 84; the quality of exalted, 114; one of the eight divine attributes, 115; theoretical (versus spiritual), 163; and Muḥammad, 177; necessity of inner, 187, 188
imam (religious leader): of legal school, 3, 33; Shīʿī, 4, 13, 14, 21, 89; Ismāʿīlī, 18; as living heir of the Prophet, 23; Twelver imam similar to directing-shaykh, 23
Imāmī Shīʿīs, 18, 20, 33, 129
īmān (faith): compared to *islām* and *iḥsān*, 4–5; appearance of and the reality of, 9; as a preliminary stage, 38; and credal affirmations, 79; related to special *fayḍ*, 118
inclusive unity (*wāḥidiyyat*) 242. See also *aḥadiyyat*
Indian rebellion of 1857, 74
initiation (*bayʿa*, Per. *bayʿat* declaring formal allegiance, initiation), 153–62; for women, xxiv, 160–61; in sufi lodges, 1, 44, 52; rituals of, 3; Uwaysī, 20, 88, 92, 93; oath of allegiance, 52; and a proper connection to God, 83; and activating the disciple's subtle entities, 105; and *shaktipāt*, 117; after a spectacular cure, 154; multiple, 157; renewing bonds of, 166; as sunna, 187, 188–89
insān al-kāmil, al- (the perfect human), xx
intercession: of mediating-shaykhs, 10; of Muḥammad, 11; Naqshbandī-Aḥrārī, 63; of Salīm Chishtī, 66; government landgrants in exchange for, 71; affiliation of, 157; disciple's growth depends on, 181; people barred from any hope of, 199; and Aḥmad Riḍā, 200; and the need for a mediator, 210
intermediary: Muḥammad as, 11; between Muḥammad and believer, 12; between God and humanity, 15, 42, 148, 156; of an Uwaysī guide, 122; necessity of shaykh as, 132, 137, 188, 210; and mediating-shaykh, 200
intimate of God. See *walī*
intoxication, 65, 93, 123, 136, 139, 142
Iqbāl, Muḥammad (d. 1938), 224, 232; modern Islamic ideas of, 207; stressed the larger Muslim community, 209; poetry of, 209, 216; and the Qur'an, 210; and pan-Islamic notions, 215; and Arabia, 218; and Pakistan, 218
Iqbāl Mujaddidī, xxvi, 65, 171, 215
Irshād Ḥusayn Rampūrī (d. 1311/1893–94): wrote few teaching certificates, 164; association with Bādshāhī Mosque in Lahore, 171; teacher of Jamāʿat ʿAlī Shāh, 191
islām (submission to God): contrasted to *īmān* and *iḥsān*, 4–6, 38; and recollecting God, 125
Islamic worldview, xvii, 31, 226
Islamization, 46, 170
Ismāʿīlī, 18, 217; Ismāʿīlī imams, 4
isnād (continuous chain of authorities leading back to Muḥammad), 2, 27, 82, 85, 157; isnād principle, 83–84
istikhāra (requesting God for help in making a decision), 154, 158
Ittiḥād-i millat ("United Muslim Community"), 192, 213, 216

jadhba ("intoxicated" attraction to God): connection of, 87; phenomenon of, 93; associated with shaykh's spiritual power, 96; and *sayr-i anfusī*, 121; the path of attraction, 122; why

jadhba (continued)
Companions did not experience it, 123; with visualization of the shaykh, 135, 136; as explanation for shaykh's behavior, 142; and permission to teach, 244
Jaʿfar al-Khuldī (d. 358/959), 2, 33, 88
Jaʿfar aṣ-Ṣādiq (d. 148/765), 33, 85, 86
Jahāngīr, 68, 71, 172
Jamāʿat ʿAlī Shāh, 192–205; leader of the Muslim Community, xix, 213, 216; as mediating-shaykh, xxii, 13, 191, 210, 228; associated with *anjumans*, 183, 194; and publishing, 194–95, 197–99; and sufi revival movement, 194; and travel, 195–96; and spiritual training, 200, 202; and love, 201, 220, 229; and annual meeting, 203–5; attracts both rural and urban Muslims, 206, 210; and the British, 213, 214; and limited authority, 214; and the Shahīdganj Mosque, 215; and Jinnah, 217, 230; and the Muslim League, 217, 218; and the Unionist Party, 217; annual festival to celebrate, 223; and disciples, 223; community of expressed an emerging nationhood, 228
Jamāluddīn b. Badshāh Pardah Pūsh Khwarzmī (d. 1015–16/1606–7), 65
Jamʿiat al-Ulama-yi Hind, 213
Jazūlī, al- (d. 869/1465), 72, 236; Jazūliyya, 19
Jesus, 109, 115, 141, 178, 243, 252
jihād (literally, striving), 8, 155; *jihād* as war and as inner struggle, 9
Jinnah, Muhammad, 202, 217, 220, 229, 230
Jāmī. *See* ʿAbdurraḥmān Jāmī
Junayd al-Baghdādī (d. 297/910), 32, 33, 106, 123, 132, 241
jurisprudence (*fiqh*), 3, 6, 24, 33, 153
juristic sufism, xix, 8, 224, 225
jurists' (ʿulāmāʾ): *islām*, the domain of, 5; equating jurisprudence with the entirety of religious knowledge, 6; and expressions of religion, 8; as heirs of the Prophet, 14, 36; functional infallibility in decisions of, 35; as sufis, 78. *See also* religious scholar

Kaʿba, 16, 23, 42, 133, 148, 155, 177; meaning of, 43; Yūsuf Hamadānī as the Kaʿba of Khurasan, 44; as a symbol of a universal Islam, 209, 220; appearance of, 246; reality of, 246, 252; ontological superiority of, 247; superiority of over Muḥammad, 247
Kabul, 62, 64
Karrāmiyya, 46
Kāsānī. *See* Aḥmad Khwājagī b. Jalāluddīn Kāsānī
kashf (God's revealed knowledge), 17, 101
Kashmir, 66, 171, 215
Khādim Ḥusayn, son of Jamāʿat ʿAlī, 196
khafī (arcanum, one of the subtle centers), 108, 114, 120; different positions of, 105, 109, 111; associated with Jesus, 115, 243; origin of, 243, 250
Khālid Kurdī/Baghdādī (d. 1242/1827), 55, 59, 174
khalwa (seclusion), 44; solitude in society (*khalwat dar anjuman*), ix, 234
khānaqāh (sufi lodge): as tenth-century development, 2; contemporary activities in, 10; and directing-shaykh, 13, 195, 219, 230; anti-structure within, 30; development of, 44–54; compared to the Prophet's bench, 147; ritual in, 148–50;

succession in, 164–67; establishment of in colonial Panjab and Sind, 173–75; and local Islam, 215, 219; and mediatory sufism, 220; modern changes in, 228, 230, 232
khānaqāh-madrasa, 3
Khāwand Maḥmūd (d. 1052/ 1642), 65, 74, 171
Khiḍr (Khizr), 93, 94, 127, 129, 142, 158, 162
Khiḍriyya, 137
khirqa (sufi robe): and directing-shaykh, 1; and ritual in sufi lodge, 33, 44, 52; of blessing, 83; initiatory, 83; sultans abandoned the practice, 155; symbolic significance, 155; presentation by Jamāʿat ʿAlī, 194
Khomeinī, Ayatullāh: and relationship to sufism, 14
Khundian, 167, 174, 186, 216
Khurasan, 2, 3, 46
khwāja (master): way of the masters (*tarīqa-yi khwājagān*), 58
Khwāja Khurd, younger son of Bāqībillāh, 73, 74, 241
king(s): comparing God to, 41, 169; verify supernatural capabilities of sufis, 47; shaykh in lodge like, 148, 149, 150, 227; colonial district officer as, 211. *See also* ruler.
Kubrawiyya, 2, 73, 107, 109

Lahore: non-Aḥrārī Naqshbandīs settled in, 64; disciples of Muḥammad Qāḍī in, 65; tomb of Khāwand Maḥmūd in, 74; Naqshbandīs near, 174; and 1989 elections, 177; center for revivalist publications, 182; and Anjuman-i Islāmiyya, 183; Barelwi schools began in, 186; newspapers in, 192, 197; and Sikh control of 213, 215, 216; Dātā Ganjbakhsh's tomb in, 216; ulama in, 216
laṭīfa (pl. *laṭāʾif*) (subtle center, subtle body/field, subtle entity depending on context), 96, 103–16, 133, 188; as subtle center, 96, 126, 128, 146; six-*laṭīfa* systems, 109; as subtle body, 125, 129
Lawrence, Bruce, xxv, xxvi, 39, 80
Leitner, G.W., 183, 227
letters: evidence of spiritual practice in, xviii, 99, 146; sufi letters as sources, xx, 248; Sirhindī and his son writing to government officials, 69; Naqshbandīs writing to rulers, 78; used to buttress the institution of the living shaykh, 80
liminal: power, 12; crazy wise men, 22; poverty, 50;
liminality, 50, 225, 228
lineage: as a source of authority, xv, 11, 23; spiritual, 2, 12, 14, 15, 18, 19, 31, 56, 95, 188, 224; biological, 18, 20, 224; conduit for spiritual energy, 20; teaching, 20; ancestral, 21; charisma associated with, 22; sublineages of the Naqshbandiyya, 74; raised to Companion, 88; as link to Muḥammad, 154; and propagating Islam, 184; unifying various sufis, 195, 228, 239; transcending, 229
lodge. See *khānaqāh*
love (*ʿishq*): of the shaykh, xx, 131, 136, 139, 140, 141, 144, 146, 167, 180, 181, 196, 200, 201, 202, 205, 207, 228; the most subtle of human expressions, 7; unconditional for mediating-shaykh, 12, 201, 202; of an impersonal God, 39; of the Prophet, 72, 177, 185, 201, 205, 213, 223, 228, 229; and *rābiṭa*,

love (continued)
131; spontaneous development, 136, 146, 147; and visualization of the shaykh, 136, 139, 140; of Abū Bakr, 140; excessive, 141; God, 141, 144, 152, 153, 154, 201, 205; goal of spiritual practice of, 191; of intimates of God, 201; Mujaddidī practices redefined by, 201–202; of the shaykh's children, 201; of sufis, 205; Rāmānuja's bhakti-yoga, 206; universal, 210, 220; and nation-state, 227, 229; unifying the community, 229; and the contemplations, 245, 247, 251, 253
loveplay, 140, 141
Lucknow, 3, 99, 151, 152, 171, 185

Madārī lineage, 59
madrasa (religious school, typically school of higher education where Islamic sciences are taught), 3, 32, 45, 164, 186; religious schools in Pakistan 180
madrasa-*khānaqāh*, 45
Maḥbūb ʿAlam (d. 1335/1917), 85
mainstream Sunnī community (*ahl al-sunna wa'-jamāʿa*), 70
maʿiyyat (being together with God), 244
majdhūb (a person attracted to God), 21, 22, 24, 94, 121, 122. See also *jadhba*
majdhūb-i sālik, 121, 122. See also *sālik-i majdhūb*
maktūbāt (collected letters): success of the Naqshbandiyya and, 96
Maktūbāt of Aḥmad Sirhindī, 80, 96, 201, 238; Shēr Muḥammad reads, 164
Malāmatiyya, 128
Mālikī law school, 26, 33
maʿmūlāt literature, 235–39
Manrī. *See* Sharafuddīn Manrī
maqām(s) (mystical station): of correct moral behavior, 34; of Abū Bakr aṣ-Ṣiddīq, 98; *maqām-i shahādat*, 98; of greater intimacy, 99; describe the spiritual path, 100; Muḥammad's, 118; a disciple's, 120; of ten stations, 121; *maqām-i mushāhada*, 132; of the prophets, 144
maʿrifa. *See* gnosis
Maʿrūf al-Karkhī (d. 200/815), 90, 94
master-disciple relationship: mediating-shaykh had diffused power within, 13; non-existent for Tablīghī Jamāʿat group, 22; more authoritarian nature with directing-shaykh, 29; and *pīrī-murīdī* relationship, 33; like other hierarchical relationships, 47; initiation formally creates, 52; in Naqshbandī-Timurid partnership, 63; psychological processes in, 138–46; increasing hierarchical distance within, 207
mediating-shaykh: one configuration of personal authority, xv; spiritual practice defines, xvi, xviii; transformation to, xix, 168, 189, 219, 225; has become the norm, xxii; intercedes with Muḥammad, 10, 12; Āghā Khān analogous to, 23; Barelwis as, 181; new form of Naqshbandī personal authority, 190–191; compared to hereditary shrine shaykh, 191; and love, 199–200, 220; and the directing-shaykh, 199, 203, 232; and *ācāryas*, 206; combined practices of hereditary pirs with revivalist shaykhs, 210; and master-disciple relationships, 230. *See also* Jamāʿat ʿAlī
mediation: social, xvii; and sufi shaykh, 10–11, 189; sufi lodge positioned for, 46; and the *qayyūm*, 68; mediation of

Muḥammad necessary, 119; tomb-shrines a part of, 175; necessary in agrarian/herding societies, 225
mediational Islam, 180, 186
mediational paradigm, 175
mediational sufism, 168, 170, 176
mediators: Mujaddidīs as, xvi; sufis' essential role as, 31; between people and rulers and people and God, 60; between humans and God, 133, 190; social, 169; rural shrine families as, 211; directing-shakyhs as, 224
Medina, 11, 51, 73, 152, 163; as holiest place on earth, 177; replicating *hijra* to, 223
Meier, Fritz, x, 31, 45, 132
Mihr ʿAlī Shāh (d. 1355–6/1937), 170, 191, 217, 218
miʿrāj (ascension [into heaven]), 98, 106, 246; Bayazīd's ascension, 38
Mīr Dard (d. 1200–1/1785), 72, 73, 100
Mīrzā Maẓhar Jān-i jānān (d. 1195/1781), 83; and his experiernce with a hadith teacher, 17, 20, 24; tomb of, 74; and initiation practices, 158; disciples of, 236–37
missionary activity, 22, 46, 182, 183, 184
modeling one's behavior (typically on the shaykh): based on the sunna, xv, 18, 19; allows for individual transformation, 12, 145; on the teacher, 19; on mediating-shaykh, 23; unconscious, 138; as psychological tie, 140; conscious, 144
Moses, 94, 109, 115, 142, 162, 250; Reality of Moses, 252
Mughals: and Naqshbandī-Aḥrārī spiritual intercession, 63; need for religious legitimacy, 63; intermarriage with Aḥrārīs, 64; ties with the Naqshbandīs, 66; and landgrants, 71, 211; and conversion of Jat tribes, 169; British eliminate symbolic traces of, 171; court of used as model for British, 204; British imitate, 211
Muḥammad, the Prophet: obedience to, 2, 25; and Gabriel, 4; as transformative presence, 7; as intercessor, 10–12, 181; according to Sunnī dogma, 10, 12; as arbitor, 11; as divine mediator, 11; as a prophetic mediator between God and humans, 11, 200; conveyed through one's sufi shaykh, 12, 141, 180; spiritual lineage connecting to, 12, 18, 20–21, 34, 155, 224; charismatic authority of, 14, 20; to be in the presence of, 15; associated with intimacy with God, 17; modeling behavior on, 19, 162; sufi shaykhs compared to, 20, 42; as the personal symbolic center in Islamic culture, 23, 226; reality of, 23, 244, 246, 252; exemplar of human extraordinariness, 25; Muḥammadan light, 25, 176, 202; as superhuman, 25; vision/experience of, 25; connecting to, 26, 147, 156, 189; as a paternal figure, 26; central symbol of personal authority, 31; super-superhuman status of, 35; cult of, 39; Muḥammadan *tawḥid*, 39; Muḥammadan path, 72; the spirit of, 114; superiority of, 119, 120, 248, 257; *fayḍ* mediated by, 132; pictures of 134; and visualizing the shaykh, 138; and *rābiṭa*, 143; historical, 145; and sufi initiation, 154, 158; and women declaring allegiance to, 160; in mediational sufism, 169, 191, 200, 203; personal authority of, 170; and Aḥmad Riḍā, 176,

Muḥammad, the Prophet (continued)
178; Barelwi conception of, 176–77; elevating the status of, 176; veneration and love of the Prophet, 177, 197, 205; Muḥammadan electricity, 202; denying, 224, 232; as a messenger, 247; as a prophet, 247. *See also* heir of the Prophet; love; sunna
Muḥammad ʿAbdullaṭīf (d. 1398/1978): and the Pakistan movement, 172
Muḥammad Afḍal, 16, 17, 20, 24
Muḥammad Amkanagī (d. 1008/1600), 60, 66
Muḥammad ash-Shāfiʿī, 3, 35. *See* for the Shāfiʿī school, 26, 28, 33, 46
Muḥammad Ghawth Gwaliorī (d. 970/1562), 63
Muḥammad Ḥusayn Shāh (d. 1972): Jamāʿat ʿAlī's son and successor, 192, 218, 223
Muḥammad Ismāʿīl Kirmānwālī (d. 1385/1966), 175
Muḥammad Maʿṣūm (d. 1079/1668), 68, 73; as *qayyūm*, 69; wrote letters to the royal family, 69; mobilized spiritual support, 70; and concentration on the heart, 127; and activation of *laṭīfas*, 128; and need for intermediary, 137
Muḥammad Pārsā (d. 822/1420), 61, 108, 127, 135
Muḥammad Qāḍī (d. 911 or 912/1505–7), 60, 65
Muḥammad Qāsim Nānautawī (d. 1294/1877), 20, 177
Muḥammad ʿUmar Bīrbalī (d. 1387/1967): and revolution of reality, 9; and appearance of astral bodies, 136; visualizing his shaykh, 138; and revivalist Naqshbandī ideal, 151; and search for spiritual guide, 154; spiritual training of, 159; as disciple of Shēr Muḥammad, 175; and observations of twentieth-century sufis, 189
Muḥammad ʿUthmān (d. 1314/1896): searches for perfect spiritual mentor, 154–55; the last non-lineal successor, 165–66, 174; guide for Naqshbandīs of colonial Peshawar, 172; certificate of teaching permission given to, 256–57
Muḥammad Zubayr (d. 1152/1740), 69
Muhrah, 172
Muʿīnuddīn ʿAbdullḥaqq (d. 956/1549–50 or 962/1554–55), 63
Muʿīnuddīn Chishtī (d. 633/1236), 175, 203
Muḥyīddīn Quṣūrī (d. 1270/1854), 174
Mujaddidī/Mujaddidiyya: predominated over other Naqshbandī lineages, 58, 74, 96; named after Aḥmad Sirhindī, 66, 68; Shāh Walīullāh preferred, 73; spread of, 77; ignores Shīʿī imams, 90; redefinitions, 90–92; attracted many people, 95; spiritual practices of, 96, 100, 120; cosmological paradigm, 101; system of subtle centers 105–10, 120; following the path of the Companions, 117; fourfold path, 122; system of visualization, 135; Jamāʿat ʿAlī does not instruct using methods of, 200; love a religious obligation for, 201; redefined by love, 201; publications, 239
mujaddid (renewer), xv, 66, 101, 247
Multan, xxvii, 169, 211, 223
murāqabāt. *See* contemplations
murshid(s) (spiritual guide/director, sufi master): as masters of the heart, xix; heart of the sufi lodge, 5; transformative potential of, 17; as heir of the

prophet, 19; necessity for salvation, 29; indispensability of, 31; and need for a spiritual genealogy, 34; unquestioning faith in, 37; being close to God, 41; differs from the Prophet, 53; need for the disciple to be attuned with, 133; and *rābiṭa,* 135; modeling of, 138; uses behavioral and psychological strategies, 139; Prophetic ideal communicated through, 145; wields supernatural power, 148; embodies inner and outer knowledge, 151; hereditary pirs often not qualified, 151; searching for 152–54; seven criteria for, 152; ulama and, 153; going to another, 161; becoming a sufi master, 162–66

Musa Zai, 154, 155, 165, 166, 167, 172, 174

Muslim League, 208, 217, 218, 230

Mysore, 194, 196

mystery *laṭīfa.* See *sirr*

mystical experiences, 10, 18, 98, 101, 105, 123

Nadwat al-Ulama, 171

nafs (carnal soul, "ego," sense of I-ness): annihilating in the directing-shaykh, 2; inner struggle to control, 9; aligning with the shaykh's will, 16; sufis controlling, 16; correct behavior and, 32; learning how to tame, 40; minimizing is correlated with spiritual poverty, 50; performing ritual duties transforms, 104; and spiritual practices, 121; subduing, 180; trained by reciting litanies, 202; purifying, 216. *See also* ego

nafs al-ammāra, al- (the soul which incites to evil), 104

nafs al-lawwāma, al- (the soul that blames itself), 104

nafs al-muṭma'inna, al- (the tranquil soul), 7, 104, 245

nafs laṭīfa ("soul," one of the subtle centers), 105, 106, 110, 128, 256; bodily positions of, 109, 111, 129; cosmological location, 115; wayfarer travels in, 244

nafy wa-ithbāt (negation and affirmation): as advanced recollection exercise, 104, 241, 242; as a method to cultivate the *laṭīfas*, 125; called *dhikr-i khafī,* 127; taught to ʿAbdulkhāliq Ghujduwānī by Khiḍr, 129; preparation for the contemplations, 130, 163; ʿUbaydullāh Aḥrār and, 140; not important for Jamāʿat ʿAlī, 202; not discussed in the earliest Mujaddid manuals, 235

Naʿīmullāh Bahrā'ichī (d. 1218/1803), 83, 247

Najmuddīn Kubrā (d. 618/1221): founder-figure of the Kubrawiyya, 2; and the inner morphology of the human body, 107; and the closest path to God, 120; notes the limitations of asceticism, 121; and *rābiṭa*, 132; and manual of sufi etiquette, 148

Najmuddīn Rāzī (654/1256), 107, 108, 119

Naqshbandiyya Foundation, 198

Naqshbandiyya-Mujaddidiyya/Naqshbandī-Mujaddidī: universe/cosmology, 105–20; spiritual practices, 120–25; examples of behavior in sufi lodges, 147–50; criteria for a worthy shaykh, 151–54; becoming a disciple, 154–59; initiation for women, 159–62; becoming a spiritual guide, 162–67; spiritual practices abandoned, 202

Naqshbandī(s) Naqshbandiyya (often synonomous with the Naqshbandī-Mujaddidī): in

Naqshbandī(s) Naqshbandiyya (continued)
Central Asia, ix, 48, 60–61; success in the West, x; impact on social action, xv; named after Bahā'uddīn Naqshband, xv; contemporary lodges in the Panjab, xviii; and juristic sufism, xix, 18; and women shaykhas in, xxiv; return from spiritual ascent to teach, 11, 18; personal authority and a heart-to-heart connection, 17, 82; and connecting to the Prophet, 18, 85, 95; lineage and mystical practice, 20, 84; and ulama, 44, 85; definitions of "Naqshband," 55, 127; identity, 58, 187; and the Naqshbandiyya-Mujaddidiyya sublineage, 58, 74; political relationships and agenda, 61, 63, 66, 68, 70, 71, 75, 78; as military pirs, 62; Timurid partnership with, 63–66; non-Aḥrārī Naqshbandīs, 64; becomes an Indian lineage, 66; Mughal relationship with, 66–71; major Indian sublineages of, 73–74; under British rule, 79; genealogy of, 85–90; Uwaysī connections with, 89; and the "golden chain," 90; and sobriety, 92–93; Khiḍr in lineage of, 94; why people attracted to, 96; replicates the path of the Companions, 107; confluence with early Kubrawiyya practices, 109, 133; and notions of the heart, 126; recollection of the heart, 127–29; practices transmitted from the early Malāmatiyya, 128; recollection of negation and affirmation, 129–31; and *rābiṭa*, 131–33; ways to God, 131; visualization of the shaykh, 135, 140; need for annihiliation in the shaykh, 137; and loveplay, 141; shift from directing-shaykh to mediating-shaykh, 168; more prominent among Lahori Barelwi ulama, 171; in NWFP, 172; Panjab as nineteenth-century regional center of, 175; exercises of redefined in terms of love, 201. *See also* eleven guiding principles; mediating shaykh
naṣīrān-i Maḥmūd, 109
na't (devotional poetry praising Muḥammad), 177, 204, 205
Nepal, 171
night journey (of Muḥammad). See *mi'rāj*
nisba (Ar. "connection," Per. *nisbat*): to God, 16, 83, 135, 139; to the Prophet, 17, 23, 24, 82, 136, 151, 153; *nisbat-i kashifī*, 83; "proper," 83; *nisbat-i jadhba*, 86; *nisbat-i jismānī*, 89; *nisbat-i ruḥānī*, 89; of love, 140; with a perfected pir, 202
Nishapur, 2, 3, 31, 46, 128
Niẓāmuddīn Awliyā' (d. 725/1325), 142, 154
Noah, prophet associated with the *nafs laṭīfa*, 109, 115, 243
nomads: did not appreciate institutional sufis, 48; nomadic sociopolitical environment, 48; nomadic Jat tribes becoming settled, 169. *See also* agrarian
North Africa, 4, 48
Northwest Frontier Province (NWFP), xvii, 172, 218
Nūrī, an-. *See* Abū'l-Ḥusayn
NWFP. *See* Northwest Frontier Province

Pakistan, 78; Barelwi survey of ulama in, 79; the movement for, 172, 218, 223, 229; contemporary, 173, 207; religious schools in, 179; and the Muslim league, 217; and political impact of sufis, 217; and sufi shrines, 219, 232; government, 230
Pakpattan, 169, 186, 211

Pānīpatī. *See* Qāḍī Thanā'ullāh Pānīpatī
Panjab: Naqshbandī activity in, xvix, 75, 175; under British control, 74; Mujaddidīs in, 76–77, 171–75; sufi ulama in, 79; and the spread of Islam, 169; revivalist Chishtīs in, 170; Delhi notables dispersed to small towns in, 171; Wahhābīs in, 179; voluntary associations in, 182–84; Naqshbandī religious schools in, 186; mediatory Islam in, 191; shrine of Sahkī Sarvar in, 191; first sufi *anjuman* in, 194, 197, 198; Jamā'at 'Alī's activities in, 194–96; religious magazines in, 197; census reports in, 198; Muslim League victory in, 208, 217–18, 219; Mughals in, 211; rural politics in, 211–14; Sikhs in, 211, 214, 215; and Alienation of Land Act, 212; Unionist Party in, 214, 217; registered sufi shrines in, 220; destruction of indigenous education in, 227; *ma'mūlāt* genre in, 239
paradigm: Islamic, xv, 145; defined, xvi; Mujaddidī, xvi; religious authority, xxii; *isnād*, 83; religious, 99; of Mujaddidī cosmology, 101; of God, 102; of Naqshbandī spiritual travel, 105; shift from directing-shaykh to mediating-shaykh, 190; of divine intervention, 211; Barelwi mediational, 214
parda (keeping women separate from men), 151, 161
Persian court model of sufi behavior, 150
Persian kingship, 149
Persian shah, 29
Persian sources of Indian heritage, becoming estranged from, 207
personal authority. *See* Muḥammad; shaykh; sources of personal authority
Peshawar, xvii, 172, 174
pīr (Per. elder): living, 20, 88, 94, 127, 163; Naqshbandī military, 62; seeing one's future pir in a dream, 154; as a curer, 235. *See also* shaykh
pīrān-i kibār (the great masters), 250
pirism, 139
Pīr Pāgārō, 36, 212
pīrzāda (son of a pir), 164
Plato's ontology, 102: Platonic ascent/descent, 102
prestige: lineage providing, 20; of teaching-shakyh, 26; institutional affiliation affecting, 28; religious knowledge, 36; of directing-shaykh, 46, 48; of the sufi lodge, 47; crucial for rural sufi shaykh, 211; distributed by colonial district officer, 211; relationships with the colonial power, 211; British system of bestowing, 212; and of sufis and ulama, 226
printing: Arabic printing, 196; undermined local sources of authority, 208; lithograph presses, 239
profession of faith: and Iblīsian *tawḥīd*, 38; involves the tongue and the heart, 126; and *nafy wa-ithbāt*, 129, 130
propagating Islam (*tablīgh*), 22, 194
prophethood: directing-shaykh approaches the threshold of, 12; path of, 73; station of, 98; associated with the perfections of the corporeal world, 116, 117; and special *fayḍ*, 118; perfections of, 251
Prophet. *See* Muḥammad
prophets (*anbiyā'*, sing. *nabī*): non-prophets, 12, 116; intimacy with God, 14; authority of the sufi necessarily dependent on, 15; religious scholars are the heirs of, 17; imams receive divine

prophets (continued)
knowledge of, 18; religious wisdom inherited from, 85; path trodden by, 101, 117; travel to higher realities, 102; Simnānī established correspondences with, 108; Muḥammad Pārsā correlates subtle centers with, 109; Mujaddidī correspondences with *laṭīfas*, 110–11; Muḥammad Pārsā correlates subtle centers with, 109; Mujaddidī correspondences with *laṭīfas*, 110–11; receive their divine energy and grace through Muḥammad, 115; Mujaddidīs follow the path of, 116; Sunnī credal dogma, 116; differentiating *awliyā'* and, 117; realities of are just reflections of Muḥammad's reality, 119; Muḥammad as "seal" of, 120; under the foot of certain, 120; station of, 144; Muḥammad will intercede for, 178; Muḥammad as source of their prophethood, 243; intimacy of, 244; and the distinction between messengers of God, 245; perfections of prophetic realities, 246; the Great, 252
protégé of God. See *walī*
protocol in the presence of a sufi master, 148, 149, 195. See also *adab*
publication boom of magazines and newspapers in Urdu, 196. *See also* printing

Qādirī, Qādirī practices, 120, 236, 237, 255, 256: and Aḥmad Riḍā, 200
Qādiriyya: as pan-Islamic lineage, 2; and Dārā Shikūh, 70; primary affiliation of Akhund of Swat, 172; prominent in NWFP, 172
Qāḍī Thanā'ullāh Pānīpātī (d. 1225/1810): and need for mediation of sufi guide, 188–89; and seeking the sufi path incumbent on Muslims, 188; Jamā'at 'Alī's use of his ideas on love, 201; approves *Ma'mūlāt-i maẓhariyya*, 237; avoided issue of Ka'ba versus Muḥammad, 247
qālab (the physical frame, one of the subtle centers), 105, 108, 109, 110, 128, 256
qālab (heart *laṭīfa*, one of the subtle centers): speciality of theologians and philosophers, 5; location of, 105, 111; al-Ghazzālī discusses, 106; one of 'Amr al-Makkī's *laṭīfas*, 106; related to the *'arsh*, 115; Naqshbandī meaning of, 126; recollection of the heart, 127–28; remembrance of, 127; "hitting" in *nafy wa-ithbāt*, 129; bond of, 132
Qasim Zaman, xxv, 35
qawwālī (singing of sufi poetry), 127, 203
qayyūm (also *quṭb al-aqṭāb*, the one having the highest spiritual rank on earth), 68–69, 246
qibla (the direction pointing to the Ka'ba): shaykh as, 42; Prophet as, 48; Islamic customs associated with, 149; form of address to shaykh, 155
quality of comprehensive synthesis (*sha'n-i jāmi'*), 243
Qur'ān commentary, 83, 164
qurb al-farā'iḍ (achieving proximity to God by performing legally prescribed actions), 116
qurb al-nawāfil (approaching God through supererogatory practices), 116. *See also* supererogatory practices
Qushayrī al-. *See* Abū'l-Qāsim al-Qushayrī
Quṭbuddin Bakhtiyār Kākī (d. 633/1235), 154

rābiṭa (bond between the shaykh and disciple): shaykh displays

supernatural power through, 99; confirmed by a dream 113; crucial aspect of Naqshbandī spiritual methods, 125, 131–35; a way to connect to Muḥammad, 133, 143, 157; spontaneous forming of, 137; for novices inclined to love, 139; and ʿUbaydullāh Aḥrār, 140; an independent spiritual method by fifteenth century, 145; equated with the love of Muḥammad, 201;
Ramana Maharshi, 103
Rāmānuja (d. 1137 C.E.), 206
Rampur, 171
Ranjīt Singh, 211, 215
Rashīd Aḥmad Gangōhī (d. 1322–3/1905), 20, 177, 180
rāʾ y (legal decision based on independent, personal judgment), 83
Rāzī. *See* Najmuddīn Rāzī
Reality. See *ḥaqīqat*
recollection of God. See *dhikr*
red sulfur (*kibrīt aḥmar*), 32, 258
reformists: strictly interpreted islamic law and sunna, 73; and visualization of the shaykh, 134, 135; and proper place of women, 161; and revivalists defined, 170; and rural shrine practices, 176; and Deoband, 180–81; Hindu and Sikh, 182; and revivalist shaykhs, 199
religious education, 19, 22, 45, 131
religious endowments (sing. *waqf*, pl. *awqāf*, set aside for religious purposes as a charitable trust), 45, 47, 62; and the Shahīdganj mosque, 214
religious scholars (*ʿulāmāʾ*): and oral transmission of scripture, 11; as heirs of the prophets, 17; religious knowledge associated with, 18, 21; oriented to maintaining Islamic societal structures, 24; Prophetic model transmitted by, 25; teach correct behavior and act as exemplars, 34; require faith as a prerequisite to submission, 38. *See also* jurists; ulama
religious schools. *See* madrasa
remaining in God. See *baqāʾ*
renewer. See *mujaddid*
repentance, 156, 158, 159
revivalist(s): sunna and lineage as legitimizing, 20; Tablīghī Jamāʿat outwardly similar to, 22; criticism of sufi shaykhs, 150; example of one Naqshbandī ideal, 151; Shaāh Walīullāh setting standards for, 152; sufis, 154; and mediational sufism, 168; and Chishtīs, 170, 185; compared to reformists, 170; need to quote Qurʾan and hadith, 170; Shēr Muḥammad Sharaqpūrī as, 175, 220; and Deobandis, 177, 180–82; Hindu and Sikh, 182; publications, 182–83; and Islamic identity, 184; pirs, 186, 217, 220; allegiance to a sufi pir incumbent, 187; following sunna is obligatory for, 187, 199; and English-educated people, 207; and Iqbāl's poetry, 216; and the Muslim League, 217;
ribāṭ (sufi lodge), 2. See also *khānaqāh*
Risāla-yi anwār aṣ-ṣūfiyya (abbreviated *Risāla*), 197–99; established by Anwar ʿAlī, 194; goals of, 195; approximate circulation of, 215; connected the community together, 227;
rituals: going beyond required, 1; practices having the appearance of worship, 9; spiritual travel subordinated to, 18; outward adherence to, 22; various centers of, 23; of religious learning, 27, 35; structure, 52; environment, 53; prayer, 93, 125, 142, 150, 186;

rituals (continued)
credal dogma underpinning, 100, 101; diligent performance of, 104; performance, 104, 179; why performing is not sufficient for sufis, 104; purity, 127, 159; in the sufi lodge, 148; prostration, 149; initiation, 155, 157; disciple swears to perform, 156; requirements of Islam, 156, 157, 159, 232; changes in death anniversary, 205. *See* initiation
robe. See *khirqa*
rūḥ ("spirit" *laṭīfa*, one of the subtle centers): bodily locations of, 105, 109, 11; ʿAmr al-Makkī's conception of, 106; in pre-Naqshbandī *laṭīfa* configurations, 106–7; associated with the prophet David, 109; order of activation, 128; and returning to the origin of , 243; origin of, 250. *See* spirit
rulers, 8, 21, 74, 78, 99, 155; become disciples of a directing-shaykh, 225; directing-shaykhs analogous to, 228. *See also* kings
Rūmī, Jalāluddin, xxiii, 40, 43, 134, 144, 149, 150
Rundī ar-. *See* Ibn ʿAbbād ar-Rundī

Ṣadruddīn Qūnawī (d. 673/1274), 37, 242
Safavids, 14, 92
Sahl at-Tustarī (d. 283/896), 2, 25, 34, 36, 106
sajjādanishīn (principal successor, lit. "one who sits on the prayer carpet"), 175, 192; based on heredity alone, 20; as one kind of spiritual succession, 164–65; eldest son usually becomes, 165, 201, 223; at age of fourteen, 166; symbols of, 166; visualizing the newly appointed succesor, 167; and Mughals, 171, 211; invited to annual meeting, 207; political loyalty as qualification, 211; and the Muslim League, 218; functions assumed by government officials, 230
Sakhī Sarvar, 191
Sālik-i majdhūb, 121, 122
Salmān al-Fārisī (d. 36/656), 85, 86
samāʿ (listening to sufi poetry), 44, 66, 127, 181
Samarqand, 46, 56, 62, 139
sayr (spiritual journeying, spiritual travel): involves a return to everyday world, 9, 11, 41; source of authority, 11, 18, 23; shaykh facilitates, 12; duplicating the Prophetic journey, 15, 18; specialty of sufis, 17; subordinated to ritual practice, 18; sufis without, 20; considered to be the "inner" sunna, 22; associated with supernatural power, 47, 98; without attributes, 89, 101; duplicates prophetic path, 101; in Mujaddidī literature, 102, 234–40; ways of conceptualizing, 102; "subtle body" as a model for, 103, 112, 113; prerequisite is a mind free from thought, 108; in the names, 115, 131; through the contemplations, 130, 241–48; success depends on cultivating a relationship with the shaykh, 131
sayr ʿan Allāh billāh, (returning to the world of creation for God and by means of God), 123, 258
sayr fiʾl-ashyāʾ (returning to live as an apparently ordinary person), 123, 258
sayr fiʾllāh (traveling in God), 123, 258, 259
sayr-i āfāqī (traveling in the outside world), 93, 103, 121
sayr ilaʾllāh (going to God), 122, 244, 258, 259
sayr-i anfusī (traveling within oneself), 93, 103, 121
sayr wa-sulūk (the spiritual path,

the way of proceeding along the path, and the methods for the journey), 100, 120
Sayyid Aḥmad Khān, 186
Sayyid Aḥmad Shahīd Barlwī (d. 1246/1831), 72, 78
Sayyid Nūrulḥasan Bukhārī Kīliyānwālī (d. 1373/1953), 175
Schimmel, Annemarie, ix, xvii, xxvi, 114
scripturalist-minded, 79, 187
Shādhilīs/Shādhiliyya, 73, 127; spiritual path, 100; lineage includes Junayd, 106
Shāfiʿī, ash-. *See* Muḥammad ash-Shāfiʿī
Shāfiʿī school, 26, 28, 33, 46
Shāh ʿAbdulʿazīz (d. 1239/1824), 78, 170, 171; stressed dress as a symbol of Islamic identity, 185; and Ghulām ʿAlī Shāh, 239
Shāh Abūʾl-Khayr (d. 1341/1924), 64, 74, 154
Shāh Gulshan (d. 1170/1757), 72
Shahīdganj Mosque, 213–17, 228
Shāh Ismāʿīl Shahīd (d. 1831), 177
Shāh Jahān, 69–71
Shāh Kalīmullāh (d. 1142/1729), 170
Shāh Walīullāh (d. 1176/1762), 188, 227, 235, 237, 238, 239; internationally famous as a religious leader, 72; brought together all the eight major sub-lineages of the Indian Naqshbandiyya, 73; among the last Naqshbandīs to advise Indian rulers, 78; and his hadith commentary on the Naqshbandī lineage, 86; and synthesis of *laṭīfa*s, 108; and seven criteria for choosing a spiritual guide, 152; had five affiliations of blessedness, 156; as a revivalist, 170; sufi lodge of as refuge, 171; declares sufi initiation to be sunna, 188; books of dealing with spiritual practice, 235–36; and contemplations, 241; writing about sufi lineages; shaktipāt, 117
shaʾn-i jāmiʿ. *See* comprehensive synthesis
Sharafuddīn Manrī (d. 782/1381), 158, 169
shariʿa (Islamic law): the kernel protecting spiritual practice, 8; circle of sharīʿa with its center, *ḥaqīqa*, 10; Sirhindī declared strict adherence to, 100; sufi path subordinated to, 117; relation to spiritual light, 119; must go beyond the outward dictates of, 121; shaykh should follow assiduously, 142; most shaykhs in British India allegedly did not conform to, 150; when shaykh accidentally does something contrary to, 162; and admirable innovations, 179; and Deobandis, 180; and Shahīdganj Mosque agitation, 213; and Muslim League program, 217
shariʿa-minded: sufi lineages, 17, 18, 38, 94, 224, 225; often declare *samāʿ* as a forbidden activity, 128; choosing a shaykh who is, 153; shariʿa-mindedness, 153; mediating-shaykhs as, 210
sharʿī vision, 35, 48
Shaṭṭāriyya, 73
shaykh(s) (Ar. elder): as infallible, 1, 29, 36, 139, 145; unquestioning compliance to, 1, 147, 207; obedience to, 2, 41; hereditary shaykh, 3, 22, 154; and mediation, 10–13, 157, 168; as heirs of the Prophet, 13–16, 187; compared to Muḥammad, 20; and Twelver imams, 23; institutionalization of, 34, 48; psychological dependence on the shaykh, 37, 143; as wetnurse, 37; recreates the ideal Muslim community, 39, 54; intermediary

shaykh(s) (continued)
between God and humanity, 42, 169; deceased, 88, 113, 162; Uwaysī shaykh preferred over living, 89; living shaykh has preference, 94; and supernatural power, 96, 99, 119; bond (*rābiṭa*), with, 131–34; visualization of, 134–38, 179; necessity of, 138–40; loving, 140–41, 144, 201, 207; acting against the shariʿa, 141, 142, 162; as psychiatrist, 147; qualifications of, 154–53; a pointer to God, 155; Qur'anic justification for shaykh, 157; successors of, 165–67; Deobandi, 180–82; as sufis and ulama, 194; as bridge between God and the believer, 200; genealogical chains of recited, 201–2; an intimate of God, 201; *darshān* of, 205; choosing, 210; exemption from colonial court appearances, 212; political role, 217; rally for Pakistan, 218; associated with a local and personal Islam, 219, 220; development of, 224; Pakistan and a new ideology of, 230; denial of, 232; cures disease, 235. See also *adab*; directing-shaykh; heir of the Prophet; love; mediating-shaykh; mediation; *murshid*; pir; revivalist; shrine-shaykh; supernatural power; teaching-shaykh; ulama; and visualization of the shaykh

Shēr Muḥammad Sharaqpūrī (d. 1347/1928), 133, 154, 159, 175, 220; and visualization of the shaykh, 137–38; gave spiritual education, 163; and English dress, 185–86; declared *mustaḥabb* practices to be required, 187

shrine caretaker, 164–65, 230

shrine custodians, 212

shrine-shaykh, 191, 211

shuhūdī position (subjective witnessing the oneness of God and Creation), 72

shu'ūn-i dhātiyya (essential qualities), 115, 238, 240

Sialkot, 192, 196, 197, 206, 213, 223

Ṣiddīqiyya, 59

ṣifāt (attributes), 118, 242; eight immutable divine attributes, 115; Simnānī's conception of essential attributes, 115; general *fayḍ* coming from attributes, 118; reflections of God's attributes, 122; Naqshbandī goal to travel in the *dhāt* not the attributes, 242

ṣifāt-i fiʿliyya (active attributes), 115, 243

ṣifāt-i salbiyya (attributes of negation or *ṣifāt-i tanzīhiyya*), 115, 243, 245

Sikhs, 172, 201, 217; razed Sirhind, 64, 171; graves of holy, 169; reaction to Christian conversions, 182; reformist and revivalist movements, 182; used as a positive example by Shr Muḥammad, 185–86; government of in Panjab, 211; and the Shahīdganj Mosque, 213–16; and diversity, 219; and indigenous education, 227

silsila (genealogical chain), 57, 79, 82, 92, 97, 120, 218; Bakrī, 88. *See* lineage

Simnānī. *See* ʿAlā'uddawla Simnānī

Sind, 168, 172, 173, 174, 211, 218, 239

Sirhind, 171, 175

Sirhindī. *See* Aḥmad Sirhindī

Sirājuddīn (d. 1333/1933), 174; his succession at the Musa Zai sufi lodge, 164–67

sirr (mystery *laṭīfa*, one of the subtle centers): bodily location of, 105, 109, 111; in pre-Naqshbandī *laṭīfa* configurations, 106–7;

associated with Moses, 109; associated with the *kursī*, 115; order of activation, 128; travel in, 243; origin of, 250
sobriety: and the Naqshbandiyya, 90; over intoxication in sufi identity, 65. See also *jadhba*
sources of authority: utilized by sufis, xv, 21, 23, 97; four sources identified, 11; as ways of connecting to God, 16–17; converge on the Prophet, 18; type of succession that drastically altered, 165
spirit (*rūḥ*): *laṭīfas* related to, 110. See *rūḥ*
spiritual director. See *murshid*, shaykh, pir
spiritual energy. *See* divine energy/power
spiritual exercises. See *sulūk*
spiritual genealogy. *See* lineage; *silsila*
spiritual hierarchy, xxiv, 18, 99, 169. See also *abdāl*
spiritual journeying. See *sayr*
spiritual lineage. *See* lineage
spiritual master. See *murshid*; pir; shaykh
spiritual mentor. See *murshid*; pir; shaykh
spiritual power. *See* divine energy/power
spiritual travel. See *sayr*
station. See *maqām*
Successors: Uways as the best of, 93
sufi affiliation. *See* lineage; *silsila*
sufi etiquette. See *adab*
sufi *ijtihād*. See *ijtihād*
sufi lodge. See *khānaqāh*
sufi master. See *murshid*; pir; shaykh
sufi robe. See *khirqa*
sufism: early development of, 1, 4, 32; institutional development of, 4, 37, 48; and Islam, 4–5; and *iḥsān*, 5; an expression of religion, a transformational process, 8; and antinomian tendencies, 20; theoretical sufism, a field of knowledge, 31, 80, 225; so-called stagnation of Sufism, 81; completely perfect behavior (*adab*), 148; institutionalized, 168, 230; opposition to, 168, 179, 187; revivalist, 170; and Deobandis, 177; and Indo-Muslim identity, 184; Muḥammadan Sufism Society, 194; newly defined Sufiism, 195; propagating, 195; service to the knowledge of, 198; Pakistani government trying to control, 230, 232. *See also* juristic sufism; mediational sufism
ṣuḥbat. *See* companionship
Suhrawardiyya, 2, 73, 169
Sulamī, as-. *See* Abū ʿAbdurraḥmān as-Sulamī
sulūk (mystical practices, spiritual exercises to progress on the path), 83, 101, 112, 122, 157, 165; abandoning of spiritual exercises, 208
sunna (example of the Prophet): the inner sunna, 11, 23, 97, 147; as source of personal authority, 17; modeling one's behavior on, 18; only outwardly following, 22; incumbent on Muslims to imitate, 26, 187; rituals of transmission of knowledge developed from, 27; rules of sufi lodge based on, 36, 44; and the early Naqshbandīs, 89; practices based on in colonial India, 151; and admirable innovations, 179; and Deobandi teachers as exemplars of, 180; Barelwi notions of, 181; and revivalist stress on, 184–85; in conflict with British dress and customs, 185–86; ritually mandatory for

sunna (continued)
Naqshbandīs, 187; sufi initiation considered as, 187, 188; as following his *hijra*, 223
super-arcanum. See *akhfā*
supererogatory practices, 116, 187; prayer, 51, 105; rituals, 52. See *qurb an-nawāfil*
supernatural power (*himma, taṣarruf, tawajjuh*, the manipulation of divine energy/power or *fayḍ*): shaykh as a nexus of 12, 53; perception that sufis possessed, 18, 36, 99; liminality of pir fosters the development of, 50; derived from spiritual travel, 98; *rābiṭa* related to, 99; focused to benefit others, 119; based on being an heir to the Prophet, 148; Jamāʿat ʿAlī did not exhibit, 200; not recognized in mediational sufism, 200, 208. *See also* divine energy/power; *fayḍ*; *tawajjuh*
Supreme Council of Sufi Lineages, 232
Surat, 64, 65
Swat, 172

taʿayyun-i awwal (the primary manifestation of the Essence), 114
taʿayyun-i thānī (the secondary manifestion of the Essence), 115
tabarruk (pl. *tabarrukāt, baraka*-impregnated objects), 58, 156, 158
tablīgh. *See* propagating Islam
Tablīghī Jamāʿat, 22, 151, 185
tahajjud (supererogatory prayers performed typically between midnight and the sunrise prayer), 202
Tahirids, 2, 46
tahlīl (repeating *lā ilāh illā Allāh*, there is no God but God), 129, 130
Taoists, 109, 110
taqlīd (unquestioning obedience to the precedents of one legal school, the opposite of *ijtihād*), 83
ṭarīqa (literally, path or method, a path to God differentiated from shariʿa, a specific spiritual lineage): pan-Islamic, 2; compared to the circle of shariʿa, 10; ṭarīqa Shīʿīsm, 23; "Muḥammadan path," 72; equation of *nisba* and *ṭarīqa*, 83; as a spiritual path, 117; Naqshabandī as closest, 120
ṭarīq-i jadhba (the "short" path of attraction): a much faster way to God than doing regular practices, 93; traversing the path through the intermediary of an Uwaysī guide, 122
ṭarīq-i sulūk, the path of regular practice, 93; traversing the path through a living guide, 122
tawajjuh (literally, concentration; the shaykh's concentration of supernatural power on the disciple to facilitate the disciple's progress), 131–34: and Uwaysī experience, 89; heart-to-heart communication associated with, 96; and *rābiṭa*, 99; in initiation, 127, 160; giving, 133; reactions to, 152; importance in looking for a shaykh, 153; contrasted with theoretical training, 163; associated with directing-shaykhs, 195; related to spiritual territory, 195; redefined by love, 201; and British modern worldview, 208. *See also* divine power/energy; supernatural power
tawakkul (absolute trust in God for one's needs), 121, 137, 175
tawassul (mediation of holy people between the believer and God to facilitate the believer becoming

closer to God), 102, 158, 188; *bay'at-i tawassul*, 157
tawba (repentance), 156, 159
tawḥīd (the affirmation of the unity of God), 5, 100, 114
Ṭayfūriyya, 59
teaching-shaykh(s) (*shahkh al-ta'līm*), 26–29: as a configuration of personal authority, xv, 23; shift to directing-shaykh, xix, 12, 29–35; and mediation of divine scripture, 11
teaching permission (*ijāza*): unrestricted permission (*ijāza-yi muṭlaq*), 113, 164–66, 254, 256; required formally to teach, 152; conditional permission (*ijāza-yi muqayyad*) 164, 165, 254
tekke (Turk.). See *khānaqāh*
T'hānawī. *See* Ashraf 'Alī
throne (*'arsh*), 105, 115, 116
Timurids, 56, 59, 60, 61, 192
Tīmūr (d. 807/1405), 59, 60
tombs, 162, 168, 180
tomb-shrines, 45, 51, 169. *See also* shrine caretakers/custodians
towns (Urdu, sing. *qaṣabat*), 170
transformation: transformations in sufism, 1; and configurations associated with sources of authority, 10; sufis and imams facilitate, 23;
transmission of religious knowledge: as a source of authority, xvi; associated with stringent behavioral patterns, 35
Transoxiana, 56, 61
Tughluq Tīmūr (r. 748/1347–763/1362), 59
turban, 185, 194: and sunna, 151, 185; in initiation, 159, 161, 165, 166, 167
Turgut Özal, ix
Turkestan, 59, 60
Turkey, xvi, 48, 61, 174
Turner, Victor, xvi, 49, 53, 228, 229
Tustarī, Sahl at-. *See* Sahl at-Tustarī
Twelver Shī'īs, 4, 14, 18, 41, 176
'Ubaydullāh Aḥrār (d. 895/1490), 60–65, 66, 70, 73, 196: three methods of reaching God, 131; and *rābiṭa*, 132, 133, 135, 139–41
ulama: defined religious knowledge as comprising the Qur'ān and hadith, 3; and sufis, 6, 27, 35, 36, 43, 44, 54, 70, 78, 153, 194, 213, 225; as specialists of *islām*, 8; authority derived from transmitted knowledge, 14, 83; not a clear-cut category, 24; Naqshbandīs definition of true, 85; "The ulama are to my people as the prophets were to the sons of Israel," 85; and political decline of the Mughals, 171; scattered to towns in northern India, 171; in Panjab, 171; support of mediational sufism, 176–79; of Ahl-i Hadith, 179; of Deoband, 180–82; Jamā'at 'Alī attracts, 192; authority undermined by printed books, 209; Mughals used as mediators, 211; and Iqbāl's poetry, 216; and mosques as identity markers, 216; keep local Islam on the periphery, 219; and the indigenous educational system, 226; found jobs in British courts, 227. *See also* jurists; reformists; religious scholars; revivalists
undifferentiated existence (*lā ta'ayyun*), 113
Unionist Party, 208, 214, 215, 217, 218
United Provinces, 168
unity of existence. See *waḥdat al-wujūd*
unity of witnessing. See *waḥdat al-shuhūd*
Urdu publications, 215
Uwaysī: Uwaysī initiations discouraged, 20, 92–95; as a connection directly to Muḥammad, 88, 89; model for

Uwaysī (continued)
initiation by the imaginal form of deceased shaykhs, 88; in the early Naqshbandiyya, 89, 93; and well-developed subtle body, 113; as a quick path, 122
Uwaysī instruction, 244
Uways al-Qaranī, 88, 93, 114
Uzbekistan, ix, x, 55

Vernacular Press Act, 197
visualization of the shaykh (*taṣawwur-i shaykh*), 54, 134, 135, 136, 137, 140

waḥdat al-shuhūd (unity of witnessing, testimonial unity), 109, 114, 123
waḥdat al-wujūd ("unity of existence" or existential unity), 114, 123, 243
Wahhābīs, 79, 179, 194
walī, or *walī Allāh* (p. *awliyā'*, a person close to God, a protégé, an intimate, or friend of God): kinds of, 13–14; as an intermediary between humanity and God, 14–15, 133; sufis as, 17, 43, 104, 139; and supernatural power, 18, 99; as social mediators, 30; and prophets, 39, 42, 73, 117; functionally equated with the Prophet, 40–41; always exist, 41; as the real Ka'ba, 43; receive the special *fayḍ*, 118; and the Companions, 123, 163; and love, 141, 152; mistakes of, 143; religious obligation to love, 201; companionship with gives eternal life, 202; Jinnah as, 217, 230; presences of, 256
waqf. *See* religious endowments
wasīla (the means one uses to approach God), 131, 157, 200
Weber, Max, 14, 22
wilāya (Per. *wilāyat*, intimacy with or closeness to God), 188; linguistic contrast with *walāya*, 13, 99; and prophethood, 73; and *nisba*, 83; and supernatural power, 98; and special *fayḍ*, 118; losing 144; as spiritual territory, 195; *wilāyat-i anbiyā'*, 244
wilāyat-i kubrā (greater intimacy with God), 98, 116, 123, 164, 244
wilāyat-i ṣughrā (lesser intimacy with God), 98, 116, 122, 164, 244
wilāyat-i ṣughrā, kubrā, 'ulyā (circles of the three intimacies), 256
wilāyat-i 'ulyā (greatest intimacy with God), 123, 245
women, 181; sufis, xxiv; and seclusion from non-familial males, 151, 161; and initiation, 160–61; disciples, 161
wujūdī position (the objective declaration that God and Creation were identical), 72
wuqūf ("concentration" when discussing the *laṭīfa*s and "understanding" in the context of contemplation): meaning in different contexts, 127; awareness of time (*wuqūf-i zamānī*), 234; counting of *dhikr* repetitions (*wuqūf-i 'adadī*), 234; a heart constantly attentive to God (*wuqūf-i qalbī*), 234

Yemen, 4, 28, 88, 113, 114
Yūsuf Hamadānī (d. 535/1140), 44, 58, 234

Ẓafar 'Alī Khān, 192, 215, 216
Zaydī imams, 4; Zaydīs, 18
Zen Buddhists, 9
zāwiyya (sufi lodge). See *khānaqāh*

www.ingramcontent.com/pod-product-compliance
Lightning Source LLC
Chambersburg PA
CBHW021342300426
44114CB00012B/1049